George Stephenson.

Engraved by W. Holl, after the portrait by John Lucas.

NEW YORK, HARPER & BROTHERS.

THE LIFE

OF

GEORGE STEPHENSON

AND OF HIS SON

ROBERT STEPHENSON;

COMPRISING ALSO

A HISTORY OF THE INVENTION AND INTRODUCTION
OF THE RAILWAY LOCOMOTIVE.

By SAMUEL SMILES,
AUTHOR OF "SELF-HELP," "THE HUGUENOTS," ETC.

With Portraits and Numerous Illustrations.

NEW YORK:
HARPER & BROTHERS, PUBLISHERS,
FRANKLIN SQUARE.
1868.

PREFACE.

THE present is a revised edition of the Life of George Stephenson and of his son Robert Stephenson, to which is prefixed a history of the Railway and the Locomotive in its earlier stages, uniform with the early history of the Steam-engine given in vol. iv. of "Lives of the Engineers" containing the memoirs of Boulton and Watt. A memoir of Richard Trevithick has also been included in this introductory portion of the book, which will probably be found more complete than any notice which has yet appeared of that distinguished mechanical engineer.

Since the appearance of this Life in its original form ten years ago, the construction of Railways has continued to make extraordinary progress. The length of lines then open in Europe was estimated at about 18,000 miles: it is now more than 50,000 miles. Although Great Britain, first in the field, had then, after about twenty-five years' work, expended nearly 300 millions sterling in the construction of 8300 miles of double railway, it has during the last ten years expended about 200 millions more in constructing 5600 additional miles.

But the construction of railways has proceeded with equal rapidity on the Continent. France has now 9624 miles at work; Germany (including Austria), 13,392 miles; Spain, 3161 miles; Sweden, 1100 miles; Belgium, 1073 miles; Switzerland, 795 miles; Holland, 617 miles; besides railways in other states. These have, for the most part, been constructed and opened during the last ten years, while a considerable length is still under construction. Austria is actively engaged in carrying new lines across the plains of Hungary to the frontier of Turkey, which Turkey is preparing to meet by lines carried up the valley of the Lower Danube; and Russia, with 2800 miles already at work, is occupied with extensive schemes for connecting Petersburg and Moscow with her ports in the Black Sea on the one hand, and with the frontier towns of her Asiatic empire on the other.

Italy also is employing her new-born liberty in vigorously extending railways throughout her dominions. The length of Italian lines in operation in 1866 was 2752 miles, of which not less than 680 were opened in that year. Already has a direct line of communication been opened between Germany and Italy through the Brenner Pass, by which it is now possible to make the entire journey by railway (excepting only the short sea-passage across the English Channel) from London to Brindisi on the southeastern extremity of the Italian peninsula; and, in the course of a few more years, a still shorter route will be opened through France, when that most formidable of all railway borings, the seven-mile tunnel under Mont Cenis, has been completed.

During the last ten years, nearly the whole of the existing Indian railways have been made. When Edmund Burke in 1783 arraigned the British government for their neglect of India in his speech on Mr. Fox's Bill, he said, "England has built no bridges, made no high roads, cut no navigations, dug out no reservoirs. . . . . Were we to be driven out of India this day, nothing would remain to tell that it had been possessed, during the inglorious period of our dominion, by any thing better than the orang-outang or the tiger." But that reproach no longer applies. Some of the greatest bridges erected in modern times—such as those over the Sone near Patna, and over the Jamna at Allahabad—have been erected in connection with the Indian railways, of which there are already 3637 miles at work, and above 2000 more under construction. When these lines have been completed, at an expenditure of about £88,000,000 of British capital guaranteed by the British government, India will be provided with a magnificent system of internal communication, connecting the capitals of the three Presidencies—uniting Bombay with Madras on the south, and with Calcutta on the northeast—while a great main line, 2200 miles in extent, passing through the northwestern provinces, and connecting Calcutta with Lucknow, Delhi, Lahore, Moultan, and Kurrachee, will unite the mouths of the Hooghly in the Bay of Bengal with those of the Indus in the Arabian Sea.

When the first edition of this work appeared in the beginning of 1857, the Canadian system of railways was but in its infancy. The Grand Trunk was only begun, and the Victoria Bridge—the greatest of all railway structures—was not half erected. Now, that fine colony has more than 2200 miles in active operation along the great valley of the St. Lawrence, connecting Rivière du Loup at the mouth of that river, and the harbor of Portland in the State of Maine, *via* Montreal and Toronto, with Sarnia on Lake Huron, and with Windsor, opposite Detroit, in the State of Michigan. The Australian Colonies also have during the same time been actively engaged in providing themselves with railways, many of which are at work, and others are in course of formation. Even the Cape of Good Hope has several lines open, and others making. France also has constructed about 400 miles in Algeria, while the Pasha of Egypt is the proprietor of 360 miles in operation across the Egyptian desert.

But in no country has railway construction been prosecuted with greater vigor than in the United States. There the railway furnishes not only the means of intercommunication between already established settlements, as in the Old World, but it is regarded as the pioneer of colonization, and as instrumental in opening up new and fertile territories of vast extent in the west —the food-grounds of future nations. Hence railway construction in that country was scarcely interrupted even by the great Civil War; at the commencement of which Mr. Seward publicly expressed the opinion that "physical bonds, such as highways, railroads, rivers, and canals, are vastly more powerful for holding civil communities together than any mere covenants, though written on parchment or engraved on iron."

The people of the United States were the first to follow the example of England, after the practicability of steam locomotion had been proved on the Stockton and Darlington and Liverpool and Manchester Railways. The first sod of the Baltimore and Ohio Railway was cut on the 4th of July, 1828, and the line was completed and opened for traffic in the following year, when it was worked partly by horse-power, and partly by a locomotive built at Baltimore, which is still preserved in the Company's workshops. In 1830 the Hudson and Mohawk Railway was begun, while other lines were under construction in Pennsylvania, Massachusetts, and New Jersey; and in the course of ten years, 1843 miles were finished and in operation. In ten more years, 8827 miles were at work; at the end of 1864, not less than 35,000 miles, mostly single tracks; while about 15,000 miles more were under construction. One of the most extensive trunk-lines still unfinished is the Great Pacific Railroad, connecting the lines in the valleys of the Mississippi and the Missouri with the city of San Francisco on the shores of the Pacific, by which, when completed, it will be possible to make the journey from England to Hong Kong, *via* New York, in little more than a month.

The results of the working of railways have been in many respects different from those anticipated by their projectors. One of the most unexpected has been the growth of an immense passenger-traffic. The Stockton and Darlington line was projected as a coal line only, and the Liverpool and Manchester as a merchandise line. Passengers were not taken into account as a source of revenue; for, at the time of their projection, it was not believed that people would trust themselves to be drawn upon a railway by an "explosive machine," as the locomotive was described to be. Indeed, a writer of eminence declared that he would as soon think of being fired off on a ricochet rocket as travel on a railway at twice the speed of the old stage-coaches. So great was the alarm which existed as to the locomotive, that the Liverpool and Manchester Committee pledged themselves in their second prospectus, issued in 1825, "not to require any clause empowering its use;" and as late as 1829, the Newcastle and Carlisle Act was conceded on the express condition that it should not be worked by locomotives, but by horses only.

Nevertheless, the Liverpool and Manchester Company obtained powers to make and work their railway without any such restriction; and when the line was made and opened, a locomotive passenger-train was ordered to be run upon it by way of experiment. Greatly to the surprise of the directors, more passengers presented themselves as travelers by the train than could conveniently be carried.

The first arrangements as to passenger-traffic were of a very primitive character, being mainly copied from the old stage-coach system. The passengers were "booked" at the railway office, and their names were entered in a way-bill which was given to the guard when the train started. Though the usual stage-coach bugleman could not conveniently accompany the passengers, the trains were at first played out of the terminal stations by a lively tune performed by a trumpeter at the end of the platform, and this continued to be done at the Manchester Station until a comparatively recent date.

But the number of passengers carried by the Liverpool and Manchester line was so unexpectedly great, that it was very soon found necessary to remodel the entire system. Tickets were introduced, by which a great saving of time was effected. More roomy and commodious carriages were provided, the original first-class compartments being seated for four passengers only. Every thing was found to have been in the first instance made too light and too slight. The prize "Rocket," which weighed only 4½ tons when loaded with its coke and water, was found quite unsuited for drawing the increasingly heavy loads of passengers. There was also this essential difference between the old stage-coach and the new railway train, that, whereas the former was "full" with six inside and ten outside, the latter must be able to accommodate whatever number of passengers came to be carried. Hence heavier and more powerful engines, and larger and more substantial carriages, were from time to time added to the carrying stock of the railway.

The speed of the trains was also increased. The first locomotives used in hauling coal-trains ran at from four to six miles an hour. On the Stockton and Darlington line the speed was increased to about ten miles an hour; and on the Liverpool and Manchester line the first passenger-trains were run at the average speed of seventeen miles an hour, which at that time was considered very fast. But this was not enough. When the London and Birmingham line was opened, the mail-trains were run at twenty-three miles an hour; and gradually the speed went up, until now the fast trains are run at from fifty to sixty miles an hour—the pistons in the cylinders, at sixty miles, traveling at the inconceivable rapidity of 800 feet per minute!

To bear the load of heavy engines run at high speeds, a much stronger and heavier road was found necessary; and shortly after the opening of the Liverpool and Manchester line, it was entirely relaid with stronger materials. Now that express passenger-engines are from thirty to thirty-five tons each, the weight of the rails has been increased from 35 lbs. to 75 lbs. or 86 lbs. to the yard. Stone blocks have given place to wooden sleepers; rails with loose ends resting on the chairs, to rails with their ends firmly "fished" together; and in many places, where the traffic is unusually heavy, iron rails have been replaced by those of steel.

And now see the enormous magnitude to which railway passenger-traffic has grown. In the year 1866, 274,293,668 passengers were carried by day tickets in Great Britain alone. But this was not all; for in that year 110,227 periodical tickets were issued by the different railways; and assuming half of them to be annual, one fourth half-yearly, and the remainder quarterly tickets, and that their holders made only five journeys each way weekly, this would give an additional number of 39,405,600 journeys, or a total of 313,699,268 passengers carried in Great Britain in one year.

It is difficult to grasp the idea of the enormous number of persons represented by these figures. The mind is merely bewildered by them, and can form no adequate notion of their magnitude. To reckon them singly would occupy twenty years, counting at the rate of one a second for twelve hours every day. Or take another illustration. Supposing every man, woman, and child in Great Britain to make ten journeys by rail yearly, the number would fall short of the passengers carried in 1866.

Mr. Porter, in his "Progress of the Nation," estimated that thirty millions of passengers, or about eighty-two thousand a day, traveled by coaches in Great Britain in 1834, an average distance of twelve miles each, at an average cost of 5*s.* a passenger, or at the rate of 5*d.* a mile; whereas above 313 millions are now carried by railway an average distance of 8½ miles each, at an average cost of 1*s.* 1½*d.* per passenger, or about three halfpence per mile, in considerably less than half the time.

But, besides the above number of passengers, one hundred and twenty-four million tons of minerals and merchandise were carried by railway in the United Kingdon in 1866, and fifteen millions of cattle, besides mails, parcels, and other traffic. The distance run by passenger and goods trains in the year was 142,807,853 miles, to accomplish which it is estimated that four miles of railway on an average must be covered by running trains during every second all the year round.

To perform this service, there were, in 1866, 8125 locomotives at work in the United Kingdom, consuming about three million tons of coal and coke, and flashing into the air every minute some thirty tons of water in the form of steam in a high state of elasticity. There were also 19,228 passenger-carriages, 7276 vans and breaks attached to passenger-trains, and 242,947 trucks, wagons, and other vehicles appropriated to merchandise. Buckled together, buffer to buffer, the locomotives and tenders would extend for a length of about 54 miles, or more than the distance from London to Brighton; while the carrying vehicles, joined together, would form two trains occupying a double line of railway extending from London to beyond Inverness.

A notable feature in the growth of railway traffic of late years has been the increase in the number of third-class passengers, compared with first and second class. Sixteen years since, the third-class passengers constituted only about one third; ten years later they were about one half; whereas now they form nearly two thirds of the whole number carried. Thus George Stephenson's prediction "that the time would come when it would be cheaper for a working man to make a journey by railway than to walk on foot" is already realized.

The degree of safety with which this great traffic has been conducted is not the least remarkable of its features. Of course, so long as railways are worked by men, they will be liable to the imperfections belonging to all things human. Though their machinery may be perfect, and their organization as complete as skill and forethought can make it, workmen will at times be forgetful and listless, and a moment's carelessness may lead to the most disastrous results. Yet, taking all circumstances into account, the wonder is that traveling by railway at high speeds should have been rendered comparatively so safe.

To be struck by lightning is one of the rarest of all causes of death, yet more persons were killed by lightning in Great Britain, in 1866, than were killed on railways from causes beyond their own control; the number in the former case having been nineteen, and in the latter fifteen, or one in every twenty millions of passengers carried. Most persons would consider the probability of their dying by hanging to be extremely remote; yet, according to the Registrar General's returns for 1867, it is thirty times greater than that of being killed by railway accident. Taking the number of persons who traveled in Great Britain in 1866 at 313,699,268, of whom fifteen were accidentally killed, it would appear that, even supposing a person to have a permanent existence, and to make a journey by railway daily, the probability of his being killed in an accident would occur on an average once in above 50,000 years.

The remarkable safety with which railway traffic is on the whole conducted, is due to constant watchfulness and highly-applied skill. The men who work the railways are for the most part the picked men of the country, and every railway station may be regarded as a practical school of industry, attention, and punctuality. Where railways fail in these respects, it will usually be found that it is because the men are personally defective, or because better men are not to be had. It must also be added that the onerous and responsible duties which railway workmen are called upon to perform require a degree of consideration on the part of the public which is not very often extended to them.

Few are aware of the complicated means and agencies that are in constant operation on railways day and night to insure the safety of the passengers to their journeys' end. The road is under a system of continuous inspection, under gangs of men—about twelve to every five miles, under a foreman or "ganger"—whose duty it is to see that the rails and chairs are sound, all their fastenings complete, and the line clear of obstructions.

Then, at all the junctions, sidings, and crossings, pointsmen are stationed, with definite instructions as to the duties to be performed by them. At these places signals are provided, worked from the station platforms, or from special signal-boxes, for the purpose of protecting the stopping or passing trains. When the first railways were opened the signals were of a very simple kind. The station-men gave them with their arms stretched out in different positions; then flags of different colors were used; next fixed signals, with arms or discs, or of rectangular or triangular shape. These were followed by a complete system of semaphore signals, near and distant, protecting all junctions, sidings, and crossings.

When government inspectors were first appointed by the Board of Trade to examine and report upon the working of railways, they were alarmed by the number of trains following each other at some stations in what then seemed to be a very rapid succession. A passage from a Report written in 1840 by Sir Frederick Smith, as to the traffic at "Taylor's Junction," on the York and North Midland Railway, contrasts curiously with the railway life and activity of the present day: "Here," wrote the alarmed inspector, "the passenger trains from York, as well as Leeds and Selby, meet four times a day. No less than 23 passenger-trains stop at or pass this station in the 24 hours—an amount of traffic requiring not only the most perfect arrangements on the part of the management, but the utmost vigilance and energy in the servants of the Company employed at this place." Contrast this with the state of things now. On the Metropolitan Line, 667 trains pass a given point in one direction or the other during the eighteen hours of the working day, or an average of 36 trains an hour. At the Cannon-street Station of the Southeastern Railway, 527 trains pass in and out daily, many of them crossing each others' tracks under the protection of the station signals. Forty-five trains run in and out between 9 and 10 A.M., and an equal number between 4 and 5 P.M. Again, at the Clapham Junction, near London, about 700 trains pass or stop daily; and though to the casual observer the succession of trains coming and going, running and stopping, coupling and shunting, appears a scene of inextricable confusion and danger, the whole is clearly intelligible to the signal-men in their boxes, who work the trains in and out with extraordinary precision and regularity.

The inside of a signal-box reminds one of a piano-forte on a large scale, the lever-handles corresponding with the keys of the instrument; and, to an uninstructed person, to work the one would be as difficult as to play a tune on the other. The signal-box outside Cannon-street Station contains 67 lever-handles, by means of which the signal-men are enabled at the same moment to communicate with the drivers of all the engines on the line within an area of 800 yards. They direct by signs, which are quite as intelligible as words, the drivers of the trains starting from inside the station, as well as those of the trains arriving from outside. By pulling a lever-handle, a distant signal, perhaps out of sight, is set some hundred yards off, which the approaching driver—reading it quickly as he comes along—at once interprets, and stops or advances, as the signal may direct.

The precision and accuracy of the signal-machinery employed at important stations and junctions have of late years been much improved by an ingenious contrivance, by means of which the setting of the signal prepares the road for the coming train. When the signal is set at "Danger," the points are at the same time worked, and the road is "locked" against it; and when at "Safety," the road is open—the signal and the points exactly corresponding.

The Electric Telegraph has also been found a valuable auxiliary in insuring the safe working of large railway traffics. Though the locomotive may run at sixty miles an hour, electricity, when at its fastest, travels at the rate of 288,000 miles a second, and is therefore always able to herald the coming train. The electric telegraph may, indeed, be regarded as the nervous system of the railway. By its means the whole line is kept throbbing with intelligence. The method of working electric signals varies on different lines; but the usual practice is to divide a line into so many lengths, each protected by its signal-stations, the fundamental law of telegraph working being that two engines are not to be allowed to run on the same line between two signal-stations at the same time. When a train passes one of such stations, it is immediately signaled on—usually by electric signal-bells—to the station in advance, and that interval of railway is "blocked" until the signal has been received from the station in advance that the train has passed it. Thus *an interval of space* is always secured between trains following each other, which are thereby alike protected before and behind. And thus, when a train starts on a journey of it may be hundreds of miles, it is signaled on from station to station, and "lives along the line," until at length it reaches its destination, and the last signal of "train in" is given. By this means an immense number of trains can be worked with regularity and safety. On the South-eastern Railway, where the system has been brought to a state of high efficiency, it is no unusual thing during Easter week to send 570,000 passengers through the London Bridge Station alone; and on some days as many as 1200 trains a day.

While such are the expedients adopted to insure safety, others equally ingenious are adopted to insure speed. In the case of express and mail trains, the frequent stopping of the engines to take in a fresh supply of water occasions a considerable loss of time on a long journey, each stoppage for this purpose occupying from ten to fifteen minutes. To avoid such stoppages larger tenders have been provided, capable of carrying as much as 2000 gallons of water each. But as a considerable time is occupied in filling these, a plan has been contrived by Mr. Ramsbottom, the locomotive engineer of the London and Northwestern Railway, by which the engines are made to *feed themselves* while running at full speed! The plan is as follows: An open trough, about 440 feet long, is laid longitudinally between the rails. Into this trough, which is filled with water, a dip-pipe, or scoop attached to the bottom of the tender of the running train, is lowered, and, at a speed of 50 miles an hour, as much as 1070 gallons of water are scooped up in the course of a few minutes. The first of such troughs was laid down between Chester and Holyhead, to enable the Express Mail to run the distance of 84¾ miles in two hours and five minutes without stopping; and similar troughs have since been laid down at Bushey, near London; at Castlethorpe, near Wolverton; and at Parkside, near Liverpool. At these four troughs about 130,000 gallons of water are scooped up daily.

Wherever railways have been made, new towns have sprung up, and old towns and cities been quickened into new life. When the first English lines were projected, great were the prophecies of disaster to the inhabitants of the districts through which they were proposed to be forced. Such fears have long since been dispelled in this country. The same prejudices existed in France. When the railway from Paris to Marseilles was projected to pass through Lyons, a local prophet predicted that if the line were made the city would be ruined—"*Ville traversée, ville perdue;*" while a local priest denounced the locomotive and the electric telegraph as heralding the reign of Antichrist. But such nonsense is no longer uttered. Now it is the city without the railway that is regarded as the "city lost;" for it is in a measure shut out from the rest of the world, and left outside the pale of civilization.

Perhaps the most striking of all the illustrations that could be offered of the extent to which railways facilitate the locomotion, the industry, and the subsistence of the population of large towns and cities, is afforded by the working of the railway system in connection with the capital of Great Britain.

The extension of railways to London has been of comparatively recent date, the whole of the lines connecting it with the provinces and terminating at its outskirts having been opened during the last thirty years, while the lines inside London have for the most part been opened within the last ten years.

The first London line was the Greenwich Railway, part of which was opened for traffic to Deptford in February, 1836. The working of this railway was first exhibited as a show, and the usual attractions were employed to make it "draw." A band of musicians in the garb of the Beef-eaters was stationed at the

London end, and another band at Deptford. For cheapness' sake, the Deptford band was shortly superseded by a large barrel-organ, which played in the passengers; but when the traffic became established, the barrel-organ, as well as the Beef-eater band at the London end, were both discontinued. The whole length of the line was lit up at night by a row of lamps on either side like a street, as if to enable the locomotives or the passengers to see their way in the dark; but these lamps also were eventually discontinued as unnecessary.

As a show, the Greenwich Railway proved tolerably successful. During the first eleven months it carried 456,750 passengers, or an average of about 1300 a day. But the railway having been found more convenient to the public than either the river boats or the omnibuses, the number of passengers rapidly increased. When the Croydon, Brighton, and Southeastern Railways began to pour their streams of traffic over the Greenwich Viaduct, its accommodation was found much too limited, and it was widened from time to time, until now nine lines of railway are laid side by side, over which more than twenty millions of passengers are carried yearly, or an average of about 60,000 a day all the year round.

Since the partial opening of the Greenwich Railway in 1836, a large extent of railways has been constructed in and about the metropolis, and convenient stations have been established almost in the heart of the city. Sixteen of these stations are within a circle of half a mile radius from the Mansion House, and above three hundred stations are in actual use or in course of construction within about five miles of Charing Cross. The most important lines recently opened for the accommodation of the London local traffic have been the London, Chatham and Dover Metropolitan Extensions (1861), the Metropolitan (1863), the North London Extension to Liverpool Street (1865), the Charing Cross and Cannon-street Extensions of the Southeastern Railway (1864–6), and the South London Extension of the Brighton

Railway (1866). Of these railways, the London, Chatham and Dover carried 5,228,418 passengers in 1867; the Metropolitan, 23,405,282; the North London, 17,535,502; the Southeastern, 17,473,934; and the Brighton, 12,686,417. The total number carried into and out of London, as well as from station to station in London, in the same year, was 104 millions of passengers.

To accommodate this vast traffic, not fewer than 3600 local trains are run in and out daily, besides 340 trains which depart to and arrive from distant places, north, south, east, and west. In the morning hours, between 8 30 and 10 30, when business men are proceeding inward to their offices and counting-houses, and in the afternoon between four and six, when they are returning outward to their homes, as many as two thousand stoppages are made in the hour, within the metropolitan district, for the purpose of taking up and setting down passengers, while about two miles of railway are covered by the running trains.

One of the remarkable effects of railways has been to extend the residential area of all large towns and cities. This is especially notable in the case of London. Before the introduction of railways, the residential area of the metropolis was limited by the time occupied by business men in making the journey outward and inward daily; and it was for the most part bounded by Bow on the east, by Hampstead and Highgate on the north, by Paddington and Kensington on the west, and by Clapham and Brixton on the south. But now that stations have been established near the centre of the city, and places so distant as Waltham, Barnet, Watford, Hanwell, Richmond, Epsom, Croydon, Reigate, and Erith can be more quickly reached by rail than the old suburban quarters were by omnibus, the metropolis has become extended in all directions along its railway lines, and the population of London, instead of living in the city or its immediate vicinity as formerly, have come to occupy a residential area of not less than six hundred square miles!

The number of new towns which have consequently sprung

into existence near London within the last twenty years has been very great; towns numbering from ten to twenty thousand inhabitants, which before were but villages, if, indeed, they existed. This has especially been the case along the lines south of the Thames, principally in consequence of the termini of those lines being more conveniently situated for city men of business. Hence the rapid growth of the suburban towns up and down the river, from Richmond and Staines on the west, to Erith and Gravesend on the east, and the hives of population which have settled on the high grounds south of the Thames, in the neighborhood of Norwood and the Crystal Palace, rapidly spreading over the Surrey Downs, from Wimbledon to Guildford, and from Bromley to Croydon, Epsom, and Dorking. And now that the towns on the south and southeast coast can be reached by city men in little more time than it takes to travel to Clapham or Bayswater by omnibus, such places have become, as it were, parts of the great metropolis, and Brighton and Hastings are but marine suburbs of London.

The improved state of the communications of the city with the country has had a marked effect upon its population. While the action of the railways has been to add largely to the number of persons living in London, it has also been accompanied by their dispersion over a much larger area. Thus the population of the central parts of London is constantly decreasing, whereas that of the suburban districts is as constantly increasing. The population of the city fell off more than 10,000 between 1851 and 1861; and during the same period, that of Holborn, the Strand, St. Martin's-in-the-Fields, St. James's, Westminster, East and West London, showed a considerable decrease. But, as regards the whole mass of the metropolitan population, the increase has been enormous, especially since the introduction of railways. Thus, starting from 1801, when the population of London was 958,863, we find it increasing in each decennial period at the rate of between two and three hundred thousand, until the year 1841, when it amounted to 1,948,369. Railways had by that time reached London, after which its population increased at nearly double the former ratio. In the ten years ending 1851, the increase was 413,867; and in the ten years ending 1861, 441,753; until now, to quote the words of the Registrar General in his last annual Report, "the population within the registration limits is by estimate 2,993,513; but beyond this central mass there is a ring of life growing rapidly, and extending along railway lines over a circle of fifteen miles from Charing Cross. The population within that circle, patrolled by the metropolitan police, is about 3,463,771!"

The aggregation of so vast a number of persons within so comparatively limited an area — the immense quantity of food required for their daily sustenance, as well as of fuel, clothing, and other necessaries — would be attended with no small inconvenience and danger but for the facilities again provided by the railways. The provisioning of a garrison of even four thousand men is considered a formidable affair; how much more so the provisioning of nearly four millions of people!

The whole mystery is explained by the admirable organization of the railway service, and the regularity and dispatch with which it is conducted. We are enabled by the courtesy of the general managers of the London railways to bring together the following brief summary of facts relating to the food supply of London, which will probably be regarded by most readers as of a very remarkable character.

Generally speaking, the railways to the south of the Thames contribute comparatively little toward the feeding of London. They are, for the most part, passenger and residential lines, traversing a limited and not very fertile district bounded by the seacoast, and, excepting in fruit and vegetables, milk and hops, they probably carry more food from London than they bring to it. The principal supplies of grain, flour, potatoes, and fish are brought by railway from the eastern counties of England and

Scotland; and of cattle and sheep, beef and mutton, from the grazing counties of the west and northwest of Britain, as far as from the Highlands of Scotland, which, through the instrumentality of railways, have become part of the great grazing-grounds of the metropolis.

Take first "the staff of life"—bread and its constituents. Of wheat, not less than 222,080 quarters were brought into London by railway in 1867, besides what was brought by sea; of oats, 151,757 quarters; of barley, 70,282 quarters; of beans and peas, 51,448 quarters. Of the wheat and barley, by far the largest proportion was brought by the Great Eastern Railway, which delivered in London last year 155,000 quarters of wheat and 45,500 quarters of barley, besides 600,429 quarters more in the form of malt. The largest quantity of oats was brought by the Great Northern Railway, principally from the north of England and the east of Scotland—the quantity delivered by that company in 1867 having been 97,500 quarters, besides 24,664 quarters of wheat, 5560 quarters of barley, and 103,917 quarters of malt. Again, of 1,250,566 sacks of flour and meal delivered in London last year, the Great Eastern brought 654,000 sacks, the Great Northern 232,022 sacks, and the Great Western 136,312 sacks; the principal contribution of the London and Northwestern Railway toward the London bread-stores being 100,760 boxes of American flour, besides 24,300 sacks of English. The total quantity of malt delivered at the London railway stations in 1867 was thirteen hundred thousand sacks.

Next, as to flesh meat. Last year not fewer than 172,300 head of cattle were brought into London by railway, though this was considerably less than the number carried before the cattle plague, the Great Eastern Railway alone having carried 44,672 less than in 1864. But this loss has since been more than made up by the increased quantities of fresh beef, mutton, and other kinds of meat imported in lieu of the live animals. The principal supplies of cattle are brought, as we have said, by the western, northern, and eastern lines: by the Great Western from the western counties and Ireland; by the London and Northwestern, the Midland, and the Great Northern, from the northern counties and from Scotland; and by the Great Eastern from the eastern counties, and from the ports of Harwich and Lowestoft.

Last year also, 1,147,609 sheep were brought to London by railway, of which the Great Eastern delivered not less than 265,371 head. The London and Northwestern and Great Northern between them brought 390,000 head from the northern English counties, with a large proportion from the Scotch Highlands; while the Great Western brought up 130,000 head from the Welsh mountains, and from the rich grazing districts of Wilts, Gloucester, Somerset, and Devon. Another important freight of the London and Northwestern Railway consists of pigs, of which they delivered 54,700 in London last year, principally Irish; while the Great Eastern brought up 27,500 of the same animal, partly foreign.

While the cattle plague has had the effect of greatly reducing the number of live-stock brought into London yearly, it has given a considerable impetus to the Fresh Meat traffic. Thus, in addition to the above large numbers of cattle and sheep delivered in London last year, the railways brought 76,175 tons of meat, which—taking the meat of an average beast at 800 lbs., and of an average sheep at 64 lbs.—would be equivalent to about 112,000 more cattle, and 1,267,500 more sheep. The Great Northern brought the largest quantity; next, the London and Northwestern—these two companies having brought up between them, from distances as remote as Aberdeen and Inverness, about 42,000 tons of fresh meat in 1867, at an average freight of about ½*d.* a lb.

Again, as regards Fish, of which six tenths of the whole quantity consumed in London is now brought by rail. The Great Eastern and the Great Northern are by far the largest importers of this article, and justify their claim to be regarded as the great food lines of London. Of the 61,358 tons of fish brought by railway in 1867, not less than 24,500 tons were delivered by the former, and 22,000 tons, brought from much longer distances, by the latter company. The London and Northwestern brought about 6000 tons last year, the principal part of which was salmon from Scotland and Ireland. The Great Western also brought about 4000 tons, partly salmon, but the greater part mackerel from the southwest coast. During the mackerel season, as much as a hundred tons at a time are brought into the Paddington Station by express fish-train from Cornwall.

The Great Eastern and Great Northern Companies are also the principal carriers of turkeys, geese, fowls, and game, the quantity delivered in London last year by the former company having been 5042 tons. In Christmas week no fewer than 30,000 turkeys and geese were delivered at the Bishopsgate Station, besides about 300 tons of poultry, 10,000 barrels of beer, and immense quantities of fish, oysters, and other kinds of food. As much as 1600 tons of poultry and game were brought last year by the Southwestern Railway; 600 tons by the Great Northern Railway; and 130 tons of turkeys, geese, and fowls by the London, Chatham and Dover line, principally from France.

Of miscellaneous articles, the Great Northern and Midland each brought about 3000 tons of cheese, the Southwestern 2600 tons, and the London and Northwestern 10,034 cheeses in number; while the Southwestern and Brighton lines brought a splendid contribution to the London breakfast-table in the shape of 11,259 *tons* of French eggs; these two companies delivering between them an average of more than three millions of eggs a week all the year round! The same companies last year delivered in London 14,819 tons of butter, for the most part the produce of the farms of Normandy, the greater cleanness and neatness with which the Normandy butter is prepared for market rendering it a favorite both with dealers and consumers of late years compared with Irish butter. The London, Chatham and Dover Company also brought from Calais 96 tons of eggs.

Next, as to the potatoes, vegetables, and fruit brought by rail. Forty years since, the inhabitants of London relied for their supply of vegetables on the garden-grounds in the immediate neighborhood of the metropolis, and the consequence was that they were both very dear and limited in quantity. But railways, while they have extended the grazing-grounds of London as far as the Highlands, have at the same time extended the garden-grounds of London into all the adjoining counties—into East Kent, Essex, Suffolk, and Norfolk, the vale of Gloucester, and even as far as Penzance in Cornwall. The London, Chatham and Dover, one of the youngest of our main lines, brought up from East Kent last year 5279 tons of potatoes, 1046 tons of vegetables, and 5386 tons of fruit, besides 542 tons of vegetables from France. The Southeastern brought 25,163 tons of the same produce. The Great Eastern brought from the eastern counties 21,315 tons of potatoes, and 3596 tons of vegetables and fruit; while the Great Northern brought no less than 78,505 tons of potatoes—a large part of them from the east of Scotland —and 3768 tons of vegetables and fruit. About 6000 tons of early potatoes were last year brought from Cornwall, with about 5000 tons of brocoli, and the quantities are steadily increasing. "Truly London hath a large belly," said old Fuller two hundred years since. But how much more capacious is it now!

One of the most striking illustrations of the utility of railways in contributing to the supply of wholesome articles of food to the population of large cities is to be found in the rapid growth of the traffic in Milk. Readers of newspapers may remember the descriptions published some years since of the horrid dens in which London cows are penned, and of the odious compound sold by the name of milk, of which the least deleterious ingredient in it was supplied by the "cow with the iron tail." That state of affairs is now completely changed. What with the greatly improved state of the London dairies and the better quality of the milk supplied by them, together with the large quantities brought by railway from a range of a hundred miles and more all round London, even the poorest classes in the metropolis are now enabled to obtain as wholesome a supply of the article as the inhabitants of most country towns.

The milk traffic has in some cases been rapid, almost sudden, in its growth. Though the Great Western is at present the greatest of the milk lines, it brought very little into London prior to the year 1865. In the month of August in that year it brought 23,474 gallons, and in the month of October following the quantity had increased to 103,214 gallons. Last year the total quantity delivered in London by this single railway was 1,514,836 gallons, or an average of 30,000 gallons a week. The largest proportion of this milk was brought from beyond Swindon in Wiltshire, about 100 miles from London; but considerable quantities were also brought from the vale of Gloucester and from Somerset. The London and Southwestern also is a great milk-carrying line, having brought as much as 1,480,272 gallons to London last year, or an average of 28,000 gallons a week. The Great Eastern brought nearly the same quantity, 1,322,429 gallons, or an average of about 25,400 gallons a week. The London and Northwestern ranks next, having brought 643,432 gallons in 1867; then the Great Northern, 455,916 gallons; the Southeastern, 435,668 gallons; and the Brighton, 419,254 gallons. The total quantity of milk delivered in London by railway last year was 6,309,446 gallons, or above 120,000 gallons a week. Yet this traffic, large though it may appear, is as yet but in its infancy, and in the course of a few more years it will be found very largely increased, according as facilities are provided for its accommodation and transit.

These great streams of food, which we have thus so summarily described, flow into London so continuously and uninterruptedly, that comparatively few persons are aware of the magnitude and importance of the process thus daily going forward. Though gathered from an immense extent of country—embracing England, Scotland, Wales, and Ireland—the influx is so unintermitted that it is relied upon with as much certainty as if it only came from the counties immediately adjoining London. The express meat-train from Aberdeen arrives in town as punctually as the Clapham omnibus, and the express milk-train from Aylesbury is as regular in its delivery as the penny post. Indeed, London now depends so much upon railways for its subsistence, that it may be said to be fed by them from day to day, having never more than a few days' food in stock. And the supply is so regular and continuous, that the possibility of its being interrupted never for a moment occurs to any one. Yet, in these days of strikes among workmen, such a contingency is quite within the limits of possibility. Another contingency, arising in a state of war, is probably still more remote. But, were it possible for a war to occur between England and a combination of foreign powers possessed of stronger iron-clads than ours, and that they were able to ram our ships back into port and land an enemy of overpowering force on the Essex coast, it would be sufficient for them to occupy or cut the railways leading from the north, to starve London into submission in less than a fortnight.

Besides supplying London with food, railways have also been instrumental in insuring the more regular and economical supply of fuel—a matter of almost as vital importance to the population in a climate such as that of England. So long as the market was supplied with coal brought by sea in sailing ships, fuel in winter often rose to a famine price, especially during long-continued easterly winds. But, now that railways are in full work, the price is almost as steady in winter as in summer, and the supply is more regular at all seasons. The following statement of the coals brought into London by sea and by railway, at decennial periods since 1827, as supplied by Mr. J. R. Scott, Registrar of the Coal Exchange, shows the effect of railways in increasing the supply of fuel, at the same time that they have lowered the price to the consumer:

Years.	Sea-borne Coal.	Coals brought by Railway.	Price per Ton.
	Tons.	Tons.	s. d.
1827	1,882,321	nil	28 6
1847	3,280,420	19,336	20 10
1857	3,133,459	1,206,775	18 8
1867	3,016,416	3,295,652	20 8

Thus the price of coal has been reduced 7*s.* 10*d.* a ton since 1827, while the quantity delivered has been enormously increased, the total saving on the quantity consumed in the metropolis in 1867, compared with 1827, being equal to £2,388,000.

But the carriage of food and fuel to London forms but a small part of the merchandise traffic carried by railway. Above 600,000 tons of goods of various kinds yearly pass through one station only, that of the London and Northwestern Company, at Camden Town; and sometimes as many as 20,000 parcels daily. Every other metropolitan station is similarly alive with traffic inward and outward, London having since the introduction of railways become more than ever a great distributive centre, to which merchandise of all kinds converges, and from which it is distributed to all parts of the country. Mr. Bazley, M.P., stated at a late public meeting at Manchester that it would probably require ten millions of horses to convey by road the merchandise traffic which is now annually carried by railway.

Railways have also proved of great value in connection with the Cheap Postage system. By their means it has become possible to carry letters, newspapers, books, and post parcels in any quantity, expeditiously and cheaply. The Liverpool and Manchester line was no sooner opened in 1830 than the Post-office authorities recognized its utility, and used it for carrying the mails between the two towns. When the London and Birmingham line was opened eight years later, mail trains were at once put on, the directors undertaking to perform the distance of 113 miles within 5 hours by day and 5½ hours by night. As additional lines were opened, the old four-horse mail-coaches were gradually discontinued, until, in 1858, the last of them, the "Derby Dilly," which ran between Manchester and Derby, was taken off on the opening of the Midland line to Rowsley.

The increased accommodation provided by railways was found of essential importance, more particularly after the adoption of the Cheap Postage system; and that such accommodation was needed will be obvious from the extraordinary increase which has taken place in the number of letters and packets sent by post. Thus, in 1839, the number of chargeable letters carried was only 76 millions, and of newspapers 44½ millions; whereas, in 1865, the number of letters had increased to 720 millions, and in 1867 to 775 millions, or more than tenfold, while the number of newspapers, books, samples, and patterns (a new branch of postal business begun in 1864) had increased, in 1865, to 98½ millions.

To accommodate this largely-increasing traffic, the bulk of which is carried by railway, the mileage run by mail trains in the United Kingdom has increased from 25,000 miles a day in 1854 (the first year of which we have any return of the mileage run) to 60,000 miles a day in 1867, or an increase of 240 per cent. The Post-office expenditure on railway service has also increased, but not in like proportion, having been £364,000 in the former year, and £559,575 in the latter, or an increase of 154 per cent. The revenue, gross and net, has increased still more rapidly. In 1841, the first complete year of the Cheap Postage system, the gross revenue was £1,359,466, and the net revenue £500,789; in 1854, the gross revenue was £2,574,407, and the net revenue £1,173,723; and in 1867, the gross revenue was £4,548,129, and the net revenue £2,127,125, being an increase of 420 per cent. compared with 1841, and of 180 per cent. compared with 1854. How much of this net increase might fairly be credited to the Railway Postal service we shall not pretend to say, but assuredly the proportion must be very considerable.

One of the great advantages of railways in connection with the postal service is the greatly increased frequency of communication which they provide between all the large towns. Thus

Liverpool has now six deliveries of Manchester letters daily, while every large town in the kingdom has two or more deliveries of London letters daily. In 1863, 393 towns had two mails daily from London; 50 had three mails daily; 7 had four mails a day *from* London, and 15 had four mails a day *to* London; while 3 towns had five mails a day *from* London, and 6 had five mails a day *to* London.

Another feature of the railway mail train, as of the passenger train, is its capacity to carry any quantity of letters and post parcels that may require to be carried. In 1838, the aggregate weight of all the evening mails dispatched from London by twenty-eight mail-coaches was 4 tons 6 cwt., or an average of about 3¼ cwt. each, though the maximum contract weight was 15 cwt. The mails now are necessarily much heavier, the number of letters and packets having, as we have seen, increased more than tenfold since 1839. But it is not the ordinary so much as the extraordinary mails that are of considerable weight, more particularly the American, the Continental, and the Australian mails. It is no unusual thing, we are informed, for the last-mentioned mail to weigh as much as 40 tons. How many of the old mail-coaches it would take to carry such a mail the 79 miles' journey to Southampton, with a relay of four horses every five or seven miles, is a problem for the arithmetician to solve. But even supposing each coach to be loaded to the maximum weight of 15 cwt. per coach, it would require about sixty vehicles and about 1700 horses to carry the 40 tons, besides the coachmen and guards.

A few words, in conclusion, as to the number of men employed in working and maintaining railways. According to Mr. Mills,* 166,047 men and officers were employed in the working of 13,289 miles open in the United Kingdom in 1865, besides 53,923 employed on lines then under construction. The most numerous

* "The Railway Service, its Exigencies, Provisions, and Requirements." By W. F. Mills. London, 1867.

body of workmen is that of the laborers (81,284) employed in the maintenance of the permanent way. Being mostly picked men from the laboring class of the adjoining districts, they are paid considerably higher wages, and hence one of the direct effects of railways on the laboring population (besides affording them greater facilities for locomotion) has been to raise the standard of wages of ordinary labor at least 2*s.* a week in all the districts into which they have penetrated. The workmen next in number is that of the artificers (40,167) employed in constructing and repairing the rolling-stock; the porters (25,381), the plate-layers (12,901), guards and brakesmen (5799), firemen (5266), and engine-drivers (5171). But, besides the employés directly engaged in the working and maintenance of railways, large numbers of workmen are also occupied in the manufacture of locomotives and rolling-stock, and in providing the requisite materials for the permanent way. Thus the consumption of rails alone averages nearly 400,000 tons a year in the United Kingdom alone, while the replacing of decayed sleepers requires about 10,000 acres of forest to be cut down annually and sawn into sleepers. Taking the various railway workmen into account, with their families, it will be found that they represent a total of about three quarters of a million persons, or about one in fifty of our population, who are dependent on railways for their subsistence.

While the practical working of railways has, on the whole, been so satisfactory, the case has been very different as regards their direction and financial management. The men employed in the working of railways make it their business to learn it, and, being responsible, they are under the necessity of taking pains to do it well; whereas the men who govern and direct them are practically irresponsible, and may possess no qualification whatever for the office excepting only the holding of so much stock. The consequence has been much blundering on the part of these amateurs, and great loss on the part of the public. Indeed, what between the confused, contradictory, and often unjust legislation of Parliament on the one hand, and the carelessness or incompetency of directors on the other, many once flourishing concerns have been thrown into a state of utter confusion and muddle, until railway government has become a by-word of reproach.

And this state of things will probably continue until the fatal defect of government by Boards—an extremely limited responsibility, or no responsibility at all—has been rectified by the appointment, as in France, of executives consisting of a few men of special ability and trained administrative skill, personally responsible to their constituents for the due performance of their respective functions. But the discussion of this subject would require a treatise, whereas we are now but writing a preface.

Whatever may be said of the financial mismanagement of railways, there can be no doubt as to the great benefits conferred by them on the public wherever made. Even those railways which have exhibited the most "frightful examples" of scheming and financing, so soon as placed in the hands of practical men to work, have been found to prove of unquestionable public convenience and utility. And notwithstanding all the faults and imperfections that are alleged against railways have been admitted, we think that they must, nevertheless, be recognized as by far the most valuable means of communication between men and nations that has yet been given to the world.

The author's object in publishing this book in its original form, some ten years since, was to describe, in connection with the "Life of George Stephenson," the origin and progress of the railway system, and to show by what moral and material agencies its founders were enabled to carry their ideas into effect, and to work out results which even then were of a remarkable character, though they have since, as above described, become so much more extraordinary. The favor with which successive editions of the book have been received has justified the author in his anticipation that such a narrative would prove of general, if not of permanent interest, and he has taken pains, in preparing for the press the present, and probably final edition, to render it, by careful amendment and revision, more worthy of the public acceptance.

London, May, 1868.

PREFACE

TO THE EIGHTH EDITION, 1864.

The following is a revised and improved edition of "The Life of George Stephenson," with which is incorporated a Memoir of his son Robert, late President of the Institute of Civil Engineers. Since its original appearance in 1857, much additional information has been communicated to the author relative to the early history of Railways and the men principally concerned in establishing them, of which he has availed himself in the present edition.

In preparing the original work for publication, the author enjoyed the advantage of the cordial co-operation and assistance of Robert Stephenson, on whom he mainly relied for information as to the various stages through which the Locomotive passed, and especially as to his father's share in its improvement. Through Mr. Stephenson's instrumentality also, the author was enabled to obtain much valuable information from gentlemen who had been intimately connected with his father and himself in their early undertakings—among others, from Mr. Edward Pease, of Darlington; Mr. Dixon, C.E.; Mr. Sopwith, F.R.S.; Mr. Charles Parker; and Sir Joshua Walmsley.

Most of the facts relating to the early period of George Stephenson's career were collected from colliers, brakesmen, enginemen, and others, who had known him intimately, or been fellow-workmen with him, and were proud to communicate what they remembered of his early life. The information obtained from these old men—most of them illiterate, and some broken down by hard work—though valuable in many respects, was confused, and sometimes contradictory; but, to insure as much accuracy and consistency of narrative as possible, the author submitted the MS. to Mr. Stephenson, and had the benefit of his revision of it previous to publication.

Mr. Stephenson took a lively interest in the improvement of the "Life" of his father, and continued to furnish corrections and additions for insertion in the successive editions of the book which were called for by the public. After the first two editions had appeared, he induced several gentlemen, well qualified to supply additional authentic information, to communicate their recollections of his father, among whom may be mentioned Mr. T. L. Gooch, C.E.; Mr. Vaughan, of Snibston; Mr. F. Swanwick, C.E.; and Mr. Binns, of Clayross, who had officiated as private secretaries to George Stephenson at different periods of his life, and afterward held responsible offices either under him or in conjunction with him.

The author states these facts to show that the information contained in this book is of an authentic character, and has been obtained from the most trustworthy sources. Whether he has used it to the best purpose or not, he leaves others to judge. This much, however, he may himself say—that he has endeavored, to the best of his ability, to set forth the facts communicated to him in a simple, faithful, and straightforward manner; and, even if he has not wholly succeeded in doing this, he has, at all events, been the means of collecting information on a subject originally unattractive to professional literary men, and thereby rendered its farther prosecution comparatively easy to those who may feel called upon to undertake it.

The author does not pretend to have steered clear of errors in treating a subject so extensive, and, before he undertook the labor, comparatively uninvestigated; but, wherever errors have been pointed out, he has taken the earliest opportunity of correcting them. With respect to objections taken to the book because of the undue share of merit alleged to be therein attributed to the Stephensons in respect of the Railway and the Locomotive, there will necessarily be various opinions. There is scarcely an invention or improvement in mechanics but has been the subject of dispute, and it was to be expected that those who had counter claims would put them forward in the present case; nor has the author any reason to complain of the manner in which this has been done.

While George Stephenson is the principal subject in the following book, his son Robert also forms an essential part of it. Father and son were so intimately associated in the early period of their career, that it is difficult, if not impossible, to describe the one apart from the other. The life and achievements of the son were in a great measure the complement of the life and achievements of the father. The care, also, with which the elder Stephenson, while occupying the position of an obscure engine-wright, devoted himself to his son's education, and the gratitude with which the latter repaid the affectionate self-denial of his father, furnish some of the most interesting illustrations of the personal character of both.

These views were early adopted by the author and carried out by him in the preparation of the original work, with the concurrence of Robert Stephenson, who supplied the necessary particulars relating to himself. Such portions of these were accordingly embodied in the narrative as could with propriety be published during his life-time, and the remaining portions are now added with the object of rendering more complete the record of the son's life, as well as the early history of the Railway System.

CONTENTS.

PART I.

CHAPTER I.

SCHEMERS AND PROJECTORS.

Man's Desire for rapid Transit.—Origin of the Railway.—Early Coal Wagon-ways in the North of England.—Early Attempts to apply the Power of Wind to drive Carriages.—Sailing-coaches.—Sir Isaac Newton's Proposal to employ Steam-power.—Dr. Darwin's Speculations on the Subject.—Mr. Edgeworth's Speculations.—Dr. Darwin's Prophecy .... Page 47

CHAPTER II.

EARLY LOCOMOTIVE MODELS.

Watt and Robison's proposed Steam-carriage.—Memoir of Joseph Cugnot and his Road-locomotive.—Francis Moore.—James Watt's Specification of a Locomotive-engine.—William Murdoch's Model.—William Symington's model Steam-carriage.—Oliver Evans's model Locomotive 60

CHAPTER III.

THE CORNISH LOCOMOTIVE—MEMOIR OF TREVITHICK.

Early Welsh Railway Acts.—Wandsworth, Croydon, and Merstham Railway.—Boyhood of Trevithick.—Becomes an Engineer.—His Career.—Constructs a Steam-carriage.—Its Exhibition in London.—Constructs a Tram-engine.—Its Trial on the Merthyr Railroad.—Trevithick's Improvements in the Steam-engine.—Attempts to construct a Tunnel under the Thames.—His numerous Inventions and Patents.—Engines ordered of him for Peru.—Trevithick a Mining Engineer in South America.—Is ruined by the Peruvian Revolution.—His return Home.—His last Patents.—Death and Characteristics 73

PART II.

CHAPTER I.

THE NEWCASTLE COAL-FIELD—GEORGE STEPHENSON'S EARLY YEARS.

Newcastle in ancient Times.—The Coal-trade.—Modern Newcastle.—The Colliery Workmen.—The Pumping-engines.—The Pitmen.—The Keelmen.—Wylam Colliery and Village.—George Stephenson's Birthplace.—The Stephenson Family.—Old Robert Stephenson.—George's Boyhood.—Employed as a Herd-boy.—Makes Clay Engines.—Employed as Corf-bitter.—Drives the Gin-horse.—Appointed assistant Fireman 97

CHAPTER II.

NEWBURN AND CALLERTON—GEORGE STEPHENSON LEARNS TO BE AN ENGINE-MAN.

Stephenson's Life at Newburn.—Appointed Engine-man.—Duties of Plugman.—Study of the Steam-engine.—Experiments in Bird-hatching.—Learns to Read.—His Schoolmasters.—Progress in Arithmetic.—His Dog.—Learns to Brake.—Duties of Brakesman.—Begins Shoe-mending.—Fight with a Pitman ...Page 111

CHAPTER III.

ENGINE-MAN AT WILLINGTON QUAY AND KILLINGWORTH.

Sobriety and Studiousness.—Removal to Willington Quay, and Marriage.—Attempts a Perpetual-motion Machine.—William Fairbairn, C.E., and George Stephenson.—Ballast-heaving.—Cottage Chimney takes fire.—Birth of his son Robert.—Removal to West Moor, Killingworth.—Death of his Wife.—Appointed Engine-man at Montrose.—Return to Killingworth.—Appointed Brakesman at West Moor.—Is drawn for the Militia.—Thinks of Emigrating.—Takes a contract for Brakeing.—Improves the Winding-engine.—Cures a Pumping-engine.—Is appointed Engine-wright of the Colliery 121

CHAPTER IV.

THE STEPHENSONS AT KILLINGWORTH—EDUCATION AND SELF-EDUCATION.

Efforts at Self-improvement.—John Wigham.—Studies in Natural Philosophy.—Education of Robert Stephenson.—Sent to Bruce's School, Newcastle.—His boyish Tricks.—Stephenson's Cottage, West Moor.—Mechanical Contrivances.—The Sun-dial at West Moor.—Stephenson's various Duties as Colliery Engineer ... 137

CHAPTER V.

THE LOCOMOTIVE ENGINE—GEORGE STEPHENSON BEGINS ITS IMPROVEMENT.

Slow Progress heretofore made in the Improvement of the Locomotive.—The Wylam Wagon-way.—Mr. Blackett orders a Locomotive.—Mr. Blenkinsop's Leeds Locomotive.—Mr. Blackett's second Engine a Failure.—The improved Wylam Engine.—George Stephenson's Study of the Subject.—His first Locomotive constructed.—His Improvement of the Engine, as described by his Son.—Invention of the Steam-blast 152

CHAPTER VI.

INVENTION OF THE "GEORDY" SAFETY-LAMP.

Frequency of Colliery Explosions.—Accidents in the Killingworth Pit.—Stephenson's heroic Conduct.—Proposes to invent a Safety-lamp.—His first Lamp and its Trial.—Cottage Experiments with Coal-gas.—His second and third Lamps.—Scene at the Newcastle Institute.—The Stephenson and Davy Controversy.—The Davy and Stephenson Testimonials.—Merits of the "Geordy" Lamp 175

CHAPTER VII.

GEORGE STEPHENSON'S FARTHER IMPROVEMENTS IN THE LOCOMOTIVE—ROBERT STEPHENSON AS VIEWER'S APPRENTICE AND STUDENT.

Stephenson's Improvements in the Mine-machinery.—Farther Improvements in the Locomotive and in the Road.—Experiments on Friction.—Early Neglect of the Locomotive.—Stephenson again meditates emigrating to America.—Employed as

Engineer of the Hetton Railway.—Robert Stephenson put Apprentice to a Coal-viewer.—His Father sends him to Edinburg University.—His Studies there.—Geological Tour in the Highlands........Page 198

CHAPTER VIII.

GEORGE STEPHENSON ENGINEER OF THE STOCKTON AND DARLINGTON RAILWAY.

Failure of the first public Railways near London.—Want of improved communications in the Bishop Auckland Coal-district.—Various Projects devised.—A Railway projected at Darlington.—Edward Pease.—George Stephenson employed as Engineer.—Mr. Pease's Visit to Killingworth.—A Locomotive Factory begun at Newcastle.—The Stockton and Darlington Line constructed.—The public Opening.—The Coal-traffic.—The first Passenger-traffic by Railway.—The Town of Middlesborough-on-Tees created by the Railway........ 216

CHAPTER IX.

THE LIVERPOOL AND MANCHESTER RAILWAY PROJECTED.

Insufficiency of the Communication between Liverpool and Manchester.—A Tram-road projected by Mr. Sandars.—The Line surveyed by William James.—The Survey a failure.—George Stephenson appointed Engineer.—A Company formed and a Railroad projected.—The first Prospectus issued.—Opposition to the Survey.—Speculations as to Railway Speed.—George Stephenson's Views thought extravagant.—Article in the "Quarterly"........ 247

CHAPTER X.

PARLIAMENTARY CONTEST ON THE LIVERPOOL AND MANCHESTER BILL.

The Bill before Parliament.—The Evidence.—George Stephenson in the Witness-box.—Examined as to Speed.—His Cross-examination.—Examined as to the possibility of constructing a Line on Chat Moss.—Mr. Harrison's Speech.—Mr. Giles's Evidence as to Chat Moss.—Mr. Alderson's Speech.—The Bill lost.—Stephenson's Vexation.—The Bill revived, with the Messrs. Rennie as Engineers.—Sir Isaac Coffin's prophecies of Disaster.—The Act passed........ 265

CHAPTER XI.

CHAT MOSS—CONSTRUCTION OF THE LIVERPOOL AND MANCHESTER RAILWAY.

George Stephenson again appointed Engineer of the Railway.—Chat Moss described.—The resident Engineers of the Line.—George Stephenson's Theory of a Floating Road on the Moss.—Operations begun.—The Tar-barrel Drains.—The Embankment sinks in the Moss.—Proposed Abandonment of the Works.—Stephenson's Perseverance.—The Obstacles conquered.—The Tunnel at Liverpool.—The Olive Mount Cutting.—The Sankey Viaduct.—Stephenson's great Labors.—His daily Life.—Evenings at Home........ 281

CHAPTER XII.

ROBERT STEPHENSON'S RESIDENCE IN COLOMBIA AND RETURN—THE "BATTLE OF THE LOCOMOTIVE."

Robert Stephenson appointed Mining Engineer in Colombia.—Mule Journey to Bogotá.—Mariquita.—Silver Mining.—Difficulties with the Cornishmen.—His Cottage at Santa Anna.—Resigns his Appointment.—Meeting with Trevithick.—Voyage to New York, and Shipwreck.—Returns to Newcastle, and takes Charge of the Locomotive Factory.—Discussion as to the Working Power of the Liverpool and Manchester Railway.—Walker and Rastrick's Report.—A Prize offered for the best Locomotive.—Invention of the Multitubular Boiler.—Henry Booth.—Construction of the "Rocket."—The Locomotive Competition at Rainhill.—Triumph of the "Rocket" .... Page 301

CHAPTER XIII.

OPENING OF THE LIVERPOOL AND MANCHESTER RAILWAY, AND EXTENSION OF THE RAILWAY SYSTEM.

The Railway finished.—Organization of the Working.—The public Opening.—Fatal Accident to Mr. Huskisson.—The Traffic begun.—Improvements in the Road, Rolling Stock, and Locomotive.—Steam-carriages tried on common Roads.—New Railway Projects.—Opposition to Railways in the South of England.—Robert Stephenson appointed Engineer of Leicester and Swannington Railway.—George removes to Snibston and sinks for Coal.—His character as a Master........ 329

CHAPTER XIV.

ROBERT STEPHENSON CONSTRUCTS THE LONDON AND BIRMINGHAM RAILWAY.

The London and Birmingham Railway projected.—George and Robert Stephenson appointed Engineers.—An Opposition organized.—Public Meetings against the Scheme.—Robert Stephenson's Interview with Sir A. Cooper.—The Survey obstructed.—The Line resurveyed.—The Bill in Parliament.—Thrown out in the Lords.—The Project revived.—The Act obtained.—The Works let in Contracts. —Difficulties of the Undertaking.—The Line described.—Blisworth Cutting.—Primrose Hill Tunnel.—Kilsby Tunnel.—Its Construction described.—Failures of Contractors.—Magnitude of the Works.—The Railway navvies........ 349

CHAPTER XV.

MANCHESTER AND LEEDS, MIDLAND, AND OTHER RAILWAYS—GENERAL EXTENSION OF RAILWAYS AND THEIR RESULTS.

Projection of new Lines.—Dutton Viaduct on the Grand Junction.—The Manchester and Leeds.—Incident in Committee.—Summit Tunnel, Littleborough.—The Midland Railway.—The Works compared with the Simplon Road.—Slip near Ambergate.—Bull Bridge.—The York and North Midland.—The Scarborough Branch.—George Stephenson on Estimates.—Stephenson on his Surveys.—His quick Observation.—His extensive Labors.—Traveling and Correspondence.—Life at Alton Grange.—Stephenson's London Office.—Journeys to Belgium.—Interviews with the King.—Public Openings of English Railways.—Stephenson's Assistants.—Results of Railroads........ 365

CHAPTER XVI.

GEORGE STEPHENSON'S COAL-MINES—OPINIONS ON RAILWAY SPEEDS—RAILWAY MANIA.

George Stephenson on Railways and Coal Traffic.—Leases the Claycross Estate.—His Residence at Tapton.—His Appearance at Mechanics' Institutes.—His Views on Railway Speed.—Undulating Lines favored.—Stephenson on Railway Speculation.—Atmospheric Railways projected.—Opposed by Stephenson.—The Railway Mania.—Action of Parliament.—Rage for direct Lines.—Stephenson's Letter to Peel.—George Hudson, the "Railway King."—His Fall.—Stephenson again visits Belgium.—Interview with King Leopold.—Journey into Spain........ 392

CHAPTER XVII.

ROBERT STEPHENSON'S CAREER—EAST COAST ROUTE TO SCOTLAND—HIGH-LEVEL BRIDGE, NEWCASTLE.

Robert Stephenson's Career.—His extensive Employment as Parliamentary Engineer.—His rival, Brunel.—The Great Western Railway.—Width of Gauge.—Robert Stephenson's caution as to Investments.—The Newcastle and Berwick Railway.—Contest in Parliament.—George Stephenson's Interview with Lord Howick. —The Royal Border Bridge, Berwick.—Progress of Iron Bridge-building.—Robert Stephenson constructs the High-Level Bridge, Newcastle.—Pile-driving by Steam.—Merits of the Structure.—The through Railway to Scotland completed .... Page 421

CHAPTER XVIII.

CHESTER AND HOLYHEAD RAILWAY—MENAI AND CONWAY BRIDGES.

George Stephenson Surveys a line from Chester to Holyhead.—Robert Stephenson afterward appointed Engineer.—The Railway Works under Penmaen Mawr.—The Crossing of the Menai Strait.—Various Plans proposed.—A Tubular Beam determined on.—Strength of wrought-iron Tubes.—Mr. William Fairbairn consulted.—His Experiments.—Professor Hodgkinson.—Chains proposed, and eventually discarded.—The Bridge Works.—The Conway Bridge.—Britannia Bridge described.—Floating of the Tubes.—Robert Stephenson's great Anxiety.—Raising of the Tubes.—The Hydraulic Press bursts.—The Works completed.—Merits of the Britannia Bridge 438

CHAPTER XIX.

CLOSING YEARS OF GEORGE STEPHENSON'S LIFE—ILLNESS AND DEATH.

George Stephenson's Life at Tapton.—Experiments in Horticulture.—His Farming Operations.—Affection for Animals.—Bee-keeping.—Reading and Conversation. —Rencounter with Lord Denman.—Hospitality at Tapton.—His Microscope.—A "Crowdie Night."—Visits to London.—Visits Sir Robert Peel at Drayton Manor.—His Conversation.—Encounter with Dr. Buckland.—Coal formed by the Sun's Light.—Opening of the Trent Valley Line and its Celebration.—Meeting with Emerson.—Illness, Death, and Funeral.—Statues of George Stephenson.—Personal Characteristics 460

CHAPTER XX.

ROBERT STEPHENSON'S VICTORIA BRIDGE, LOWER CANADA—ILLNESS AND DEATH —THE STEPHENSON CHARACTERISTICS.

Robert Stephenson's gradual Retirement from the profession of Engineer.—His Tubular Bridge over the Nile.—Railways in Canada.—Proposed Bridge at Montreal. —A Tubular Bridge proposed.—Robert Stephenson appointed Engineer.—Design of the Victoria Bridge.—The Piers.—Getting in of the Foundations.—Progress of the Works.—Erection of the Tubes.—Scene at the breaking-up of the Ice in 1858.—The Night-work.—Erection of main central Tube.—Completion of the Works.—Robert Stephenson in Parliament.—His Opinion of the Suez Canal.—His Honors.—Launch of the Great Eastern.—Last Illness and Death.—The Stephenson Characteristics.—Conclusion 474

INDEX 497

LIST OF ILLUSTRATIONS.

PAGE

Portrait of George Stephenson *to face Title Page.*
Portrait of Trevithick.................. 46
Tyne Coal-staith.......................... 49
Flange-rail.................................. 50
Cugnot's Steam-carriage.............. 62
Murdock's Model Locomotive......... 66
Symington's Model Steam-carriage.. 69
Oliver Evans's Model Locomotive.... 71
Trevithick's Tram-engine.............. 81
High-Level Bridge, Newcastle........ 96
Map of Newcastle District............ 98
Wylam.. 103
High-Street House, Wylam........... 104
Colliery Wagons........................... 110
Newburn..................................... 111
Colliery Gin................................. 120
Stephenson's Cottage at Willington Quay...................................... 121
Stephenson's Signature................ 123
West Moor Colliery...................... 127
Killingworth High Pit.................. 136
Glebe Farm-house, Benton........... 137
Rutter's School-house at Long Benton.. 140
Bruce's School, Newcastle............ 142
Stephenson's Cottage, West Moor.... 146
Sun-dial, Killingworth.................. 149
Colliers' Cottages, Long Benton...... 151
Blenkinsop's Leeds Engine............ 155
The Wylam Engine....................... 160
Spur-gear.................................... 164
Killingworth Locomotive (Section).. 168
Colliery Whimsey......................... 174
Pit-head, West Moor..................... 177
Davy's and Stephenson's Safety-lamps...................................... 187
Literary and Philosophical Institute, Newcastle................................ 189
The Stephenson Tankard.............. 197
Half-lap Joint.............................. 200
Old Killingworth Locomotive.......... 201
West Moor Pit, Killingworth.......... 214
Portrait of Edward Pease.............. 223
Map of Stockton and Darlington Railway..................................... 224

PAGE

Opening of Stockton and Darlington Railway..................................... 238
The First Railway Coach.............. 241
No. 1 Engine at Darlington............ 244
Middlesborough-on-Tees............... 246
Map of Liverpool and Manchester Railway............................... 250–1
Surveying on Chat Moss................ 264
Olive Mount Cutting..................... 291
Sankey Viaduct............................ 292
Baiting-place at Sankey................ 296
Chat Moss—Works in progress....... 299
Robert Stephenson's Cottage at Santa Anna.................................. 306
The "Rocket"............................... 321
Locomotive Competition at Rainhill. 324
Railway *versus* Road.................... 328
Map of Leicester and Swannington Railway..................................... 343
Alton Grange............................... 346
Portrait of Robert Stephenson........ 348
Map of London and Birmingham Railway..................................... 354
Blisworth Cutting......................... 355
Shafts, Kilsby Tunnel.................... 357
Kilsby Tunnel (North end)............ 363
Dutton Viaduct............................ 366
Littleborough Tunnel (West entrance)..................................... 368
Littleborough Tunnel (Walsden end) 369
Map of Midland Railway................ 370
Land-slip, Ambergate.................... 372
Bull Bridge.................................. 373
Coalville and Snibston Colliery........ 391
Tapton House.............................. 392
Lime-works, Ambergate................. 394
Forth-Street Works, Newcastle....... 396
Claycross Works.......................... 420
Newcastle from High-Level Bridge.. 421
Royal Border Bridge, Berwick........ 430
Elevation and Plan of Arch, High-Level Bridge.............................. 436
Railway at Penmaen Mawr............ 440
Map of Menai Strait...................... 442
Construction of Britannia Tube on Staging..................................... 450

	PAGE
Conway Bridge	451
Menai Bridge	457
Floating First Tube, Conway Bridge	459
View in Tapton Gardens	460
Footpath to Tapton House	465
Trinity Church, Chesterfield	471
Tablet in Trinity Church	473
Victoria Bridge, Montreal	474
Elevation of Pier, Victoria Bridge	478
Works in Progress, Victoria Bridge	480
Erection of the Main Central Tube, Victoria Bridge	483
Stephenson Memorial Schools, Willington	496

EARLY INVENTORS IN LOCOMOTION.

RICHARD TREVITHICK, C.E.

EARLY INVENTORS IN LOCOMOTION.

CHAPTER I.

SCHEMERS AND PROJECTORS.

It is easy to understand how rapid transit from place to place should, from the earliest times, have been an object of desire. The marvelous gift of speed conferred by Fortunatus's Wishing Cap was what all must have envied: it conferred power. It also conferred pleasure. "Life has not many things better than this," said Samuel Johnson as he rolled along in the post-chaise. But it also conferred comfort and well-being; and hence the easy and rapid transit of persons and commodities became in all countries an object of desire in proportion to their growth in civilization.

We have elsewhere* endeavored to describe the obstructions to the progress of society occasioned by the defective internal communications of Britain in early times, which were to a considerable extent removed by the adoption of the canal system, and the improvement of our roads and highways, toward the end of last century. But the progress of industry was so rapid—the invention of new tools, machines, and engines so greatly increased the productive wealth of the nation—that some forty years since it was found that these roads and canals, numerous and excellent though they might be, were altogether inadequate for the accommodation of the traffic of the country, which was increasing in almost a direct ratio with the increased application of steam-power to the purposes of productive industry.

The inventive minds of the nation, always on the alert—the "schemers" and the "projectors," to whom society has in all times been so greatly indebted—proceeded to apply themselves to the solution of the problem of how the communications of the country were best to be improved; and the result was, that the power

* "Lives of the Engineers," vols. i. and ii.

of steam itself was applied to remedy the inconveniences which it had caused.

Like most inventions, that of the Steam Locomotive was very gradually made. The idea of it, born in one age, was revived in the ages that followed. It was embodied first in one model, then in another—the labors of one inventor being taken up by his successors—until at length, after many disappointments and many failures, the practicable working locomotive was achieved.

The locomotive engine was not, however, sufficient for the purposes of cheap and rapid transit. Another expedient was absolutely essential to its success—that of the Railway: the smooth rail to bear the load, as well as the steam-engine to draw it.

Expedients were early adopted for the purpose of diminishing friction between the wheels of vehicles and the roads along which they were dragged by horse-power. The Romans employed stone blocks with that object; and the streets of the long-buried city of Pompeii still bear the marks of the ancient Roman chariot-wheels, as the stone track for heavy vehicles on our modern London Bridge shows the wheel-marks of the wagons which cross it. These stone blocks were merely a simple expedient to diminish friction, and were the first steps toward a railroad.

The railway proper doubtless originated in the coal districts of the North of England and Wales, where it was found useful in facilitating the transport of coals from the pits to the shipping-places. At an early period the coal was carried to the boats in panniers, or in sacks upon horses' backs. Next carts were used, and tram-ways of flag-stone were laid down, along which they were easily hauled. The carts were then converted into wagons, and mounted on four wheels instead of two.

Still farther to facilitate the haulage of the wagons, pieces of planking were laid parallel upon wooden sleepers, or imbedded in the ordinary track. It is said that these wooden rails were first employed by a Mr. Beaumont, a gentleman from the South, who, about the year 1630, adventured in the northern mines with about thirty thousand pounds, and after introducing many improvements in the working of the coal, as well as in the methods of transporting it to the staithes on the river, was ruined by his enterprise, and "within a few Years," to use the words of the ancient chronicler, "he consumed all his Money, and rode Home upon his light Horse."*

COAL-STAITH ON THE TYNE. [By R. P. Leitch.]

The use of wooden rails gradually extended, and they were laid down between most of the collieries on the Tyne and the places at which the coal was shipped. Roger North, in 1676, found the practice had become extensively adopted, and he speaks of the large sums then paid for way-leave—that is, the permission granted by the owners of lands lying between the coal-pits and the river-side to lay down a tram-way for the purpose of connecting the one with the other.

A century later, Arthur Young observed that not only had these roads become greatly multiplied, but formidable works had been constructed to carry them along upon the same level. "The coal wagon-roads from the pits to the water," he says, "are great works, carried over all sorts of inequalities of ground, so far as the distance of nine or ten miles. The tracks of the wheels are marked with pieces of wood let into the road for the wheels of the wagons to run on, by which one horse is enabled to draw, and that with ease, fifty or sixty bushels of coals."†

Saint Fond, the French traveler, who visited Newcastle in 1791, described the colliery wagon-ways in that neighborhood as superior to any thing of the kind he had seen. The wooden rails

* Harleian MSS., vol. iii., 269.

† "Six Months' Tour," vol. iii., 9.

were formed with a rounded upper surface, like a projecting moulding, and the wagon-wheels being "made of cast iron, and hollowed in the manner of a metal pulley," readily fitted the rounded surface of the rails. The economy with which the coal was thus hauled to the shipping-places was urged by Saint Fond as an inducement to his own countrymen to adopt a like method of transit.*

Similar wagon-roads were early laid down in the coal districts of Wales, Cumberland, and Scotland. At the time of the Scotch rebellion in 1745, a tram-road existed between the Tranent coal-pits and the small harbor of Cockenzie, in East Lothian; and a portion of the line was selected by General Cope as a position for his cannon at the battle of Prestonpans.

In these rude wooden tracks we find the germ of the modern railroad. Improvements were gradually made in them. Thus, at some collieries, thin plates of iron were nailed upon their upper surface, for the purpose of protecting the parts most exposed to friction. Cast-iron rails were also tried, the wooden rails having been found liable to rot. The first iron rails are supposed to have been laid down at Whitehaven as early as 1738. This cast-iron road was denominated a "plate-way," from the plate-like form in which the rails were cast. In 1767, as appears from the books of the Coalbrookdale Iron Works, in Shropshire, five or six tons of rails were cast, as an experiment, on the suggestion of Mr. Reynolds, one of the partners; and they were shortly after laid down to form a road.

In 1776, a cast-iron tram-way, nailed to wooden sleepers, was laid down at the Duke of Norfolk's colliery near Sheffield. The person who designed and constructed this coal line was Mr. John Curr, whose son has erroneously claimed for him the invention of the cast-iron railway. He certainly adopted it early, and thereby met the fate of men before their age; for his plan was opposed by the laboring people of the colliery, who got up a riot, in which they tore up the road and burned the coal-staith, while Mr. Curr

* "Travels in England, Scotland, and the Hebrides," vol. i., 142.

fled into a neighboring wood for concealment, and lay there *perdu* for three days and nights, to escape the fury of the populace.* The plates of these early tram-ways had a ledge cast on their outer edge to guide the wheel along the road, after the manner shown in the preceding cut.

In 1789, Mr. William Jessop constructed a railway at Loughborough, in Leicestershire, and there introduced the cast-iron edge-rail, with flanches cast upon the tire of the wagon-wheels to keep them on the track, instead of having the margin or flanch cast upon the rail itself; and this plan was shortly after adopted in other places. In 1800, Mr. Benjamin Outram, of Little Eaton, Derbyshire (father of the distinguished General Outram), used stone props instead of timber for supporting the ends or joinings of the rails. Thus the use of railroads, in various forms, gradually extended, until they became generally adopted in the mining districts.

Such was the growth of the railroad, which, it will be observed, originated in necessity, and was modified according to experience; progress in this, as in all departments of mechanics, having been effected by the exertions of many men; one generation entering upon the labors of that which preceded it, and carrying them onward to farther stages of improvement. The invention of the locomotive was in like manner made by successive steps. It was not the invention of one man, but of a succession of men, each working at the proper hour, and according to the needs of that hour; one inventor interpreting only the first word of the problem which his successors were to solve after long and laborious efforts and experiments. "The locomotive is not the invention of one man," said Robert Stephenson at Newcastle, "but of a nation of mechanical engineers."

Down to the end of last century, and indeed down almost to our own time, the only power used in haulage was that of the horse. Along the common roads of the country the poor horses were "tearing their hearts out" in dragging cumbersome vehicles behind them, and the transport of merchandise continued to be slow, dear, and in all respects unsatisfactory. Many expedients were suggested with the view of getting rid of the horse. The

* "Railway Locomotion and Steam Navigation, their Principles and Practice." By John Curr. London, 1847.

power of wind was one of the first expedients proposed. It was cheap, though by no means regular. It impelled ships by sea; why should it not be used to impel carriages by land?

The first sailing-coach was invented by one Simon Stevinius, or Stevins, a Fleming, toward the end of the sixteenth century. Pierre Gassendi gives an account of its performances as follows:

"Purposing to visit Grotius, Peireskius went to Scheveling that he might satisfy himself of the carriage and swiftness of a coach a few years before invented, and made with that artifice that with expanded sails it would fly upon the shore as a ship upon the sea. He had formerly heard that Count Maurice, a little after his victory at Nieuport [1600], had put himself thereinto, together with Francis Mendoza, his prisoner, on purpose to make trial thereof, and that, within two hours, they arrived at Putten, which is distant from Scheveling fourteen leagues, or two-and-forty miles. He had, therefore, a mind to make the experiment himself, and he would often tell us with what admiration he was seized when he was carried with a quick wind and yet perceived it not, the coach's motion being equally quick."*

The sailing-coach, however, was only a curiosity. As a practicable machine, it proved worthless, for the wind could not be depended upon for land locomotion. The coach could not tack as the ship did. Sometimes the wind did not blow at all, while at other times it blew a hurricane. After being used for some time as a toy, the sailing-coach was given up as impracticable, and the project speedily dropped out of sight."

But, strange to say, the expedient of driving coal-wagons by the wind was revived in Wales about a century later. On this occasion, Sir Humphry Mackworth, an ingenious coal-miner at Neath, was the projector. Waller, in his "Essay on Mines," published in 1698, takes the opportunity of eulogizing Sir Humphry's "new sailing-wagons, for the cheap carriage of his coal to the water-side, whereby one horse does the work of ten at all times; but when any wind is stirring (which is seldom wanting near the sea), one man and a small sail do the work of twenty."† It does

* A curious account of this early project is to be found in the library of the British Museum, under the name "Stevin, 1652."

† The writer adds—"I believe he (Sir Humphry Mackworth) is the first gentleman

not, however, appear that any other coal-owner had the courage to follow Sir Humphry's example, and the sailing-wagon was forgotten until, after the lapse of another century, it was revived by Mr. Edgeworth.

The employment of steam-power as a means of land locomotion was the subject of much curious speculation long before any practical attempt was made to carry it into effect. The merit of promulgating the first idea with reference to it probably belongs to no other than the great Sir Isaac Newton. In his "Explanation of the Newtonian Philosophy," written in 1680, he figured a spherical generator, supported on wheels, and provided with a seat for a passenger in front, and a long jet-pipe behind, and stated that "the whole is to be mounted on little wheels, so as to move easily on a horizontal plane, and if the hole, or jet-pipe, be opened, the vapor will rush out violently one way, and the wheels and the ball at the same time will be carried the contrary way." This, it will be observed, was but a modification of the earliest known steam-engine, or Œolopile, of Hero of Alexandria. It is not believed that Sir Isaac Newton ever made any experiment of his proposed method of locomotion, or did more than merely throw out the idea for other minds to work upon.

The idea of employing steam in locomotion was revived from time to time, and formed the subject of much curious speculation. About the middle of last century we find Benjamin Franklin, then agent in London for the United Provinces of America, Matthew Boulton, of Birmingham, and Erasmus Darwin, of Lichfield, engaged in a correspondence relative to steam as a motive power. Boulton had made a model of a fire-engine, which he sent to London for Franklin's inspection; and though the original purpose for which the engine had been contrived was the pumping of water, it was believed to be practicable to employ it also as a means of locomotion. Franklin was too much occupied at the time by grave political questions to pursue the subject; but the sanguine and speculative mind of Erasmus Darwin was inflamed by the idea of a "fiery chariot," and he pressed his

in this part of the world that hath set up sailing engines on land, driven by the wind; not for any curiosity or vain applause, but for real profit; whereby he could not fail of Bishop Malkin's blessing on his undertakings, in case he were in a capacity to bestow it."

friend Boulton to prosecute the contrivance of the necessary steam machine.*

Erasmus Darwin was in many respects a remarkable man. In his own neighborhood he was highly esteemed as a physician, and by many intelligent readers of his day he was greatly prized as a poet. Horace Walpole said of his "Botanic Garden" that it was "the most delicious poem upon earth," and he declared that he "could read it over and over again forever." The doctor was accustomed to write his poems with a pencil on little scraps of paper while riding about among his patients in his "sulky." The vehicle, which was worn and bespattered outside, had room within it for the doctor and his appurtenances only. On one side of him was a pile of books reaching from the floor to nearly the front window of the carriage, while on the other was a hamper containing fruit and sweetmeats, with a store of cream and sugar, with which the occupant regaled himself during his journey. Lashed on to the place usually appropriated to the "boot" was a large pail for watering the horses, together with a bag of oats and a bundle of hay. Such was the equipage of a fashionable country physician of the last century.

Dr. Darwin was a man of large and massive person, bearing a rather striking resemblance to his distinguished townsman, Dr. Johnson, in manner, deportment, and force of character. He was full of anecdote, and his conversation was most original and entertaining. He was a very outspoken man, vehemently enunciating theories which some thought original and others dangerous. As he drove through the country in his "sulky," his mind teemed with speculation on all subjects, from zoonomy, botany, and physiology, to physics, æsthetics, and mental philosophy. Though his speculations were not always sound, they were clever and ingenious, and, at all events, they had the effect of setting other minds a-thinking and speculating on science and the methods for its advancement. From his "Loves of the Plants"—afterward so cleverly parodied by George Canning in his "Loves of the Triangles"—it would appear that the doctor even entertained a theory of managing the winds by a little philosophic artifice. His scheme of a steam locomotive was of a more prac-

* See farther, "Lives of the Engineers," vol. iv., Boulton and Watt, p. 182–4.

tical character. This idea, like so many others, first occurred to him in his "sulky."

"As I was riding home yesterday," he wrote to his friend Boulton in the year 1765, "I considered the scheme of the fiery chariot, and the longer I contemplated this favorite idea, the more practicable it appeared to me. I shall lay my thoughts before you, crude and undigested though they may appear to be, telling you as well what I thought would not do as what would do, as by those hints you may be led into various trains of thinking upon this subject, and by that means (if any hints can assist your genius, which, without hints, is above all others I am acquainted with) be more likely to improve or disapprove. And as I am quite mad of this scheme, I beg you will not mention it, or show this paper to Wyat or any body.

"These things are required: 1st, a rotary motion; 2d, easily altering its direction to any other direction; 3d, to be accelerated, retarded, destroyed, revived instantly and easily; 4th, the bulk, the weight, and expense of the machine to be as small as possible in proportion to its use."*

He then goes on to throw out various suggestions as to the form and arrangement of the machine, the number of wheels on which it was to run, and the mode of applying the power. The text of this letter is illustrated by rough diagrams, showing a vehicle mounted on three wheels, the foremost or guiding wheel being under the control of the driver; but in a subsequent passage he says, "I think four wheels will be better."

"Let there be two cylinders," he proceeds. "Suppose one piston up, and the vacuum made under it by the *jet d'eau froid.* That piston can not yet descend because the cock is not yet opened which admits the steam into its antagonist cylinder. Hence the two pistons are in equilibrio, being either of them pressed by the atmosphere. Then I say, if the cock which admits the steam into the antagonist cylinder be opened gradually and not with a jerk, that the first-mentioned [piston in the] cylinder will descend gradually and not less forcibly. Hence, by the management of the steam cocks, the motion may be accelerated, retarded, destroyed, revived instantly and easily. And if this answers in practice as it does in theory, the machine can not fail of success! Eureka!

* Soho MSS.

"The cocks of the cold water may be moved by the great work, but the steam cocks must be managed by the hand of the charioteer, who also directs the rudder-wheel. [Then follow his rough diagrams.] The central wheel ought to have been under the rollers, so as it may be out of the way of the boiler."*

After farther explaining himself, he goes on to say:

"If you could learn the expense of coals to a common fire-engine and the weight of water it draws, some certain estimate may be made if such a scheme as this would answer. Pray don't show Wyat this scheme, for if you think it feasible and will send me a critique upon it, I will certainly, if I can get somebody to bear half the expense with me, endeavor to build a fiery chariot, and, if it answers, get a patent. If you choose to be partner with me in the profit, and expense, and trouble, let me know, as I am determined to execute it if you approve of it.

"Please to remember the pulses of the common fire-engines, and say in what manner the piston is so made as to keep out the air in its motion. By what way is the *jet d'eau froid* let out of the cylinder? How full of water is the boiler? How is it supplied, and what is the quantity of its waste of water?"†

It will be observed from these remarks that the doctor's notions were of the crudest sort, and, as he obviously contemplated but a modification of the Newcomen engine, then chiefly employed in pumping water from mines, the action of which was slow, clumsy, and expensive, the steam being condensed by injection of cold water, it is clear that, even though Boulton had taken up and prosecuted Darwin's idea, it could not have issued in a practicable or economical working locomotive.

But, although Darwin himself—his time engrossed by his increasing medical practice—proceeded no farther with his scheme of a "fiery chariot," he succeeded in inflaming the mind of his young friend, Richard Lovell Edgeworth, who had settled for a time in his neighborhood, and induced him to direct his attention to the introduction of improved means of locomotion by steam. In a letter written by Dr. Small to Watt in 1768, we find him describing Edgeworth as "a gentleman of fortune, young, mechanical, and indefatigable, who has taken a resolution to move land and water carriages by steam, and has made considerable

* Soho MSS.

† Ibid.

progress in the short space of time that he has devoted to the study."

One of the first-fruits of Edgeworth's investigations was his paper "On Railroads," which he read before the Society of Arts in 1768, and for which he was awarded the society's gold medal. He there proposed that four iron railroads be laid down on one of the great roads out of London; two for carts and wagons, and two for light carriages and stage-coaches. The post-chaises and gentlemen's carriages might, he thought, be made to go at eight miles an hour, and the stage-coaches at six miles an hour, drawn by a single horse. He urged that such a method of transport would be attended with great economy of power and consequent cheapness. Many years later, in 1802, he published his views on the same subject in a more matured form. By that time Watt's steam-engine had come into general use, and he suggested that small stationary engines should be fixed along his proposed railroad, and made, by means of circulating chains, to draw the carriages along with a great diminution of horse labor and expense.

It is creditable to Mr. Edgeworth's forethought that both the models proposed by him have since been adopted. Horse-traction of carriages on railways is now in general use in the towns of the United States; and omnibuses on the same principle regularly ply between the Place de la Concorde at Paris and St. Cloud, both being found highly convenient for the public, and profitable to the proprietors. The system of working railways by fixed engines was also regularly employed on some lines in the infancy of the railway system, though it has since fallen into disuse, in consequence of the increased power given to the modern locomotive, which enables it to surmount gradients formerly considered impracticable.

Besides his speculations on railways worked by horse and steam power, Mr. Edgeworth—unconscious of the early experiments of Stevins and Mackworth—made many attempts to apply the power of the wind with the same object. It is stated in his "Memoirs" that he devoted himself to locomotive traction by various methods for a period of about forty years, during which he made above a hundred working models, in a great variety of forms; and though none of his schemes were attended with practical success, he adds that he gained far more in amusement than he lost by his unsuccessful labors. "The only mortification that affected me," he says, "was my discovery, many years after I had taken out my patent [for the sailing-carriage], that the rudiments of my whole scheme were mentioned in an obscure memoir of the French Academy."

The sailing-wagon scheme, as revived by Mr. Edgeworth, was doubtless of a highly ingenious character, though it was not practicable. One of his expedients was a portable railway, of a kind somewhat similar to that since revived by Mr. Boydell. Many experiments were tried with the new wagons on Hare Hatch Common, but they were attended with so much danger when the wind blew strong—the vehicles seeming to fly rather than roll along the ground—that farther experiments were abandoned, and Mr. Edgeworth himself at length came to the conclusion that a power so uncertain as that of the wind could never be relied upon for the safe conduct of ordinary traffic. His thoughts finally settled on steam as the only practicable power for this purpose; but, though his enthusiasm in the cause of improved transit of persons and of goods remained unabated, he was now too far advanced in life to prosecute his investigations in that direction. When an old man of seventy he wrote to James Watt (7th August, 1813): "I have always thought that steam would become the universal lord, and that we should in time scorn post-horses. An iron railroad would be a cheaper thing than a road on the common construction. Four years later he died, and left the problem, which he had nearly all his life been trying ineffectually to solve, to be worked out by younger men.

Dr. Darwin had long before preceded him into the silent land. Down to his death in 1802, Edgeworth had kept up a continuous correspondence with him on his favorite topic; but it does not appear that Darwin ever revived his project of the "fiery chariot." He was satisfied to prophesy its eventual success in the lines which are perhaps more generally known than any he has written—for, though Horace Walpole declared that he could "read the Botanic Garden over and over again forever," the poetry of Darwin is now all but forgotten. The following was his prophecy, published in 1791, before any practical locomotive or steam boat had been invented:

> "Soon shall thy arm, unconquered steam, afar
> Drag the slow barge, or drive the rapid car;
> Or on wide-waving wings expanded bear
> The flying chariot through the fields of air.
> Fair crews triumphant, leaning from above,
> Shall wave their flutt'ring kerchiefs as they move;
> Or warrior bands alarm the gaping crowd,
> And armies shrink beneath the shadowy cloud."

The prophecy embodied in the first two lines of the passage has certainly been fulfilled, but the triumph of the steam balloon has yet to come.

CHAPTER II.

EARLY LOCOMOTIVE MODELS.

THE application of steam-power to the driving of wheel-carriages on common roads was in 1759 brought under the notice of James Watt by his young friend John Robison, then a student at the University of Glasgow. Robison prepared a rough sketch of his suggested steam-carriage, in which he proposed to place the cylinder with its open end downward, to avoid the necessity for using a working beam. Watt was then only twenty-three years old, and was very much occupied in conducting his business of a mathematical instrument maker, which he had only recently established. Nevertheless, he proceeded to construct a model locomotive provided with two cylinders of tin-plate, intending that the pistons and their connecting-rods should act alternately on two pinions attached to the axles of the carriage-wheels. But the model, when made, did not answer Watt's expectations; and when, shortly after, Robison left college to go to sea, he laid the project aside, and did not resume it for many years.

In the mean time, an ingenious French mechanic had taken up the subject, and proceeded to make a self-moving road engine worked by steam-power. It has been incidentally stated that a M. Pouillet was the first to make a locomotive machine,* but no particulars are given of the invention, which is more usually attributed to Nicholas Joseph Cugnot, a native of Void, in Lorraine, where he was born in 1729. Not much is known of Cugnot's early history beyond that he was an officer in the army, that he published several works on military science, and that on leaving the army he devoted himself to the invention of a steam-carriage to be run on common roads.

It appears from documents collected by M. Morin that Cugnot

* "Portfeuille du Conservatoire des Arts et Métiers," Livraison 1, p. 3.

constructed his first carriage at the Arsenal in 1769, at the cost of the Comte de Saxe, by whom he was patronized and liberally helped. It ran on three wheels, and was put in motion by an engine composed of two single-acting cylinders, the pistons of which acted alternately on the single front wheel. While this machine was in course of construction, a Swiss officer, named Planta, brought forward a similar project; but, on perceiving that Cugnot's carriage was superior to his own, he proceeded no farther with it.

When Cugnot's carriage was ready, it was tried in the presence of the Duc de Choiseul, the Comte de Saxe, and other military officers. On being first set in motion, it ran against a stone wall which stood in its way, and threw it down. There was thus no doubt about its power, though there were many doubts about its manageableness. At length it was got out of the Arsenal and put upon the road, when it was found that, though only loaded with four persons, it could not travel faster than about two and a quarter miles an hour; and that, the size of the boiler not being sufficient, it would not continue at work for more than twelve or fifteen minutes, when it was necessary to wait until sufficient steam had been raised to enable it to proceed farther.

The experiment was looked upon with great interest, and admitted to be of a very remarkable character; and, considering that it was a first attempt, it was not by any means regarded as unsuccessful. As it was believed that such a machine, if properly proportioned, might be employed to drag cannon into the field independent of horse-power, the Minister of War authorized Cugnot to proceed with the construction of a new and improved machine, which was finished and ready for trial in the course of the following year. The new locomotive was composed of two parts, one being a carriage supported on two wheels, somewhat resembling a small brewer's cart, furnished with a seat for the driver, while the other contained the machinery, which was supported on a single driving-wheel 4 ft. 2 in. in diameter. The engine consisted of a round copper boiler with a furnace inside provided with two small chimneys, two single-acting 13-in. brass cylinders communicating with the boiler by a steam-pipe, and the arrangements for communicating the motion of the pistons to the driving-wheel, together with the steering-gear.

CUGNOT'S ENGINE.

The two parts of the machine were united by a movable pin and a toothed sector fixed on the framing of the front or machine part of the carriage. When one of the pistons descended, the piston-rod drew with it a crank, the catch of which caused the driving-wheel to make a quarter of a revolution by means of the ratchet-wheel fixed on the axle of the driving-wheel. At the same time, a chain fixed to the crank on the same side also descended and moved a lever, the opposite end of which was thereby raised, restoring the second piston to its original position at the top of the cylinder by the interposition of a second chain and crank. The piston-rod of the descending piston, by means of a catch, set other levers in motion, the chain fixed to them turning a half-way cock so as to open the second cylinder to the steam and the first to the atmosphere. The second piston, then descending in turn, caused the driving-wheel to make another quarter revolution, restoring the first piston to its original position; and the process being repeated, the machine was thereby kept in motion. To enable it to run backward, the catch of the crank was arranged in such a manner that it could be made to act either above or below, and thereby reverse the action of the machinery on the driving-wheel. It will thus be observed that Cugnot's locomotive presented a simple and ingenious form of a high-pressure engine; and, though of rude construction, it was a highly-creditable piece of work, considering the time of its appearance and the circumstances under which it was constructed.

Several successful trials were made with the new locomotive in the streets of Paris, which excited no small degree of interest. Unhappily, however, an accident which occurred to it in one of the trials had the effect of putting a stop to farther experiments. Turning the corner of a street near the Madeleine one day, when the machine was running at a speed of about three miles an hour, it became overbalanced, and fell over with a crash; after which, the running of the vehicle being considered dangerous, it was thenceforth locked up securely in the Arsenal to prevent its doing farther mischief.

The merit of Cugnot was, however, duly recognized. He was granted a pension of 300 livres, which continued to be paid to him until the outbreak of the Revolution. The Girondist Roland was appointed to examine the engine and report upon it to the Convention; but his report, which was favorable, was not adopted; on which the inventor's pension was stopped, and he was left for a time without the means of living. Some years later, Bonaparte, on his return from Italy after the peace of Campo Formio, interested himself in Cugnot's invention, and expressed a favorable opinion of his locomotive before the Academy; but his attention was shortly after diverted from the subject by the Expedition to Egypt. Napoleon, however, succeeded in restoring Cugnot's pension, and thus soothed his declining years. He died in Paris in 1804, at the age of seventy-five. Cugnot's locomotive is still to be seen in the Museum of the Conservatoire des Arts et Métiers at Paris; and it is, without exception, the most venerable and interesting of all the machines extant connected with the early history of locomotion.

While Cugnot was constructing his first machine at Paris, one Francis Moore, a linen-draper, was taking out a patent in London for moving wheel-carriages by steam. On the 14th of March, 1769, he gave notice of a patent for "a machine made of wood or metal, and worked by fire, water, or air, for the purpose of moving bodies on land or water," and on the 13th of July following he gave notice of another "for machines made of wood and metal, moved by power, for the carriage of persons and goods, and for accelerating boats, barges, and other vessels." But it does not appear that Moore did any thing beyond lodging the titles of his inventions, so that we are left in the dark as to what was their precise character.

James Watt's friend and correspondent, Dr. Small, of Birmingham, when he heard of Moore's intended project, wrote to the Glasgow inventor with the object of stimulating him to perfect his steam-engine, then in hand, and urging him to apply it, among other things, to purposes of locomotion. "I hope soon," said Small, "to travel in a fiery chariot of your invention." Watt replied to the effect that "if Linen-draper Moore does not use my engines to drive his carriages, he can't drive them by steam. If he does, I will stop them." But Watt was still a long way from perfecting his invention. The steam-engine capable of driving carriages was a problem that remained to be solved, and it was a problem to the solution of which Watt never fairly applied himself. It was enough for him to accomplish the great work of perfecting his condensed engine, and with that he rested content.

But Watt continued to be so strongly urged by those about him to apply steam-power to purposes of locomotion that, in his comprehensive patent of the 24th of August, 1784, he included an arrangement with that object. From his specification we learn that he proposed a cylindrical or globular boiler, protected outside by wood strongly hooped together, with a furnace inside entirely surrounded by the water to be heated except at the ends. Two cylinders working alternately were to be employed, and the pistons working within them were to be moved by the elastic force of the steam; "and after it has performed its office," he says, "I discharge it into the atmosphere by a proper regulating valve, or I discharge it into a condensing vessel made air-tight, and formed of thin plates and pipes of metal, having their outsides exposed to the wind;" the object of this latter arrangement being to economize the water, which would otherwise be lost. The power was to be communicated by a rotative motion (of the nature of the "sun and planet" arrangement) to the axle of one or more of the wheels of the carriage, or to another axis connected with the axle by means of toothed wheels; and in other cases he proposed, instead of the rotative machinery, to employ "toothed racks, or sectors of circles, worked with reciprocating motion by the engines, and acting upon ratched wheels fixed on the axles of the carriage." To drive a carriage containing two persons would, he estimated, require an engine with a cylinder 7 in. in diameter, making sixty strokes per minute of 1 ft. each, and so constructed as to act both on the ascent and descent of the piston; and, finally, the elastic force of the steam in the boiler must be such as to be occasionally equal to supporting a pillar of mercury 30 in. high.

Though Watt repeatedly expressed his intention of constructing a model locomotive after his specification, it does not appear that he ever carried it out. He was too much engrossed with other work; and, besides, he never entertained very sanguine views as to the practicability of road locomotion by steam. He continued, however, to discuss the subject with his partner Boulton, and from his letters we gather that his mind continued undetermined as to the best plan to be pursued. Only four days after the date of the above specification (*i. e.*, on the 28th of August, 1784) we find him communicating his views on the subject to Boulton at great length, and explaining his ideas as to how the proposed object might best be accomplished. He first addressed himself to the point of whether 80 lbs. was a sufficient power to move a post-chaise on a tolerably good and level road at four miles an hour; secondly, whether 8 ft. of boiler surface exposed to the fire would be sufficient to evaporate a cube foot of water per hour without much waste of fuel; thirdly, whether it would require steam of more than eleven and a half times atmospheric density to cause the engine to exert a power equal to 6 lbs. on the inch. "I think," he observed, "the cylinder must either be made larger or make more than sixty strokes per minute. As to working gear, stopping and backing, with steering the carriage, I think these things perfectly manageable."

"My original ideas on the subject," he continued, "were prior to my invention of these improved engines, or before the crank, or any other of the rotative motions were thought of. My plan then was to have two inverted cylinders, with toothed racks instead of piston-rods, which were to be applied to two ratchet-wheels on the axle-tree, and to act alternately; and I am partly of opinion that this method might be applied with advantage yet, because it needs no fly and has some other conveniences. From what I have said, and from much more which a little reflection will suggest to you, you will see that without several circumstances turn out more favorable than has been stated, the machine will be clumsy and defective, and that it will cost much time to bring it to any tolerable degree of perfection, and that for me to interrupt the career of our business would be imprudent; I even grudge the time I have taken to make these comments on it. There is, however, another way in which much mechanism might be saved if it be in itself practicable, which is to apply to it one of the self-moving rotatives, which has no regulators, but turns like a mill-wheel by the constant influx and efflux of steam; but this would not abridge the size of the boiler, and I am not sure that such engines are practicable."

It will be observed from these explanations that Watt's views as to road locomotion were still crude and undefined; and, indeed, he never carried them farther. While he was thus discussing the subject with Boulton, William Murdock, one of the most skilled and ingenious workmen of the Soho firm—then living at Redruth, in Cornwall—was occupying himself during his leisure hours, which were but few, in constructing a model locomotive after a design of his own. He had doubtless heard of the proposal to apply steam to locomotion, and, being a clever inventor, he forthwith set himself to work out the problem. The plan he pursued was very simple and yet efficient. His model was of small dimensions, standing little more than a foot high, but it was sufficiently large to demonstrate the soundness of the principle on which it was constructed. It was supported on three wheels, and carried a small copper boiler, heated by a spirit-lamp, with a flue passing obliquely through it. The cylinder, of $\frac{3}{4}$ in. diameter and 2 in. stroke, was fixed in the top of the boiler, the piston-rod being connected with the vibrating beam attached to the connecting-rod which worked the crank of the driving-wheel. This little engine worked by the expansive force of the steam only, which was discharged into the atmosphere after it had done its work of alternately raising and depressing the piston in the cylinder.

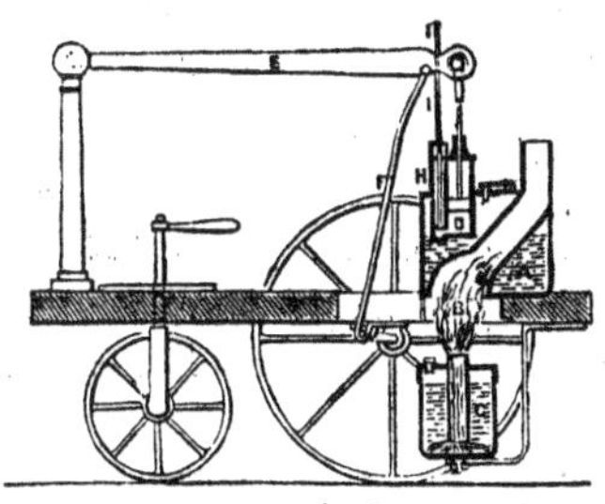
SECTION OF MURDOCK'S MODEL.

Mr. Murdock's son informed the author that this model was invented and constructed in 1781, but, from the correspondence of Boulton and Watt, we infer that it was not ready for trial until 1784. The first experiment with it was made in Murdock's own house at Redruth, when it successfully hauled a model wagon round the room—the single wheel placed in front of the engine, and working in a swivel frame, enabling it to run round in a circle.

Another experiment was made out of doors, on which occasion, small though the engine was, it fairly outran the speed of its inventor. It seems that one night, after returning from his duties at the Redruth mine, Murdock determined to try the working of his model locomotive. For this purpose he had recourse to the walk leading to the church, about a mile from the town. It was rather narrow, and was bounded on each side by high hedges. The night was dark, and Murdock set out alone to try his experiment. Having lit his lamp, the water soon boiled, when off started the engine, with the inventor after it. Shortly after he heard distant shouts of terror. It was too dark to perceive objects; but he found, on following up the machine, that the cries proceeded from the worthy pastor of the parish, who, going toward the town, was met on this lonely road by the hissing and fiery little monster, which he subsequently declared he had taken to be the Evil One in *propria persona!*

Watt was by no means pleased when he learned that Murdock was giving his mind to these experiments. He feared that it might have the effect of withdrawing him from the employment of the firm, to which his services had become almost indispensable; for there was no more active, skillful, or ingenious workman in all their concern. Watt accordingly wrote to Boulton, recommending him to advise Murdock to give up his locomotive-engine scheme; but, if he could not succeed in that, then, rather than lose Murdock's services, Watt proposed that he should be allowed an advance of £100 to enable him to prosecute his experiments, and if he succeeded within a year in making an engine capable of drawing a post-chaise carrying two passengers and the driver at four miles an hour, it was suggested that he should be taken as partner into the locomotive business, for which Boulton and Watt were to provide the necessary capital.

Two years later (in September, 1786) we find Watt again expressing his regret to Boulton that Murdock was "busying himself with the steam-carriage." "I have still," said he, "the same opinion concerning it that I had, but to prevent as much as possible more fruitless argument about it, I have one of some size under hand, and am resolved to try if God will work a miracle in favor of these carriages. I shall in some future letter send you the words of my specification on that subject. In the mean time I wish William could be brought to do as we do, to mind the business in hand, and let such as Symington and Sadler throw away their time and money in hunting shadows." In a subsequent letter Watt expressed his gratification at finding "that William applies to his business." From that time Murdock as well as Watt dropped all farther speculation on the subject, and left it to others to work out the problem of the locomotive engine. Murdock's model remained but a curious toy, which he himself took pleasure in exhibiting to his intimate friends; and though he long continued to speculate about road locomotion, and was persuaded of its practicability, he refrained from embodying his ideas of it in any more complete working form.

Symington and Sadler, the "hunters of shadows" referred to by Watt, did little to advance the question. Of Sadler we know nothing beyond that in 1786 he was making experiments as to the application of steam-power to the driving of wheel-carriages. This came to the knowledge of Boulton and Watt, who gave him notice, on the 4th of July of the same year, that "the sole privilege of making steam-engines by the elastic force of steam acting on a piston, with or without condensation, had been granted to Mr. Watt by Act of Parliament, and also that among other improvements and applications of his principle he hath particularly specified the application of steam-engines for driving wheel carriages in a patent which he took out in the year 1784." They accordingly cautioned him against proceeding farther in the matter; and as we hear no more of Sadler's steam-carriage, it is probable that the notice had its effect.

The name of William Symington is better known in connection with the history of steam locomotion by sea. He was born at Leadhills, in Scotland, in 1763. His father was a practical mechanic, who superintended the engines and machinery of the Mining Company at Wanlockhead, where one of Boulton and Watt's pumping-engines was at work. Young Symington was of an ingenious turn of mind from his boyhood, and at an early period he seems to have conceived the idea of employing the steam-engine to drive wheel-carriages. His father and he worked together, and by the year 1786, when the son was only twenty-three years of age, they succeeded in completing a working model of a road locomotive. Mr. Meason, the manager of the mine, was so much pleased with the model, the merit of which principally belonged to young Symington, that he sent him to Edinburg for the purpose of exhibiting it before the scientific gentlemen of that city, in the hope that it might lead, in some way, to his future advancement in life. Mr. Meason also allowed the model to be exhibited at his own house there, and he invited many gentlemen of distinction to inspect it.

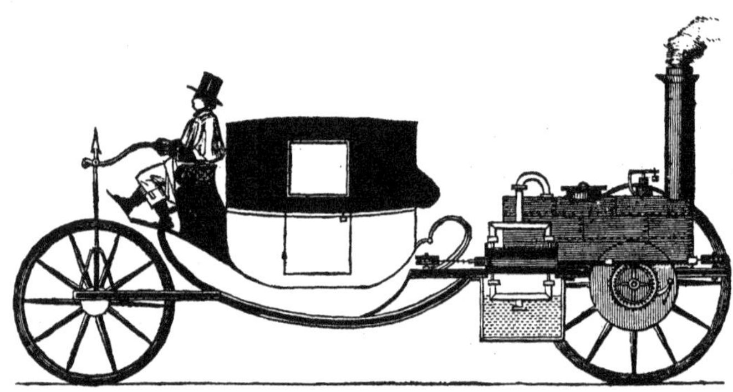

SYMINGTON'S MODEL STEAM-CARRIAGE, 1786.

The machine consisted of a carriage and locomotive behind, supported on four wheels. The boiler was cylindrical, communicating by a steam-pipe with the two horizontal cylinders, one on each side of the engine. When the piston was raised by the action of the steam, a vacuum was produced by the condensation of the steam in a cold-water tank placed underneath the engine, on which the piston was again forced back by the pressure of the atmosphere. The motion was communicated to the wheels by rack-rods connected with the piston-rod, which worked on each side of a drum fixed on the hind axle, the alternate action of which rods upon the tooth and ratchet wheels with which the drum was provided producing the rotary motion. It will thus be observed that Symington's engine was partly atmospheric and partly condensing, the condensation being effected by a separate vessel and air-pump, as patented by Watt; and though the arrangement was ingenious, it is clear that, had it ever been brought into use, the traction by means of such an engine would have been of the very slowest kind.

But Symington's engine was not destined to be applied to road locomotion. He was completely diverted from employing it for that purpose by his connection with Mr. Miller, of Dalswinton, then engaged in experimenting on the application of mechanical power to the driving of his double paddle-boat. The power of men was first tried, but the labor was found too severe; and when Mr. Miller went to see Symington's model, and informed the inventor of his difficulty in obtaining a regular and effective power for driving his boat, Symington—his mind naturally full of his own invention—at once suggested his steam-engine for the purpose. The suggestion was adopted, and Mr. Miller authorized him to proceed with the construction of a steam-engine to be fitted into his double pleasure boat on Dalswinton Lock, where it was tried in October, 1788. This was followed by farther experiments, which eventually led to the construction of the *Charlotte Dundas* in 1801, which may be regarded as the first practical steam-boat ever built.

Symington took out letters patent in the same year, securing the invention, or rather the novel combination of inventions, embodied in his steam-boat, but he never succeeded in getting it introduced into practical use. From the date of completing his invention, fortune seemed to run steadily against him. The Duke of Bridgewater, who had ordered a number of Symington's steam-boats for his canal, died, and his executors countermanded the order. Symington failed in inducing any other canal company to make trial of his invention. Lord Dundas also took the *Charlotte Dundas* off the Forth and Clyde Canal, where she had been at work, and from that time the vessel was never more tried. Symington had no capital of his own to work upon, and he seems to have been unable to make friends among capitalists. The rest of his life was for the most part thrown away. Toward the close of it his principal haunt was London, amid whose vast population he was one of the many waifs and strays. He succeeded in obtaining a grant of £100 from the Privy Purse in 1824, and afterward an annuity of £50, but he did not live long to enjoy it, for he died in March, 1831, and was buried in the church-yard of St. Botolph, Aldgate, where there is not even a stone to mark the grave of the inventor of the first practicable steam-boat.

While the inventive minds of England were thus occupied, those of America were not idle. The idea of applying steam-power to the propulsion of carriages on land is said to have occurred to John Fitch in 1785; but he did not pursue the idea "for more than a week," being diverted from it by his scheme of applying the same power to the propulsion of vessels on the water.* About the same time, Oliver Evans, a native of Newport, Delaware, was occupied with a project for driving steam-carriages on common roads; and in 1786 the Legislature of Mary-

OLIVER EVANS'S MODEL LOCOMOTIVE.

land granted him the exclusive right for that state. Several years, however, passed before he could raise the means for erecting a model carriage, most of his friends regarding the project as altogether chimerical and impracticable. In 1800 or 1801, Evans began a steam-carriage at his own expense; but he had not proceeded far with it when he altered his intention, and applied the engine intended for the driving of a carriage to the driving of a small grinding-mill, in which it was found efficient. In 1804 he constructed at Philadelphia a second engine of five-horse power, working on the high-pressure principle, which was placed on a large flat or scow, mounted upon wheels. "This," says his biographer, "was considered a fine opportunity to show

* This statement is made in "The Life of John Fitch," by Thompson Westcott, Philadelphia, 1857. Mr. Thompson there states that the idea of employing a steam-engine to propel carriages on land occurred to John Fitch at a time when, he avers, "he was altogether ignorant that a steam-engine had ever been invented!" (p. 120). Such a statement is calculated to damage the credibility of the entire book, in which the invention of the steam-boat, as well as of the screw propeller, is unhesitatingly claimed for John Fitch.

the public that his engine could propel both land and water conveyances. When the machine was finished, Evans fixed under it, in a rough and temporary manner, wheels with wooden axletrees. Although the whole weight was equal to two hundred barrels of flour, yet his small engine propelled it up Market Street, and round the circle to the water-works, where it was launched into the Schuylkill. A paddle-wheel was then applied to its stern, and it thus sailed down that river to the Delaware, a distance of sixteen miles, in the presence of thousands of spectators."* It does not, however, appear that any farther trial was made of this engine as a locomotive; and, having been dismounted and applied to the driving of a small grinding-mill, its employment as a traveling engine was shortly forgotten.

* Horne's "Memoirs of the Most Eminent American Mechanics," New York, 1858, p. 76.

CHAPTER III.

THE CORNISH LOCOMOTIVE—MEMOIR OF RICHARD TREVITHICK.

WHILE the discussion of steam-power as a means of locomotion was proceeding in England, other projectors were advocating the extension of wagon-ways and railroads. Mr. Thomas, of Denton, near Newcastle-on-Tyne, read a paper before the Philosophical Society of that town in 1800, in which he urged the laying down of railways throughout the country, on the principle of the coal wagon-ways, for the general carriage of goods and merchandise; and Dr. James Anderson, of Edinburg, about the same time published his "Recreations of Agriculture," wherein he recommended that railways should be laid along the principal turnpike-roads, and worked by horse-power, which, he alleged, would have the effect of greatly reducing the cost of transport, and thereby stimulating all branches of industry.

Railways were indeed already becoming adopted in places where the haulage of heavy loads was for short distances; and in some cases lines were laid down of considerable length. One of the first of such lines constructed under the powers of an Act of Parliament was the Cardiff and Merthyr railway or tram-road, about twenty-seven miles in length, for the accommodation of the iron-works of Plymouth, Pen-y-darran, and Dowlais, all in South Wales, the necessary Act for which was obtained in 1794. Another, the Sirhoway railroad, about twenty-eight miles in length, was constructed under the powers of an act obtained in 1801; it accommodated the Tredegar and Sirhoway Iron-works and the Trevill Lime-works, as well as the collieries along its route.

In the immediate neighborhood of London there was another very early railroad, the Wandsworth and Croydon tram-way, about ten miles long, which was afterward extended southward to Merstham, in Surrey, for about eight miles more, making a total length of nearly eighteen miles. The first act for the purpose of authorizing the construction of this road was obtained in 1800.

All these lines were, however, worked by horses, and in the case of the Croydon and Merstham line, donkeys shared in the work, which consisted chiefly in the haulage of stone, coal, and lime. No proposal had yet been made to apply the power of steam as a substitute for horses on railways, nor were the rails then laid down of a strength sufficient to bear more than a loaded wagon of the weight of three tons, or, at the very outside, of three and a quarter tons.

It was, however, observed from the first that there was an immense saving in the cost of haulage; and on the day of opening the southern portion of the Merstham Railroad in 1805, a train of twelve wagons laden with stone, weighing in all thirty-eight tons, was drawn six miles in an hour by one horse, with apparent ease, down an incline of 1 in 120; and this was bruited about as an extraordinary feat, highly illustrative of the important uses of the new iron-ways.

About the same time, the subject of road locomotion was again brought into prominent notice by an important practical experiment conducted in a remote corner of the kingdom. The experimenter was a young man, then obscure, but afterward famous, who may be fairly regarded as the inventor of the railway locomotive, if any single individual be entitled to that appellation. This was Richard Trevithick, a person of extraordinary mechanical skill but of marvelous ill fortune, who, though the inventor of many ingenious contrivances, and the founder of the fortunes of many, himself died in cold obstruction and in extreme poverty, leaving behind him nothing but his great inventions and the recollection of his genius.

Richard Trevithick was born on the 13th of April, 1771, in the parish of Illogan, a few miles west of Redruth, in Cornwall. In the immediate neighborhood rises Castle-Carn-brea, a rocky eminence, supposed by Borlase to have been the principal seat of Druidic worship in the West of England. The hill commands an extraordinary view over one of the richest mining fields of Cornwall, from Chacewater and Redruth to Camborne.

Trevithick's father acted as purser at several of the mines. Though a man in good position and circumstances, he does not seem to have taken much pains with his son's education. Being an only child, he was very much indulged—among other things, in his dislike for the restraints and discipline of school; and he was left to wander about among the mines, spending his time in the engine-rooms, picking up information about pumping-engines and mining machinery.

His father, observing the boy's strong bent toward mechanics, placed him for a time as pupil with William Murdock, while the latter lived at Redruth superintending the working and repairs of Boulton and Watt's pumping-engines in that neighborhood. During his pupilage, young Trevithick doubtless learned much from that able mechanic. It is probable that he got his first idea of the high-pressure road locomotive which he afterward constructed from Murdock's ingenious little model above described, the construction and action of which must have been quite familiar to him, for no secret was ever made of it, and its performances were often exhibited.

Many new pumping-engines being in course of erection in the neighborhood about that time, there was an unusual demand for engineers, which it was found difficult to supply; and young Trevithick, whose skill was acknowledged, had no difficulty in getting an appointment. The father was astonished at his boy's presumption (as he supposed it to be) in undertaking such a responsibility, and he begged the mine agents to reconsider their decision. But the result showed that they were justified in making the appointment; for young Trevithick, though he had not yet attained his majority, proved fully competent to perform the duties devolving upon him as engineer.

So long as Boulton and Watt's patent continued to run, constant attempts were made in Cornwall and elsewhere to upset it. Their engines had cleared the mines of water, and thereby rescued the mine lords from ruin, but it was felt to be a great hardship that they should have to pay for the right to use them. They accordingly stimulated the ingenuity of the local engineers to contrive an engine that should answer the same purpose, and enable them to evade making any farther payments to Boulton and Watt. The first to produce an engine that seemed likely to answer the purpose was Jonathan Hornblower, who had been employed in erecting Watt's engines in Cornwall. After him one

Edward Bull, who had been first a stoker and then an assistant-tender of Watt's engines, turned out another pumping-engine, which promised to prove an equally safe evasion of the existing patent. But Boulton and Watt having taken the necessary steps to defend their right, several actions were tried, in which they proved successful, and then the mine lords were compelled to disgorge. When they found that Hornblower could be of no farther use to them, they abandoned him—threw him away like a sucked orange; and shortly after we find him a prisoner for debt in the King's Bench, almost in a state of starvation. Nor do we hear any thing more of Edward Bull after the issue of the Boulton and Watt trial.

Like the other Cornish engineers, young Trevithick took an active part from the first in opposing the Birmingham patent, and he is said to have constructed several engines, with the assistance of William Bull (formerly an erector of Watt's machines), with the object of evading it. These engines are said to have been highly creditable to their makers, working to the entire satisfaction of the mine-owners. The issue of the Watt trial, however, which declared all such engines to be piracies, brought to an end for a time a business which would otherwise have proved a very profitable one, and Trevithick's partnership with Bull then came to an end.

While carrying on his business, Trevithick had frequent occasion to visit Mr. Harvey's iron foundery at Hayle, then a small work, but now one of the largest in the West of England, the Cornish pumping-engines turned out by Harvey and Co. being the very best of their kind. During these visits Trevithick became acquainted with the various members of Mr. Harvey's family, and in course of time he contracted an engagement with one of his daughters, Miss Jane Harvey, to whom he was married in November, 1797.

A few years later we find Trevithick engaged in partnership with his cousin, Andrew Vivian, also an engineer. They carried on their business of engine-making at Camborne, a mining town situated in the midst of the mining district, a few miles south of Redruth. Watt's patent-right expired in 1800, and from that time the Cornish engineers were free to make engines after their own methods. Trevithick was not content to follow in the beaten paths, but, being of a highly speculative turn, he occupied himself in contriving various new methods of employing steam with the object of economizing fuel and increasing the effective power of the engine.

From an early period he entertained the idea of making the expansive force of steam act directly on both sides of the piston on the high-pressure principle, and thus getting rid of the process of condensation as in Watt's engines. Although Cugnot had employed high-pressure steam in his road locomotive, and Murdock in his model, and although Watt had distinctly specified the action of steam at high-pressure as well as low in his patents of 1769, 1782, and 1784, the idea was not embodied in any practicable working engine until the subject was taken in hand by Trevithick. The results of his long and careful study were embodied in the patent which he took out in 1802, in his own and Vivian's name, for an improved steam-engine, and "the application thereof for driving carriages and for other purposes."

The arrangement of Trevithick's engine was exceedingly ingenious. It exhibited a beautiful simplicity of parts; the machinery was arranged in a highly effective form, uniting strength with solidity and portability, and enabling the power of steam to be employed with very great rapidity, economy, and force. Watt's principal objection to using high-pressure steam consisted in the danger to which the boiler was exposed of being burst by internal pressure. In Trevithick's engine, this was avoided by using a cylindrical wrought-iron boiler, being the form capable of presenting the greatest resistance to the expansive force of steam. Boilers of this kind were not, however, new. Oliver Evans, of Delaware, had made use of them in his high-pressure engines prior to the date of Trevithick's patent; and, as Evans did not claim the cylindrical boiler, it is probable that the invention was in use before his time. Nevertheless, Trevithick had the merit of introducing the round boilers into Cornwall, where they are still known as "Trevithick boilers." The saving in fuel effected by their use was such that in 1812 the Messrs. Williams, of Scorrier, made Trevithick a present of £300, in acknowledgment of the benefits arising to their mines from that source alone.

Trevithick's steam-carriage was the most compact and handsome vehicle of the kind that had yet been invented, and, indeed, as regards arrangement, it has scarcely to this day been surpassed. It consisted of a carriage capable of accommodating some half-dozen passengers, underneath which was the engine and machinery inclosed, about the size of an orchestra drum, the whole being supported on four wheels—two in front, by which it was guided, and two, behind, by which it was driven. The engine had but one cylinder. The piston-rod outside the cylinder was double, and drove a cross-piece, working in guides, on the opposite side of the cranked axle to the cylinder, the crank of the axle revolving between the double parts of the piston-rod. Toothed wheels were attached to this axle, which worked into other toothed wheels fixed on the axle of the driving-wheels. The steam-cocks were opened and shut by a connection with the crank-axle; and the force-pump, with which the boiler was supplied with water, was also worked from it, as were the bellows to blow the fire and thereby keep up the combustion in the furnace.

The specification clearly alludes to the use of the engine on railroads as follows: "It is also to be noticed that we do occasionally, or in certain cases, make the external periphery of the wheels uneven by projecting heads of nails or bolts, or cross grooves or fittings to railroads where required, and that in cases of hard pull we cause a lever, belt, or claw to project through the rim of one or both of the said wheels, so as to take hold of the ground, but that, in general, the ordinary structure or figure of the external surface of those wheels will be found to answer the intended purpose."

The specification also shows the application of the high-pressure engine on the same principle to the driving of a sugar-mill, or for other purposes where a fixed power is required, dispensing with condenser, cistern, air-pump, and cold-water pump. In the year 1803, a small engine of this kind was erected after Trevithick's plan at Marazion, which worked by steam of at least 30 lbs. on the inch above atmospheric pressure, and gave much satisfaction.

The first experimental steam-carriage was constructed by Trevithick and Vivian in their workshops at Camborne in 1803, and was tried by them on the public road adjoining the town, as well as in the street of the town itself. John Petherick, a native of Camborne, who was alive in 1858, stated in a letter to Mr. Edward Williams that he well remembered seeing the engine, worked by Mr. Trevithick himself, come through the place, to the great wonder of the inhabitants. He says, "The experiment was satisfactory only as long as the steam pressure could be kept up. During that continuance Trevithick called upon the people to 'jump up,' so as to create a load on the engine; and it soon became covered with men, which did not seem to make any difference to the power or speed so long as the steam was kept up. This was sought to be done by the application of a cylindrical horizontal bellows worked by the engine itself; but the attempt to keep up the power of the steam for any considerable time proved a failure."

Trevithick, however, made several alterations in the engine which had the effect of improving it, and its success was such that he determined to take it to London and exhibit it there as the most recent novelty in steam mechanism. It was successfully run by road from Camborne to Plymouth, a distance of about ninety miles. At Plymouth it was shipped for London, where it shortly after arrived in safety, and excited considerable curiosity. It was run on the waste ground in the vicinity of the present Bethlehem Hospital, as well as on Lord's cricket-ground. There Sir Humphry Davy, Mr. Davies Gilbert, and other scientific gentlemen inspected the machine and rode upon it. Several of them took the steering of the carriage by turns, and they expressed their satisfaction with the mechanism by which it was directed. Sir Humphry, writing to a friend in Cornwall, said, "I shall soon hope to hear that the roads of England are the haunts of Captain Trevithick's dragons—a characteristic name." After the experiment at Lord's, the carriage was run along the New-road, and down Gray's-Inn Lane, to the premises of a carriage-builder in Long Acre. To show the adaptability of the engine for fixed uses, Trevithick had it taken from the carriage on the day after this trial and removed to the shop of a cutler, where he applied it with success to the driving of the machinery.

The steam-carriage shortly became the talk of the town, and the public curiosity being on the increase, Trevithick resolved on inclosing a piece of ground on the site of the present Euston station of the London and Northwestern Railway, and admitting persons to see the exhibition of his engine at so much a head.

He had a tram-road laid down in an elliptical form within the inclosure, and the carriage was run round it on the rails in the sight of a great number of spectators. On the second day another crowd collected to see the exhibition, but, for what reason is not known, although it is said to have been through one of Trevithick's freaks of temper, the place was closed and the engine removed. It is, however, not improbable that the inventor had come to the conclusion that the state of the roads at that time was such as to preclude its coming into general use for purposes of ordinary traffic.

While the steam-carriage was being exhibited, a gentleman was laying heavy wagers as to the weight which could be hauled by a single horse on the Wandsworth and Croydon iron tram-way; and the number and weight of wagons drawn by the horse were something surprising. Trevithick very probably put the two things together—the steam-horse and the iron-way—and kept the performance in mind when he proceeded to construct his second or railway locomotive. In the mean time, having dismantled his steam-carriage, sent back the phaeton to the coach-builder to whom it belonged, and sold the little engine which had worked the machine, he returned to Camborne to carry on his business. In the course of the year 1803 he went to Pen-y-darran, in South Wales, to erect a forge engine for the iron-works there; and, when it was finished, he began the erection of a railway locomotive—the first ever constructed. There were already, as above stated, several lines of rail laid down in the district for the accommodation of the coal and iron works. That between Merthyr Tydvil and Cardiff was the longest and most important, and it had been at work for some years. It had probably occurred to Trevithick that here was a fine opportunity for putting to practical test the powers of the locomotive, and he proceeded to construct one accordingly in the workshops at Pen-y-darran.

This first railway locomotive was finished and tried upon the Merthyr tram-road on the 21st of February, 1804. It had a cylindrical wrought-iron boiler with flat ends. The furnace and flue were inside the boiler, the flue returning, having its exit at the same end at which it entered, so as to increase the heating surface. The cylinder, 4¾ in. in diameter, was placed horizontally in the end of the boiler, and the waste steam was thrown into the stack. The wheels were worked in the same manner as in the carriage engine already described; and a fly-wheel was added on one side, to secure a continuous rotary motion at the end of each stroke of the piston. The pressure of the steam was about 40 lbs. on the inch. The engine ran upon four wheels, coupled by cog-wheels, and those who remember the engine say that the four wheels were smooth.

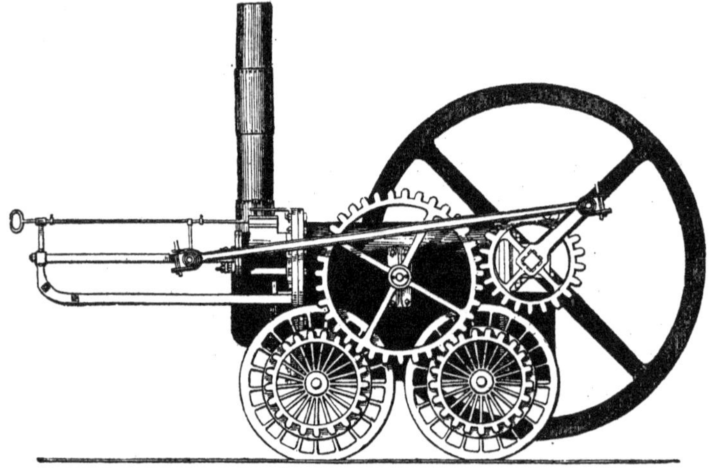

TREVITHICK'S HIGH-PRESSURE TRAM-ENGINE.

On the first trial, this engine drew for a distance of nine miles ten tons of bar iron, together with the necessary carriages, water, and fuel, at the rate of five and a half miles an hour. Rees Jones, an old engine-fitter, who helped to erect the engine, and was alive in 1858, gave Mr. Menelaus the following account of its performances: "When the engine was finished, she was used for bringing down metal from the old forge. She worked very well; but frequently, from her weight, broke the tram-plates, and also the hooks between the trams. After working for some time in this way, she took a journey of iron from Pen-y-darran down the Basin Road, upon which road she was intended to work. On the journey she broke a great many of the tram-plates; and, before reaching the Basin, she ran off the road, and was brought back to Pen-y-darran by horses. The engine was never used as a locomotive after this; but she was used as a stationary engine, and worked in this way for several years."

So far as the locomotive was concerned it was a remarkable success. The defect lay not in the engine so much as in the road. This was formed of plate-rails of cast iron, with a guiding flange upon the rail instead of on the engine wheels, as in the modern locomotive. The rails were also of a very weak form, considering the quantity of iron in them; and, though they were sufficient to bear the loaded wagons mounted upon small wheels, as ordinarily drawn along them by horses, they were found quite insufficient to bear the weight of Trevithick's engine. To relay the road of sufficient strength would have involved a heavy outlay, which the owners were unwilling to incur, not yet perceiving the advantage, in an economical point of view, of employing engine in lieu of horse power. The locomotive was accordingly taken off the road, and the experiment, successful though it had been, was brought to an end.

Trevithick had, however, by means of his Pen-y-darran engine, in a great measure solved the problem of steam locomotion on railways. He had produced a compact engine, working on the high-pressure principle, capable of carrying fuel and water sufficient for a journey of considerable length, and of drawing loaded wagons at five and a half miles an hour. He had shown by his smooth-wheeled locomotive that the weight of the engine had given sufficient adhesion for the haulage of the load. He had discharged the steam into the chimney, though not for the purpose of increasing the draught, as he employed bellows for that purpose. It appears, however, that Trevithick's friend, Mr. Davies Gilbert, afterward President of the Royal Society, especially noticed the effect of discharging the waste steam into the chimney of the Pen-y-darran engine. He observed that when the engine moved, at each puff the fire brightened, while scarcely any visible steam or smoke came from the chimney.

Mr. Gilbert published the result of his observations in "Nicholson's Journal" for September, 1805, and the attention of Mr. Nicholson, the editor, having thereby been called to the subject, he proceeded to make a series of experiments, the result of which was that in 1806 he took out a patent for a steam-blasting apparatus, by which he proposed to apply high-pressure steam to force along currents of air for various useful purposes, including the urging of furnace and other fires. It is thus obvious that the principle of the blast-pipe was known to both Gilbert and Nicholson at this early period; but it is somewhat remarkable that Trevithick himself should have remained skeptical as to its use, for as late as 1815 we find him taking out a patent, in which, among other improvements, he included a method of urging his fire by fanners, similar to a winnowing machine.

In the mean time Trevithick occupied himself in carrying on the various business of a general engineer, and was ready to embark in any enterprise likely to give scope for his inventive skill. In whatever work he was employed, he was sure to introduce new methods and arrangements, if not new inventions. He was full of speculative enthusiasm, a great theorist, and yet an indefatigable experimenter. At the beginning of 1806—the year after the locomotive had been taken off the Merthyr Tydvil tram-road—he made arrangements for entering into a contract for ballasting all the shipping in the Thames. At the end of a letter written by him on the 18th of February in that year to Davies Gilbert, respecting a *puffer* engine, he said, "I am about to enter into a contract with the Trinity Board for lifting up ballast out of the bottom of the Thames for all the shipping. The first quantity stated was 300,000 tons a year, but now they state 500,000 tons. I am to do nothing but wind up the chain for 6*d.* per ton, which is now done by men. They never lift it above twenty-five feet high—a man will now get up ten tons for 7*s.* My engine at Dalcoath has lifted about 100 tons that height with one bushel of coals. I have two engines already finished for the purpose, and shall be in town in about fifteen days for to set them to work. They propose to engage with me for twenty-one years."* The contract was not, however, entered into. Trevithick quarreled with the capitalists who had found the money for the trials, and the "Blazer" and "Plymouth," the vessels in which his engines and machinery had been fitted, fell into other hands.

Trevithick, nevertheless, seems to have been on the highway to fortune, for, at the beginning of 1806, he had received orders for nine engines in one month, all for Cornwall; and he expected orders for four others. He had also in view the construction of a railway; but nothing came of this project. More hopeful still, as regarded immediate returns, was the Cornish engine business,

* Weale's "Papers on Engineering," vol. i., "On the Dredging Machine," p. 7.

which presented a very wide field. Now that the trade had been thrown open by the expiry of Boulton and Watt's patent, competition had sprung up, and many new makers and inventors of engines were ready to supply the demand.

Among the most prominent of these were Trevithick and Woolf. Trevithick was the most original and speculative, Woolf the most plodding and practical, and the most successful. Trevithick's ingenuity exhibited itself in his schemes for working Boulton and Watt's pumping-engine by high-pressure steam, by means of his cylindrical wrought-iron boiler. He proposed to expand the steam down to low pressure previous to condensation, thereby anticipating by many years the Cornish engine now in use. The suggestion was not, however, then acted on, and he fell back on his original design of a simple non-condensing high-pressure engine. One of these was erected at Dalcoath mine to draw the ores there. It was called "the puffer" by the mining people, from its puffing the steam direct into the air; but its performances did not compare favorably with those of the ordinary condensing engines of Boulton and Watt, and the engine did not come into general use.

Trevithick was not satisfied to carry on a prosperous engine business in Cornwall. Camborne was too small for him, and the Cornish mining districts presented too limited a field for his ambitious spirit. So he came to London, the Patent-office drawing him as the loadstone does the needle. In 1808 he took out two patents, one for "certain machinery for towing, driving, or forcing and discharging ships and other vessels of their cargoes," and the other for "a new method of stowing cargoes of ships." In 1809 he took out another patent for constructing docks, ships, etc., and propelling vessels.

In these patents, Trevithick was associated with one Robert Dickinson, of Great Queen Street, but his name stands first in the specification, wherein he describes himself as "of Rotherhithe, in the county of Surrey, engineer." By the first of these patents he proposed to tow vessels by means of a rowing wheel shaped like an undershot water-wheel furnished with floats placed vertically in a box, and worked by a steam-engine, which he also proposed to employ in the loading and unloading of the vessel, but it is not known that the plan was ever introduced into practical use. The patent of 1809 included a floating dock or caisson made of wrought-iron plates, in which a ship might be docked while afloat, and, after the water had been pumped out of the caisson, repaired without moving her stores, masts, or furniture. This invention has since been carried out in practice by the Messrs. Rennie in the floating iron dock which they have recently constructed for the Spanish government. Another invention included in the specification was the construction of merchant and war ships of wrought-iron plates strongly riveted together, with their decks supported by wrought-iron beams, and the masts, bowsprits, and booms also of tubular wrought iron, thereby anticipating by many years the form and structure of vessels now in common use.

While Trevithick lived at Rotherhithe, he entered upon a remarkable enterprise—no less than the construction of a tunnel under the Thames—a work which was carried out with so much difficulty by Sir Isambard Brunel some twenty years later. Several schemes had been proposed at different times for connecting the two banks of the river by an underground communication. As early as 1798, Ralph Dodd suggested a tunnel under the Thames between Gravesend and Tilbury, and in 1802 Mr. Vazie projected a tunnel from Rotherhithe to Limehouse. A company was formed to carry out the latter scheme, and a shaft was sunk, at considerable expense, to a depth of 76 feet below high water. The works were from time to time suspended, and it was not until the year 1807, when Trevithick was appointed engineer of the work, that arrangements were made for proceeding with the driftway under the bed of the Thames. After about five months' working, the drift was driven for a length of 953 feet, when the roof gave way and the water burst in. The opening was, however, plugged by clay in bags thrown into the river, and the work proceeded until 1028 feet had been accomplished. Then the water burst in again, and the process of plugging and pumping the water out of the drift was repeated. After seventy more feet had been added to the excavation, there was another irruption, which completely flooded the driftway, and the water rose nearly to the top of the shaft. This difficulty was, however, again overcome, and with great danger twenty more feet were accomplished; but the bursts of water became so frequent and unmanageable that at length the face of the drift was timbered up and the work abandoned. Trevithick, who had been promised a reward of £1000 if the tunnel succeeded, thus lost both his labor and his reward. The only remuneration he received from the Company was a hundred guineas, which were paid to him according to agreement, provided he carried the excavation to the extent of 1000 yards, which he did.

Trevithick returned to Camborne in 1809, where we find him busily occupied with new projects, and introducing his new engine worked by water-power, the first of which was put up at the Druid mine, as well as in perfecting his high-pressure engine and its working by expansion. One of the first of such engines was erected at the Huel Prosper mine, of which he was engineer; and this, as well as others subsequently constructed on the same principle, proved quite successful.

In 1815 Trevithick took out a farther patent, embodying several important applications of steam-power. One of these consisted in "causing steam of a high pressure to spout out against the atmosphere, and by its recoiling force to produce motion in a direction contrary to the issuing steam, similar to the motion produced in a rocket, or to the recoil of a gun." This was, however, but a revival of the ancient Œolipile described by Hero, and known as "Hero's engine."

In another part of his specification Trevithick described the screw-propeller as "a screw or a number of leaves placed obliquely round an axis similar to the vanes of a smoke-jack, which shall be made to revolve with great speed in a line with the required motion of the ship, or parallel to the same line of motion." In a second part of the specification, he described a plunger or pole-engine in which the steam worked at high-pressure. The first engine of this kind was erected by Trevithick at Herland in 1815, but the result was not equal to his expectations, though the principle was afterward successfully applied by Mr. William Sims, who purchased the patent-right.

In this specification Trevithick also described a tubular boiler of a new construction for the purpose of more rapidly producing high-pressure steam, the heating surface being extended by constructing the boiler of a number of small perpendicular tubes, closed at the bottom, but all opening at the top into a common reservoir, from whence they received their water, and into which the steam of all the tubes was united.

While Trevithick was engaged in these ingenious projects, an event occurred which, though it promised to issue in the most splendid results, proved the greatest misfortune of his life. We refer to his adventures in connection with the gold mines of Peru. Many of the richest of them had been drowned out, the pumping machinery of the country being incapable of clearing them of water. The districts in which they were situated were almost inaccessible to ordinary traffic, all transport being conducted on the backs of men or of mules. The parts of an ordinary condensing engine were too ponderous to be carried up these mountain heights, and it was evident that, unless some lighter sort of engine could be employed, the mines in question must be abandoned.

Mr. Uvillé, a Swiss gentleman interested in South American mining, came over from Peru to England in 1811 for the purpose of making inquiries about such an engine, but he received no encouragement. He was about to return to Lima, in despair of accomplishing his object, when, one day, accidentally passing a shop-window in Fitzroy Square, he caught sight of an engine exposed for sale which immediately attracted his attention. It was the engine constructed by Trevithick for his first locomotive, which he had sold some years before, on the sudden abandonment of the exhibition of its performances in London. Mr. Uvillé was so much pleased with its construction and mode of action that he at once purchased it and took it out with him to South America. Arrived there, he had the engine transported across the mountains to the rich mining district of Pasco, about a hundred miles north of Lima, to try its effects on the highest mountain ridges.

The experiment was so satisfactory that an association of influential gentlemen was immediately formed to introduce the engine on a large scale, and enter into contracts with the mine-owners for clearing their shafts of the water which drowned them. The Viceroy of Peru approved the plan, and the association dispatched Mr. Uvillé to England to purchase the requisite engines. He took ship for Falmouth about the end of 1812 for the purpose of finding out Trevithick. He only knew of Trevithick by name, and that he lived in Cornwall, but nothing farther. Being full of his subject, however, he could not refrain from conversing on the subject with the passengers on board the ship by which he sailed, and it so happened that one of them—a Mr. Teague—was a relative of Trevithick, who promised, shortly after their landing, to introduce him to the inventor.

Mr. Teague was as good as his word, and in the course of a few days Uvillé was enabled to discuss the scheme with Trevithick at his own house at Camborne, where he still resided. The result was an order for a number of high-pressure pumping-engines, which were put in hand at once; and on the 1st of September, 1814, nine of them were shipped at Portsmouth for Lima, accompanied by Uvillé and three Cornish engineers, one of whom was William Bull, of Chasewater, Trevithick's first partner.

The engines reached Lima in safety, and were welcomed by a royal salute and with public rejoicings. Such, however, was the difficulty of transporting the materials across the mountains, that it was not until the middle of the year 1816 that the first engine was erected and set to work to pump out the Santa Rosa mine, in the royal mineral territory of Yaüricocha. The association of gentlemen to whom the engines belonged had entered into a contract to drain this among other mines, on condition of sharing in the gross produce of the ores to the extent of about 25 per cent. of the whole amount raised. The result of the first working of the engine was so satisfactory that the projectors were filled with no less astonishment than delight, and they characterized the undertaking as one from which they "anticipated a torrent of silver that would fill surrounding nations with astonishment."

In the mean time Trevithick was proceeding at home with the manufacture of the remaining engines, as well as new coining apparatus for the Peruvian mint, and furnaces for purifying silver ore by fusion; and with these engines and apparatus he set sail for America in October, 1816, reaching Lima in safety in the following February. He was received with almost royal honors. The government "Gazette" officially announced "the arrival of Don Ricardo Trevithick, an eminent professor of mechanics, machinery, and mineralógy, inventor and constructor of the engines of the last patent, and who directed in England the execution of the machinery now at work in Pasco." The lord warden was ordered by the viceroy to escort Trevithick to the mines accompanied by a guard of honor. The news of his expected arrival there occasioned great rejoicings, and the chief men of the district came down the mountains to meet and welcome him. Uvillé wrote to his associates that Trevithick had been sent out "by heaven for the prosperity of the mines, and that the lord warden proposed to erect his statue in solid silver." Trevithick himself wrote home to his friends in Cornwall that he had before him the prospect of almost boundless wealth, having, in addition to his emoluments as patentee, obtained a fifth share in the Lima Company, which, he expected, on a moderate computation, would yield him about £100,000 a year!

But these brilliant prospects were suddenly blasted by the Peruvian revolution which broke out in the following year. While Mr. Boaze was reading his paper* before the Royal Geological Society of Cornwall, in which these anticipations of Trevithick's fame and fortune were so glowingly described, Lord Cochrane was on his way to South America to take the command of the Chilian fleet in its attack of the ports of Peru, still in the possession of the Spaniards.

Toward the end of 1818, Lord Cochrane hoisted his flag, and shortly after proceeded to assail the Spanish fleet in Callao Harbor. This proved the signal for a general insurrection, during the continuance of which the commercial and industrial affairs of the province were completely paralyzed. The pumping-engines of Trevithick were now of comparatively little use in pumping water out of mines in which the miners would no longer work. Although Lima was abandoned by the Spaniards toward the end of 1821, the civil war continued to rage for several years longer, until at length the independence of Peru was achieved; but it was long before the population were content to settle down as before, and follow the ordinary pursuits of industry and commerce.

The result to Trevithick was, that he and his partners in the Mining Company were consigned to ruin. It has been said that the engineer joined the patriotic party, and invented for Lord

* Paper read by Henry Boaze, Esq., "On Captain Trevithick's Adventures," at the Anniversary Meeting of September, 1817.—"Transactions of Royal Geological Society of Cornwall," vol. i., p. 212.

Cochrane an ingenious gun-carriage centred and equally balanced on pivots, and easily worked by machinery; but of this no mention is made by Lord Cochrane in his "Memoirs." The Patriots kept Trevithick on the mountains as a sort of patron and protector of their interests; but for this very reason he became proportionately obnoxious to the Royalists, who, looking upon him as the agent through whom the patriotic party obtained the sinews of war, destroyed his engines, and broke up his machinery wherever they could. At length he determined to escape from Peru, and fled northward across the mountains, accompanied by a single friend, making for the Isthmus of Panamá. In the course of this long, toilsome, and dangerous journey, he encountered great privations; he slept in the forest at night, traveled on foot by day, and crossed the streams by swimming. At length, his clothes torn, worn, and hanging almost in shreds, and his baggage all lost, he succeeded in reaching the port of Cartagena, on the Gulf of Darien, almost destitute.

Here he encountered Robert Stephenson, who was waiting at the one inn of the place until a ship was ready to set sail for England. Stephenson had finished his engagement with the Colombian Mining Company for which he had been working, and was eager to return home. When Trevithick entered the room in which he was sitting, Stephenson at once saw that he was an Englishman. He stood some six feet in height, and, though well proportioned when in ordinary health, he was now gaunt and hollow, the picture of privation and misery.

Stephenson made up to the stranger, and was not a little surprised to find that he was no other than the famous engineer, Trevithick, the builder of the first patent locomotive, and who, when he last heard of him, was accumulating so gigantic a fortune in Peru! Though now penniless, Trevithick was as full of speculation as ever, and related to Stephenson that he was on his way home for the purpose of organizing another gold-mining company, which should make the fortunes of all who took part in it. He was, however, in the mean time, unable to pay for his passage, and Stephenson lent him the requisite money for the purpose of reaching his home in Cornwall.

As there was no vessel likely to sail for England for some time, Stephenson and Trevithick took the first ship bound for New

York. After a stormy passage, full of adventure and peril, the vessel was driven on a lee-shore, and the passengers and crew barely escaped with their lives. On reaching New York, Trevithick immediately set sail for England, and he landed safe at Falmouth in October, 1827, bringing back with him a pair of silver spurs, the only remnant which he had preserved of those "torrents of silver" which his engines were to raise from the mines of Peru.

Immediately on his return home, Trevithick memorialized the government for some remuneration adequate to the great benefit which the country had derived from his invention of the high-pressure steam-engine, and his introduction of the cylindrical boiler. The petition was prepared in December, 1827, and was cheerfully signed by the leading mine-owners and engineers in Cornwall; but there their efforts on his behalf ended.

He took out two more patents—one in 1831, for a new method of heating apartments, and another in 1832, for improvements in the steam-engine, and the application of steam-power to navigation and locomotion; but neither of them seems to have proved of any service to him. His new improvement in the steam-engine was neither more nor less than the invention of an apparatus similar to that which has quite recently come into use for employing superheated steam as a means of working the engine more effectively and economically. The patent also included a method of propelling ships by ejecting water through a tube with great force and speed in a direction opposite to the course of the vessel, a method since reinvented in many forms, though not yet successfully introduced in practice.

Strange to say, though Trevithick had been so intimately connected with the practical introduction of the Locomotive, he seems to have taken but little interest in its introduction upon railways, but confined himself to advocating its employment on common roads as its most useful application.* Though in many things he was before his age, here he was unquestionably behind

* On the 12th of August, 1831, by which time the Liverpool and Manchester line was in full work, Trevithick appeared as a witness before the select committee of the House of Commons on the employment of steam-carriages on common roads. He said "he had been abroad a good many years, and had had nothing to do with steam-carriages until very lately. He had it now, however, in contemplation to do a great deal on common roads, and, with that view, had taken out a patent for an entirely

it. But Trevithick was now an old man; his constitution was broken, and his energy worked out. Younger men were in the field, less ingenious and speculative, but more practical and energetic; and in the blaze of their fame the Cornish engineer was forgotten.

During the last year of his life Trevithick resided at Dartford, in Kent. He had induced the Messrs. Hall, the engineers of that place, to give him an opportunity of testing the value of his last invention—that of a vessel driven by the ejection of water through a tube—and he went there to superintend the construction of the necessary engine and apparatus. The vessel was duly fitted up, and several experiments were made with it in the adjoining creek, but it did not realize a speed of more than four miles an hour. Trevithick, being of opinion that the engine-power was insufficient, proceeded to have a new engine constructed, to the boiler of which, within the furnace, numerous tubes were attached, round which the fire played. So much steam was raised by this arrangement that the piston "blew;" but still the result of the experiments was unsatisfactory. While laboring at these inventions, and planning new arrangements never to be carried out, the engineer was seized by the illness of which he died, on the 22d of April, 1833, in the 62d year of his age.

As Trevithick was entirely without means at his death, besides being some sixty pounds in debt to the landlord of the Bull Inn, where he had been lodging for nearly a year, he would probably have been buried at the expense of the parish but for the Messrs. Hall and their workmen, who raised a sum sufficient to give the "great inventor" a decent burial; and they followed his remains to the grave in Deptford Church-yard, where he lies without a stone to mark his resting-place.

There can be no doubt as to the great mechanical ability of Trevithick. He was a man of original and intuitive genius in invention. Every mechanical arrangement which he undertook to study issued from his hands transformed and improved. But there he rested. He struck out many inventions, and left them to take care of themselves. His great failing was the want of

new engine, the arrangements in which were calculated to obviate all the difficulties which had hitherto stood in the way of traveling on common roads."

perseverance. His mind was always full of projects; but his very genius led him astray in search of new things, while his imagination often outran his judgment. Hence his life was but a series of beginnings.

Look at the extraordinary things that Trevithick began. He made the first railway locomotive, and cast the invention aside, leaving it to others to take it up and prosecute it to a successful issue. He introduced, if he did not invent, the cylindrical boiler and the high-pressure engine, which increased so enormously the steam-power of the world; but he reaped the profits of neither. He invented an oscillating engine and a screw propeller; he took out a patent for using superheated steam, as well as for wrought-iron ships and wrought-iron floating docks; but he left it to others to introduce these several inventions.

Never was there such a series of splendid mechanical beginnings. He began a Thames Tunnel and abandoned it. He went to South America with the prospect of making a gigantic fortune, but he had scarcely begun to gather in his gold than he was forced to fly, and returned home destitute. This last event, however, was a misfortune which no efforts on his part could have prevented. But even when he had the best chances, Trevithick threw them away. When he had brought his road locomotive to London to exhibit, and was beginning to excite the curiosity of the public respecting it, he suddenly closed the exhibition in a fit of caprice, removed the engine, and returned to Cornwall in a tiff. The failure, also, of the railroad on which his locomotive traveled so provoked him that he at once abandoned the enterprise in disgust.

There may have been some moral twist in the engineer's character, into which we do not seek to pry; but it seems clear that he was wanting in that resolute perseverance, that power of fighting an up-hill battle, without which no great enterprise can be conducted to a successful issue. In this respect the character of Richard Trevithick presents a remarkable contrast to that of George Stephenson, who took up only one of the many projects which the other had cast aside, and by dint of application, industry, and perseverance, carried into effect one of the most remarkable but peaceful revolutions which has ever been accomplished in any age or country.

We now proceed to describe the history of this revolution in connection with the Life of George Stephenson, and to trace the locomotive through its several stages of development until we find it recognized as one of the most vigorous and untiring workers in the entire world of industry.

LIVES

OF

GEORGE AND ROBERT STEPHENSON.

NEWCASTLE-UPON-TYNE AND THE HIGH-LEVEL BRIDGE.

[By R. P. Leitch, after his Original Drawing.]

LIFE OF GEORGE STEPHENSON, Etc.

CHAPTER I.

THE NEWCASTLE COAL-FIELD—GEORGE STEPHENSON'S EARLY YEARS.

In no quarter of England have greater changes been wrought by the successive advances made in the practical science of engineering than in the extensive colliery districts of the North, of which Newcastle-upon-Tyne is the centre and the capital.

In ancient times the Romans planted a colony at Newcastle, throwing a bridge across the Tyne near the site of the low-level bridge shown in the prefixed engraving, and erecting a strong fortification above it on the high ground now occupied by the Central Railway Station. North and northwest lay a wild country, abounding in moors, mountains, and morasses, but occupied to a certain extent by fierce and barbarous tribes. To defend the young colony against their ravages, a strong wall was built by the Romans, extending from Wallsend on the north bank of the Tyne, a few miles below Newcastle, across the country to Burgh-upon-Sands on the Solway Frith. The remains of the wall are still to be traced in the less populous hill-districts of Northumberland. In the neighborhood of Newcastle they have been gradually effaced by the works of succeeding generations, though the "Wallsend" coal consumed in our household fires still serves to remind us of the great Roman work.

After the withdrawal of the Romans, Northumbria became planted by immigrant Saxons from North Germany and Norsemen from Scandinavia, whose eorls or earls made Newcastle their principal seat. Then came the Normans, from whose *New* Castle, built some eight hundred years since, the town derives its present name. The keep of this venerable structure, black with age and smoke, still stands entire at the northern end of the noble high-level bridge—the utilitarian work of modern times thus confronting the warlike relic of the older civilization.

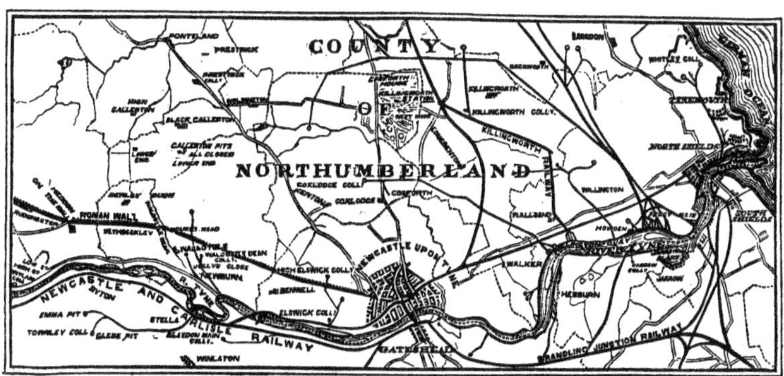

MAP OF NEWCASTLE DISTRICT.

The nearness of Newcastle to the Scotch Border was a great hinderance to its security and progress in the middle ages of English history. Indeed, the district between it and Berwick continued to be ravaged by moss-troopers long after the union of the crowns. The gentry lived in their strong Peel castles; even the larger farm-houses were fortified; and blood-hounds were trained for the purpose of tracking the cattle-reavers to their retreats in the hills. The judges of Assize rode from Carlisle to Newcastle guarded by an escort armed to the teeth. A tribute called "dagger and protection money" was annually paid by the sheriff of Newcastle for the purpose of providing daggers and other weapons for the escort; and, though the need of such protection has *long since ceased, the tribute continues to be paid in broad gold* pieces of the time of Charles the First.

Until about the middle of last century the roads across Northumberland were little better than horse-tracks, and not many years since the primitive agricultural cart with solid wooden wheels was almost as common in the western parts of the county as it is in Spain now. The track of the old Roman road long continued to be the most practicable route between Newcastle and Carlisle, the traffic between the two towns having been carried on pack-horses until within a comparatively recent period.

Since that time great changes have taken place on the Tyne. When wood for firing became scarce and dear, and the forests of the South of England were found inadequate to supply the increasing demand for fuel, attention was turned to the rich stores of coal lying underground in the neighborhood of Newcastle and Durham. It then became an article of increasing export, and "sea-coal" fires gradually superseded those of wood. Hence an old writer describes Newcastle as "the Eye of the North, and the Hearth that warmeth the South parts of this kingdom with Fire." Fuel became the staple product of the district, the quantity exported increasing from year to year, until the coal raised from these northern mines amounts to upward of sixteen millions of tons a year, of which not less than nine millions are annually conveyed away by sea.

Newcastle has in the mean time spread in all directions far beyond its ancient boundaries. From a walled mediæval town of monks and merchants, it has been converted into a busy centre of commerce and manufactures inhabited by nearly 100,000 people. It is no longer a Border fortress—a "shield and defense against the invasions and frequent insults of the Scots," as described in ancient charters—but a busy centre of peaceful industry, and the outlet for a vast amount of steam-power, which is exported in the form of coal to all parts of the world. Newcastle is in many respects a town of singular and curious interest, especially in its older parts, which are full of crooked lanes and narrow streets, wynds, and chares, formed by tall, antique houses, rising tier above tier along the steep northern bank of the Tyne, as the similarly precipitous streets of Gateshead crowd the opposite shore.

All over the coal region, which extends from the Coquet to the Tees, about fifty miles from north to south, the surface of the soil exhibits the signs of extensive underground workings. As you pass through the country at night, the earth looks as if it were bursting with fire at many points, the blaze of coke-ovens, iron-furnaces, and coal-heaps reddening the sky to such a distance that the horizon seems like a glowing belt of fire.

Among the upper-ground workmen employed at the coal-pits, the principal are the firemen, engine-men, and brakesmen, who fire and work the engines, and superintend the machinery by means of which the collieries are worked. Previous to the introduction of the steam-engine, the usual machine employed for the purpose was what is called a "gin." The gin consists of a large drum placed horizontally, round which ropes attached to buckets and corves are wound, which are thus drawn up or sent down the shafts by a horse traveling in a circular track or "gin race." This method was employed for drawing up both coals and water, and it is still used for the same purpose in small collieries; but where the quantity of water to be raised is great, pumps worked by steam-power are called into requisition.

Newcomen's atmospheric engine was first made use of to work the pumps, and it continued to be so employed long after the more powerful and economical condensing engine of Watt had been invented. In the Newcomen or "fire-engine," as it was called, the power is produced by the pressure of the atmosphere forcing down the piston in the cylinder, on a vacuum being produced within it by condensation of the contained steam by means of cold-water injection. The piston-rod is attached to one end of a lever, while the pump-rod works in connection with the other, the hydraulic action employed to raise the water being exactly similar to that of a common sucking-pump.

The working of a Newcomen engine was a clumsy and apparently a very painful process, accompanied by an extraordinary amount of wheezing, sighing, creaking, and bumping. When the pump descended, there was heard a plunge, a heavy sigh, and a loud bump; then, as it rose, and the sucker began to act, there was heard a creak, a wheeze, another bump, and then a rush of water as it was lifted and poured out. Where engines of a more powerful and improved description were used, as is now the case, the quantity of water raised is enormous—as much as a million and a half gallons in the twenty-four hours.

The pitmen, or "the lads belaw," who work out the coal below ground, are a peculiar class, quite distinct from the workmen on the surface. They are a people with peculiar habits, manners, and character, as much so as fishermen and sailors, to whom, indeed, they bear, in some respects, a considerable resemblance. Some fifty years since, they were a much rougher and worse educated class than they are now; hard workers, but very wild and uncouth; much given to "steeks," or strikes; and distinguished, in their hours of leisure and on pay-nights, for their love of cock-fighting, dog-fighting, hard drinking, and cuddy races. The pay-night was a fortnightly saturnalia, in which the pitman's character was fully brought out, especially when the "yel" was good. Though earning much higher wages than the ordinary laboring population of the upper soil, the latter did not mix nor intermarry with them, so that they were left to form their own communities, and hence their marked peculiarities as a class. Indeed, a sort of traditional disrepute seems long to have clung to the pitmen, arising perhaps from the nature of their employment, and from the circumstance that the colliers were among the last classes enfranchised in England, as they were certainly the last in Scotland, where they continued bondmen down to the end of last century. The last thirty years, however, have worked a great improvement in the moral condition of the Northumbrian pitmen; the abolition of the twelve months' bond to the mine, and the substitution of a month's notice previous to leaving, having given them greater freedom and opportunity for obtaining employment; and day-schools and Sunday-schools, together with the important influences of railways, have brought them fully up to a level with the other classes of the laboring population.

The coals, when raised from the pits, are emptied into the wagons placed alongside, from whence they are sent along the rails to the staiths erected by the river-side, the wagons sometimes descending by their own gravity along inclined planes, the wagoner standing behind to check the speed by means of a convoy or wooden brake bearing upon the rims of the wheels. Arrived at the staiths, the wagons are emptied at once into the ships waiting alongside for cargo. Any one who has sailed down the Tyne from Newcastle Bridge can not but have been struck with the appearance of the immense staiths, constructed of timber, which are erected at short distances from each other on both sides of the river.

But a great deal of the coal shipped from the Tyne comes from above-bridge, where sea-going craft can not reach, and is floated down the river in "keels," in which the coals are sometimes piled up according to convenience when large, or, when the coal is small or tender, it is conveyed in tubs to prevent breakage. These keels are of a very ancient model—perhaps the oldest extant in England: they are even said to be of the same build as those in which the Norsemen navigated the Tyne centuries ago. The keel is a tubby, grimy-looking craft, rounded fore and aft, with a single large square sail, which the keel-bullies, as the Tyne watermen are called, manage with great dexterity; the vessel being guided by the aid of the "swape," or great oar, which is used as a kind of rudder at the stern of the vessel. These keelmen are an exceedingly hardy class of workmen, not by any means so quarrelsome as their designation of "bully" would imply—the word being merely derived from the obsolete term "boolie," or beloved, an appellation still in familiar use among brother workers in the coal districts. One of the most curious sights on the Tyne is the fleet of hundreds of these black-sailed, black-hulled keels, bringing down at each tide their black cargoes for the ships at anchor in the deep water at Shields and other parts of the river below Newcastle.

These preliminary observations will perhaps be sufficient to explain the meaning of many of the occupations alluded to, and the phrases employed, in the course of the following narrative, some of which might otherwise have been comparatively unintelligible to the reader.

The colliery village of Wylam is situated on the north bank of the Tyne, about eight miles west of Newcastle. The Newcastle and Carlisle Railway runs along the opposite bank; and the traveler by that line sees the usual signs of a colliery in the unsightly pumping-engines surrounded by heaps of ashes, coal-dust, and slag, while a neighboring iron-furnace in full blast throws out dense smoke and loud jets of steam by day and lurid flames at night. These works form the nucleus of the village, which is almost entirely occupied by coal-miners and iron-furnace-men. The place is remarkable for its large population, but not for its cleanness or neatness as a village; the houses, as in most colliery villages, being the property of the owners or lessees, who employ them in temporarily accommodating the work-people, against whose earnings there is a weekly set-off for house and coals. About the end of last century, the estate of which Wylam forms part belonged to Mr. Blackett, a gentleman of considerable celebrity in coal-mining, then more generally known as the proprietor of the "Globe" newspaper.

There is nothing to interest one in the village itself. But a few hundred yards from its eastern extremity stands a humble detached dwelling, which will be interesting to many as the birth-

WYLAM COLLIERY AND VILLAGE. [By R. P. Leitch.]

place of one of the most remarkable men of our times—George Stephenson, the Railway Engineer. It is a common, two-storied, red-tiled, rubble house, portioned off into four laborers' apartments. It is known by the name of High-street House, and was originally so called because it stands by the side of what used to be the old riding post-road or street between Newcastle and Hexham, along which the post was carried on horseback within the memory of persons living.

The lower room in the west end of this house was the home of the Stephenson family, and there George Stephenson was born, the second of a family of six children, on the 9th of June, 1781. The apartment is now, what it was then, an ordinary laborer's dwelling; its walls are unplastered, its floor is of clay, and the bare rafters are exposed overhead.

Robert Stephenson, or "Old Bob," as the neighbors familiarly called him, and his wife Mabel, were a respectable couple, careful and hard-working. Robert Stephenson's father was a Scotchman, who came into England in the capacity of a gentleman's servant.* Mabel, his wife, was the second daughter of Robert Carr, a dyer at Ovingham. The Carrs were for several genera-

HIGH-STREET HOUSE, WYLAM. [By R. P. Leitch.]

tions the owners of a house in that village adjoining the church-yard; and the family tomb-stone may still be seen standing against the east end of the chancel of the parish church, underneath the centre lancet window, as the tomb-stone of Thomas Bewick, the wood-engraver, occupies the western gable. Mabel Stephenson was a woman of somewhat delicate constitution, and troubled occasionally, as her neighbors said, with "the vapors." But those who remembered her concurred in describing her as "a real canny body;" and a woman of whom this is said by general consent in the Newcastle district may be pronounced a worthy person indeed, for it is about the highest praise of a woman which Northumbrians can express.

* A tradition exists in the family that Robert Stephenson's father came across the Border on the loss of considerable property. Miss Stephenson, the daughter of Robert's third son, John, has stated that a suit was commenced for recovery of the property, but was dropped for want of the requisite means to prosecute it.

For some time after their marriage, Robert resided with his wife at Walbottle, a village situated between Wylam and Newcastle, where he was employed as a laborer at the colliery; after which the family removed to Wylam, where he found employment as fireman of the old pumping-engine at that colliery.

George Stephenson was the second of a family of six children.* It does not appear that the birth of any of the children was registered in the parish books, the author having made an unsuccessful search in the registers of Ovingham and Heddon-on-the-Wall to ascertain the fact.

An old Wylam collier, who remembered George Stephenson's father, thus described him: "Geordie's fayther war like a peer o' deals nailed thegither, an' a bit o' flesh i' th' inside; he war as queer as Dick's hatband—went thrice aboot, an' wudn't tie. His wife Mabel war a delicat' boddie, an' varry flighty. They war an honest family, but sair hadden doon i' th' world." Indeed, the earnings of old Robert did not amount to more than twelve shillings a week; and, as there were six children to maintain, the family, during their stay at Wylam, were necessarily in very straitened circumstances. The father's wages being barely sufficient, even with the most rigid economy, for the sustenance of the household, there was little to spare for clothing, and nothing for education, so that none of the children were sent to school.

Old Robert was a general favorite in the village, especially among the children, whom he was accustomed to draw about him while tending the engine-fire, and feast their young imaginations with tales of Sinbad the Sailor and Robinson Crusoe, besides oth-

* The family Bible of Robert and Mabel Stephenson, which seems to have come into their possession in November, 1790, contains the following record of the births of these children, evidently written by one hand and at one time:

"A Rechester of the children belonging Robert and Mabel Stepheson—

"James Stepheson Was Born March the 4 day 1779

"George Stepheson Was Born June 9 day 1781

"Elender Stepheson Was Born April the 16 day 1784

"Robert Stepheson Was Born March the 10 day 1788

"John Stepheson Was Born November the 4 day 1789

"Ann Stepheson Was Born July the 19 day 1792."

Of the two daughters, Eleanor married Stephen Liddell, afterward employed in the Locomotive Factory in Newcastle. Ann married John Nixon, with whom she emigrated to the United States; she died at Pittsburg in 1860. John Stephenson was accidentally killed at the Locomotive Factory in January, 1831.

ers of his own invention; so that "Bob's engine-fire" came to be the most popular resort in the village. Another feature in his character, by which he was long remembered, was his affection for birds and animals; and he had many tame favorites of both sorts, which were as fond of resorting to his engine-fire as the boys and girls themselves. In the winter time he had usually a flock of tame robins about him; and they would come hopping familiarly to his feet to pick up the crumbs which he had saved for them out of his humble dinner. At his cottage he was rarely without one or more tame blackbirds, which flew about the house, or in and out at the door. In summer time he would go bird-nesting with his children; and one day he took his little boy George to see a blackbird's nest for the first time. Holding him up in his arms, he let the wondering boy peep down, through the branches held aside for the purpose, into a nest full of young birds—a sight which the boy never forgot, but used to speak of with delight to his intimate friends when he himself had grown an old man.

The boy George led the ordinary life of working people's children. He played about the doors; went bird-nesting when he could; and ran errands to the village. He was also an eager listener, with the other children, to his father's curious tales, and he early imbibed from him his affection for birds and animals. In course of time he was promoted to the office of carrying his father's dinner to him while at work, and at home he helped to nurse his younger brothers and sisters. One of his earliest duties was to see that the other children were kept out of the way of the chaldron wagons, which were then dragged by horses along the wooden tram-road immediately in front of the cottage door.

This wagon-way was the first in the northern district on which the experiment of a locomotive engine was tried. But, at the time of which we speak, the locomotive had scarcely been dreamt of in England as a practicable working power; horses only were used to haul the coal; and one of the first sights with which the boy was familiar was the coal-wagons dragged by them along the wooden railway at Wylam.

Thus eight years passed; after which, the coal having been worked out on the north side, the old engine, which had grown "dismal to look at," as an old workman described it, was pulled down; and then old Robert, having obtained employment as a fireman at the Dewley Burn Colliery, removed with his family to that place.

Dewley Burn, at this day, consists of a few old-fashioned, low-roofed cottages standing on either side of a babbling little stream. They are connected by a rustic wooden bridge, which spans the rift in front of the doors. In the central one-roomed cottage of this group, on the right bank, Robert Stephenson lived for a time with his family, the pit at which he worked standing in the rear of the cottages.

Young though he was, George was now of an age to be able to contribute something toward the family maintenance; for, in a poor man's house, every child is a burden until his little hands can be turned to profitable account. That the boy was shrewd and active, and possessed of a ready mother-wit, will be evident enough from the following incident. One day his sister Nell went into Newcastle to buy a bonnet, and Geordie went with her "for company." At a draper's shop in the Bigg Market Nell found a "chip" quite to her mind, but on pricing it, alas! it was found to be fifteen pence beyond her means. Girl-like, she had set her mind upon that bonnet, and no other would please her. She accordingly left the shop very much dejected. But Geordie said, "Never heed, Nell; come wi' me, and I'll see if I canna win siller enough to buy the bonnet; stand ye there till I come back." Away ran the boy, and disappeared amid the throng of the market, leaving the girl to wait his return. Long and long she waited, until it grew dusk, and the market-people had nearly all left. She had begun to despair, and fears crossed her mind that Geordie must have been run over and killed, when at last up he came running, almost breathless. "I've gotten the siller for the bonnet, Nell!" cried he. "Eh, Geordie!" she said, "but hoo hae ye gotten it?" "Hauddin the gentlemen's horses!" was the exultant reply. The bonnet was forthwith bought, and the two returned to Dewley in triumph.

George's first regular employment was of a very humble sort. A widow, named Grace Ainslie, then occupied the neighboring farm-house of Dewley. She kept a number of cows, and had the privilege of grazing them along the wagon-ways. She needed a boy to herd the cows, to keep them out of the way of the wagons, and prevent their straying or trespassing on the neighbors' "liberties;" the boy's duty was also to bar the gates at night after all the wagons had passed. George petitioned for this post, and, to his great joy, he was appointed, at the wage of twopence a day.

It was light employment, and he had plenty of spare time on his hands, which he spent in bird-nesting, making whistles out of reeds and scrannel straws, and erecting Liliputian mills in the little water-streams that ran into the Dewley bog. But his favorite amusement at this early age was erecting clay engines in conjunction with his playmate, Bill Thirlwall. The place is still pointed out where the future engineers made their first essays in modeling. The boys found the clay for their engines in the adjoining bog, and the hemlocks which grew about supplied them with imaginary steam-pipes. They even proceeded to make a miniature winding-machine in connection with their engine, and the apparatus was erected upon a bench in front of the Thirlwalls' cottage. Their corves were made out of hollowed corks; their ropes were supplied by twine; and a few bits of wood gleaned from the refuse of the carpenters' shop completed their materials. With this apparatus the boys made a show of sending the corves down the pit and drawing them up again, much to the marvel of the pitmen. But some mischievous person about the place seized the opportunity early one morning of smashing the fragile machinery, greatly to the grief of the young engineers. We may mention, in passing, that George's companion afterward became a workman of repute, and creditably held the office of engineer at Shilbottle, near Alnwick, for a period of nearly thirty years.

As Stephenson grew older and abler to work, he was set to lead the horses when plowing, though scarce big enough to stride across the furrows; and he used afterward to say that he rode to his work in the mornings at an hour when most other children of his age were asleep in their beds. He was also employed to hoe turnips, and do similar farm-work, for which he was paid the advanced wage of fourpence a day. But his highest ambition was to be taken on at the colliery where his father worked; and he shortly joined his elder brother James there as a "corf-bitter," or "picker," to clear the coal of stones, bats, and dross. His wages were then advanced to sixpence a day, and afterward to eightpence when he was sent to drive the gin-horse.

Shortly after, George went to Black Callerton Colliery to drive the gin there; and, as that colliery lies about two miles across the fields from Dewley Burn, the boy walked that distance early in the morning to his work, returning home late in the evening. One of the old residents at Black Callerton, who remembered him at that time, described him to the author as "a grit growing lad, with bare legs an' feet;" adding that he was "very quick-witted, and full of fun and tricks: indeed, there was nothing under the sun but he tried to imitate." He was usually foremost also in the sports and pastimes of youth.

Among his first strongly developed tastes was the love of birds and animals, which he inherited from his father. Blackbirds were his special favorites. The hedges between Dewley and Black Callerton were capital bird-nesting places, and there was not a nest there that he did not know of. When the young birds were old enough, he would bring them home with him, feed them, and teach them to fly about the cottage unconfined by cages. One of his blackbirds became so tame that, after flying about the doors all day, and in and out of the cottage, it would take up its roost upon the bed-head at night. And, most singular of all, the bird would disappear in the spring and summer months, when it was supposed to go into the woods to pair and rear its young, after which it would reappear at the cottage, and resume its social habits during the winter. This went on for several years. George had also a stock of tame rabbits, for which he built a little house behind the cottage, and for many years he continued to pride himself upon the superiority of his breed.

After he had driven the gin for some time at Dewley and Black Callerton, he was taken on as assistant to his father in firing the engine at Dewley. This was a step of promotion which he had anxiously desired, his only fear being lest he should be found too young for the work. Indeed, he afterward used to relate how he was wont to hide himself when the owner of the colliery went round, in case he should be thought too little a boy to earn the wages paid him. Since he had modeled his clay engines in the bog, his young ambition was to be an engine-man;

and to be an assistant fireman was the first step toward this position. Great, therefore, was his joy when, at about fourteen years of age, he was appointed assistant fireman, at the wage of a shilling a day.

But the coal at Dewley Burn being at length worked out, the pit was ordered to be "laid in," and old Robert and his family were again under the necessity of shifting their home; for, to use the common phrase, they must "follow the wark."

NEWBURN ON THE TYNE. [By R. P. Leitch.]

CHAPTER II.

NEWBURN AND CALLERTON—GEORGE STEPHENSON LEARNS TO BE AN ENGINE-MAN.

On quitting their humble home at Dewley Burn, the Stephenson family removed to a place called Jolly's Close, a few miles to the south, close behind the village of Newburn, where another coal-mine belonging to the Duke of Northumberland, called "the Duke's Winnin," had recently been opened out.

One of the old persons in the neighborhood, who knew the family well, describes the dwelling in which they lived as a poor cottage of only one room, in which the father, mother, four sons, and two daughters lived and slept. It was crowded with three low-poled beds. The one apartment served for parlor, kitchen, sleeping-room, and all.

The children of the Stephenson family were now growing apace, and several of them were old enough to be able to earn money at various kinds of colliery work. James and George, the two eldest sons, worked as assistant firemen; and the younger boys worked as wheelers or pickers on the bank-tops; while the two girls helped their mother with the household work.

Other workings of the coal were opened out in the neighborhood, and to one of these George was removed as fireman on his own account. This was called the "Mid Mill Winnin," where he had for his mate a young man named Coe. They worked together there for about two years, by twelve-hour shifts, George firing the engine at the wage of a shilling a day. He was now fifteen years old. His ambition was as yet limited to attaining the standing of a full workman, at a man's wages, and with that view he endeavored to attain such a knowledge of his engine as would eventually lead to his employment as engine-man, with its accompanying advantage of higher pay. He was a steady, sober, hard-working young man, but nothing more in the estimation of his fellow-workmen.

One of his favorite pastimes in by-hours was trying feats of strength with his companions. Although in frame he was not particularly robust, yet he was big and bony, and considered very strong for his age. At throwing the hammer George had no compeer. At lifting heavy weights off the ground from between his feet, by means of a bar of iron passed through them—placing the bar against his knees as a fulcrum, and then straightening his spine and lifting them sheer up—he was also very successful. On one occasion he lifted as much as sixty stones' weight—a striking indication of his strength of bone and muscle.

When the pit at Mid Mill was closed, George and his companion Coe were sent to work another pumping-engine erected near Throckley Bridge, where they continued for some months. It was while working at this place that his wages were raised to 12*s.* a week—an event to him of great importance. On coming out of the foreman's office that Saturday evening on which he received the advance, he announced the fact to his fellow-workmen, adding triumphantly, "I am now a made man for life!"

The pit opened at Newburn, at which old Robert Stephenson worked, proving a failure, it was closed, and a new pit was sunk at Water-row, on a strip of land lying between the Wylam wagon-way and the River Tyne, about half a mile west of Newburn Church. A pumping-engine was erected there by Robert Hawthorn, the duke's engineer, and old Stephenson went to work it as fireman, his son George acting as the engine-man or plugman. At that time he was about seventeen years old—a very youthful age at which to fill so responsible a post. He had thus already got ahead of his father in his station as a workman; for the plugman holds a higher grade than the fireman, requiring more practical knowledge and skill, and usually receiving higher wages.

George's duties as plugman were to watch the engine, to see that it kept well in work, and that the pumps were efficient in drawing the water. When the water-level in the pit was lowered, and the suction became incomplete through the exposure of the suction-holes, it was then his duty to proceed to the bottom of the shaft and plug the tube so that the pump should draw: hence the designation of "plugman." If a stoppage in the engine took place through any defect which he was incapable of remedying, it was his duty to call in the aid of the chief engineer to set it to rights.

But from the time that George Stephenson was appointed fireman, and more particularly afterward as engine-man, he applied himself so assiduously and successfully to the study of the engine and its gearing—taking the machine to pieces in his leisure hours for the purpose of cleaning it and understanding its various parts—that he soon acquired a thorough practical knowledge of its construction and mode of working, and very rarely needed to call the engineer of the colliery to his aid. His engine became a sort of pet with him, and he was never wearied of watching and inspecting it with admiration.

There is, indeed, a peculiar fascination about an engine to the person whose duty it is to watch and work it. It is almost sublime in its untiring industry and quiet power; capable of performing the most gigantic work, yet so docile that a child's hand may guide it. No wonder, therefore, that the workman who is the daily companion of this life-like machine, and is constantly watching it with anxious care, at length comes to regard it with a degree of personal interest and regard. This daily contemplation of the steam-engine, and the sight of its steady action, is an education of itself to an ingenious and thoughtful man. And it is a remarkable fact, that nearly all that has been done for the improvement of this machine has been accomplished, not by philosophers and scientific men, but by laborers, mechanics, and engine-men. Indeed, it would appear as if this were one of the departments of practical science in which the higher powers of the human mind must bend to mechanical instinct.

Stephenson was now in his eighteenth year, but, like many of his fellow-workmen, he had not yet learned to read. All that he could do was to get some one to read for him by his engine-fire, out of any book or stray newspaper which found its way into the neighborhood. Bonaparte was then overrunning Italy, and astounding Europe by his brilliant succession of victories; and there was no more eager auditor of his exploits, as read from the newspaper accounts, than the young engine-man at the Water-row Pit.

There were also numerous stray bits of information and intelligence contained in these papers which excited Stephenson's interest. One of them related to the Egyptian method of hatching birds' eggs by means of artificial heat. Curious about every thing relating to birds, he determined to test it by experiment. It was spring time, and he forthwith went bird-nesting in the adjoining woods and hedges. He gathered a collection of eggs of various sorts, set them in flour in a warm place in the engine-house, covered the whole with wool, and waited the issue. The heat was kept as steady as possible, and the eggs were carefully turned every twelve hours; but, though they chipped, and some of them exhibited well-grown chicks, they never hatched. The experiment failed, but the incident shows that the inquiring mind of the youth was fairly at work.

Modeling of engines in clay continued to be another of his favorite occupations. He made models of engines which he had seen, and of others which were described to him. These attempts were an improvement upon his first trials at Dewley Burn bog, when occupied there as a herd-boy. He was, however, anxious to know something of the wonderful engines of Boulton and Watt, and was told that they were to be found fully described in books, which he must search for information as to their construction, action, and uses. But, alas! Stephenson could not read; he had not yet learned even his letters.

Thus he shortly found, when gazing wistfully in the direction of knowledge, that to advance farther as a skilled workman, he must master this wonderful art of reading—the key to so many other arts. Only thus could he gain an access to books, the depositories of the wisdom and experience of the past. Although a grown man, and doing the work of a man, he was not ashamed to confess his ignorance, and go to school, big as he was, to learn his letters. Perhaps, too, he foresaw that, in laying out a little of his spare earnings for this purpose, he was investing money judiciously, and that, in every hour he spent at school, he was really working for better wages.

His first schoolmaster was Robin Cowens, a poor teacher in the village of Walbottle. He kept a night-school, which was attended by a few of the colliers' and laborers' sons in the neighborhood. George took lessons in spelling and reading three nights in the week. Robin Cowen's teaching cost threepence a week; and though it was not very good, yet George, being hungry for knowledge and eager to acquire it, soon learned to read. He also practiced "pot-hooks," and at the age of nineteen he was proud to be able to write his own name."

A Scotch dominie, named Andrew Robertson, set up a night-school in the village of Newburn in the winter of 1799. It was more convenient for George to attend this school, as it was nearer his work, being only a few minutes' walk from Jolly's Close. Besides, Andrew had the reputation of being a good arithmetician, and this was a branch of knowledge that Stephenson was very desirous of acquiring. He accordingly began taking lessons from him, paying fourpence a week. Robert Gray, junior fireman at the Water-row Pit, began arithmetic at the same time; and Gray afterward told the author that George learned "figuring" so much faster than he did, that he could not make out how it was—"he took to figures so wonderful." Although the two started together from the same point, at the end of the winter George had mastered "reduction," while Robert Gray was still struggling with the difficulties of simple division. But George's secret was his perseverance. He worked out the sums in his by-hours, improving every minute of his spare time by the engine-fire, there studying the arithmetical problems set for him upon his slate by the master. In the evenings he took to Robertson the sums which he had "worked," and new ones were "set" for him to study out the following day. Thus his progress was rapid, and, with a willing heart and mind, he soon became well advanced in arithmetic. Indeed, Andrew Robertson became very proud of his scholar; and shortly after, when the Water-row Pit was closed, and George removed to Black Callerton to work there, the poor schoolmaster, not having a very extensive connection in Newburn, went with his pupils, and set up his night-school at Black Callerton, where he continued his lessons.

George still found time to attend to his favorite animals while working at the Water-row Pit. Like his father, he used to tempt the robin-redbreasts to hop and fly about him at the engine-fire by the bait of bread-crumbs saved from his dinner. But his chief favorite was his dog—so sagacious that he almost daily carried George's dinner to him at the pit. The tin containing the meal was suspended from the dog's neck, and, thus laden, he proceeded faithfully from Jolly's Close to Water-row Pit, quite through the village of Newburn. He turned neither to left nor right, nor heeded the barking of curs at his heels. But his course was not unattended with perils. One day the big, strange dog of a passing butcher, espying the engine-man's messenger with the tin can about his neck, ran after and fell upon him. There was a terrible tussle and worrying, which lasted for a brief while, and, shortly after, the dog's master, anxious for his dinner, saw his faithful servant approaching, bleeding but triumphant. The tin can was still round his neck, but the dinner had been spilled in the struggle. Though George went without his dinner that day, he was prouder of his dog than ever when the circumstances of the combat were related to him by the villagers who had seen it.

It was while working at the Water-row Pit that Stephenson learned the art of brakeing an engine. This being one of the higher departments of colliery labor, and among the best paid, George was very anxious to learn it. A small winding-engine having been put up for the purpose of drawing the coals from the pit, Bill Coe, his friend and fellow-workman, was appointed the brakesman. He frequently allowed George to try his hand at the machine, and instructed him how to proceed. Coe was, however, opposed in this by several of the other workmen, one of whom, a banksman named William Locke,* went so far as to stop the working of the pit because Stephenson had been called

* Father of Mr. Locke, M.P., the engineer. He afterward removed to Barnsley, in Yorkshire.

in to the brake. But one day, as Mr. Charles Nixon, the manager of the pit, was observed approaching, Coe adopted an expedient which put a stop to the opposition. He called upon Stephenson to "come into the brake-house and take hold of the machine." Locke, as usual, sat down, and the working of the pit was stopped. When requested by the manager to give an explanation, he said that "young Stephenson couldn't brake, and, what was more, never would learn, he was so clumsy." Mr. Nixon, however, ordered Locke to go on with the work, which he did; and Stephenson, after some farther practice, acquired the art of brakeing.

After working at the Water-row Pit and at other engines near Newburn for about three years, George and Coe went to Black Callerton early in 1810. Though only twenty years of age, his employers thought so well of him that they appointed him to the responsible office of brakesman at the Dolly Pit. For convenience' sake, he took lodgings at a small farmer's in the village, finding his own victuals, and paying so much a week for lodging and attendance. In the locality this was called "picklin in his awn poke neuk." It not unfrequently happens that the young workman about the collieries, when selecting a lodging, contrives to pitch his tent where the daughter of the house ultimately becomes his wife. This is often the real attraction that draws the youth from home, though a very different one may be pretended.

George Stephenson's duties as brakesman may be briefly described. The work was somewhat monotonous, and consisted in superintending the working of the engine and machinery by means of which the coals were drawn out of the pit. Brakesmen are almost invariably selected from those who have had considerable experience as engine-firemen, and borne a good character for steadiness, punctuality, watchfulness, and "mother wit." In George Stephenson's day the coals were drawn out of the pit in corves, or large baskets made of hazel rods. The corves were placed together in a cage, between which and the pit-ropes there was usually from fifteen to twenty feet of chain. The approach of the corves toward the pit mouth was signaled by a bell, brought into action by a piece of mechanism worked from the shaft of the engine. When the bell sounded, the brakesman checked the speed by taking hold of the hand-gear connected with the steam-valves, which were so arranged that by their means he could regulate the speed of the engine, and stop or set it in motion when required. Connected with the fly-wheel was a powerful wooden brake, acting by pressure against its rim, something like the brake of a railway carriage against its wheels. On catching sight of the chain attached to the ascending corve-cage, the brakesman, by pressing his foot upon a foot-step near him, was enabled, with great precision, to stop the revolutions of the wheel, and arrest the ascent of the corves at the pit mouth, when they were forthwith landed on the "settle-board." On the full corves being replaced by empty ones, it was then the duty of the brakesman to reverse the engine, and send the corves down the pit to be filled again.

The monotony of George Stephenson's occupation as a brakesman was somewhat varied by the change which he made, in his turn, from the day to the night shift. His duty, on the latter occasions, consisted chiefly in sending men and materials into the mine, and in drawing other men and materials out. Most of the workmen enter the pit during the night shift, and leave it in the latter part of the day, while coal-drawing is proceeding. The requirements of the work at night are such that the brakesman has a good deal of spare time on his hands, which he is at liberty to employ in his own way. From an early period, George was accustomed to employ those vacant night hours in working the sums set for him by Andrew Robertson upon his slate, practicing writing in his copy-book, and mending the shoes of his fellow-workmen. His wages while working at the Dolly Pit amounted to from £1 15*s.* to £2 in the fortnight; but he gradually added to them as he became more expert at shoe-mending, and afterward at shoe-making.

Probably he was stimulated to take in hand this extra work by the attachment he had by this time formed for a young woman named Fanny Henderson, who officiated as servant in the small farmer's house in which he lodged. We have been informed that the personal attractions of Fanny, though these were considerable, were the least of her charms. Mr. William Fairbairn, who afterward saw her in her home at Willington Quay, describes her as a very comely woman. But her temper was one of the sweetest; and those who knew her were accustomed to speak of the charming modesty of her demeanor, her kindness of disposition, and, withal, her sound good sense.

Among his various mendings of old shoes at Callerton, George was on one occasion favored with the shoes of his sweetheart to sole. One can imagine the pleasure with which he would linger over such a piece of work, and the pride with which he would execute it. A friend of his, still living, relates that, after he had finished the shoes, he carried them about with him in his pocket on the Sunday afternoon, and that from time to time he would pull them out and hold them up, exclaiming "what a capital job he had made of them!"

Not long after he began to work at Black Callerton as brakesman he had a quarrel with a pitman named Ned Nelson, a roystering bully, who was the terror of the village. Nelson was a great fighter, and it was therefore considered dangerous to quarrel with him. Stephenson was so unfortunate as not to be able to please this pitman by the way in which he drew him out of the pit, and Nelson swore at him grossly because of the alleged clumsiness of his brakeing. George defended himself, and appealed to the testimony of the other workmen. Nelson had not been accustomed to George's style of self-assertion, and, after a great deal of abuse, he threatened to kick the brakesman, who defied him to do so. Nelson ended by challenging Stephenson to a pitched battle, and the latter accepted the challenge, when a day was fixed on which the fight was to come off.

Great was the excitement at Black Callerton when it was known that George Stephenson had accepted Nelson's challenge. Every body said he would be killed. The villagers, the young men, and especially the boys of the place, with whom George was a great favorite, all wished that he might beat Nelson, but they scarcely dared to say so. They came about him while he was at work in the engine-house to inquire if it was really true that he was "goin' to fight Nelson." "Ay; never fear for me; I'll fight him." And fight him he did. For some days previous to the appointed day of battle, Nelson went entirely off work for the purpose of keeping himself fresh and strong, whereas Stephenson went on doing his daily work as usual, and appeared not in the least disconcerted by the prospect of the affair. So, on the evening appointed, after George had done his day's labor, he went into the Dolly Pit Field, where his already exulting rival was ready to meet him. George stripped, and "went in" like a practiced pugilist, though it was his first and last fight. After a few rounds, George's wiry muscles and practiced strength enabled him severely to punish his adversary and to secure an easy victory.

This circumstance is related in illustration of Stephenson's personal pluck and courage, and it was thoroughly characteristic of the man. He was no pugilist, and the reverse of quarrelsome. But he would not be put down by the bully of the colliery, and he fought him. There his pugilism ended; they afterward shook hands, and continued good friends. In after life Stephenson's mettle was often as hardly tried, though in a different way, and he did not fail to exhibit the same courage in contending with the bullies of the railway world as he showed in his encounter with Ned Nelson, the fighting pitman of Callerton.

STEPHENSON'S COTTAGE AT WILLINGTON QUAY. [By R. P. Leitch.]

CHAPTER III.

ENGINE-MAN AT WILLINGTON QUAY AND KILLINGWORTH.

George Stephenson had now acquired the character of an expert workman. He was diligent and observant while at work, and sober and studious when the day's work was done. His friend Coe described him to the author as "a standing example of manly character." On pay-Saturday afternoons, when the pitmen held their fortnightly holiday, occupying themselves chiefly in cock-fighting and dog-fighting in the adjoining fields, followed by adjournments to the "yel-house," George was accustomed to take his engine to pieces, for the purpose of obtaining "insight," and he cleaned all the parts and put the machine in thorough working order before leaving her. His amusements continued to be principally of the athletic kind, and he found few that could beat him at lifting heavy weights, leaping, and throwing the hammer.

In the evenings he improved himself in the arts of reading and writing, and occasionally he took a turn at modeling. It was at Callerton, his son Robert informed us, that he began to try his hand at original invention, and for some time he applied his attention to a machine of the nature of an engine-brake, which reversed itself by its own action. But nothing came of the contrivance, and it was eventually thrown aside as useless. Yet not altogether so; for even the highest skill must undergo the inevitable discipline of experiment, and submit to the wholesome correction of occasional failure.

After working at Callerton for about two years, Stephenson received an offer to take charge of the engine on Willington Ballast Hill at an advanced wage. He determined to accept it, and at the same time to marry Fanny Henderson, and begin housekeeping on his own account. Though he was only twenty-one years old, he had contrived, by thrift, steadiness, and industry, to save as much money as enabled him, with the help of Fanny's small hoard, to take a cottage dwelling at Willington Quay, and furnish it in a humble but comfortable style for the reception of his bride.

Willington Quay lies on the north bank of the Tyne, about six miles below Newcastle. It consists of a line of houses straggling along the river side, and high behind it towers up the huge mound of ballast emptied out of the ships which resort to the quay for their cargoes of coal for the London market. The ballast is thrown out of the ships' holds into wagons laid alongside. When filled, a train of these is dragged to the summit of the Ballast Hill, where they are run out, and their contents emptied on to the monstrous accumulation of earth, chalk, and Thames mud already laid there, probably to form a puzzle for future antiquaries and geologists when the origin of these immense hills along the Tyne has been forgotten. At the foot of this great mound of shot rubbish was a fixed engine, which drew the trains of laden wagons up the incline by means of ropes working over pulleys, and of this engine George Stephenson acted as brakesman.

The cottage in which he took up his abode was a small two-storied dwelling, standing a little back from the quay, with a bit of garden ground in front;* but he only occupied the upper

* The Stephenson Memorial Schools have since been erected on the site of the old cottage at Willington Quay represented in the engraving at the head of this chapter. A vignette of the Memorial Schools will be found at the end of the volume.

room in the west end of the cottage. Close behind rose the Ballast Hill.

When the cottage dwelling had been made snug and was ready for his wife's reception, the marriage took place. It was celebrated in Newburn Church on the 28th of November, 1802. George Stephenson's signature, as it stands in the register, is that of a person who seems to have just learned to write. With all the writer's care, however, he had not been able to avoid a blotch. The name of Frances Henderson has the appearance of being written by the same hand.

George Stephenson

Frances Henderson

After the ceremony, George and his newly-wedded partner proceeded to the house of old Robert Stephenson and his wife Mabel at Jolly Close. The old man was now becoming infirm, though he still worked as an engine-fireman, and contrived with difficulty "to keep his head above water." When the visit had been paid, the bridal party prepared to set out for their new home at Willington Quay. They went in a style which was quite common before traveling by railway had been invented. Two farm-horses, borrowed from a neighboring farmer, were each provided with a saddle and a pillion, and George having mounted one, his wife seated herself behind him, holding on by her arms round his waist. The brideman and bridemaid in like manner mounted the other horse, and in this wise the wedding party rode across the country, passing through the old streets of Newcastle, and then by Wallsend to Willington Quay—a long ride of about fifteen miles.

George Stephenson's daily life at Willington was that of a steady workman. By the manner, however, in which he continued to improve his spare hours in the evening, he was silently and surely paving the way for being something more than a manual laborer. He diligently set himself to study the principles of mechanics, and to master the laws by which his engine worked. For a workman, he was even at that time more than ordinarily speculative, often taking up strange theories, and trying to sift out the truth that was in them. While sitting by the side of his young wife in his cottage dwelling in the winter evenings, he was usually occupied in studying mechanical subjects or in modeling experimental machines.

Among his various speculations while at Willington, he tried to discover a means of Perpetual Motion. Although he failed, as so many others had done before him, the very efforts he made tended to whet his inventive faculties and to call forth his dormant powers. He actually went so far as to construct the model of a machine for the purpose. It consisted of a wooden wheel, the periphery of which was furnished with glass tubes filled with quicksilver; as the wheel rotated, the quicksilver poured itself down into the lower tubes, and thus a sort of self-acting motion was kept up in the apparatus, which, however, did not prove to be perpetual. Where he had first obtained the idea of this machine —whether from conversation, or reading, or his own thoughts, is not known; but his son Robert was of opinion that he had heard of an apparatus of this kind as described in the "History of Inventions." As he had then no access to books, and, indeed, could scarcely yet read, it is probable that he had been told of the invention, and set about testing its value according to his own methods.

Much of his spare time continued to be occupied by labor more immediately profitable, regarded in a pecuniary point of view. In the evenings, after his day's labor at his engine, he would occasionally employ himself for a few hours in casting ballast out of the collier ships, by which means he was enabled to earn a few shillings weekly. Mr. William Fairbairn, of Manchester, has informed the author that, while Stephenson was employed at the Willington Ballast Hill, he himself was working in the neighborhood as an engine apprentice at the Percy Main Colliery. He was very fond of George, who was a fine, hearty fellow, besides being a capital workman. In the summer evenings young Fairbairn was accustomed to go down to Willington to see his friend, and on such occasions he would frequently take charge of George's engine for a few hours, to enable him to take a two or three hours' turn at heaving ballast out of the ships' holds. It is pleasant to think of the future President of the British Association thus helping the future Railway Engineer to earn a few extra shillings by overwork in the evenings, at a time when both occupied the rank but of humble working men in an obscure northern village.

Mr. Fairbairn was also a frequent visitor at George's cottage on the Quay, where, though there was no luxury, there was comfort, cleanness, and a pervading spirit of industry. Even at home George was never for a moment idle. When there was no ballast to heave, he took in shoes to mend; and from mending he proceeded to making them, as well as shoe-lasts, in which he was admitted to be very expert. William Coe, who continued to live at Willington in 1851, informed the author that he bought a pair of shoes from George Stephenson for 7*s.* 6*d.*, and he remembered that they were a capital fit, and wore very well.

But an accident occurred in Stephenson's household about this time which had the effect of directing his industry into a new and still more profitable channel. The cottage chimney took fire one day in his absence, when the alarmed neighbors, rushing in, threw quantities of water upon the flames; and some, in their zeal, even mounted the ridge of the house, and poured buckets of water down the chimney. The fire was soon put out, but the house was thoroughly soaked. When George came home, he found the water running out of the door, every thing in disorder, and his new furniture covered with soot. The eight-day clock, which hung against the wall—one of the most highly-prized articles in the house—was seriously damaged by the steam with which the room had been filled. Its wheels were so clogged by the dust and soot that it was brought to a complete stand-still.

George was advised to send the article to the clock-maker, but that would cost money; and he declared that he would repair it himself—at least he would try. The clock was accordingly taken to pieces and cleaned; the tools which he had been accumulating for the purpose of constructing his Perpetual Motion machine readily enabled him to do this, and he succeeded so well that, shortly after, the neighbors sent him their clocks to clean, and he soon became one of the most expert clock-cleaners in the neighborhood.

It was while living at Willington Quay that George Stephenson's only son was born on the 16th of October, 1803.* The child was from the first, as may well be imagined, a great favorite with his father, and added much to the happiness of his evening hours. George Stephenson's strong "philoprogenitiveness," as phrenologists call it, had in his boyhood expended itself on birds, and dogs, and rabbits, and even on the poor old gin-horses which he had driven at the Callerton Pit, and now he found in his child a more genial object for the exercise of his affection.

The christening of the boy took place in the school-house at Wallsend, the old parish church being at the time in so dilapidated a condition from the "creeping" or subsidence of the ground, consequent upon the excavation of the coal, that it was considered dangerous to enter it.† On this occasion, Robert Gray and Anne Henderson, who had officiated as brideman and bridemaid at the wedding, came over again to Willington, and stood godfather and godmother to little Robert, as the child was named, after his grandfather.

After working for about three years as a brakesman at the Willington machine, George Stephenson was induced to leave his situation there for a similar one at the West Moor Colliery, Killingworth. It was not without considerable persuasion that he was induced to leave the Quay, as he knew that he should thereby give up the chance of earning extra money by casting ballast from the keels. At last, however, he consented, in the hope of making up the loss in some other way.

The village of Killingworth lies about seven miles north of Newcastle, and is one of the best-known collieries in that neigh-

* No register was made of Robert Stephenson's birth, and he himself was in doubt whether he was born in October, November, or December. For instance, a dinner was given to him by the contractors of the London and Birmingham Railway on the 16th of November, 1839, that day being then supposed by his father to have been his birthday. When preparing the "Life of George Stephenson," Robert stated to the author that the 16th of December was the correct day. But, after the book had passed through four editions, he desired the date to be corrected to the 16th of October, which, on the whole, he thought the right date, and it was so altered accordingly.

† The congregation in a church near Newcastle were one Sunday morning plentifully powdered with chips from the white ceiling of the church, which had been *crept under*, being above an old mine. "It is only the pit a-creeping," said the parish clerk, by way of encouragement to the people to remain. But it would not do; for there was a sudden *creep out* of the congregation. The clerk went at last, with a powdered head, crying out, "It's only a creep."—"Our Coal-Fields and our Coal-Pits."

WEST MOOR COLLIERY. [By R. P. Leitch.]

borhood. The workings of the coal are of vast extent, and give employment to a large number of work-people. To this place Stephenson first came as a brakesman about the end of 1804. He had not been long in his new home ere his wife died of consumption, leaving him with his only child Robert. George deeply felt the loss, for his wife and he had been very happy together. Their lot had been sweetened by daily successful toil. George had been hard-working, and his wife had made his hearth so bright and his home so snug, that no attraction could draw him from her side in the evening hours. But this domestic happiness was all to pass away, and the bereaved husband felt for a time as one that had thenceforth to tread the journey of life alone.

Shortly after this event, while his grief was still fresh, he received an invitation from some gentlemen concerned in large spinning-works near Montrose, in Scotland, to proceed thither and superintend the working of one of Boulton and Watt's engines. He accepted the offer, and made arrangements to leave Killingworth for a time.

Having left his boy in charge of a respectable woman who acted as his housekeeper, he set out on the journey to Scotland on foot, with his kit upon his back. While working at Montrose, he gave a striking proof of that practical ability in contrivance for which he was afterward so distinguished. It appears that the water required for the purposes of his engine, as well as for the use of the works, was pumped from a considerable depth, being supplied from the adjacent extensive sand strata. The pumps frequently got choked by the sand drawn in at the bottom of the well through the snore-holes, or apertures through which the water to be raised is admitted. The barrels soon became worn, and the bucket and clack leathers destroyed, so that it became necessary to devise a remedy; and with this object, the engine-man proceeded to adopt the following simple but original expedient. He had a wooden box or boot made, twelve feet high, which he placed in the sump or well, and into this he inserted the lower end of the pump. The result was, that the water flowed clear from the outer part of the well over into the boot, and was drawn up without any admixture of sand, and the difficulty was thus conquered.*

During his stay in Scotland, Stephenson, being paid good wages, contrived to save a sum of £28, which he took back with him to Killingworth, after an absence of about a year. Longing to get back to his kindred, and his heart yearning for the boy whom he had left behind, our engine-man bade adieu to his Montrose employers, and trudged back to Killingworth on foot as he had gone. He related to his friend Coe, on his return, that when on the borders of Northumberland, late one evening, footsore and wearied with his long day's journey, he knocked at a small farmer's cottage door, and requested shelter for the night. It was refused; and then he entreated that, being sore tired and unable to proceed any farther, they would permit him to lie

* This incident was related by Robert Stephenson during a voyage to the north of Scotland in 1857, when off Montrose, on board his yacht *Titania;* and the reminiscence was immediately communicated to the author by the late Mr. William Kell, of Gateshead, who was present, at Mr. Stephenson's request, as being worthy of insertion in his father's biography. Mr. George Elliott, one of the most skilled coal-viewers in the North, was of the party, and expressed his admiration at the ready skill with which the difficulty had been overcome, the expedient of the boot being then unknown in the Northumberland and Durham mines. He acknowledged it to be "a wrinkle," adding that its application would, in several instances within his own knowledge, have been of great practical value.

down in the out-house, for that a little clean straw would serve him. The farmer's wife appeared at the door, looked at the traveler, then retiring with her husband, the two confabulated a little apart, and finally they invited Stephenson into the cottage. Always full of conversation and anecdote, he soon made himself at home in the farmer's family, and spent with them some pleasant hours. He was hospitably entertained for the night, and when he left the cottage in the morning, he pressed them to make some charge for his lodging, but they refused to accept any recompense. They only asked him to remember them kindly, and if he ever came that way, to be sure and call again. Many years after, when Stephenson had become a thriving man, he did not forget the humble pair who had thus succored and entertained him on his way; he sought their cottage again when age had silvered their hair; and when he left the aged couple on that occasion, they may have been reminded of the old saying that we may sometimes "entertain angels unawares."

Reaching home, Stephenson found that his father had met with a serious accident at the Blucher Pit, which had reduced him to great distress and poverty. While engaged in the inside of an engine, making some repairs, a fellow-workman inadvertently let in the steam upon him. The blast struck him full in the face; he was terribly scorched, and his eyesight was irretrievably lost. The helpless and infirm man had struggled for a time with poverty; his sons who were at home, poor as himself, were little able to help him, while George was at a distance in Scotland. On his return, however, with his savings in his pocket, his first step was to pay off his father's debts, amounting to about £15; and, shortly after, he removed the aged pair from Jolly's Close to a comfortable cottage adjoining the tram-road near the West Moor at Killingworth, where the old man lived for many years, supported by his son.

Stephenson was again taken on as a brakesman at the West Moor Pit. He does not seem to have been very hopeful as to his prospects in life at the time. Indeed, the condition of the working classes was then very discouraging. England was engaged in a great war, which pressed upon the industry, and severely tried the resources of the country. Heavy taxes were imposed upon all the articles of consumption that would bear them.

There was a constant demand for men to fill the army, navy, and militia. Never before had England witnessed such drumming and fifing for recruits. In 1805, the gross forces of the United Kingdom amounted to nearly 700,000 men, and early in 1808 Lord Castlereagh carried a measure for the establishment of a local militia of 200,000 men. These measures were accompanied by general distress among the laboring classes. There were riots in Manchester, Newcastle, and elsewhere, through scarcity of work and lowness of wages. The working people were also liable to be pressed for the navy, or drawn for the militia; and though people could not fail to be discontented under such circumstances, they scarcely dared even to mutter their discontent to their neighbors.

George Stephenson was one of those drawn for the militia. He must therefore either quit his work and go a-soldiering, or find a substitute. He adopted the latter course, and borrowed £6, which, with the remainder of his savings, enabled him to provide a militia-man to serve in his stead. Thus the whole of his hard-won earnings were swept away at a stroke. He was almost in despair, and contemplated the idea of leaving the country, and emigrating to the United States. Although a voyage thither was then a much more formidable thing for a working man to accomplish than a voyage to Australia is now, he seriously entertained the project, and had all but made up his mind to go. His sister Ann, with her husband, emigrated about that time, but George could not raise the requisite money, and they departed without him. After all, it went sore against his heart to leave his home and his kindred, the scenes of his youth and the friends of his boyhood, and he struggled long with the idea, brooding over it in sorrow. Speaking afterward to a friend of his thoughts at the time, he said: "You know the road from my house at the West Moor to Killingworth. I remember once when I went along that road I wept bitterly, for I knew not where my lot in life would be cast." But his poverty prevented him from prosecuting the idea of emigration, and rooted him to the place where he afterward worked out his career so manfully and victoriously.

In 1808, Stephenson, with two other brakesmen, took a small contract under the colliery lessees, brakeing the engines at the

West Moor Pit. The brakesmen found the oil and tallow; they divided the work among them, and were paid so much per score for their labor. There being two engines working night and day, two of the three men were always on duty, the average earnings of each amounting to from 18*s.* to 20*s.* a week. It was the interest of the brakesmen to economize the working as much as possible, and George no sooner entered upon the contract than he proceeded to devise ways and means of making the contract "pay." He observed that the ropes with which the coal was drawn out of the pit by the winding-engine were badly arranged; they "glued" and wore each other to tatters by the perpetual friction. There was thus great wear and tear, and a serious increase in the expenses of the pit. George found that the ropes which, at other pits in the neighborhood, lasted about three months, at the West Moor Pit became worn out in about a month. He accordingly set himself to ascertain the cause of the defect; and, finding that it was occasioned by excessive friction, he proceeded, with the sanction of the head engine-wright and of the colliery owners, to shift the pulley-wheels so that they worked immediately over the centre of the pit. By this expedient, accompanied by an entire rearrangement of the gearing of the machine, he shortly succeeded in greatly lessening the wear and tear of the ropes, to the advantage of the owners as well as of the workmen, who were thus enabled to labor more continuously and profitably.

About the same time he attempted an improvement in the winding-engine which he worked, by placing a valve between the air-pump and condenser. This expedient, although it led to no practical result, showed that his mind was actively engaged in studying new mechanical adaptations. It continued to be his regular habit, on Saturdays, to take his engine to pieces, for the purpose at the same time of familiarizing himself with its action, and of placing it in a state of thorough working order; and by mastering the details of the engine, he was enabled, as opportunity occurred, to turn to practical account the knowledge thus diligently and patiently acquired.

Such an opportunity was not long in presenting itself. In the year 1810, a pit was sunk by the "Grand Allies" (the lessees of the mines) at the village of Killingworth, now known as the Killingworth High Pit. An atmospheric or Newcomen engine, originally made by Smeaton, was fixed there for the purpose of pumping out the water from the shaft; but, somehow or other, the engine failed to clear the pit. As one of the workmen has since described the circumstance—"She couldn't keep her jack-head in water: all the engine-men in the neighborhood were tried, as well as Crowther of the Ouseburn, but they were clean bet." The engine had been fruitlessly pumping for nearly twelve months, and came to be regarded as a total failure. Stephenson had gone to look at it when in course of erection, and then observed to the over-man that he thought it was defective; he also gave it as his opinion that if there were much water in the mine, the engine could never keep it under. Of course, as he was only a brakesman, his opinion was considered to be worth very little on such a point. He continued, however, to make frequent visits to the engine to see "how she was getting on." From the bank-head where he worked his brake he could see the chimney smoking at the High Pit; and as the workmen were passing to and from their work, he would call out and inquire "if they had gotten to the bottom yet." And the reply was always to the same effect—the pumping made no progress, and the workmen were still "drowned out."

One Saturday afternoon he went over to the High Pit to examine the engine more carefully than he had yet done. He had been turning the subject over in his mind, and, after a long examination, he seemed to have satisfied himself as to the cause of the failure. Kit Heppel, one of the sinkers, asked him, "Weel, George, what do you mak' o' her? Do you think you could do any thing to improve her?" "Man," said George, in reply, "I could alter her and make her draw: in a week's time from this I could send you to the bottom."

Heppel at once reported this conversation to Ralph Dodds, the head viewer, who, being now quite in despair, and hopeless of succeeding with the engine, determined to give George's skill a trial. George had already acquired the character of a very clever and ingenious workman, and, at the worst, he could only fail, as the rest had done. In the evening Dodds went in search of Stephenson, and met him on the road, dressed in his Sunday's suit, on his way to "the preaching" in the Methodist Chapel, which he at that time attended. "Well, George," said Dodds, "they tell me that you think you can put the engine at the High Pit to rights." "Yes, sir," said George, "I think I could." "If that's the case, I'll give you a fair trial, and you must set to work immediately. We are clean drowned out, and can not get a step farther. The engineers hereabouts are all bet; and if you really succeed in accomplishing what they can not do, you may depend upon it I will make you a man for life."

Stephenson began his operations early next morning. The only condition that he made, before setting to work, was that he should select his own workmen. There was, as he knew, a good deal of jealousy among the "regular" men that a colliery brakesman should pretend to know more about their engine than they themselves did, and attempt to remedy defects which the most skilled men of their craft, including the engineer of the colliery, had failed to do. But George made the condition a *sine quâ non.* "The workmen," said he, "must either be all Whigs or all Tories." There was no help for it, so Dodds ordered the old hands to stand aside. The men grumbled, but gave way; and then George and his party went in.

The engine was taken entirely to pieces. The cistern containing the injection water was raised ten feet; the injection cock, being too small, was enlarged to nearly double its former size, and it was so arranged that it should be shut off quickly at the beginning of the stroke. These and other alterations were necessarily performed in a rough way, but, as the result proved, on true principles. Stephenson also, finding that the boiler would bear a greater pressure than five pounds to the inch, determined to work it at a pressure of ten pounds, though this was contrary to the directions of both Newcomen and Smeaton.

The necessary alterations were made in about three days, and many persons came to see the engine start, including the men who had put her up. The pit being nearly full of water, she had little to do on starting, and, to use George's words, "came bounce into the house." Dodds exclaimed, "Why, she was better as she was; now, she will knock the house down." After a short time, however, the engine got fairly to work, and by ten o'clock that night the water was lower in the pit than it had ever been before. The engine was kept pumping all Thursday, and by the Friday afternoon the pit was cleared of water, and the workmen were "sent to the bottom," as Stephenson had promised. Thus the alterations effected in the pumping apparatus proved completely successful.*

Mr. Dodds was particularly gratified with the manner in which the job had been done, and he made Stephenson a present of ten pounds, which, though very inadequate when compared with the value of the work performed, was accepted with gratitude. George was proud of the gift as the first marked recognition of his skill as a workman; and he used afterward to say that it was the biggest sum of money he had up to that time earned in one lump. Ralph Dodds, however, did more than this; he released the brakesman from the handles of his engine at West Moor, and appointed him engine-man at the High Pit, at good wages, during the time the pit was sinking—the job lasting for about a year; and he also kept him in mind for farther advancement.

Stephenson's skill as an engine-doctor soon became noised abroad, and he was called upon to prescribe remedies for all the old, wheezy, and ineffective pumping-machines in the neighborhood. In this capacity he soon left the "regular" men far behind, though they, in their turn, were very much disposed to treat the Killingworth brakesman as no better than a quack. Nevertheless, his practice was really founded upon a close study of the principles of mechanics, and on an intimate practical acquaintance with the details of the pumping-engine.

Another of his smaller achievements in the same line is still told by the people of the district. At the corner of the road leading to Long-Benton there was a quarry from which a peculiar and scarce kind of ochre was taken. In the course of working it out, the water had collected in considerable quantities; and there being no means of draining it off, it accumulated to such an extent that the farther working of the ochre was almost entirely stopped. Ordinary pumps were tried, and failed; and then a windmill was tried, and failed too. On this, George was asked what ought to be done to clear the quarry of the water. He said "he would set up for them an engine, little bigger than a kail-

* As different versions have been given of this affair, it may be mentioned that the above statement is made on the authority of the late Robert Stephenson, and of George Stephenson himself, as communicated by the latter to his friend Thomas L. Gooch, C.E., who has kindly supplied the author with his memoranda on the subject.

pot, that would clear them out in a week." And he did so. A little engine was speedily erected, by means of which the quarry was pumped dry in the course of a few days. Thus his skill as a pump-doctor soon became the marvel of the district.

In elastic muscular vigor Stephenson was now in his prime, and he still continued zealous in measuring his strength and agility with his fellow-workmen. The competitive element in his nature was always strong, and his success in these feats of rivalry was certainly remarkable. Few, if any, could lift such weights, throw the hammer and put the stone so far, or cover so great a space at a standing or running leap. One day, between the engine hour and the rope-rolling hour, Kit Heppel challenged him to leap from one high wall to another, with a deep gap between. To Heppel's surprise and dismay, George took the standing leap, and cleared the eleven feet at a bound. Had his eye been less accurate, or his limbs less agile and sure, the feat must have cost him his life.

But so full of redundant muscular vigor was he, that leaping, putting, or throwing the hammer, were not enough for him. He was also ambitious of riding on horseback; and, as he had not yet been promoted to an office enabling him to keep a horse of his own, he sometimes borrowed one of the gin-horses for a ride. On one of these occasions he brought the animal back reeking, when Tommy Mitcheson, the bank horse-keeper, a rough-spoken fellow, exclaimed to him, "Set such fellows as you on horseback, and you'll soon ride to the De'il." But Tommy Mitcheson lived to tell the story, and to confess that, after all, there had been a better issue of George's horsemanship than what he had predicted.

Old Cree, the engine-wright at Killingworth High Pit, having been killed by an accident, George Stephenson was, in 1812, appointed engine-wright of the colliery at the salary of £100 a year. He was also allowed the use of a galloway to ride upon in his visits of inspection to the collieries leased by the "Grand Allies" in that neighborhood.

The "Grand Allies" were a company of gentlemen, consisting of Sir Thomas Liddell (afterward Lord Ravensworth), the Earl of Strathmore, and, and Mr. Stuart Wortley (afterward Lord Wharncliffe), the lessees of the Killingworth collieries. Having been informed of the merits of Stephenson, of his indefatigable industry, and the skill which he had displayed in the repairs of the pumping-engines, they readily acceded to Mr. Dodds's recommendation that he should be appointed the colliery engine-wright; and, as we shall afterward find, they continued to honor him by distinguished marks of their approval.

KILLINGWORTH HIGH PIT.

GLEBE FARM-HOUSE, BENTON. [By R. P. Leitch.]

CHAPTER IV.

THE STEPHENSONS AT KILLINGWORTH—EDUCATION AND SELF-EDUCATION OF FATHER AND SON.

George Stephenson had now been diligently employed for several years in the work of self-improvement, and he experienced the usual results in increasing mental strength, capability, and skill. Perhaps the secret of every man's best success in life is to be found in the alacrity and industry with which he takes advantage of the opportunities which present themselves for well-doing. Our engine-man was an eminent illustration of the importance of cultivating this habit of life. Every spare moment was laid under contribution by him, either for the purpose of adding to his earnings or to his knowledge. He missed no opportunity of extending his observations, especially in his own department of work, aiming at improvement, and trying to turn all that he did know to useful practical account.

He continued his attempts to solve the mystery of Perpetual Motion, and contrived several model machines with the object of embodying his ideas in a practical working shape. He afterward used to lament the time he had lost in these futile efforts, and said that if he had enjoyed the opportunities which most young men now have, of learning from books what previous experimenters had accomplished, he would have been spared much labor and mortification. Not being acquainted with what other mechanics had done, he groped his way in pursuit of some idea originated by his own independent thinking and observation, and, when he had brought it into some definite form, lo! he found that his supposed invention had long been known and recorded in scientific books. Often he thought he had hit upon discoveries which he subsequently found were but old and exploded fallacies. Yet his very struggle to overcome the difficulties which lay in his way was of itself an education of the best sort. By wrestling with them, he strengthened his judgment and sharpened his skill, stimulating and cultivating his inventiveness and mechanical ingenuity. Being very much in earnest, he was compelled to consider the subject of his special inquiry in all its relations, and thus he gradually acquired practical ability through his very efforts after the impracticable.

Many of his evenings were spent in the society of John Wigham, whose father occupied the Glebe farm at Benton close at hand. John was a fair penman and good arithmetician, and Stephenson frequented his society chiefly for the purpose of improving himself in writing and "figuring." Under Andrew Robertson he had never quite mastered the Rule of Three, and it was only when Wigham took him in hand that he made progress in the higher branches of arithmetic. He generally took his slate with him to the Wighams' cottage, when he had his sums set, that he might work them out while tending his engine on the following day. When too busy with other work to be able to call upon Wigham in person, he sent the slate by a fellow-workman to have the former sums corrected and new ones set. Sometimes also, at leisure moments, he was enabled to do a little "figuring" with chalk upon the sides of the coal-wagons. So much patient perseverance could not but eventually succeed; and by dint of practice and study, Stephenson was enabled to master the successive rules of arithmetic.

John Wigham was of great use to his pupil in many ways. He was a good talker, fond of argument, an extensive reader as country reading went in those days, and a very suggestive thinker. Though his store of information might be comparatively small when measured with that of more highly cultivated minds, much of it was entirely new to Stephenson, who regarded him as a very clever and extraordinary person. Wigham also taught him to draw plans and sections, though in this branch Stephenson proved so apt that he soon surpassed his master. A volume of "Ferguson's Lectures on Mechanics" which fell into their hands was a great treasure to both the students. One who remembers their evening occupations says he "used to wonder what they meant by weighing the air and water in so odd a way." They were trying the specific gravities of objects; and the devices which they employed, the mechanical shifts to which they were put, were often of the rudest kind. In these evening entertainments the mechanical contrivances were supplied by Stephenson, while Wigham found the scientific rationale. The opportunity thus afforded to the former of cultivating his mind by contact with one wiser than himself proved of great value, and in after life Stephenson gratefully remembered the assistance which, when a humble workman, he had received from John Wigham, the farmer's son.

His leisure moments thus carefully improved, it will be inferred that Stephenson continued a sober man. Though his notions were never extreme on this point, he was systematically temperate. It appears that on the invitation of his master, Ralph Dodds —and an invitation from a master to a workman is not easy to resist—he had, on one or two occasions, been induced to join him in a forenoon glass of ale in the public house of the village. But one day, about noon, when Mr. Dodds had got him as far as the public-house door, on his invitation to "come in and take a glass o' yel," Stephenson made a dead stop, and said, firmly, "No, sir, you must excuse me; I have made a resolution to drink no more at this time of day." And he went back. He desired to retain the character of a steady workman; and the instances of men about him who had made shipwreck of their character through intemperance were then, as now, unhappily too frequent.

But another consideration besides his own self-improvement had already begun to exercise an important influence upon his life. This was the training and education of his son Robert, now growing up an active, intelligent boy, as full of fun and tricks as his father had been. When a little fellow, scarce big enough to reach so high as to put a clock-head on when placed upon the table, his father would make him mount a chair for the purpose; and to "help father" was the proudest work which the boy then, and ever after, could take part in. When the little engine was set up at the Ochre Quarry to pump it dry, Robert was scarcely absent for an hour. He watched the machine very eagerly when it was set to work, and he was very much annoyed at the fire burning away the grates. The man who fired the engine was a sort of wag, and thinking to get a laugh at the boy, he said, "Those bars are getting varra bad, Robert; I think we maun cut up some of that hard wood, and put it in instead." "What would be the use of that, you fool?" said the boy, quickly. "You would no sooner have put them in than they would be burnt out again!"

So soon as Robert was of a proper age, his father sent him over to the road-side school at Long Benton, kept by Rutter, the

RUTTER'S SCHOOL-HOUSE, LONG BENTON. [By R. P. Leitch.]

parish clerk. But the education which he gave was of a very limited kind, scarcely extending beyond the primer and pothooks. While working as a brakesman on the pit-head at Killingworth, the father had often bethought him of the obstructions he had himself encountered in life through his want of schooling, and he formed the determination that no labor, nor pains, nor self-denial on his part should be spared to furnish his son with the best education that it was in his power to bestow.

It is true, his earnings were comparatively small at that time.

He was still maintaining his infirm parents, and the cost of living continued excessive. But he fell back, as before, upon his old expedient of working up his spare time in the evenings at home, or during the night shifts when it was his turn to tend the engine, in mending and making shoes, cleaning clocks and watches, making shoe-lasts for the shoemakers of the neighborhood, and cutting out the pitmen's clothes for their wives; and we have been told that to this day there are clothes worn at Killingworth made after "Geordy Steevie's cut." To give his own words: "In the earlier period of my career," said he, "when Robert was a little boy, I saw how deficient I was in education, and I made up my mind that he should not labor under the same defect, but that I would put him to a good school, and give him a liberal training. I was, however, a poor man; and how do you think I managed? I betook myself to mending my neighbors' clocks and watches at nights, after my daily labor was done, and thus I procured the means of educating my son."*

By dint of such extra labor in his by-hours, with this object, Stephenson contrived to save a sum of £100, which he accumulated in *guineas*, each of which he afterward sold to Jews, who went about buying up gold coins (then dearer than silver), at twenty-six shillings apiece; and he lent out the proceeds at interest. He was now, therefore, a comparatively thriving man.

When he was appointed engine-wright of the colliery, he was, of course, still easier in his circumstances; and, carrying out the resolution which he had formed as to his boy's education, Robert was sent to Mr. Bruce's school in Percy Street, Newcastle, at midsummer, 1815, when he was about twelve years old. His father bought for him a donkey, on which he rode into Newcastle and back daily; and there are many still living who remember the little boy, dressed in his suit of homely gray stuff cut out by his father, cantering along to school upon the "cuddy," with his wallet of provisions for the day and his bag of books slung over his shoulder.

When Robert went to Mr. Bruce's school he was a shy, unpolished country lad, speaking the broad dialect of the pitmen; and the other boys would occasionally tease him, for the purpose of

* Speech at Newcastle, on the 18th of June, 1844, at the meeting held in celebration of the opening of the Newcastle and Darlington Railway.

provoking an outburst of his Killingworth Doric. As the shyness got rubbed off by familiarity, his love of fun began to show itself, and he was found able enough to hold his own among the other boys. As a scholar he was steady and diligent, and his master was accustomed to hold him up to the laggards of the

BRUCE'S SCHOOL, NEWCASTLE. [By R. P. Leitch.]

school as an example of good conduct and industry. But his progress, though satisfactory, was by no means extraordinary. He used in after life to pride himself on his achievements in mensuration, though another boy, John Taylor, beat him at arithmetic. He also made considerable progress in mathematics; and in a letter written to the son of his teacher, many years after, he said, "It was to Mr. Bruce's tuition and methods of modeling the mind that I attribute much of my success as an engineer, for it was from him that I derived my taste for mathematical pursuits, and the facility I possess of applying this kind of knowledge to practical purposes, and modifying it according to circumstances."

During the time Robert attended school at Newcastle, his father made the boy's education instrumental to his own. Robert was accustomed to spend some of his spare time at the rooms of the Literary and Philosophical Institute, and when he went home in the evening he would recount to his father the results of his reading. Sometimes he was allowed to take with him to Killingworth a volume of the "Repertory of Arts and Sciences," which father and son studied together. But many of the most valuable works belonging to the Newcastle Library were not permitted to be removed from the rooms; these Robert was instructed to read and study, and bring away with him descriptions and sketches for his father's information. His father also practiced him in the reading of plans and drawings without at all referring to the written descriptions. He used to observe to his son, "A good drawing or plan should always explain itself;" and, placing a drawing of an engine or machine before the youth, he would say, "There, now, describe that to me—the arrangement and the action." Thus he taught him to read a drawing as easily as he would read a page of a book. Both father and son profited by this excellent practice, which shortly enabled them to apprehend with the greatest facility the details of even the most difficult and complicated mechanical drawing.

While Robert went on with his lessons in the evenings, his father was usually occupied with his watch and clock cleaning, or contriving models of pumping-engines, or endeavoring to embody in a tangible shape the mechanical inventions which he found described in the odd volumes on Mechanics which fell in his way. This daily and unceasing example of industry and application, working on before the boy's eyes in the person of a loving and beloved father, imprinted itself deeply upon his mind in characters never to be effaced. A spirit of self-improvement was thus early and carefully planted and fostered in him, which continued to influence his character through life; and toward the close of his career he was proud to confess that if his professional success had been great, it was mainly to the example and training of his father that he owed it.

Robert was not, however, exclusively devoted to study, but, like most boys full of animal spirits, he was very fond of fun and play, and sometimes of mischief. Dr. Bruce relates that an old Killingworth laborer, when asked by Robert, on one of his last visits to Newcastle, if he remembered him replied with emotion, "Ay, indeed! Haven't I paid your head many a time when you came with your father's bait, for you were always a sad hempy?"

The author had the pleasure, in the year 1854, of accompanying Robert Stephenson on a visit to his old home and haunts at Killingworth. He had so often traveled the road upon his donkey to and from school that every foot of it was familiar to him, and each turn in it served to recall to mind some incident of his boyish days.* His eyes glistened when he came in sight of Killingworth pit head. Pointing to a humble red-tiled house by the roadside at Benton, he said, "You see that house—that was Rutter's, where I learned my A B C, and made a beginning of my school learning; and there," pointing to a colliery chimney on the left, "there is Long Benton, where my father put up his first pumping-engine; and a great success it was. And this humble clay-floored cottage you see here is where my grandfather lived till the close of his life. Many a time have I ridden straight into the house, mounted on my cuddy, and called upon grandfather to admire his points. I remember the old man feeling the animal all over—he was then quite blind—after which he would dilate upon the shape of his ears, fetlocks, and quarters, and usually end by pronouncing him to be a 'real blood.' I was a great favorite with the old man, who continued very fond of animals, and cheerful to the last; and I believe nothing gave him greater pleasure than a visit from me and my cuddy."

On the way from Benton to High Killingworth, Mr. Stephenson pointed to a corner of the road where he had once played a boyish trick upon a Killingworth collier. "Straker," said he, "was a great bully, a coarse, swearing fellow, and a perfect tyrant among the women and children. He would go tearing into old Nanny the huxter's shop in the village, and demand in a savage voice, 'What's ye'r best ham the pund?' 'What's floor the hunder?' 'What d'ye ax for prime bacon?'—his categories usually ending with the miserable order, accompanied with a tremendous oath, of 'Gie's a penny rrow (roll) an' a baubee herrin'!' The poor woman was usually set 'all of a shake' by a visit from this fellow. He was also a great boaster, and used to crow over the robbers whom he had put to flight; mere men in buckram,

* At one part of the road he was once pulled off his donkey by some mischievous boys, and released by a young man named James Burnet. Many years after, Burnet was taken on as a workman at the Newcastle factory, probably owing his selection in some measure to the above circumstance.

as every body knew. We boys," he continued, "believed him to be a great coward, and determined to play him a trick. Two other boys joined me in waylaying Straker one night at that corner," pointing to it. "We sprang out and called upon him, in as gruff voices as we could assume, to 'stand and deliver!' He dropped down upon his knees in the dirt, declaring he was a poor man, with a sma' family, asking for 'mercy,' and imploring us, as 'gentlemen, for God's sake, t' let him a-be!' We couldn't stand this any longer, and set up a shout of laughter. Recognizing our boys' voices, he sprang to his feet again and rattled out a volley of oaths, on which we cut through the hedge, and heard him shortly after swearing his way along the road to the yelhouse."

On another occasion Robert played a series of tricks of a somewhat different character. Like his father, he was very fond of reducing his scientific reading to practice; and after studying Franklin's description of the lightning experiment, he proceeded to expend his store of Saturday pennies in purchasing about half a mile of copper wire at a brazier's shop in Newcastle. Having prepared his kite, he set it up in the field opposite his father's door, and bringing the wire, insulated by means of a few feet of silk cord, over the backs of some of Farmer Wigham's cows, he soon had them skipping about the field in all directions with their tails up. One day he had his kite flying at the cottage-door as his father's galloway was hanging by the bridle to the paling, waiting for the master to mount. Bringing the end of the wire just over the pony's crupper, so smart an electric shock was given it that the brute was almost knocked down. At this juncture his father issued from the house, riding-whip in hand, and was witness to the scientific trick just played off upon his galloway. "Ah! you mischievous scoondrel!" cried he to the boy, who ran off, himself inwardly chuckling with pride, nevertheless, at Robert's successful experiment.*

At this time, and for many years after, Stephenson dwelt in a

* Robert Stephenson was, perhaps, prouder of this little boyish experiment than he was of many of his subsequent achievements. Not having been quite accurately stated in the first edition of this book, Mr. Stephenson noted the correction for the second, and wrote to the author (Sept. 18th, 1857) as follows: "In the kite experiment, will you say that the copper wire was insulated by a few feet of silk cord; without this, the experiment can not be made."

cottage standing by the side of the road leading from the West Moor Pit to Killingworth. The railway from West Moor crosses this road close by the easternmost end of the cottage. The dwelling originally consisted of but one apartment on the ground floor, with a garret overhead, to which access was obtained by means

STEPHENSON'S COTTAGE, WEST MOOR. [By R. P. Leitch.]

of a step-ladder. With his own hands Stephenson built an oven, and in the course of time he added rooms to the cottage, until it became expanded into a comfortable four-roomed dwelling, in which he remained as long as he lived at Killingworth.

He continued as fond of birds and animals as ever, and seemed to have the power of attaching them to him in a remarkable degree. He had a blackbird at Killingworth so fond of him that it would fly about the cottage, and on holding out his finger the bird would come and perch upon it directly. A cage was built for "blackie" in the partition between the passage and the room, a square of glass forming its outer wall; and Robert used afterward to take pleasure in describing the oddity of the bird, imitating the manner in which it would cock its head on his father's entering the house, and follow him with its eye into the inner apartment.

Neighbors were accustomed to call at the cottage and have their clocks and watches set to rights when they went wrong. One day, after looking at the works of a watch left by a pitman's wife, George handed it to his son: "Put her in the oven, Robert," said he, "for a quarter of an hour or so." It seemed an odd way of repairing a watch; nevertheless, the watch was put into the oven, and at the end of the appointed time it was taken out, going all right. The wheels had merely got clogged by the oil congealed by the cold, which at once explains the rationale of the remedy adopted.

There was a little garden attached to the cottage, in which, while a workman, Stephenson took a pride in growing gigantic leeks and astonishing cabbages. There was great competition in the growing of vegetables among the villagers, all of whom he excelled excepting one, whose cabbages sometimes outshone his. To protect his garden-crops from the ravages of the birds, he invented a strange sort of "fley-craw," which moved its arms with the wind; and he fastened his garden-door by means of a piece of ingenious mechanism, so that no one but himself could enter it. His cottage was quite a curiosity-shop of models of engines, self-acting planes, and perpetual-motion machines. The last named contrivances, however, were only unsuccessful attempts to solve a problem which had already baffled hundreds of preceding inventors.

His odd and eccentric contrivances often excited great wonder among the Killingworth villagers. He won the women's admiration by connecting their cradles with the smoke-jack, and making them self-acting. Then he astonished the pitmen by attaching an alarm to the clock of the watchman whose duty it was to call them betimes in the morning. He also contrived a wonderful lamp which burned under water, with which he was afterward wont to amuse the Brandling family at Gosforth—going into the fish-pond at night, lamp in hand, attracting and catching the fish, which rushed wildly toward the flame.

Dr. Bruce tells of a competition which Stephenson had with the joiner at Killingworth as to which of them could make the best shoe-last; and when the former had done his work, either for the humor of the thing or to secure fair play from the appointed judge, he took it to the Morrisons in Newcastle, and got them to put their stamp upon it; so that it is possible the Killingworth brakesman, afterward the inventor of a safety-lamp and originator of the locomotive railway system, and John Morrison, the last-maker, afterward the translator of the Scriptures into the Chinese language, may have confronted each other in solemn contemplation of the successful last, which won the verdict coveted by its maker.

Sometimes George would endeavor to impart to his fellow-workmen the results of his scientific reading. Every thing that he learned from books was so new and so wonderful to him, that he regarded the facts he drew from them in the light of discoveries, as if they had been made but yesterday. Once he tried to explain to some of the pitmen how the earth was round, and kept turning round. But his auditors flatly declared the thing to be impossible, as it was clear that "at the bottom side they must fall off!" "Ah!" said George, "you don't quite understand it yet." His son Robert also early endeavored to communicate to others the information which he had gathered at school; and Dr. Bruce relates that, when visiting Killingworth on one occasion, he found him engaged in teaching algebra to such of the pitmen's boys as would become his pupils.

While Robert was still at school, his father proposed to him during the holidays that he should construct a sun-dial, to be placed over their cottage-door at West Moor. "I expostulated with him at first," said Robert, "that I had not learned sufficient astronomy and mathematics to enable me to make the necessary calculations. But he would have no denial. 'The thing is to be done,' said he, 'so just set about it at once.' Well, we got a 'Ferguson's Astronomy,' and studied the subject together. Many a sore head I had while making the necessary calculations to adapt the dial to the latitude of Killingworth. But at length it was fairly drawn out on paper, and then my father got a stone, and we hewed, and carved, and polished it, until we made a very respectable dial of it; and there it is, you see," pointing to it over the cottage door, "still quietly numbering the hours when the sun shines. I assure you, not a little was thought of that piece of work by the pitmen when it was put up, and began to tell its tale of time." The date carved upon the dial is "August 11th, MDCCCXVI." Both father and son were in after life very proud of

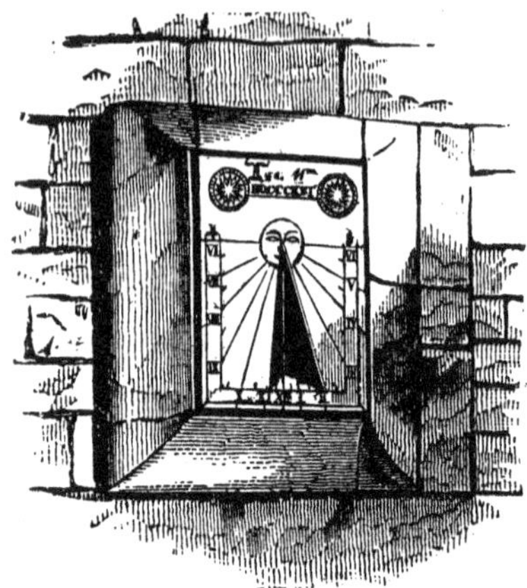

their joint production. Many years after, George took a party of savans, when attending the meeting of the British Association at Newcastle, over to Killingworth to see the pits, and he did not fail to direct their attention to the sun-dial; and Robert, on the last visit which he made to the place, a short time before his death, took a friend into the cottage, and pointed out to him the very desk, still there, at which he had sat when making his calculations of the latitude of Killingworth.

From the time of his appointment as engineer at the Killingworth Pit, George Stephenson was in a measure relieved from the daily routine of manual labor, having, as we have seen, advanced himself to the grade of a higher-class workman. He had not ceased to be a worker, though he employed his industry in a different way. It might, indeed, be inferred that he had now the command of greater leisure; but his spare hours were as much as ever given to work, either necessary or self-imposed. So far as regarded his social position, he had already reached the summit of his ambition; and when he had got his hundred a year, and his dun galloway to ride on, he said he never wanted to be any higher. When Robert Wetherly offered to give him an old gig, his traveling having so much increased of late, he accepted it with great reluctance, observing that he should be ashamed to get into it, "people would think him so proud."

When the High Pit had been sunk and the coal was ready for working, Stephenson erected his first winding-engine to draw the coals out of the pit, and also a pumping-engine for Long Benton colliery, both of which proved quite successful. Among other works of this time, he projected and laid down a self-acting incline along the declivity which fell toward the coal-loading place near Willington, where he had formerly officiated as brakesman; and he so arranged it that the full wagons, descending, drew the empty wagons up the railroad. This was one of the first self-acting inclines laid down in the district.

The following is Stephenson's own account of his various duties and labors at this period of his life, as given before a Committee of the House of Commons in 1835:*

"After making some improvements in the steam-engines above ground, I was requested by the manager of the colliery to go underground along with him, to see if any improvements could be made in the mines by employing machinery as a substitute for manual labor and horse-power in bringing the coals out of the deeper workings of the mine. On my first going down the Killingworth pit, there was a steam-engine underground for the purpose of drawing water from a pit that was sunk at some distance from the first shaft. The Killingworth coal-field is considerably dislocated. After the colliery was opened, at a very short distance from the shaft, one of those dislocations was met with. The coal was thrown down about forty yards. Considerable time was spent in sinking another pit to this depth. And on my going down to examine the work, I proposed making the engine (which had been erected some time previously) to draw the coals up an inclined plane which descended immediately from the place where it was fixed. A considerable change was accordingly made in the mode of working the colliery, not only in applying the machinery, but in employing putters instead of horses in bringing the coals from the hewers; and by those changes the number of horses in the pit was reduced from about 100 to 15 or 16. During the time I was engaged in making these important alterations, I went round the workings in the pit with the viewer almost every time that he went into the mine, not only at Killingworth, but at Mountmoor, Derwentcrook, Southmoor, all of which collieries belonged to Lord Ravensworth and his partners; and the whole of the machinery in all these collieries was put under my charge."

It will thus be observed that Stephenson had now much better opportunities for improving himself in mechanics than he had heretofore possessed. His practical knowledge of the steam-engine could not fail to prove of the greatest value to him. His shrewd insight, together with his intimate acquaintance with its mechanism, enabled him to apprehend, as if by intuition, its most abstruse and difficult combinations. The study which he had

* Evidence given before the Select Committee on Accidents in Mines, 1835.

given to it when a workman, and the patient manner in which he had groped his way through all the details of the machine, gave him the power of a master in dealing with it as applied to colliery purposes.

Sir Thomas Liddell was frequently about the works, and took pleasure in giving every encouragement to the engine-wright in his efforts after improvement. The subject of the locomotive engine was already occupying Stephenson's careful attention, although it was still regarded in the light of a curious and costly toy, of comparatively little real use. But he had at an early period recognized its practical value, and formed an adequate conception of the might which as yet slumbered within it, and he now proceeded to bend the whole faculties of his mind to the development of its powers.

COLLIERS' COTTAGES AT LONG BENTON. [By R. P. Leitch.]

CHAPTER V.

THE LOCOMOTIVE ENGINE—GEORGE STEPHENSON BEGINS ITS IMPROVEMENT.

THE rapid increase in the coal-trade of the Tyne about the beginning of the present century had the effect of stimulating the ingenuity of mechanics, and encouraging them to devise improved methods of transporting the coal from the pits to the shipping-places. From our introductory chapter, it will have been observed that the improvements which had thus far been effected were confined almost entirely to the road. The railway wagons still continued to be drawn by horses. By improving and flattening the tram-way, considerable economy in horse-power had been secured; but, unless some more effective method of mechanical traction could be devised, it was clear that railway improvement had almost reached its limits.

Notwithstanding Trevithick's comparatively successful experiment with the first railway locomotive on the Merthyr Tydvil tram-road in 1804, described in a former chapter, he seems to have taken no farther steps to bring his invention into notice. He was probably discouraged by the breakage of the cast-iron plates, of which the road was formed, which were crushed under the load of his engine, and could not induce the owners of the line to relay it with better materials so as to give his locomotive a fair trial.

An imaginary difficulty, also, seems to have tended, among other obstacles, to prevent the adoption of the locomotive, viz., the idea that, if a heavy weight were placed behind the engine, the "grip" or "bite" of its smooth wheels upon the equally smooth iron rail must necessarily be so slight that they would whirl round upon it, and, consequently, that the machine would not make any progress.* Hence Trevithick, in his patent, pro-

* The same fallacy seems long to have held its ground in France; for M. Granier tells us that some time after the first of George Stephenson's locomotives had been

vided that the periphery of the driving-wheels should be made rough by the projection of bolts or cross-grooves, so that the adhesion of the wheels to the road might thereby be better secured.

Trevithick himself does not seem to have erected another engine, but we gather from the evidence given by Mr. Rastrick in the committee on the Liverpool and Manchester Bill in 1825, that ten or twelve years before that time he had made an engine for Trevithick after his patent, and that the engine was exhibited in London. "A circular railroad was laid down," said Mr. Rastrick, and it was stated that this engine was to run against a horse, and that which went a sufficient number of miles was to win." It is not known what afterward became of this engine.

There were, however, at a much earlier period, several wealthy and enterprising men, both in Yorkshire and Northumberland, who were willing to give the locomotive a fair trial; and had Trevithick but possessed the requisite tenacity of purpose—had he not been too soon discouraged by partially successful experiments—he might have risen to both fame and fortune, not only as the inventor of the locomotive, but as the practical introducer of railway locomotion.

One of Trevithick's early friends and admirers was Mr. Blackett, of Wylam. The Wylam wagon-way is one of the oldest in the north of England. Down to the year 1807 it was formed of wooden spars or rails, laid down between the colliery at Wylam —where old Robert Stephenson worked—and the village of Lemington, some four miles down the Tyne, where the coals were loaded into keels or barges, and floated down past Newcastle, to be shipped for London. Each chaldron-wagon had a man in charge of it, and was originally drawn by one horse. The rate at which the wagons were hauled was so slow that only two journeys were performed by each man and horse in one day, and three on the day following. This primitive wagon-way passed, as before stated, close in front of the cottage in which George Stephenson was born, and one of the earliest sights which met his infant eyes was this wooden tram-road worked by horses.

placed on the Liverpool and Manchester line, a model of one was exhibited before the Academy. After it had been examined, a member of that learned body said, smiling, "Yes, this is all very ingenious, no doubt, but unfortunately the machine will never move. The wheels will turn round and round in the same place."

Mr. Blackett was the first colliery owner in the North who took an active interest in the locomotive. He had witnessed the first performances of Trevithick's steam-carriage in London, and was so taken with the idea of its application to railway locomotion that he resolved to have an engine erected after the new patent for use upon his tram-way at Wylam. He accordingly obtained from Trevithick, in October, 1804, a plan of his engine, provided with "friction-wheels," and employed Mr. John Whinfield, of Pipewellgate, Gateshead, to construct it at his foundery there. The engine was made under the superintendence of one John Steele,* an ingenious mechanic, who had been in Wales, and worked under Trevithick in fitting the engine at Pen-y-darran. When the Gateshead locomotive was finished, a temporary way was laid down in the works, on which it was run backward and forward many times. For some reason or other, however—it is said because the engine was too light for drawing the coal-trains—it never left the works, but was dismounted from the wheels, and set to blow the cupola of the foundery, in which service it long continued to be employed.

Several years elapsed before Mr. Blackett took any farther steps to carry out his idea. The final abandonment of Trevithick's locomotive at Pen-y-darran perhaps contributed to deter him from proceeding farther; but he had the Wylam wooden tram-way taken up in 1808, and a plate-way of cast iron laid

* John Steele was one of the many "born mechanics" of the Northumberland district. When a boy at Colliery Dykes, his native place, he was noted for his "turn for machinery." He used to take his playfellows home to see and admire his imitations of pit-engines. While a mere youth he lost his leg by an accident; and those who remember him at Whinfield's speak of his hopping about the locomotive, of which he was very proud, upon his wooden leg. It was a great disappointment to him when Mr. Blackett refused to take the engine. One day he took a friend to look at it when reduced to its degraded office of blowing the cupola bellows; and, referring to the cause of its rejection, he observed that he was certain it would succeed, if made sufficiently heavy. "Our master," he continued, "will not be at the expense of following it up; but depend upon it the day will come when such an engine will be fairly tried, and then it will be found to answer." Steele was afterward extensively employed by the British government in raising sunken ships; and later in life he established engine-works at Rouen, where he made marine-engines for the French government. He was unfortunately killed by the explosion of an engine-boiler (with the safety-valve of which something had gone wrong) when on an experimental trip with one of the steamers fitted up by himself, and on his way to England to visit his family near Newcastle.

down instead—a single line furnished with sidings to enable the laden wagons to pass the empty ones. The new iron road proved so much smoother than the old wooden one, that a single horse, instead of drawing one, was enabled to draw two, or even three laden wagons.

Although the locomotive seemed about to be lost sight of, it was not forgotten. In 1811, Mr. Blenkinsop, the manager of the Middleton Collieries, near Leeds, revived the idea of employing it in lieu of horses to haul the coals along his tram-way. Mr. Blenkinsop, in the patent which he took out for his proposed engine, followed in many respects the design of Trevithick; but, with the help of Matthew Murray, of Leeds, one of the most ingenious mechanics of his day, he introduced several important and valuable modifications. Thus he employed two cylinders of 8 in. diameter instead of one, as in Trevithick's engine. These cylinders were placed vertically, and immersed for more than half their length in the steam space of the boiler. The eduction

BLENKINSOP'S LEEDS ENGINE.

pipes met in a single tube at the top, and threw the steam into the air. The boiler was cylindrical in form, but of cast iron. It had one flue, the fire being at one end and the chimney at the other. The engine was supported on a carriage without springs, resting directly upon two pairs of wheels and axles unconnected with the working parts, and which merely served to carry the engine upon the rails. The motion was effected in this way: the piston-rods, by means of cross-heads, worked the connecting-rods, which came down to two cranks on each side below the boiler, placed at right angles in order to pass their centres with certainty. These cranks worked two shafts fixed across the engine, on which were small-toothed wheels working into a larger one between them; and on the axis of this large wheel, outside the framing, were the driving-wheels, one of which was toothed, and worked into a rack on one side of the railway.

It will be observed that the principal new features in this engine were the two cylinders and the toothed-wheel working into a rack-rail. Mr. Blenkinsop contrived the latter expedient in order to insure sufficient adhesion between the wheel and the road, supposing that smooth wheels and smooth rails would be insufficient for the purpose. Clumsy and slow though the engine was compared with modern locomotives, it was nevertheless a success. It was the first engine that plied regularly upon any railway, doing useful work; and it continued so employed for more than twenty years. What was more, it was a commercial success, for its employment was found to be economical compared with horse-power. In a letter to Sir John Sinclair, Mr. Blenkinsop stated that his engine weighed five tons; consumed two thirds of a hundred weight of coals and fifty gallons of water per hour; drew twenty-seven wagons, weighing ninety-four tons, on a dead level, at three and a half miles an hour, or fifteen tons up an ascent of 2 in. in the yard; that when "lightly loaded" it traveled at a speed of ten miles an hour; that it did the work of sixteen horses in twelve hours; and that its cost was £400. Such was Mr. Blenkinsop's own account of the performances of his engine, which was for a long time regarded as one of the wonders of the neighborhood.*

* Thomas Gray, a native of Leeds, was an enthusiastic believer in the new tractive power, and wherever he went he preached up railways and Blenkinsop's locomotive.

The Messrs. Chapman, of Newcastle, in 1812 endeavored to overcome the same fictitious difficulty of the want of adhesion between the wheel and the rail by patenting a locomotive to work along the road by means of a chain stretched from one end of it to the other. This chain was passed once round a grooved barrel-wheel under the centre of the engine, so that when the wheel turned, the locomotive, as it were, dragged itself along the railway. An engine constructed after this plan was tried on the Heaton Railway, near Newcastle; but it was so clumsy in action, there was so great a loss of power by friction, and it was found to be so expensive and difficult to keep in repair, that it was very soon abandoned. Another remarkable expedient was adopted by Mr. Brunton, of the Butterley Works, Derbyshire, who in 1813 patented his Mechanical Traveler, to go *upon legs* working alternately like those of a horse.* But this engine never got beyond the experimental state, for, at its very first trial, the driver, to make sure of a good start, overloaded the safety-valve, when the boiler burst and killed a number of the by-standers, wounding many more. These, and other contrivances with the same object, projected about the same time, show that invention was busily at work, and that many minds were anxiously laboring to solve the problem of steam locomotion on railways.

Mr. Blackett, of Wylam, was encouraged by the success of Mr. Blenkinsop's experiment, and again he resolved to make a trial of the locomotive upon his wagon-way. Accordingly, in 1812, he ordered a second engine, which was so designed as to work with a toothed driving-wheel upon a rack-rail as at Leeds. This

While he was living at Brussels in 1816, a canal to Charleroi was under consideration, on which he seized the opportunity of urging the superior merits of a railway. When he returned to England in 1820, he wrote a book upon the subject, entitled, "Observations on a General Iron Railway," in which he strongly advocated the advantages of railways generally, giving as a frontispiece to the book an engraving of Blenkinsop's engine. And several years after the opening of the Liverpool and Manchester Railway we find Thomas Gray, true to his first love, urging in the "Mechanics' Magazine" the superiority of Blenkinsop's cogged wheel and rail over the smooth road and rail of the modern railway.

* Other machines with legs were patented in the following year by Lewis Gompertz and by Thomas Tindall. In Tindall's specification it is provided that the power of the engine is to be assisted by a *horizontal windmill;* and the four pushers, or legs, are to be caused to come successively in contact with the ground, and impel the carriage.

locomotive was constructed by Thomas Waters, of Gateshead, under the superintendence of Jonathan Foster, Mr. Blackett's principal engine-wright. It was a combination of Trevithick's and Blenkinsop's engines; but it was of a more awkward construction than either. Like Trevithick's, it had a single cylinder with a fly-wheel, which Blenkinsop had discarded. The boiler was of cast iron. Jonathan Foster described it to the author in 1854 as "a strange machine, with lots of pumps, cog-wheels, and plugs, requiring constant attention while at work." The weight of the whole was about six tons.

When finished, it was conveyed to Wylam on a wagon, and there mounted upon a wooden frame, supported by four pairs of wheels, which had been constructed for its reception. A barrel of water, placed on another frame upon wheels, was attached to it as a tender. After a great deal of labor, the cumbrous machine was got upon the road. At first it would not move an inch. Its maker, Tommy Waters, became impatient, and at length enraged, and, taking hold of the lever of the safety-valve, declared in his desperation that "either *she* or *he* should go." At length the machinery was set in motion, on which, as Jonathan Foster described to the author, "she flew all to pieces, and it was the biggest wonder i' the world that we were not all blewn up." The incompetent and useless engine was declared to be a failure; it was shortly after dismounted and sold; and Mr. Blackett's praiseworthy efforts thus far proved in vain.

He was still, however, desirous of testing the practicability of employing locomotive power in working the coal down to Lemington, and he determined on making yet another trial. He accordingly directed his engine-wright, Jonathan Foster, to proceed with the building of a third engine in the Wylam workshops. This new locomotive had a single 8-inch cylinder, was provided with a fly-wheel like its predecessor, and the driving-wheel was cogged on one side to enable it to travel in the rack-rail laid along the road. The engine proved more successful than the former one, and it was found capable of dragging eight or nine loaded wagons, though at the rate of little more than a mile an hour, from the colliery to the shipping-place. It sometimes took six hours to perform the journey of five miles. Its weight was found too great for the road, and the cast-iron plates were constantly breaking. It was also very apt to get off the rack-rail, and then it stood still. The driver was one day asked how he got on. "Get on?" said he, "we don't get on; we only get off!" On such occasions, horses had to be sent out to drag the wagons as before, and others to haul the engine back to the workshops. It was constantly getting out of order; its plugs, pumps, or cranks got wrong, and it was under repair as often as at work. At length it became so cranky that the horses were usually sent after it to drag it along when it gave up, and the workmen generally declared it to be a "perfect plague." Mr. Blackett did not obtain credit among his neighbors for these experiments. Many laughed at his machines, regarding them only in the light of crotchets —frequently quoting the proverb of "a fool and his money are soon parted." Others regarded them as absurd innovations on the established method of hauling coal, and pronounced that they would "never answer."

Notwithstanding, however, the comparative failure of the second locomotive, Mr. Blackett persevered with his experiments. He was zealously assisted by Jonathan Foster, the engine-wright, and William Hedley, the viewer of the colliery, a highly ingenious person, who proved of great use in carrying out the experiments to a successful issue. One of the chief causes of failure being the rack-rail, the idea occurred to Mr. Hedley that it might be possible to secure sufficient adhesion between the wheel and the rail by the mere weight of the engine, and he proceeded to make a series of experiments for the purpose of determining this problem. He had a frame placed on four wheels, and fitted up with windlasses attached by gearing to the several wheels. The frame having been properly weighted, six men were set to work the windlasses, when it was found that the adhesion of the smooth wheels on the smooth rails was quite sufficient to enable them to propel the machine without slipping. Having then found the proportion which the power bore to the weight, he demonstrated by successive experiments that the weight of the engine would of itself produce sufficient adhesion to enable it to draw upon a smooth railroad the requisite number of wagons in all kinds of weather. And thus was the fallacy which had heretofore prevailed on this subject completely exploded, and it was satisfactorily proved that rack-rails, toothed wheels, endless chains, and legs, were alike unnecessary for the efficient traction of loaded wagons upon a moderately level road.*

From this time forward, considerably less difficulty was experienced in working the coal-trains upon the Wylam tram-road. At length the rack-rail was dispensed with. The road was laid with heavier rails; the working of the old engine was improved; and a new engine was shortly after built and placed upon the road, still on eight wheels, driven by seven rack-wheels working inside them—with a wrought-iron boiler through which the flue was returned so as largely to increase the heating surface, and thus give increased power to the engine.† Below is a representation of this improved Wylam engine.

WYLAM ENGINE.

* Mr. Hedley took out a patent to secure his invention, dated the 13th of March, 1813. Specification No. 3666. If it be true, as alleged, that the wheels of Trevithick's first locomotive were smooth, it seems strange that the fallacy should ever have existed.

† By the year 1825, the progress made on the Wylam Railroad was thus described by Mr. Mackenzie in his "History of Northumberland:" "A stranger," said he, "is struck with surprise and astonishment on seeing a locomotive engine moving majestically along the road at the rate of four or five miles an hour, drawing along from ten to fourteen loaded wagons, weighing about 21½ tons; and his surprise is increased on witnessing the extraordinary facility with which the engine is managed. This invention is a noble triumph of science."

As may readily be imagined, the jets of steam from the piston, blowing off into the air at high pressure while the engine was in motion, caused considerable annoyance to horses passing along the Wylam road, at that time a public highway. The nuisance was felt to be almost intolerable, and a neighboring gentleman threatened to have it put down. To diminish the noise as much as possible, Mr. Blackett gave orders that so soon as any horse, or vehicle drawn by horses, came in sight, the locomotive was to be stopped, and the frightful blast of the engine thus suspended until the passing animals had got out of sight. Much interruption was thus caused to the working of the railway, and it excited considerable dissatisfaction among the workmen. The following plan was adopted to abate the nuisance: a reservoir was provided immediately behind the chimney (as shown in the opposite cut) into which the waste steam was thrown after it had performed its office in the cylinder, and from this reservoir the steam gradually escaped into the atmosphere without noise. This arrangement was devised with the express object of preventing a blast in the chimney, the value of which, as we shall subsequently find, was not detected until George Stephenson, adopting it with a preconceived design and purpose, demonstrated its importance and value—as being, in fact, the very life-breath of the locomotive engine.

While Mr. Blackett was thus experimenting and building locomotives at Wylam, George Stephenson was anxiously studying the same subject at Killingworth. He was no sooner appointed engine-wright of the collieries than his attention was directed to the means of more economically hauling the coal from the pits to the river side. We have seen that one of the first important improvements which he made, after being placed in charge of the colliery machinery, was to apply the surplus power of a pumping steam-engine fixed underground, for the purpose of drawing the coals out of the deeper workings of the Killingworth mines, by which he succeeded in effecting a large reduction in the expenditure on manual and horse labor.

The coals, when brought above ground, had next to be laboriously dragged by means of horses to the shipping staiths on the Tyne, several miles distant. The adoption of a tram-road, it is true, had tended to facilitate their transit; nevertheless, the haulage was both tedious and expensive. With the view of economizing labor, Stephenson laid down inclined planes where the nature of the ground would admit of this expedient being adopted. Thus a train of full wagons let down the incline by means of a rope running over wheels laid along the tram-road, the other end of which was attached to a train of empty wagons placed at the bottom of the parallel road on the same incline, dragged them up by the simple power of gravity. But this applied only to a comparatively small part of the road. An economical method of working the coal-trains, instead of by means of horses—the keep of which was at that time very costly, in consequence of the high price of corn—was still a great desideratum, and the best practical minds in the collieries were actively engaged in trying to solve the problem.

In the first place, Stephenson resolved to make himself thoroughly acquainted with what had already been done. Mr. Blackett's engines were working daily at Wylam, past the cottage where he had been born, and thither he frequently went* to inspect the improvements made by Mr. Blackett from time to time both in the locomotive and in the plate-way along which it worked. Jonathan Foster informed us that, after one of these visits, Stephenson declared to him his conviction that a much more effective engine might be made, that should work more steadily and draw the load more effectively.

He had also the advantage, about the same time, of seeing one of Blenkinsop's Leeds engines, which was placed on the tram-way leading from the collieries of Kenton and Coxlodge, on the 2d of September, 1813. This locomotive drew sixteen chaldron wagons, containing an aggregate weight of seventy tons, at the rate of about three miles an hour. George Stephenson and several of the Killingworth men were among the crowd of spectators that

* At the Stephenson Memorial meeting at Newcastle-on-Tyne, 26th of October, 1858, Mr. Hugh Taylor, chairman of the Northern Coal-owners, gave the following account of one of such visits made by Stephenson to Wylam, in the company of Mr. Nicholas Wood and himself: "It was, I think, in 1812, that Mr. Stephenson and Mr. Wood came to my house, then at Newburn, and after we had dined, we went and examined the locomotive then on Mr. Blackett's wagon-way. At that early date it went by a sort of cog-wheel; there was also something of a chain to it. There was no idea that the machine would be sufficiently adhesive to the rails by the action of its own weight; but I remember a man going before—that was after the chain was abrogated—and scattering ashes on the rails, in order to give it adhesiveness, and two or three miles an hour was about the rate of progress."

day; and after examining the engine and observing its performances, he remarked to his companions that "he thought he could make a better engine than that, to go upon legs." Probably he had heard of the invention of Brunton, whose patent had by this time been published, and proved the subject of much curious speculation in the colliery districts. Certain it is that, shortly after the inspection of the Coxlodge engine, he contemplated the construction of a new locomotive, which was to surpass all that had preceded it. He observed that those engines which had been constructed up to this time, however ingenious in their arrangements, were in a great measure practical failures. Mr. Blackett's was as yet both clumsy and expensive. Chapman's had been removed from the Heaton tram-way in 1812, and was regarded as a total failure. And the Blenkinsop engine at Coxlodge was found very unsteady and costly in its working; besides, it pulled the rails to pieces, the entire strain being upon the rack-rail on one side of the road. The boiler, however, having shortly blown up, there was an end of that engine, and the colliery owners did not feel encouraged to try any farther experiment.

An efficient and economical working locomotive engine, therefore, still remained to be invented, and to accomplish this object Stephenson now applied himself. Profiting by what his predecessors had done, warned by their failures and encouraged by their partial successes, he commenced his labors. There was still wanting the man who should accomplish for the locomotive what James Watt had done for the steam-engine, and combine in a complete form the best points in the separate plans of others, embodying with them such original inventions and adaptations of his own as to entitle him to the merit of inventing the working locomotive, as James Watt is to be regarded as the inventor of the working condensing engine. This was the great work upon which George Stephenson now entered, though probably without any adequate idea of the ultimate importance of his labors to society and civilization.

He proceeded to bring the subject of constructing a "Traveling Engine," as he then denominated the locomotive, under the notice of the lessees of the Killingworth Colliery, in the year 1813. Lord Ravensworth, the principal partner, had already formed a very favorable opinion of the new colliery engine-wright from the improvements which he had effected in the colliery engines, both above and below ground; and, after considering the matter, and hearing Stephenson's explanations, he authorized him to proceed with the construction of a locomotive, though his lordship was by some called a fool for advancing money for such a purpose. "The first locomotive that I made," said Stephenson, many years after,* when speaking of his early career at a public meeting in Newcastle, "was at Killingworth Colliery, and with Lord Ravensworth's money. Yes, Lord Ravensworth and partners were the first to intrust me, thirty-two years since, with money to make a locomotive engine. I said to my friends, there was no limit to the speed of such an engine, if the works could be made to stand."

Our engine-wright had, however, many obstacles to encounter before he could get fairly to work with the erection of his locomotive. His chief difficulty was in finding workmen sufficiently skilled in mechanics and in the use of tools to follow his instructions and embody his designs in a practical shape. The tools then in use about the collieries were rude and clumsy, and there were no such facilities as now exist for turning out machinery of an entirely new character. Stephenson was under the necessity of working with such men and tools as were at his command, and he had in a great measure to train and instruct the workmen himself. The engine was built in the workshops at the West Moor, the leading mechanic being John Thirlwall, the colliery blacksmith, an excellent mechanic in his way, though quite new to the work now intrusted to him.

In this first locomotive constructed at Killingworth, Stephenson to some extent followed the plan of Blenkinsop's engine. The wrought-iron boiler was cylindrical, eight feet in length and thirty-four inches in diameter, with an internal flue-tube twenty inches wide passing through it. The engine had two vertical cylinders of eight inches diameter and two feet stroke let into the boiler, which worked the propelling gear with cross-heads and connecting-rods. The power of the two cylinders was combined

THE SPUR-GEAR.

* Speech at the opening of the Newcastle and Darlington Railway, June 18, 1844.

by means of spur-wheels, which communicated the motive power to the wheels supporting the engine on the rail, instead of, as in Blenkinsop's engine, to cog-wheels which acted on the cogged rail independent of the four supporting wheels. The engine thus worked upon what is termed the second motion. The chimney was of wrought iron, round which was a chamber extending back to the feed-pumps, for the purpose of heating the water previous to its injection into the boiler. The engine had no springs, and was mounted on a wooden frame supported on four wheels. In order to neutralize as much as possible the jolts and shocks which such an engine would necessarily encounter from the obstacles and inequalities of the then very imperfect plateway, the water-barrel which served for a tender was fixed to the end of a lever and weighted, the other end of the lever being connected with the frame of the locomotive carriage. By this means the weight of the two was more equally distributed, though the contrivance did not by any means compensate for the total absence of springs.

The wheels of the locomotive were all smooth, Stephenson having satisfied himself by experiment that the adhesion between the wheels of a loaded engine and the rail would be sufficient for the purpose of traction. Robert Stephenson informed us that his father caused a number of workmen to mount upon the wheels of a wagon moderately loaded, and throw their entire weight upon the spokes on one side, when he found that the wagon could thus be easily propelled forward without the wheels slipping. This, together with other experiments, satisfied him, as it had already satisfied Mr. Hedley, of the expediency of adopting smooth wheels on his engine, and it was so made accordingly.

The engine was, after much labor and anxiety, and frequent alterations of parts, at length brought to completion, having been about ten months in hand. It was placed upon the Killingworth Railway on the 25th of July, 1814, and its powers were tried on the same day. On an ascending gradient of 1 in 450, the engine succeeded in drawing after it eight loaded carriages of thirty tons' weight at about four miles an hour; and for some time after it continued regularly at work.

Although a considerable advance upon previous locomotives, "Blucher" (as the engine was popularly called) was nevertheless a somewhat cumbrous and clumsy machine. The parts were huddled together. The boiler constituted the principal feature; and, being the foundation of the other parts, it was made to do duty not only as a generator of steam, but also as a basis for the fixings of the machinery and for the bearings of the wheels and axles. The want of springs was seriously felt; and the progress of the engine was a succession of jolts, causing considerable derangement to the machinery. The mode of communicating the motive power to the wheels by means of the spur-gear also caused frequent jerks, each cylinder alternately propelling or becoming propelled by the other, as the pressure of the one upon the wheels became greater or less than the pressure of the other; and, when the teeth of the cog-wheels became at all worn, a rattling noise was produced during the traveling of the engine.

As the principal test of the success of the locomotive was its economy as compared with horse-power, careful calculations were made with the view of ascertaining this important point. The result was, that it was found the working of the engine was at first barely economical; and at the end of the year the steam-power and the horse-power were ascertained to be as nearly as possible upon a par in point of cost.

We give the remainder of the history of George Stephenson's efforts to produce an economical working locomotive in the words of his son Robert, as communicated to the author in 1856, for the purposes of his father's "Life."

"A few months of experience and careful observation upon the operation of this (his first) engine convinced my father that the complication arising out of the action of the two cylinders being combined by spur-wheels would prevent their coming into practical application. He then directed his attention to an entire change in the construction and mechanical arrangements, and in the following year took out a patent, dated February 28th, 1815, for an engine which combined in a remarkable degree the essential requisites of an economical locomotive—that is to say, few parts, simplicity in their action, and great simplicity in the mode by which power was communicated to the wheels supporting the engine.

"This second engine consisted as before of two vertical cylinders, which communicated directly with each pair of the four wheels that supported the engine by a cross-head and a pair of connecting-rods;

but, in attempting to establish a direct communication between the cylinders and the wheels that rolled upon the rails, considerable difficulties presented themselves. The ordinary joints could not be employed to unite the engine, which was a rigid mass, with the wheels rolling upon the irregular surface of the rails; for it was evident that the two rails of the line of railway could not always be maintained at the same level with respect to each other—that one wheel at the end of the axle might be depressed into a part of the line which had subsided, while the other would be elevated. In such a position of the axle and wheels it was clear that a rigid communication between the cross-head and the wheels was impracticable. Hence it became necessary to form a joint at the top of the piston-rod where it united with the cross-head, so as to permit the cross-head always to preserve complete parallelism with the axle of the wheels with which it was in communication.

"In order to obtain the flexibility combined with direct action which was essential for insuring power and avoiding needless friction and jars from irregularities in the rail, my father employed the 'ball and socket' joint for effecting a union between the ends of the cross-heads where they united with the connecting-rods, and between the end of the connecting-rods where they were united with the crank-pins attached to each driving-wheel. By this arrangement the parallelism between the cross-head and the axle was at all times maintained, it being permitted to take place without producing jar or friction upon any part of the machine.

"The next important point was to combine each pair of wheels by some simple mechanism, instead of the cog-wheels which had formerly been used. My father began by inserting each axle into two cranks at right angles to each other, with rods communicating horizontally between them. An engine was made on this plan, and answered extremely well. But at that period (1815) the mechanical skill of the country was not equal to the task of forging cranked axles of the soundness and strength necessary to stand the jars incident to locomotive work; so my father was compelled to fall back upon a substitute which, though less simple and less efficient, was within the mechanical capabilities of the workmen of that day, either for construction or repair. He adopted a chain which rolled over indented wheels placed on the centre of each axle, and so arranged that the two pairs of wheels were effectually coupled and made to keep pace with each other. But these chains after a few years' use became stretched, and then the engines were liable to irregularity in their working, especially in changing from working back to forward again. Nevertheless, these engines continued in profitable use upon the Killingworth Colliery Railway for some years. Eventually the chain was laid aside, and the front and hind wheels were united by rods on the *outside*, instead of by rods and crank-ankles *inside*, as specified in the original patent; and this expedient completely answered the purpose required, without involving any expensive or difficult workmanship.

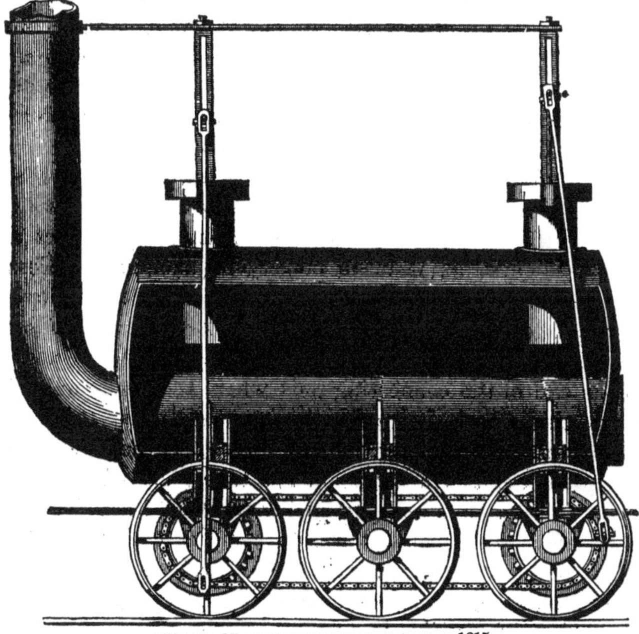

SECTION OF KILLINGWORTH LOCOMOTIVE, 1815.

"Another important improvement was introduced in this engine. The eduction steam had hitherto been allowed to escape direct into the open atmosphere; but my father, having observed the great velocity with which the waste-steam escaped, compared with the velocity with which the smoke issued from the chimney of the same engine, thought that by conveying the eduction steam into the chimney, and there allowing it to escape in a vertical direction, its velocity would be imparted to the smoke from the engine, or to the ascending current of air in the chimney. The experiment was no sooner made than the power of the engine became more than doubled; combustion was stimulated, as it were, by a blast; consequently, the power of the boiler for generating steam was increased, and, in the same proportion, the useful duty of the engine was augmented.

"Thus, in 1815, my father had succeeded in manufacturing an engine which included the following important improvements on all previous attempts in the same direction: simple and direct communication between the cylinder and the wheels rolling upon the rails; joint adhesion of all the wheels, attained by the use of horizontal connecting-rods; and, finally, a beautiful method of exciting the combustion of fuel by employing the waste steam which had formerly been allowed uselessly to escape. It is, perhaps, not too much to say that this engine, as a mechanical contrivance, contained the germ of all that has since been effected. It may be regarded, in fact, as a type of the present locomotive engine.

"In describing my father's application of the waste steam for the purpose of increasing the intensity of combustion in the boiler, and thus increasing the power of the engine without adding to its weight, and while claiming for this engine the merit of being a type of all those which have been successfully devised since the commencement of the Liverpool and Manchester Railway, it is necessary to observe that the next great improvement in the same direction, the 'multitubular boiler,' which took place some years later, could never have been used without the help of that simple expedient, *the steam-blast*, by which power only the burning of coke was rendered possible.

"I can not pass over this last-named invention of my father's without remarking how slightly, as an original idea, it has been appreciated; and yet how small would be the comparative value of the locomotive engine of the present day without the application of that important invention!

"Engines constructed by my father in the year 1818 upon the principles just described are in use on the Killingworth Colliery Railway to this very day (1856), conveying, at the speed of perhaps five or six miles an hour, heavy coal-trains, probably as economically as any of the more perfect engines now in use.

"There was another remarkable piece of ingenuity in this machine, which was completed so many years before the possibility of steam-locomotion became an object of general commercial interest and Parliamentary inquiry. I have before observed that up to and after the year 1818 there was no such class of skilled mechanics, nor were there such machinery and tools for working in metals, as are now at the disposal of inventors and manufacturers. Among other difficulties of a similar character, it was not possible at that time to construct springs of sufficient strength to support the improved engines. The rails then used being extremely light, the roads became worn down by the traffic, and occasionally the whole weight of the engine, instead of being uniformly distributed over four wheels, was thrown almost diagonally upon two. In order to avoid the danger arising from such irregularities in the road, my father arranged the boiler so that it was supported upon the frame of the engine by four cylinders which opened into the interior of the boiler. These cylinders were occupied by pistons with rods, which passed downward and pressed upon the upper side of the axles. The cylinders, opening into the interior of the boiler, allowed the pressure of steam to be applied to the upper side of the piston, and that pressure being nearly equal to the support of one fourth of the weight of the engine, each axle, whatever might be its position, had the same amount of weight to bear, and consequently the entire weight was at all times nearly equally distributed among the wheels. This expedient was more necessary in this case, as the weight of the new locomotive engines far exceeded that of the carriages which had hitherto been used upon colliery railways, and therefore subjected the rails to much greater risk from breakage. And this mode of supporting the engine remained in use until the progress of spring-making had considerably advanced, when steel springs of sufficient strength superseded this highly ingenious mode of distributing the weight of the engine uniformly among the wheels."

The invention of the Steam-blast by George Stephenson in 1815 was fraught with the most important consequences to railway locomotion, and it is not saying too much to aver that the success of the locomotive has been in a great measure the result of its adoption. Without the steam-blast, by means of which the intensity of combustion is maintained at its highest point, producing a correspondingly rapid evolution of steam, high rates of speed could not have been kept up; the advantages of the multitubular boiler (afterward invented) could never have been fully tested; and locomotives might still have been dragging themselves unwieldily along at little more than five or six miles an hour.

As this invention has been the subject of considerable controversy, it becomes necessary to add a few words respecting it in this place. It has been claimed as the invention of Trevithick in 1804, of Hedley in 1814, of Goldsworthy Gurney in 1820, and of Timothy Hackworth in 1829. With respect to Trevithick, it appears that he discharged the waste steam into the chimney of his engine, but without any intention of thereby producing a blast;* and that he attached no value to the expedient is sufficiently obvious from the fact that in 1815 he took out a patent for urging the fire by means of fanners, similar to a winnowing machine. The claim put forward on behalf of William Hedley, that he invented the blast-pipe for the Wylam engine, is sufficiently contradicted by the fact that the Wylam engine had *no* blast-pipe. "I remember the Wylam engine," Robert Stephenson wrote to the author in 1857, "and I am positive there was no blast-pipe." On the contrary, the Wylam engine embodied a contrivance for the express purpose of *preventing* a blast. This is clearly shown by the drawing and description of it contained in the first edition of Nicholas Wood's "Practical Treatise on Railroads," published in 1825. This evidence is all the more valuable for our purpose, as it was published long before any controversy had arisen as to the authorship of the invention, and, indeed, before it was believed that any merit whatever belonged to it. And it is the more remarkable, as Nicholas Wood himself, who published the first practical work on railways, did not at that time approve of the steam-blast, and referred to the Wylam engine in illustration of how it might be prevented.

The following passage from Mr. Wood's book clearly describes the express object and purpose for which George Stephenson invented and applied the steam-blast in the Killingworth engines. Describing their action, Mr. Wood says:

"The steam is admitted to the top and bottom of the piston by means of a sliding valve, which, being moved up and down alternately, opens a communication between the top and bottom of the cylinder and the pipe that is *open into the chimney and turns up*

* It must, however, be mentioned that Mr. Zerah Colburn, in his excellent work on "Locomotive Engineering and the Mechanism of Railways," points out that Mr. Davies Gilbert noted the effect of the discharge of the waste steam up the chimney of Trevithick's engine in increasing the draught, and wrote a letter to "Nicholson's Journal" (Sept., 1805) on the subject; and Mr. Nicholson himself proceeded to investigate the subject, and in 1806 he took out a patent for "steam-blasting apparatus," applicable to fixed engines, which, however, does not seem to have come into use. (See *ante*, p. 82.)

within it. The steam, after performing its office within the cylinder, is thus thrown into the chimney, and the power with which it issues will be proportionate to the degree of elasticity; and *the exit being directed upward, accelerates the velocity of the current of heated air accordingly.*"*

And again, at another part of the book, he says:

"There is another great objection urged against locomotives, which is, the noise that the steam makes in escaping into the chimney; this objection is very singular, as it is not the result of any inherent form in the organization of such engines, but an accidental circumstance. When the engines *were first made*, the steam escaped into the atmosphere, and made comparatively little noise; *it was found difficult then to produce steam in sufficient quantity to keep the engine constantly working, or rather to obtain an adequate rapidity of current in the chimney to give sufficient intensity to the fire. To effect a greater rapidity, or to increase the draught of the chimney, Mr. Stephenson thought that by causing the steam to escape into the chimney through a pipe with its end turned upward, the velocity of the current would be accelerated, and such was the effect;* but, in remedying one evil, another has been produced, which, though objectionable in some places, was not considered as objectionable on a private railroad. The tube through the boiler having been increased, there is now no longer any occasion for the action of the steam to assist the motion of the heated air in the chimney. The steam thrown in this manner into the chimney acts as a trumpet, and certainly makes a very disagreeable noise. Nothing, however, is more easy to remedy, and the very act of remedying this defect will also be the means of economizing the fuel."†

Mr. Wood then proceeds to show how the noise caused by the blast—how, in fact, the blast itself, might be effectually prevented by adopting the expedient employed in the Wylam engine; which was, to send the exhaust steam, not into the chimney (where alone the blast could act with effect by stimulating the draught), but into a steam-reservoir provided for the purpose. His words are these:

"Nothing more is wanted to destroy the noise than *to cause the*

* Nicholas Wood, "Practical Treatise on Railways," ed. 1825, p. 147.
† Ibid., p. 292–3.

steam to expand itself into a reservoir, and then allow it to escape gradually to the atmosphere through the chimney. Upon the Wylam railroad the noise was made the subject of complaint by a neighboring gentleman, and they adopted this mode, which had the effect above mentioned."*

It is curious to find that Mr. Nicholas Wood continued to object to the use of the steam-blast down even to the time when the Liverpool and Manchester Railway Bill was before Parliament. In his evidence before the Committee on that Bill in 1825, he said: "Those engines [at Killingworth] *puff very much, and the object is to get an increased draught in the chimney.* Now (by enlarging the flue-tube and giving it a double turn through the boiler) we have got a sufficiency of steam without it, and I have no doubt, by allowing the steam to exhaust itself in a reservoir, it would pass quietly into the chimney without that noise." In fact, Mr. Wood was still in favor of the arrangement adopted in the Wylam engine, by which the steam-blast had been got rid of altogether.

If these statements, made in Mr. Wood's book, be correct—and they have never been disputed—they render it perfectly clear that George Stephenson invented and applied the steam-blast for the express purpose of quickening combustion in the furnace by increasing the draught in the chimney. Although urged by Wood to abandon the blast, Stephenson continued to hold by it as one of the vital powers of the locomotive engine. It is quite true that in the early engines, with only a double flue passing through the boiler, run as they were at low speeds, the blast was of comparatively less importance. It was only when the improved passenger engine, fitted with the multitubular boiler, was required to be run at high speeds that the full merits of the blast were brought out; and in detecting its essential uses in this respect, and sharpening

* Nicholas Wood, "Practical Treatise on Railways," ed. 1825, p. 294. These passages will be found in the first edition of Mr. Wood's work, published in 1825. The subsequent editions do not contain them. A few years' experience wrought great changes of opinion on many points connected with the practical working of railways, and Mr. Wood altered his text accordingly. But it is most important for our present purpose to note that, in the year 1825, long before the Liverpool and Manchester line was opened, Mr. Wood should have so clearly described the steam-blast, which had been in regular use for more than ten years in all Stephenson's locomotives employed in the working of the Killingworth railway.

it for the purpose of increasing its action, the sagacity of Timothy Hackworth, of Darlington, is entitled to due recognition.

CHAPTER VI.

INVENTION OF THE "GEORDY" SAFETY-LAMP.

EXPLOSIONS of fire-damp were unusually frequent in the coal-mines of Northumberland and Durham about the time when George Stephenson was engaged in the construction of his first locomotives. These explosions were often attended with fearful loss of life and dreadful suffering to the work-people. Killingworth Colliery was not free from such deplorable calamities; and during the time that Stephenson was employed as brakesman at the West Moor, several "blasts" took place in the pit, by which many workmen were scorched and killed, and the owners of the colliery sustained heavy losses. One of the most serious of these accidents occurred in 1806, not long after he had been appointed brakesman, by which ten persons were killed. Stephenson was near the pit mouth at the time, and the circumstances connected with the explosion made a deep impression on his mind, as appears from the graphic account which he gave of it to the Committee of the House of Commons on accidents in mines, some thirty years after the event.

"The pit," said he, "had just ceased drawing coals, and nearly all the men had got out. It was some time in the afternoon, a little after midday. There were five men that went down the pit; four of them for the purpose of preparing a place for the furnace. The fifth was a person who went down to set them to work. I sent this man down myself, and he had just got to the bottom of the shaft about two or three minutes when the explosion took place. I had left the mouth of the pit, and had gone about fifty or sixty yards away, when I heard a tremendous noise, looked round, and saw the discharge come out of the pit like the discharge of a cannon. It continued to blow, I think, for a quarter of an hour, discharging every thing that had come into the current. Wood came up, stones came up, and trusses of hay that went up into the air like balloons. Those trusses had been sent down during the day, and I think they had in some measure injured the ventilation of the mine. The ground all round the top of the pit was in a trembling state. I went as near as I durst go; every thing appeared cracking and rending about me. Part of the brattice, which was very strong, was blown away at the bottom of the pits. Very large pumps were lifted from their places, so that the engine could not work. The pit was divided into four by partitions; it was a large pit, fourteen feet in diameter, and partitions were put down at right angles, which made four compartments. The explosion took place in one of those four quarters, but it broke through into all the others at the bottom, and the brattice or partitions were set on fire at the first explosion.

"Nobody durst go near the shafts for some time, for fear of another explosion taking place. At last we considered it necessary to run the rope backward and forward, and give the miners, if there were any at the bottom of the shaft, an opportunity of catching the rope as it came to the bottom. Several men were safely got up in this way; one man, who had got hold of the rope, was being drawn up, when a farther explosion took place while he was still in the shaft, and the increased current which came about him projected him as it were up the shaft; yet he was landed without injury: it was a singular case. . . . . The pit continued to blast every two or three hours for about two days. It appears that the coal had taken fire, and as soon as the carbureted hydrogen gas collected in sufficient quantity to reach the part where it was burning, it ignited again; but none of the explosions were equal to the first, on account of many parts of the mine having become filled with azotic gas, or the *after-damp* of the mine. All the ditches in the country-side were stopped to get water to pour into the pit. We had fire-engines brought from Newcastle, and the water was poured in till it came above the fire, and then it was extinguished. The loss to the owners of the colliery by this accident must have been about £20,000."*

Another explosion took place in the same pit in 1809, by which twelve persons lost their lives. The blast did not reach the shaft as in the former case, the unfortunate persons in the pit having been suffocated by the after-damp. More calamitous still were the explosions which took place in the neighboring collieries, one of the worst being that of 1812, in the Felling Pit near Gateshead, a mine belonging to Mr. Brandling, by which no fewer than nine-

* Evidence given by George Stephenson before the Select Committee on Accidents in Mines, 26th June, 1835.

ty men and boys were suffocated or burnt to death; and a similar accident occurred in the same pit in the year following, by which twenty-two men and boys perished.

THE PIT HEAD, WEST MOOR. [By R. P. Leitch.]

It was natural that Stephenson should devote his attention to the causes of these deplorable accidents, and to the means by which they might, if possible, be prevented. His daily occupation led him to think much and deeply on the subject. As engine-wright of a colliery so extensive as that of Killingworth, where there were nearly 160 miles of gallery excavation, in which he personally superintended the working of inclined planes, along which the coals were sent to the pit entrance, he was necessarily very often under ground, and brought face to face with the dangers of fire-damp. From fissures in the roofs of the galleries carbureted hydrogen gas was constantly flowing; and in some of the more dangerous places it might be heard escaping from the crevices of the coal with a hissing noise. Ventilation, firing, and all conceivable modes of drawing out the foul air had been tried, while the more dangerous parts of the galleries were built up. Still the danger could not be wholly prevented. The miners must necessarily guide their steps through the extensive underground ways with lighted lamps or candles, the naked flame of which, coming in contact with the inflammable air, daily exposed them and their fellow-workers in the pit to the risk of death in one of its most dreadful forms.

One day in the year 1814, a workman hurried into Stephenson's cottage with the startling information that the deepest main of the colliery was on fire! He immediately hastened to the pit-head, about a hundred yards off, whither the women and children of the colliery were running, with wildness and terror depicted in every face. In a commanding voice, Stephenson ordered the engine-man to lower him down the shaft in the corve. There was danger, it might be death, before him, but he must go.

He was soon at the bottom, and in the midst of the men, who were paralyzed at the danger which threatened the lives of all in the pit. Leaping from the corve on its touching the ground, he called out, "Are there six men among you who have the courage to follow me? If so, come, and we will put the fire out." The Killingworth pitmen had the most perfect confidence in their engine-wright, and they readily volunteered to follow him. Silence succeeded the frantic tumult of the previous minute, and the men set to work with a will. In every mine, bricks, mortar, and tools enough are at hand, and by Stephenson's direction the materials were forthwith carried to the required spot, where, in a very short time, a wall was raised at the entrance to the main, he himself taking the most active part in the work. The atmospheric air was by this means excluded, the fire was extinguished, most of the people in the pit were saved from death, and the mine was preserved.

This anecdote of George Stephenson was related to the writer, near the pit-mouth, by one of the men, Kit Heppel, who had been present, and helped to build up the brick wall by which the fire was stayed, though several of the workmen were suffocated. Heppel relates that, when down the pit some days after, seeking out the dead bodies, the cause of the accident was the subject of some conversation between himself and Stephenson, and Heppel then asked him, "Can nothing be done to prevent such awful occurrences?" Stephenson replied that he thought something might be done. "Then," said Heppel, "the sooner you begin the better, for the price of coal-mining now is *pitmen's lives.*"

Fifty years since, many of the best pits were so full of the inflammable gas given forth by the coal that they could not be worked without the greatest danger, and for this reason some were altogether abandoned. The rudest possible means were adopted of producing light sufficient to enable the pitmen to work by. The phosphorescence of decayed fish-skins was tried; but this, though safe, was very inefficient. The most common method employed was what was called a steel mill, the notched wheel of which, being made to revolve against a flint, struck a succession of sparks, which scarcely served to do more than make the darkness visible. A boy carried the apparatus, working the wheel; and by the imperfect light thus given forth the miner plied his dangerous trade. Candles were only used in those parts of the pit where gas was not abundant. Under this rude system not more than one third of the coal could be worked, while two thirds were left.

What the workmen, not less than the coal-owners, eagerly desired was a lamp that should give forth sufficient light, without communicating flame to the inflammable gas which accumulated in certain parts of the pit. Something had already been done toward the invention of such a lamp by Dr. Clanny, of Sunderland, who, in 1813, contrived an apparatus to which he gave air from the mine through water, by means of bellows. This lamp went out of itself in inflammable gas. It was found, however, too unwieldy to be used by the miners for the purposes of their work, and did not come into general use. A committee of gentlemen interested in coal-mining was formed to investigate the causes of the explosions, and to devise, if possible, some means of preventing them. At the invitation of that committee, Sir Humphry Davy, then in the full zenith of his reputation, was requested to turn his attention to the subject. He accordingly visited the collieries near Newcastle on the 24th of August, 1815, and at the close of that year, on the 9th of November, 1815, he read before the Royal Society of London his celebrated paper "On the Fire-damp of Coal Mines, and on Methods of Lighting the Mine so as to prevent its Explosion."

But a humbler though not less diligent and original thinker had been at work before him, and had already practically solved the problem of the Safety-lamp. Stephenson was, of course, well aware of the desire which prevailed in the colliery districts for the invention of a lamp which should give light enough for the miners to work by without exploding the fire-damp, and the painful incidents above described only served to quicken his eagerness to master the difficulty.

For several years he had been engaged, in his own rude way, in making experiments with the fire-damp in the Killingworth mine. The pitmen used to expostulate with him on these occasions, believing the experiments to be fraught with danger. One of the sinkers, called M'Crie, observing him holding up lighted candles to the windward of the "blower" or fissure from which the inflammable gas escaped, entreated him to desist; but Stephenson's answer was, that "he was busy with a plan by which he hoped to make his experiments useful for preserving men's lives." On these occasions the miners usually got out of the way before he lit the gas.

In 1815, although he was very much occupied with the business of the collieries and the improvement of his locomotive engine, he was also busily engaged in making experiments upon the inflammable gas in the Killingworth Pit. As he himself afterward related to the Committee of the House of Commons which sat on the subject of Accidents in Mines in 1835, he imagined that if he could construct a lamp with a chimney so arranged as to cause a strong current, it would not fire at the top of the chimney, as the burnt air would ascend with such a velocity as to prevent the inflammable air of the pit from descending toward the flame; and such a lamp, he thought, might be taken into a dangerous atmosphere without risk of exploding.

Such was Stephenson's theory, when he proceeded to embody his idea of a miner's safety-lamp in a practical form. In the month of August, 1815, he requested his friend Nicholas Wood, the head viewer, to prepare a drawing of a lamp according to the description which he gave him. After several evenings' careful deliberations, the drawing was prepared, and it was shown to several of the head men about the works. "My first lamp," said Stephenson, describing it to the committee above referred to, "had a chimney at the top of the lamp, and a tube at the bottom to admit the atmospheric air, or fire-damp and air, to feed the burner or combustion of the lamp. I was not aware of the precise quantity required to feed the combustion; but to know what quantity was necessary, I had a slide at the bottom of the tube in my first lamp, to admit such a quantity of air as might eventually be found necessary to keep up the combustion."

Accompanied by his friend Wood, Stephenson went into Newcastle, and ordered a lamp to be made according to his plan by the Messrs. Hogg, tinmen, at the head of the Side—a well-known street in Newcastle. At the same time, he ordered a glass to be made for the lamp at the Northumberland Glass-house in the same town. This lamp was received from the makers on the 21st of October, and was taken to Killingworth for the purpose of immediate experiment.

"I remember that evening as distinctly as if it had been but yesterday," said Robert Stephenson, describing the circumstances to the author in 1857. "Moodie came to our cottage about dusk, and asked 'if father had got back with the lamp.' 'No.' 'Then I'll wait till he comes,' said Moodie; 'he can't be long now.' In about half an hour, in came my father, his face all radiant. He had the lamp with him! It was at once uncovered and shown to Moodie. Then it was filled with oil, trimmed, and lighted. All was ready, only the head viewer hadn't arrived. 'Run over to Benton for Nichol, Robert,' said my father to me, 'and ask him to come directly; say we're going down the pit to try the lamp.' By this time it was quite dark, and off I ran to bring Nicholas Wood. His house was at Benton, about a mile off. There was a short cut through Benton Church-yard, but just as I was about to pass the wicket I saw what I thought was a white figure moving about among the grave-stones. I took it for a ghost! My heart fluttered, and I was in a great fright, but to Nichol's house I must get, so I made the circuit of the church-yard; and when I got round to the other side I looked, and, lo! the figure was still there. But what do you think it was? Only the grave-digger, plying his work at that late hour by the light of his lantern set upon one of the grave-stones! I found Wood at home, and in a few minutes he was mounted and off to my father's. When I got home I was told they had just left—it was then about eleven—and gone down the shaft to try the lamp in one of the most dangerous parts of the mine."

Arrived at the bottom of the shaft with the lamp, the party directed their steps toward one of the foulest galleries in the pit, where the explosive gas was issuing through a blower in the roof of the mine with a loud hissing noise. By erecting some deal boarding round that part of the gallery into which the gas was escaping, the air was thus made more foul for the purpose of the experiment. After waiting about an hour, Moodie, whose practical experience of fire-damp in pits was greater than that of either Stephenson or Wood, was requested to go into the place which had thus been made foul; and, having done so, he returned, and told them that the smell of the air was such that if a lighted candle were now introduced an explosion must inevitably take place. He cautioned Stephenson as to the danger both to themselves and to the pit if the gas took fire; but Stephenson declared his confidence in the safety of his lamp, and, having lit the wick, he boldly proceeded with it toward the explosive air. The others, more timid and doubtful, hung back when they came within hearing of the blower; and, apprehensive of the danger, they retired into a safe place, out of sight of the lamp, which gradually disappeared with its bearer in the recesses of the mine. It was a critical moment, and the danger was such as would have tried the stoutest heart. Stephenson, advancing alone, with his yet untried lamp, in the depths of those underground workings, calmly venturing his life in the determination to discover a mode by which the lives of many might be saved, and death disarmed in these fatal caverns, presented an example of intrepid nerve and manly courage more noble even than that which, in the excitement of battle and the collective impetuosity of a charge, carries a man up to the cannon's mouth.

Advancing to the place of danger, and entering within the fouled air, his lighted lamp in hand, Stephenson held it firmly out, in the full current of the blower, and within a few inches of its mouth. Thus exposed, the flame of the lamp at first increased, then flickered, and then went out; but there was no explosion of the gas. Returning to his companions, who were still at a distance, he told them what had occurred. Having now acquired somewhat more confidence, they advanced with him to a point from which they could observe the experiment repeated, but still at a safe distance. They saw that when the lighted lamp was held within the explosive mixture, there was a great flame; the lamp was almost full of fire; and then it seemed to be smothered out. Again returning to his companions, he relighted the lamp, and repeated the experiment. This was done several times, with the same result. At length Wood and Moodie ventured to advance close to the fouled part of the pit; and, in making some of the later trials, Mr. Wood himself held up the lighted lamp to the blower.* Such was the result of the first experiments with the *first practical Miner's Safety-lamp*, and such was the daring resolution of its inventor in testing its qualities.

Before leaving the pit, Stephenson expressed his opinion that, by an alteration of the lamp which he contemplated, he could make it burn better. This was by a change in the slide through which the air was admitted into the lower part of the lamp, under the flame. After making some experiments on the air collected at the blower, by means of bladders which were mounted with tubes of various diameters, he satisfied himself that, when the tube was reduced to a certain diameter, the explosion would not pass through; and he fashioned his slide accordingly, reducing the diameter of the tube until he conceived it was quite safe. In about a fortnight the experiments were repeated in the pit, in a place purposely made foul as before. On this occasion a larger number of persons ventured to witness the experiments, which again proved successful. The lamp was not yet, however, so efficient as the inventor desired. It required, he observed, to be

* The accuracy of the above statement having been called in question, it is proper to state that the facts as set forth were verbally communicated to the author in the first place by Robert Stephenson, to whom the chapter was afterward read in MS. in the presence of Mr. Sopwith, F.R.S., and received his entire approval. But at the time at which Mr. Stephenson communicated the verbal information, he also handed a little book with his name written in it, still in the author's possession, saying, "Read that; you will find it all there." This little book contains, among other things, a pamphlet, entitled "Report on the Claims of Mr. George Stephenson relative to the Invention of his Safety-lamp. By the Committee appointed at a Meeting holden in Newcastle, on the 1st of November, 1817. With an Appendix containing the Evidence." Among the witnesses examined were George Stephenson, Nicholas Wood, and John Moodie, and their evidence is given in the pamphlet. Stephenson said that he tried the first lamp "in a part of the mine where the air was highly explosive. Nicholas Wood and John Moodie were his companions when the trial was made. They became frightened when they came within hearing of the blower, and would not go any farther. Mr. Stephenson went alone with the lamp to the mouth of the blower," etc. This evidence was confirmed by John Moodie, who said the air of the place where the experiment was about to be tried was such, that, if a lighted candle had been introduced, an explosion would have taken place that would have been "extremely dangerous." "Told Stephenson it was foul, and hinted at the danger; nevertheless, Stephenson *would* try the lamp, confiding in its safety. Stephenson took the lamp and went with it into the place in which Moodie had been, and Moodie and Wood, apprehensive of the danger, retired to a greater distance," etc. The accuracy of the other statements made in the text relative to the invention of the safety-lamp is confirmed by the same publication.

kept very steady when burning in the inflammable gas, otherwise it was liable to go out, in consequence, as he imagined, of the contact of the burnt air (as he then called it), or azotic gas, which lodged round the exterior of the flame. If the lamp was moved backward and forward, the azote came in contact with the flame and extinguished it. "It struck me," said he, "that if I put more tubes in, I should discharge the poisonous matter that hung round the flame by admitting the air to its exterior part."

Although he had then no access to scientific works, nor intercourse with scientific men, nor any thing that could assist him in his inquiries on the subject besides his own indefatigable spirit of inquiry, Stephenson contrived a rude apparatus, by means of which he proceeded to test the explosive properties of the gas and the velocity of current (for this was the direction of his inquiries) required to permit the explosion to pass through tubes of different diameters. In making these experiments in his cottage at the West Moor, Nicholas Wood and George's son Robert usually acted as his assistants, and sometimes the gentlemen of the neighborhood—among others, William Brandling and Matthew Bell, who were interested in coal-mining—attended as spectators. One who was present on such an occasion remembers that, when an experiment was about to be performed, and all was ready, George called to Mr. Wood, who worked the stopcocks of the gasometer, "Wise on [turn on] the hydrōgen, Nichol!"

These experiments were not performed without risk, for on one occasion the experimenting party had nearly blown off the roof of the cottage. One of these "blows up" was described by Stephenson himself before the Committee on Accidents in Coal Mines in 1835:

"I made several experiments," said he, "as to the velocity required in tubes of different diameters, to prevent explosion from fire-damp. We made the mixture in all proportions of light carbureted hydrogen with atmospheric air in the receiver, and we found by the experiments that when a current of the most explosive mixture that we could make was forced up a tube four tenths of an inch in diameter, the necessary current was nine inches in a second to prevent its coming down that tube. These experiments were repeated several times. We had two or three blows up in making the experiments, by the flame getting down into the receiver, though we had a piece of very fine wire-gauze put at the bottom of the pipe, between the receiver and the pipe through which we were forcing the current. In one of these experiments I was watching the flame in the tube, my son was taking the vibrations of the pendulum of the clock, and Mr. Wood was attending to give me the column of water as I called for it, to keep the current up to a certain point. As I saw the flame descending in the tube I called for more water, and Wood unfortunately turned the cock the wrong way; the current ceased, the flame went down the tube, and all our implements were blown to pieces, which at the time we were not very well able to replace."

The explosion of this glass receiver, which had been borrowed from the stores of the Philosophical Society at Newcastle for the purpose of making the experiments, caused the greatest possible dismay among the party, and they dreaded to inform Mr. Turner, the secretary,* of the calamity which had occurred. Fortunately, none of the experimenters were injured by the accident.

Stephenson followed up these experiments by others of a similar kind, with the view of ascertaining whether ordinary flame would pass through tubes of a small diameter, and with this object he filed off the barrels of several small keys. Placing these together, he held them perpendicularly over a strong flame, and ascertained that it did not pass upward. This was a farther proof to him of the soundness of the principle on which he had been proceeding.

In order to correct the defect of his first lamp, he accordingly proceeded to alter it so as to admit the air to the flame by several tubes of reduced diameter instead of by a single tube. He in-

* The early connection of Robert with the Philosophical and Literary Society of Newcastle had brought him into communication with the Rev. William Turner, one of the secretaries of the institution. That gentleman was always ready to assist the inquirer after knowledge, and took an early interest in the studious youth from Killingworth, with whose father he also became acquainted. Mr. Turner cheerfully helped them in their joint inquiries, and excited while he endeavored to satisfy their thirst for scientific information. Toward the close of his life Mr. Stephenson often spoke of the gratitude and esteem he felt toward his revered instructor. "Mr. Turner," he said, "was always ready to assist me with books, with instruments, and with counsel, gratuitously and cheerfully. He gave me the most valuable assistance and instruction, and to my dying day I can never forget the obligations which I owe to my venerable friend."

ferred that a sufficient quantity of air would thus be introduced into the lamp for the purposes of combustion, while the smallness of the apertures would still prevent the explosion passing downward, at the same time that the "burnt air" (the cause, in his opinion, of the lamp going out) would be more effectually dislodged. The requisite alterations were made in the lamp by Mr. Matthews, a tinman in Newcastle, and it was so altered that the air was admitted by three small tubes inserted in the bottom, the openings of which were placed on the outside of the burner, instead of having (as in the original lamp) the one tube opening directly under the flame.

This second or altered lamp was tried in the Killingworth Pit on the 4th of November, and was found to burn better than the first lamp, and to be perfectly safe. But, as it did not yet come up entirely to the inventor's expectations, he proceeded to contrive a third lamp, in which he proposed to surround the oil vessel with a number of capillary tubes. Then it struck him that if he cut off the middle of the tubes, or made holes in metal plates, placed at a distance from each other equal to the length of the tubes, the air would get in better, and the effect in preventing the communication of explosion would be the same.

He was encouraged to persevere in the completion of his safety-lamp by the occurrence of several fatal accidents about this time in the Killingworth Pit. On the 9th of November a boy was killed by a blast in the *A* pit, at the very place where Stephenson had made the experiments with his first lamp; and, when told of the accident, he observed that if the boy had been provided with his lamp, his life would have been saved. On the 20th of November he went over to Newcastle to order his third lamp from Mr. Watson, a plumber in that town. Mr. Watson referred him to his clerk, Henry Smith, whom Stephenson invited to join him at a neighboring public house, where they might quietly talk over the matter, and finally settle the plan of the new lamp. They adjourned to the "Newcastle Arms," near the present High-Level Bridge, where they had some ale, and a design of the lamp was drawn in pencil upon a half-sheet of foolscap, with a rough specification subjoined. The sketch, when shown to us by Robert Stephenson some years since, still bore the marks of the ale. It was a very rude design, but sufficient to work from. It was immediately placed in the hands of the workmen, finished in the course of a few days, and experimentally tested in the Killingworth Pit like the previous lamps on the 30th of November, by

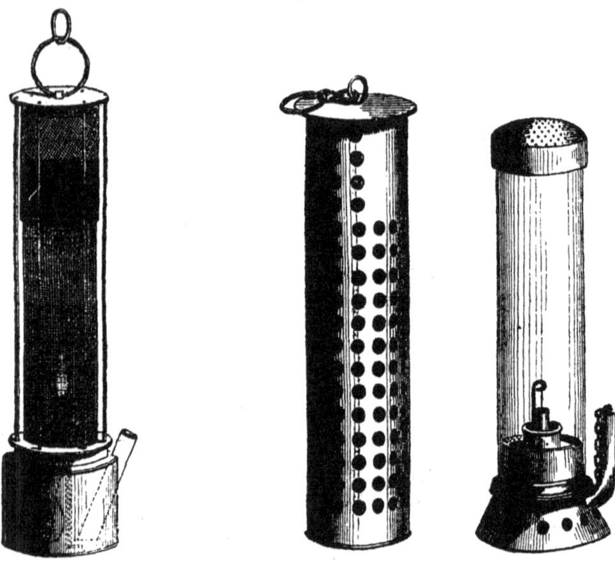

DAVY'S SAFETY-LAMP. STEPHENSON'S SAFETY-LAMP.

which date neither Stephenson nor Wood had heard of Sir Humphry Davy's experiments, nor of the lamp which that gentleman proposed to construct.

An angry controversy afterward took place as to the respective merits of George Stephenson and Sir Humphry Davy in respect of the invention of the Safety-lamp. A committee was formed on both sides, and the facts were stated in various ways. It is perfectly clear, however, that Stephenson had ascertained *the fact* that flame will not pass through tubes of a certain diameter—the principle on which the safety-lamp is constructed—before Sir Humphry Davy had formed any definite idea on the subject, or invented the model lamp afterward exhibited by him before the Royal Society. Stephenson had actually constructed a lamp on such a principle, and proved its safety, before Sir Humphry had communicated his views on the subject to any person; and by the time that the first public intimation had been given of his discovery, Stephenson's second lamp had been constructed and tested in like manner in the Killingworth Pit. The *first* was tried on the 21st of October, 1815; the *second* was tried on the 4th of November; but it was not until the 9th of November that Sir Humphry Davy presented his first lamp to the public. And by the 30th of the same month, as we have seen, Stephenson had constructed and tested his *third* safety-lamp.

Stephenson's theory of the "burnt air" and the "draught" was no doubt wrong, but his lamp was right, and that was the great fact which mainly concerned him. Torricelli did not know the rationale of his tube, nor Otto von Guericke that of his air-pump; yet no one thinks of denying them the merit of their inventions on that account. The discoveries of Volta and Galvani were in like manner independent of theory; the greatest discoveries consisting in bringing to light certain grand facts, on which theories are afterward framed. Our inventor had been pursuing the Baconian method, though he did not think of that; his sole object being to invent a safe lamp, which he knew could only be done through the process of repeated experiment. Hence his numerous experiments on the fire-damp at the blowers in the mine, as well as on carbureted hydrogen gas in his cottage by means of the apparatus above described. By experiment he distinctly ascertained that the explosion of fire-damp could not pass through small tubes; and he also did what had not before been done by any inventor—he constructed a lamp on this principle, and repeatedly proved its safety at the risk of his life. At the same time, there is no doubt that it was to Sir Humphry Davy that the merit belonged of elucidating the true law on which the safety-lamp is constructed.

The subject of this important invention excited so much interest in the northern mining districts, and Stephenson's numerous friends considered his lamp so completely successful—having stood the test of repeated experiments—that they urged him to bring his invention before the Philosophical and Literary Society of Newcastle, of whose apparatus he had availed himself in the course of his experiments on fire-damp. After much persuasion he consented to do so, and a meeting was appointed for the purpose of receiving his explanations on the evening of the 5th of December, 1815. Stephenson was at that time so diffident in manner and unpracticed in speech, that he took with him his friend

Nicholas Wood to act as his interpreter and expositor on the occasion. From eighty to a hundred of the most intelligent mem-

LITERARY AND PHILOSOPHICAL INSTITUTE, NEWCASTLE.

bers of the society were present at the meeting, when Mr. Wood stood forward to expound the principles on which the lamp had been formed, and to describe the details of its construction. Several questions were put, to which Mr. Wood proceeded to give replies to the best of his knowledge. But Stephenson, who up to that time had stood behind Wood, screened from notice, observing that the explanations given were not quite correct, could no longer control himself, and, standing forward, he proceeded in his strong Northumbrian dialect to describe the lamp down to its minutest details. He then produced several bladders full of carbureted hydrogen, which he had collected from the blowers in the Killingworth mine, and proved the safety of his lamp by numerous experiments with the gas, repeated in various ways, his earnest and impressive manner exciting in the minds of his auditors the liveliest interest both in the inventor and his invention.

Shortly after, Sir H. Davy's model lamp was received and exhibited to the coal-miners at Newcastle, on which occasion the observation was made by several gentlemen, "Why, it is the same as Stephenson's!"

Notwithstanding Stephenson's claim to be regarded as the first inventor of the Tube Safety-lamp, his merits do not seem to have been generally recognized. Sir Humphry Davy carried off the larger share of the *éclat* which attached to the discovery. What chance had the unknown workman of Killingworth with so distinguished a competitor? The one was as yet but a colliery engine-wright, scarce raised above the manual-labor class, without chemical knowledge or literary culture, pursuing his experiments in obscurity, with a view only to usefulness; the other was the scientific prodigy of his day, the pet of the Royal Society, the favorite of princes, the most brilliant of lecturers, and the most popular of philosophers.

No small indignation was expressed by the friends of Sir Humphry Davy at Stephenson's "presumption" in laying claim to the invention of the Safety-lamp. The scientific class united to ignore him entirely in the matter. In 1831, Dr. Paris, in his "Life of Sir Humphry Davy," thus wrote: "It will hereafter be scarcely believed that an invention so eminently scientific, and which could never have been derived but from the sterling treasury of science, should have been claimed on behalf of an engine-wright of Killingworth, of the name of Stephenson—a person not even possessing a knowledge of the elements of chemistry."

But Stephenson was really far above claiming for himself an invention not his own. He had already accomplished a far greater thing even than the making of a safety-lamp: he had constructed a successful locomotive, which was to be seen in daily work on the Killingworth Railway. By the improvements he had made in the engine, he might almost be said to have *invented* it; yet no one—not even the philosophers—detected as yet the significance of that wonderful machine. It excited no scientific interest, called forth no leading articles in the newspapers or the reviews, and formed the subject of no eloquent lectures at the Royal Society; for railways were as yet comparatively unknown, and the might which slumbered in the locomotive was scarcely, as yet, even dreamed of. What railways were to become rested in a great measure with that "engine-wright of Killingworth, of the name of Stephenson," though he was scarcely known as yet beyond the bounds of his own district.

As to the value of the invention of the safety-lamp there could be no doubt, and the colliery owners of Durham and Northumberland, to testify their sense of its importance, determined to present a testimonial to its inventor. The friends of Sir H. Davy met in August, 1816, to take steps to raise a subscription for the purpose. The advertised object of the meeting was to present him with a reward for the invention of *his* safety-lamp." To this no objection could be taken; for, though the principle on which the safety-lamps of Stephenson and Davy were constructed was the same, and although Stephenson's lamp was unquestionably the first successful lamp that had been constructed on such principle, and proved to be efficient, yet Sir H. Davy did invent a safety-lamp, no doubt quite independently of all that Stephenson had done; and having directed his careful attention to the subject, and elucidated the true theory of explosion of carbureted hydrogen, he was entitled to all praise and reward for his labor. But when the meeting of coal-owners proposed to raise a subscription for the purpose of presenting Sir H. Davy with a reward for "his invention of *the* safety-lamp," the case was entirely altered, and Stephenson's friends then proceeded to assert his claims to be regarded as its first inventor.

Many meetings took place on the subject, and much discussion ensued, the result of which was that a sum of £2000 was presented to Sir Humphry Davy as "the inventor of the safety-lamp;" but, at the same time, a purse of 100 guineas was voted to George Stephenson, in consideration of what he had done in the same direction. This result was, however, very unsatisfactory to Stephenson, as well as to his friends; and Mr. Brandling, of Gosforth, suggested to him that, the subject being now fairly before the public, he should publish a statement of the facts on which his claim was founded.

But this was not at all in George Stephenson's line. He had never appeared in print before, and it seemed to him a far more formidable thing to write a letter for publication in "the papers" than even to invent a safety-lamp or design a locomotive. Having called his son Robert to his assistance, he set him down before a sheet of foolscap, and when all was ready, he said, "Now, put down there just what I tell you." The composition of this letter, as we were informed by the writer of it, occupied more evenings than one; and when it was at length finished after many corrections, and fairly copied out, the father and son set out — the latter dressed in his Sunday's round jacket — to lay the joint production before Mr. Brandling, at Gosforth House. Glancing over the letter, Mr. Brandling said, "George, this will never do." "It is all true, sir," was the reply. "That may be; but it is badly written." Robert blushed, for he thought it was the penmanship that was called in question, and he had written his very best. Mr. Brandling then requested his visitors to sit down while he put the letter in a more polished form, which he did, and it was shortly after published in the local papers.

As the controversy continued for some time longer to be carried on in the Newcastle papers, Mr. Stephenson, in the year 1817, consented to publish the detailed plans, with descriptions, of the several safety-lamps which he had contrived for use in the Killingworth Colliery. The whole forms a pamphlet of only sixteen pages of letter-press.*

His friends, being fully satisfied of his claims to priority as the inventor of the safety-lamp used in the Killingworth and other collieries, proceeded to hold a public meeting for the purpose of presenting him with a reward "for the valuable service he had thus rendered to mankind." Charles J. Brandling, Esq., occupied the chair; and several resolutions were passed, of which the first and most important was as follows: "That it is the opinion of this meeting that Mr. George Stephenson, having *discovered the fact* that explosion of hydrogen gas will not pass through tubes and apertures of small dimensions, and having been *the first to apply that principle in the construction of a safety-lamp*, is entitled to a public reward."

A subscription was immediately commenced with this object, and a committee was formed, consisting of the Earl of Strathmore, C. J. Brandling, and others. The subscription list was headed by Lord Ravensworth, one of the partners in the Killingworth Colliery, who showed his appreciation of the merits of Stephenson by giving 100 guineas. C. J. Brandling and partners gave a like sum, and Matthew Bell and partners, and John Brandling and partners, gave 50 guineas each.

* "A Description of the Safety-lamp, invented by George Stephenson, and now in use in the Killingworth Colliery." London, 1817.

When the resolutions appeared in the newspapers, the scientific friends of Sir Humphry Davy in London met, and passed a series of counter-resolutions, which they published, declaring their opinion that Mr. Stephenson was *not* the author of the discovery of the fact that explosion of hydrogen will not pass through tubes and apertures of small dimensions, and that he was *not* the first to apply that principle to the construction of a safety-lamp. To these counter-resolutions were attached the well-known names of Sir Joseph Banks, P.R.S., William Thomas Brande, Charles Hatchett, W. H. Wollaston, and Thomas Young.

Mr. Stephenson's friends then, to make assurance doubly sure, and with a view to set the question at rest, determined to take evidence in detail as to the date of discovery by George Stephenson of the fact in question, and its practical application by him in the formation and actual trial of his safety-lamp. The witnesses examined were George Stephenson himself, Mr. Nicholas Wood, and John Moodie, who had been present at the first trial of the lamp; the several tinmen who made the lamps; the secretary and other members of the Literary and Philosophical Society of Newcastle, who were present at the exhibition of the third lamp; and some of the workmen who were present at the Killingworth Colliery, who had been witnesses of Stephenson's experiments on fire-damp made with the lamps at different times before Sir Humphry Davy's investigations had been heard of. This evidence was quite conclusive to the minds of the gentlemen who investigated the subject, and they published it in 1817, together with their Report, in which they declared that, "after a careful inquiry into the merits of the case, conducted, as they trust, in a spirit of fairness and moderation, they can perceive no satisfactory reason for changing their opinion."*

* The committee, in their report, after setting forth in a tabular form the dates at which Stephenson and Davy verified their theories by experiments, and brought out their respective safety-lamps, proceeded to say: "The friends of Mr. Stephenson, with this table before them, conceive their resolution to be fully borne out by the testimony of dates and facts, so far as they are known; and without the slightest idea or wish of detracting from the scientific fame, honor, or veracity of Sir Humphry Davy, they would repeat, and confine themselves to the simple assertion of their belief, that Mr. Stephenson was the first to construct a lamp upon the principle in question. And when the friends of Mr. Stephenson remember the humble and laborious station of life which he has occupied; when they consider the scanty means and opportunities which he has had for pursuing researches in practical science, and look to

The Stephenson subscription, when collected, amounted to £1000. Part of the money was devoted to the purchase of a silver tankard, which was presented to the inventor, together with the balance of the subscription, at a public dinner given in the Assembly Rooms at Newcastle.* But what gave Stephenson even greater pleasure than the silver tankard and purse of sovereigns was the gift of a silver watch, purchased by small subscriptions collected among the colliers themselves, and presented to him by them as a token of their esteem and regard for him as a man, as well as of their gratitude for the perseverance and skill with which he had prosecuted his valuable and life-saving invention to a successful issue. To the last day of his life he spoke with pride of this watch as the most highly-prized gift he had ever received.

However great may be the merits of Stephenson in connection with the invention of the tube safety-lamp, they can not be regarded as detracting in any degree from the reputation of Sir Humphry Davy. His inquiries into the explosive properties of carbureted hydrogen gas were quite original, and his discovery of the fact that explosion will not pass through tubes of a certain diameter was made independently of all that Stephenson had done in verification of the same fact. It would even appear that Mr. Smithson Tennant and Dr. Wollaston had observed the same fact several years before, though neither Stephenson nor Davy knew of it while they were prosecuting their experiments. Sir Humphry Davy's subsequent modification of the tube-lamp, by which, while diminishing the diameter, he in the same ratio shortened the tubes without danger, and in the form of wire-

the improvements and discoveries which, notwithstanding so many disadvantages, he has been enabled to make by the judicious and unremitting exercise of the energy and acuteness of his natural understanding, they can not persuade themselves that they have said any thing more than any liberal and feeling mind would most readily admit."

* The tankard bore the following inscription: "This piece of plate, purchased with a part of the sum of £1000, a subscription raised for the remuneration of Mr. GEORGE STEPHENSON for having discovered the fact that inflamed fire-damp will not pass through tubes and apertures of small dimensions, and having been *the first* to apply that principle in the construction of a safety-lamp calculated for the preservation of human life in situations formerly of the greatest danger, was presented to him at a meeting of the subscribers, Charles John Brandling, Esq., in the chair, January 12th, 1818."

gauze enveloped the safety-lamp by a multiplicity of tubes, was a beautiful application of the true theory which he had formed upon the subject.

The increased number of accidents which have occurred from explosions in coal-mines since the general introduction of the Davy lamp led to considerable doubts being entertained as to its safety, and inquiries were consequently made as to the means by which it might be farther improved; for experience has shown that, under certain circumstances, the Davy lamp is *not* safe. Stephenson was himself of opinion that the modification of his own and Sir Humphry Davy's lamp, by combining the glass cylinder with the wire-gauze, would give the best lamp. At the same time, it must be admitted that the Davy and the Geordy lamps alike failed to stand the severe tests to which they were submitted by Dr. Pereira, before the Committee on Accidents in Mines. Indeed, Dr. Pereira did not hesitate to say that, when exposed to a current of explosive gas, the Davy lamp is "decidedly unsafe," and that the experiments by which its safety had been "demonstrated" in the lecture-room had proved entirely "fallacious."

It is worthy of remark that, under circumstances in which the wire-gauze of the Davy lamp becomes red-hot from the high explosiveness of the gas, the Geordy lamp is extinguished; and we can not but think that this fact testifies to the decidedly superior safety of the Geordy. An accident occurred in the Oaks Colliery Pit at Barnsley on the 20th of August, 1857, which strikingly exemplified the respective qualities of the lamps. A sudden outburst of gas took place from the floor of the mine along a distance of fifty yards. Fortunately, the men working in the pit at the time were all supplied with safety-lamps—the hewers with Stephenson's, and the hurriers with Davy's. On this occasion, the whole of the Stephenson lamps, over a space of five hundred yards, were extinguished almost instantaneously; whereas the Davy lamps were filled with fire and became red-hot, so that several of the men using them had their hands burnt by the gauze. Had a strong current of air been blowing through the gallery at the time, an explosion would most probably have taken place—an accident which, it will be observed, could not, under such circumstances, occur from the use of the Geordy, which is immediately extinguished as soon as the air becomes explosive.*

Nicholas Wood, a good judge, has said of the two inventions, "Priority has been claimed for each of them—I believe the inventions to be parallel. By different roads they both arrived at the same result. Stephenson's is the superior lamp. Davy's is safe—Stephenson's is safer."

When the question of priority was under discussion at Mr. Lough's studio in 1857, Sir Matthew White Ridley asked Robert Stephenson, who was present, for his opinion on the subject. His answer was, "I am not exactly the person to give an unbiased

* The accident above referred to was described in the "Barnsley Times," a copy of which, containing the account, Robert Stephenson forwarded to the author, with the observation that "it is evidently written by a practical miner, and is, I think, worthy of record in my father's Life." Mr. John Browne, C.E., Barnsley, in a communication which appeared in the "Times" of December 24th, 1860, observed:

"At the period of this occurrence we had two kinds of safety-lamps in use in this pit, viz., 'Davy' and 'Stephenson,' and the gas, in going off to the upcast shaft, had to pass great numbers of men, who were at work with both kinds of lamps. The whole of the 'Davy's' became red-hot almost instantaneously from the rapid ignition of the gas within the gauze; the 'Stephenson's' were as instantly self-extinguished from the same cause, it being the prominent qualification of these lamps that, in addition to affording a somewhat better light than the 'Davy' lamp, they are suddenly extinguished when placed within a highly explosive atmosphere, so that no person can remain working and run the risk of his lamp becoming red-hot, which, under such circumstances, would be the result with the 'Davy' lamp.

"The red-hot lamps were, most fortunately, all safely put out, although the men in many cases had their hands severely burnt by the gauze; but from that time I fully resolved to adopt the exclusive use of the 'Stephenson' lamps, and not expose men to the fearful risk they must run from working with 'Davy' lamps during the probable recurrence of a similar event.

"I may remark that the 'Stephenson' lamp, originally invented by the great George Stephenson, in its present shape combines the merits of his discovery with that of Sir Humphry Davy, constituting, to my mind, the safest lamp at present known, and I speak from the long use of many hundreds daily in various collieries."

In an account given in the "Times" of the 10th of August, 1867, of a number of experiments made upon different safety-lamps at the Barnsley Gas-works, occasioned by the terrible explosion at the Lund Hill Colliery, it is stated that the different lamps were tested with the following results: "The 'Davy' lamp with no shield on the outside exploded the gas in six seconds, and with the shield inside the gauze in nine seconds. The 'Belgian' lamp exploded in ten seconds; the 'Mozard' in ten seconds; the small 'Clanny' in seven seconds, the large one in ten seconds; and the 'Stephenson' in seventy-five seconds. Although the 'Stephenson' is undoubtedly the best, it will be seen that none of the so-called safety-lamps can be depended upon when coming in contact with a *strong explosive current* of fire-damp and air."

opinion; but, as you ask me frankly, I will as frankly say, that if George Stephenson had never lived, Sir Humphry Davy could and most probably would have invented the safety-lamp; but again, if Sir Humphry Davy had never lived, George Stephenson certainly would have invented the safety-lamp, as I believe he did, independently of all that Sir Humphry Davy had done in the matter."

To this day the Geordy lamp continues in regular use in the Killingworth Collieries, and the Killingworth pitmen have expressed to the writer their decided preference for it compared with the Davy. It is certainly a strong testimony in its favor that no accident is known to have arisen from its use since it was generally introduced into the Killingworth pits.

THE STEPHENSON TANKARD.

CHAPTER VII.

GEORGE STEPHENSON'S FARTHER IMPROVEMENTS IN THE LOCOMOTIVE —THE HETTON RAILWAY—ROBERT STEPHENSON AS VIEWER'S APPRENTICE AND STUDENT.

STEPHENSON'S experiments on fire-damp, and his labors in connection with the invention of the safety-lamp, occupied but a small portion of his time, which was necessarily devoted, for the most part, to the ordinary business of the colliery. From the day of his appointment as engine-wright, one of the subjects which particularly occupied his attention was the best practical method of winning and raising the coal. Nicholas Wood has said of him that he was one of the first to introduce steam machinery underground with that object. Indeed, the Killingworth mines came to be regarded as the models of the district; and when Mr. Robert Bald, the celebrated Scotch mining engineer, was requested by Dr. (afterward Sir David) Brewster to prepare the article "Mine" for the "Edinburg Encyclopædia," he proceeded to Killingworth principally for the purpose of examining Stephenson's underground machinery. Mr. Bald has favored us with an account of his visit made with that object in 1818, and he states that he was much struck with the novelty, as well as the remarkable efficiency of Stephenson's arrangements, especially in regard to what is called the underdip working.

"I found," he says, "that a mine had been commenced near the main pit-bottom, and carried forward down the dip or slope of the coal, the rate of dip being about one in twelve; and the coals were drawn from the dip to the pit-bottom by the steam machinery in a very rapid manner. The water which oozed from the upper winning was disposed of at the pit-bottom in a barrel or trunk, and was drawn up by the power of the engine which worked the other machinery. The dip at the time of my visit was nearly a mile in length, but has since been greatly extended. As I was considerably tired by my wanderings in the galleries, when I arrived at the forehead of the dip, Mr. Stephenson said to me, 'You may very speedily be carried up to the rise by laying yourself flat upon the coal-baskets,' which were laden and ready to be taken up the incline. This I at once did, and was straightway wafted on the wings of fire to the bottom of the pit, from whence I was borne swiftly up to the light by the steam machinery on the pit-head."

The whole of the working arrangements seemed to Mr. Bald to be conducted in the most skillful and efficient manner, reflecting the highest credit on the colliery engineer.

Besides attending to the underground arrangements, the improved transit of the coals above ground from the pit-head to the shipping-place demanded an increasing share of Stephenson's attention. Every day's experience convinced him that the locomotive constructed by him after his patent of the year 1815 was far from perfect, though he continued to entertain confident hopes of its complete eventual success. He even went so far as to say that the locomotive would yet supersede every other traction-power for drawing heavy loads. It is true, many persons continued to regard his traveling engine as little better than a dangerous curiosity; and some, shaking their heads, predicted for it "a terrible blow-up some day." Nevertheless, it was daily performing its work with regularity, dragging the coal-wagons between the colliery and the staiths, and saving the labor of many men and horses.

There was not, however, so marked a saving in the expense of haulage as to induce the colliery masters to adopt locomotive power generally as a substitute for horses. How it could be improved, and rendered more efficient as well as economical, was constantly present to Stephenson's mind. He was fully conscious of the imperfections both in the road and the engine, and gave himself no rest until he had brought the efficiency of both up to a higher point. Thus he worked his way inch by inch, slowly but surely, and every step gained was made good as a basis for farther improvements.

At an early period of his labors, or about the time when he had completed his second locomotive, he began to direct his particular attention to the state of the Road, perceiving that the extended use of the locomotive must necessarily depend in a great measure upon the perfection, solidity, continuity, and smoothness of the way along which the engine traveled. Even at that early period he was in the habit of regarding the road and the locomotive as one machine, speaking of the Rail and the Wheel as "Man and Wife."

All railways were at that time laid in a careless and loose manner, and great inequalities of level were allowed to occur without much attention being paid to repairs. The consequence was a great loss of power, as well as much wear and tear of the machinery, by the frequent jolts and blows of the wheels against the rails. Stephenson's first object, therefore, was to remove the inequalities produced by the imperfect junction between rail and rail.

At that time (1816) the rails were made of cast iron, each rail being about three feet long; and sufficient care was not taken to maintain the points of junction on the same level. The chairs, or cast-iron pedestals into which the rails were inserted, were flat at the bottom, so that whenever any disturbance took place in the stone blocks or sleepers supporting them, the flat base of the chair upon which the rails rested being tilted by unequal subsidence, the end of one rail became depressed, while that of the other was elevated. Hence constant jolts and shocks, the reaction of which very often caused the fracture of the rails, and occasionally threw the engine off the road.

To remedy this imperfection, Mr. Stephenson devised a new chair, with an entirely new mode of fixing the rails therein. Instead of adopting the *butt-joint* which had hitherto been used in all cast-iron rails, he adopted the *half-lap joint*, by which means the rails extended a certain distance over each other at the ends like a scarf-joint. These ends, instead of resting on the flat chair, were made to rest upon the apex of a curve forming the bottom of the chair. The supports were also extended from three feet to three feet nine inches or four feet apart. These rails were accordingly substituted for the old cast-iron plates on the Killingworth Colliery Railway, and they were found to be a very great improvement on the previous system,

HALF-LAP JOINT.

adding both to the efficiency of the horse-power (still used on the railway) and to the smooth action of the locomotive engine, but more particularly increasing the efficiency of the latter.

This improved form of the rail and chair was embodied in a patent taken out in the joint names of Mr. Losh, of Newcastle, iron founder, and of Mr. Stephenson, bearing date the 30th of September, 1816. Mr. Losh being a wealthy, enterprising iron-manufacturer, and having confidence in George Stephenson and his improvements, found the money for the purpose of taking out the patent, which in those days was a very costly as well as troublesome affair. At the same time, Mr. Losh guaranteed Stephenson a salary of £100 per annum, with a share in the profits arising from his inventions, conditional on his attending at the Walker Iron-works two days a week—an arrangement to which the owners of the Killingworth Colliery cheerfully gave their sanction.

The specification of 1816 included various important improvements in the locomotive itself. The wheels of the engine were improved, being altered from cast to malleable iron, in whole or in part, by which they were made lighter as well as more durable and safe. The patent also included the ingenious and original

OLD KILLINGWORTH LOCOMOTIVE STILL IN USE.

contrivance by which the steam generated in the boiler was made to serve as a substitute for springs—an expedient already explained in a preceding chapter.

The result of the actual working of the new locomotive on the improved road amply justified the promises held forth in the specification. The traffic was conducted with greater regularity and economy, and the superiority of the engine, as compared with horse traction, became still more marked. And it is a fact worthy of notice, that the identical engines constructed by Stephenson in 1816 are to this day in regular useful work upon the Killingworth Railway, conveying heavy coal-trains at the speed of between five and six miles an hour, probably as economically as any of the more perfect locomotives now in use.

George Stephenson's endeavors having been attended with such marked success in the adaptation of locomotive power to railways, his attention was called by many of his friends, about the year 1818, to the application of steam to traveling on common roads. It was from this point, indeed, that the locomotive had started, Trevithick's first engine having been constructed with this special object. Stephenson's friends having observed how far behind he had left the original projector of the locomotive in its application to railroads, perhaps naturally inferred that he would be equally successful in applying it to the purpose for which Trevithick and Vivian had intended their first engine. But the accuracy with which he estimated the resistance to which loads were exposed on railways, arising from friction and gravity, led him at a very early stage to reject the idea of ever applying steam-power economically to common road traveling. In October, 1818, he made a series of careful experiments, in conjunction with Mr. Nicholas Wood, on the resistance to which carriages were exposed on railways, testing the results by means of a dynamometer of his own contrivance. The series of practical observations made by means of this instrument were interesting, as the first systematic attempt to determine the precise amount of resistance to carriages moving along railways. It was then for the first time ascertained by experiment that the friction was a constant quantity at all velocities. Although this theory had long before been developed by Vince and Coulomb, and was well known to scientific men as an established truth, yet, at the time when Stephenson made his experiments, the deductions of philosophers on the subject were neither believed in nor acted upon by practical engineers. To quote again from the MS. account supplied to the author by Robert Stephenson for the purposes of his father's "Life:"

"It was maintained by many that the results of the experiments led to the greatest possible mechanical absurdities. For instance, it was maintained that, if friction were constant at all velocities upon a level railway, when once a power was applied to a carriage which exceeded the friction of that carriage by the smallest possible amount, that same small excess of power would be able to convey the carriage along a level railway at all conceivable velocities. When this position was put by those who opposed the conclusions at which my father had arrived, he felt great hesitation in maintaining his own views; for it appeared to him at first sight really to be—as it was put by his opponents—an absurdity. Frequent repetition, however, of the experiments to which I have alluded, left no doubt upon his mind that his conclusion that friction was uniform at all velocities was a fact which must be received as positively established; and he soon afterward boldly maintained that that which was an apparent absurdity was, instead, a necessary consequence. I well remember the ridicule that was thrown upon this view by many of those persons with whom he was associated at the time. Nevertheless, it is undoubted, that, could you practically be always applying a power in excess of the resistance, a constant increase of velocity would of necessity follow without any limit. This is so obvious to most professional men of the present day, and is now so axiomatic, that I only allude to the discussion which took place when these experiments of my father were announced for the purpose of showing how small was the amount of science at that time blended with engineering practice. A few years afterward, an excellent pamphlet was published by Mr. Silvester on this question; he took up the whole subject, and demonstrated in a very simple and beautiful manner the correctness of all the views at which my father had arrived by his course of experiments.

"The other resistances to which carriages were exposed were also investigated experimentally by my father. He perceived that these resistances were mainly three—the first being upon the axles of the carriage; the second, which may be called the rolling resistance, being between the circumference of the wheel and the surface of the rail; and the third being the resistance of gravity.

"The amount of friction and gravity he accurately ascertained; but the rolling resistance was a matter of greater difficulty, for it was subject to great variation. He, however, satisfied himself that it was so great, when the surface presented to the wheel was of a rough character, that the idea of working steam-carriages economically on common roads was out of the question. Even so early as the period alluded to he brought his theoretical calculations to a practical test; he scattered sand upon the rails when an engine was running, and found that a small quantity was quite sufficient to retard and even stop the most powerful locomotive engine that he had at that time made. And he never failed to urge this conclusive experiment upon the attention of those who were wasting their money and time upon the vain attempt to apply steam to common roads.

"The following were the principal arguments which influenced his mind to work out the use of the locomotive in a directly opposite course to that pursued by a number of ingenious inventors, who, between 1820 and 1836, were engaged in attempting to apply steam-power to turnpike roads. Having ascertained that resistance might be taken as represented by 10 lbs. to a ton weight on a level railway, it became obvious to him that so small a rise as 1 in 100 would diminish the useful effort of a locomotive by upward of fifty per cent. This fact called my father's attention to the question of gradients in future locomotive lines. He then became convinced of the vital importance, in an economical point of view, of reducing the country through which a railway was intended to pass to as near a level as possible. This originated in his mind the distinctive character of railway works as contradistinguished from all other roads; for in railroads he early contended that large sums would be wisely expended in perforating barriers of hills with long tunnels, and in raising low ground with the excess cut down from the adjacent high ground. In proportion as these views fixed themselves upon his mind, and were corroborated by his daily experience, he became more and more convinced of the hopelessness of applying steam locomotion to common roads; for every argument in favor of a level railway was an argument against the rough and hilly course of a common road. He never ceased to urge upon the patrons of road steam-carriages that if, by any amount of ingenuity, an engine could be made which could by possibility traverse a turnpike road at a speed at least equal to that obtainable by horse-power, and at a less cost, such an engine, if applied to the more perfect surface of a railway, would have its efficiency enormously enhanced. For instance, he calculated that if an engine had been constructed, and had been found to travel uniformly between London and Birmingham at an average speed of 10 miles an hour—conveying, say, 20 or 30 passengers at a cost of 1*s.* per mile, it was clear that the same engine, if applied to a railway, instead of conveying 20 or 30 people, would have conveyed 200 or 300 people, and instead of a speed of 10 or 12 miles an hour, a speed of at least 30 to 40 miles an hour would have been obtained."

At this day it is difficult to understand how the sagacious and strong common-sense views of Stephenson on this subject failed to force themselves sooner upon the minds of those who were persisting in their vain though ingenious attempts to apply locomotive power to ordinary roads. For a long time they continued to hold with obstinate perseverance to the belief that for such purposes a soft road was better than a hard one—a road easily crushed better than one incapable of being crushed; and they held to this after it had been demonstrated in all parts of the mining districts that iron tram-ways were better than paved roads. But the fallacy that iron was incapable of adhesion upon iron continued to prevail, and the projectors of steam-traveling on common roads only shared in the common belief. They still considered that roughness of surface was essential to produce "bite," especially in surmounting acclivities; the truth being that they confounded roughness of surface with tenacity of surface and contact of parts, not perceiving that a yielding surface which would adapt itself to the tread of the wheel could never become an unyielding surface to form a fulcrum for its progression.

Although Stephenson's locomotive engines were in daily use for many years on the Killingworth Railway, they excited comparatively little interest. They were no longer experimental, but had become an established tractive power. The experience of years had proved that they worked more steadily, drew heavier loads, and were, on the whole, considerably more economical than horses. Nevertheless, eight years passed before another locomotive railway was constructed and opened for the purposes of coal or other traffic.

It is difficult to account for this early indifference on the part of the public to the merits of the greatest mechanical invention of the age. Steam-carriages were exciting much interest, and numerous and repeated experiments were made with them. The improvements effected by M'Adam in the mode of constructing turnpike roads were the subject of frequent discussions in the Legislature, on the grants of public money being proposed, which were from time to time made to him. Yet here at Killingworth, without the aid of a farthing of government money, a system of road locomotion had been in existence since 1814, which was destined, before many years, to revolutionize the internal communications of England and of the world, but of which the English public and the English government as yet knew nothing.

But Stephenson had no means of bringing his important invention prominently under the notice of the public. He himself knew well its importance, and he already anticipated its eventual general adoption; but, being an unlettered man, he could not give utterance to the thoughts which brooded within him on the subject. Killingworth Colliery lay far from London, the centre of scientific life in England. It was visited by no savans nor literary men, who might have succeeded in introducing to notice the wonderful machine of Stephenson. Even the local chroniclers seem to have taken no notice of the Killingworth Railway. The "Puffing Billy" was doing its daily quota of hard work, and had long ceased to be a curiosity in the neighborhood. Blenkinsop's clumsier and less successful engine—which has long since been disused, while Stephenson's Killingworth engines continue working to this day—excited far more interest, partly, perhaps, because it was close to the large town of Leeds, and used to be visited by strangers as one of the few objects of interest in that place. Blenkinsop was also an educated man, and was in communication with some of the most distinguished personages of his day on the subject of his locomotive, which thus obtained considerable celebrity.

The first engine constructed by Stephenson to order, after the Killingworth model, was made for the Duke of Portland in 1817, for use upon his tram-road, about ten miles long, extending from Kilmarnock to Troon, in Ayrshire. It was employed to haul the coals from the duke's collieries along the line to Troon harbor. Its use was, however, discontinued in consequence of the frequent breakages of the cast-iron rails, by which the working of the line was interrupted, and accordingly horses were again employed as before.*

There seemed, indeed, to be so small a prospect of introducing the locomotive into general use, that Stephenson—perhaps conscious of the capabilities within him—again recurred to his old idea of emigrating to the United States. Before entering as sleeping partner in a small foundery at Forth Banks, Newcastle, managed by Mr. John Burrell, he had thrown out the suggestion to the latter that it would be a good speculation for them to emigrate to North America, and introduce steam-boats on the great inland lakes there. The first steamers were then plying upon the Tyne before his eyes, and he saw in them the germ of a great revolution in navigation. It occurred to him that the great lakes of North America presented the finest field for trying their wonderful powers. He was an engineer, and Mr. Burrell was an iron-founder; and between them, he thought they might strike out a path to fortune in the mighty West. Fortunately, this idea remained a mere speculation so far as Stephenson was concerned, and it was left to others to do what he had dreamed of achieving. After all his patient waiting, his skill, industry, and perseverance were at length about to bear fruit.

In 1819, the owners of the Hetton Colliery, in the county of Durham, determined to have their wagon-way altered to a locomotive railroad. The result of the working of the Killingworth Railway had been so satisfactory that they resolved to adopt the same system. One reason why an experiment so long continued and so successful as that at Killingworth should have been so slow in producing results perhaps was, that to lay down a railway and furnish it with locomotives, or fixed engines where necessary, required a very large capital, beyond the means of ordinary coal-owners; while the small amount of interest felt in railways by the general public, and the supposed impracticability of working them to a profit, as yet prevented the ordinary capitalists from venturing their money in the promotion of such undertakings. The Hetton Coal Company were, however, possessed of

* The iron wheels of this engine were afterward removed, and replaced with wooden wheels, when it was again put upon the road, and continued working until quite recently. Its original cost was £750. It was sold in 1848 for £13, and broken up as old materials.

adequate means, and the local reputation of the Killingworth engine-wright pointed him out as the man best calculated to lay out their line and superintend their works. They accordingly invited him to act as the engineer of the proposed railway. Being in the service of the Killingworth Company, Stephenson felt it necessary to obtain their permission to enter upon this new work. This was at once granted. The best feeling existed between him and his employers, and they regarded it as a compliment that their colliery engineer should be selected for a work so important as the laying down of the Hetton Railway, which was to be the longest locomotive line that had, up to that time, been constructed in the neighborhood. Stephenson accepted the appointment, his brother Robert acting as resident engineer and personally superintending the execution of the works.

The Hetton Railway extended from the Hetton Colliery, situated about two miles south of Houghton-le-Spring, to the shipplaces on the banks of the Wear, near Sunderland. Its length was about eight miles; and in its course it crossed Warden Law, one of the highest hills in the district. The character of the country forbade the construction of a flat line, or one of compararatively easy gradients, except by the expenditure of a much larger capital than was placed at Stephenson's command. Heavy works could not be executed; it was therefore necessary to form the line with but little deviation from the natural conformation of the district which it traversed, and also to adapt the mechanical methods employed for its working to the character of the gradients, which in some places were necessarily heavy.

Although George Stephenson had, with every step made toward its increased utility, become more and more identified with the success of the locomotive engine, he did not allow his enthusiasm to carry him away into costly mistakes. He carefully drew the line between the cases in which the locomotive could be usefully employed and those in which stationary engines were calculated to be more economical. This led him, as in the instance of the Hetton Railway, to execute lines through and over rough countries, where gradients within the powers of the locomotive engine of that day could not be secured, employing in their stead stationary engines where locomotives were not practicable. In the present case, this course was adopted by him most successfully. On the original Hetton line there were five self-acting inclines—the full wagons drawing the empty ones up—and two inclines worked by fixed reciprocating engines of sixty-horse power each. The locomotive traveling engine, or "the iron horse," as the people of the neighborhood then styled it, worked the rest of the line. On the day of the opening of the Hetton Railway, the 18th of November, 1822, crowds of spectators assembled from all parts to witness the first operations of this ingenious and powerful machinery, which was entirely successful. On that day five of Stephenson's locomotives were at work upon the railway, under the direction of his brother Robert; and the first shipment of coal was then made by the Hetton Company at their new staiths on the Wear. The speed at which the locomotives traveled was about four miles an hour, and each engine dragged after it a train of seventeen wagons weighing about sixty-four tons.

While thus advancing step by step—attending to the business of the Killingworth Colliery, and laying out railways in the neighborhood—he was carefully watching over the education of his son. We have already seen that Robert was sent to school at Newcastle, where he remained about four years. While Robert was at school, his father, as usual, made his son's education instrumental to his own. He entered him a member of the Newcastle Literary and Philosophical Institute, the subscription to which was three guineas a year. Robert spent much of his leisure hours there, reading and studying; and when he went home in the afternoons, he was accustomed to carry home with him a volume of the "Repertory of Arts and Sciences," or of some work on practical science, which furnished the subject of interesting reading and discussion in the evening hours. Both father and son were always ready to acknowledge the great advantages they had derived from the use of so excellent a library of books; and, toward the close of his life, the latter, in recognition of his debt of gratitude to the institution, contributed a large sum for the purpose of clearing off the debt, but conditional on the annual subscription being reduced to a guinea, in order that the usefulness of the Institute might be extended.

Robert left school in the summer of 1819, and was put apprentice to Mr. Nicholas Wood, the head viewer at Killingworth, to learn the business of the colliery. He served in that capacity for about three years, during which time he became familiar with most departments of underground work. His occupation was not unattended with peril, as the following incident will show. Though the use of the Geordy lamp had become general in the Killingworth pits, and the workmen were bound, under a penalty of half a crown, not to use a naked candle, it was difficult to enforce the rule, and even the masters themselves occasionally broke it. One day Nicholas Wood, the head viewer, Moodie, the under viewer, and Robert Stephenson, were proceeding along one of the galleries, Wood with a naked candle in his hand, and Robert following him with a lamp. They came to a place where a fall of stones from the roof had taken place, on which Wood, who was first, proceeded to clamber over the stones, holding high the naked candle. He had nearly reached the summit of the heap, when the fire-damp, which had accumulated in the hollow of the roof, exploded, and instantly the whole party were blown down, and the lights extinguished. They were a mile from the shaft, and quite in the dark. There was a rush of the work-people from all quarters toward the shaft, for it was feared that the fire might extend to more dangerous parts of the pit, where, if the gas had exploded, every soul in the mine must inevitably have perished. Robert Stephenson and Moodie, on the first impulse, ran back at full speed along the dark gallery leading to the shaft, coming into collision, on their way, with the hind quarters of a horse stunned by the explosion. When they had gone half way, Moodie halted, and bethought him of Nicholas Wood. "Stop, laddie!" said he to Robert, "stop; we maun gang back and seek the maister." So they retraced their steps. Happily, no farther explosion took place. They found the master lying on the heap of stones, stunned and bruised, with his hands severely burnt. They led him to the bottom of the shaft; and he afterward took care not to venture into the dangerous parts of the mine without the protection of a Geordy lamp.

The time that Robert spent at Killingworth as viewer's apprentice was of advantage both to his father and himself. The evenings were generally devoted to reading and study, the two from this time working together as friends and co-laborers. One who used to drop in at the cottage of an evening well remembers the animated and eager discussions which on some occasions took place, more especially with reference to the growing powers of the locomotive engine. The son was even more enthusiastic than his father on the subject. Robert would suggest numerous alterations and improvements in detail. His father, on the contrary, would offer every possible objection, defending the existing arrangements—proud, nevertheless, of his son's suggestions, and often warmed and excited by his brilliant anticipations of the ultimate triumph of the locomotive.

These discussions probably had considerable influence in inducing Stephenson to take the next important step in the education of his son. Although Robert, who was only nineteen years of age, was doing well, and was certain, at the expiration of his apprenticeship, to rise to a higher position, his father was not satisfied with the amount of instruction which he had as yet given him. Remembering the disadvantages under which he had himself labored through his ignorance of practical chemistry during his investigations connected with the safety-lamp, more especially with reference to the properties of gas, as well as in the course of his experiments with the object of improving the locomotive engine, he determined to furnish his son with a better scientific culture than he had yet attained. He also believed that a proper training in technical science was indispensable to success in the higher walks of the engineer's profession, and he determined to give Robert the education, in a certain degree, which he so much desired for himself. He would thus, he knew, secure an able coworker in the elaboration of the great ideas now looming before him, and with their united practical and scientific knowledge he probably felt that they would be equal to any enterprise.

He accordingly took Robert from his labors as under viewer in the West Moor Pit, and in October, 1822, sent him for a short course of instruction to the Edinburg University. Robert was furnished with letters of introduction to several men of literary eminence in Edinburg, his father's reputation in connection with the safety-lamp being of service to him in this respect. He lodged in Drummond Street, in the immediate vicinity of the college, and attended the Chemical Lectures of Dr. Hope, the Natural Philosophy Lectures of Sir John Leslie, and the Natural History Class of Professor Jameson. He also devoted several evenings in each week to the study of practical Chemistry under Dr. John

Murray, himself one of the numerous designers of a safety-lamp. He took careful notes of the lectures, which he copied out at night before he went to bed, so that, when he returned to Killingworth, he might read them over to his father. He afterward had the notes bound up and placed in his library.

Long years after, when conversing with Thomas Harrison, C.E., at his house in Gloucester Square, he rose from his seat and took down a volume from the shelves. Mr. Harrison observed that the book was in MS., neatly written out. "What have we here?" he asked. The answer was, "When I went to college, I knew the difficulty my father had in collecting the funds to send me there. Before going I studied short-hand; while at Edinburg I took down verbatim every lecture; and in the evenings, before I went to bed, I transcribed those lectures word for word. You see the result in that range of books." From this it will be observed that the maxim of "Like father, like son," was one that strictly applied to the Stephensons.

Robert was not without the pleasure of social intercourse either during his stay at Edinburg. Among the letters of introduction which he took with him was one to Robert Bald, the mining engineer, which proved of much service to him. "I remember Mr. Bald very well," he said on one occasion, when recounting his reminiscences of his Edinburg college life. "He introduced me to Dr. Hope, Dr. Murray, and several of the distinguished men of the North. Bald was the Buddle of Scotland. He knew my father from having visited the pits at Killingworth, with the object of describing the system of working them in his article intended for the 'Edinburg Encyclopædia.' A strange adventure befell that article before it appeared in print. Bald was living at Alloa when he wrote it, and when finished he sent it to Edinburg by the hands of young Maxton, his nephew, whom he enjoined to take special care of it, and deliver it safely into the hands of the editor. The young man took passage for New Haven by one of the little steamers which then plied on the Forth; but on the voyage down the Frith she struck upon a rock nearly opposite Queen's Ferry, and soon sank. When the accident happened, Maxton's whole concern was about his uncle's article. He durst not return to Alloa if he lost it, and he must not go on to Edinburg without it. So he desperately clung to the chimney chains with the paper parcel under his arm, while most of the other passengers were washed away and drowned. And there he continued to cling until rescued by some boatmen, parcel and all, after which he made his way to Edinburg, and the article duly appeared."

Returning to the subject of his life in Edinburg, Robert continued: "Besides taking me with him to the meetings of the Royal and other societies, Mr. Bald introduced me to a very agreeable family, relatives of his own, at whose house I spent many pleasant evenings. It was there I met Jeannie M——. She was a bonnie lass, and I, being young and susceptible, fairly fell in love with her. But, like most very early attachments, mine proved evanescent. Years passed, and I had all but forgotten Jeannie, when one day I received a letter from her, from which it appeared that she was in great distress through the ruin of her relatives. I sent her a sum of money, and continued to do so for several years; but the last remittance not being acknowledged, I directed my friend Sanderson to make inquiries. I afterward found that the money had reached her at Portobello just as she was dying, and so, poor thing, she had been unable to acknowledge it."

One of the practical sciences in the study of which Robert Stephenson took special interest while at Edinburg was that of geology. The situation of the city, in the midst of a district of highly interesting geological formation, easily accessible to pedestrians, is indeed most favorable to the pursuit of such a study; and it was the practice of Professor Jameson frequently to head a band of his pupils, armed with hammers, chisels, and clinometers, and take them with him on a long ramble into the country, for the purpose of teaching them habits of observation, and reading to them from the open book of Nature itself. The professor was habitually grave and taciturn, but on such occasions he would relax and even become genial. For his own special science he had an almost engrossing enthusiasm, which on such occasions he did not fail to inspire into his pupils, who thus not only got their knowledge in the pleasantest possible way, but also fresh air and exercise in the midst of glorious scenery and in joyous company.

At the close of this session, the professor took with him a select body of his pupils on an excursion along the Great Glen of the Highlands, in the line of the Caledonian Canal, and Robert formed one of the party. They passed under the shadow of Ben Nevis, examined the famous old sea-margins known as the "parallel roads of Glen Roy," and extended their journey as far as Inverness, the professor teaching the young men, as they traveled, how to observe in a mountain country. Not long before his death, Robert Stephenson spoke in glowing terms of the great pleasure and benefit which he had derived from that interesting excursion. "I have traveled far, and enjoyed much," he said, "but that delightful botanical and geological tour I shall never forget; and I am just about to start in the *Titania* for a trip round the east coast of Scotland, returning south through the Caledonian Canal, to refresh myself with the recollection of that first and brightest tour of my life."

Toward the end of the summer the young student returned to Killingworth to re-enter upon the active business of life. The six months' study had cost his father £80—a considerable sum to him in those days; but he was amply repaid by the additional scientific culture which his son had acquired, and the evidence of ability and industry which he was enabled to exhibit in a prize for mathematics which he had won at the University.

WEST MOOR PIT, KILLINGWORTH.

We may here add that by this time George Stephenson, after remaining a widower fourteen years, had married, in 1820, his second wife, Elizabeth Hindmarsh, the daughter of a respectable farmer at Black Callerton. She was a woman of excellent character, sensible, and intelligent, and of a kindly and affectionate nature. George's son Robert, whom she loved as if he had been her own, to the last day of his life spoke of her in the highest terms; and it is unquestionable that she contributed in no small degree to the happiness of her husband's home.

The story was for some time current that, while living at Black Callerton in the capacity of engine-man, twenty years before, George had made love to Miss Hindmarsh, and, failing to obtain her hand, in despair he had married Paterson's servant. But the author has been assured by Mr. Thomas Hindmarsh, of Newcastle, the lady's brother, that the story was mere idle gossip, and altogether without foundation.

CHAPTER VIII.

GEORGE STEPHENSON ENGINEER OF THE STOCKTON AND DARLINGTON RAILWAY.

IT is not improbable that the slow progress made by railways in public estimation was, in a considerable measure, due to the comparative want of success which had attended the first projects. We do not refer to the tram-roads and railroads which connected the collieries and iron-works with the shipping-places. These were found convenient and economical, and their use became general in Durham and Northumberland, in South Wales, in Scotland, and throughout the colliery districts. But none of these were public railways. Though the Merthyr Tydvil Tram-road, the Sirhoway Railroad, and others in South Wales, were constructed under the powers of special acts,* they were exclusively used for the private purposes of the coal-owners and iron-masters at whose expense they were made.

The first *public* Railway Act was that passed in 1801, authorizing the construction of a line from Wandsworth to Croydon, under the name of "The Surrey Iron Railway." By a subsequent act, powers were obtained to extend the line to Reigate, with a branch to Godstone. The object of this railway was to furnish a more ready means for the transport of coal and merchandise from the Thames to the districts of south London, and at the same time to enable the lime-burners and proprietors of stone-quarries to send the lime and stone to London. With this object, the railroad was connected with a dock or basin in Wandsworth Creek capable of containing thirty barges, with an entrance lock into the Thames.

The works had scarcely been commenced ere the company got into difficulties, but eventually 26 miles of iron-way were con-

* The act for constructing the Merthyr Tydvil Tram-road was obtained from Parliament as early as 1794; that for the Sirhoway Railroad in 1801; the Carmarthenshire Railroad was sanctioned in the same year; and the Oystermouth Railway in 1803.

structed and opened for traffic. Any person was then at liberty to put wagons on the line, and to carry goods within the prescribed rates, the wagons being worked by horses, mules, and donkeys. Notwithstanding the very sanguine expectations which were early formed as to the paying qualities of this railway, it never realized any adequate profit to the owners. But it continued to be worked, principally by donkeys for the sake of cheapness, down to the passing of the act for constructing the London and Brighton line in 1837, when the proprietors disposed of their undertaking to the new company. The line was accordingly dismantled; the stone blocks and rails were taken up and sold; and all that remains of the Wandsworth, Croydon, and Merstham Railway is the track still observable to the south of Croydon, along Smitham Bottom, nearly parallel with the line of the present Brighton Railway, and an occasional cutting and embankment, which still mark the route of this first public railway.

The want of success of this undertaking doubtless had the effect of deterring projectors from embarking in any similar enterprise. If a line of the sort could not succeed near London, it was thought improbable that it should succeed any where else. The Croydon and Merstham line was a beacon to warn capitalists against embarking in railways, and many years passed before another was ventured upon.

Sir Richard Phillips was one of the few who early recognized the important uses of the locomotive and its employment on a large scale for the haulage of goods and passengers by railway. In his "Morning Walk to Kew" he crossed the line of the Wandsworth and Croydon Railway, when the idea seems to have occurred to him, as it afterwards did to Thomas Gray, that in the locomotive and the railway were to be found the germs of a great and peaceful social revolution:

"I found delight," said Sir Richard, in his book published in 1813, "in witnessing at Wandsworth the economy of horse labor on the iron railway. Yet a heavy sigh escaped me as I thought of the inconceivable millions of money which have been spent about Malta, four or five of which might have been the means of extending double lines of iron railway from London to Edinburg, Glasgow, Holyhead, Milford, Falmouth, Yarmouth, Dover, and Portsmouth. A reward of a single thousand would have supplied coaches and other vehicles, of various degrees of speed, with the best tackle for readily turning out; and we might, ere this, have witnessed our mail-coaches running at the rate of ten miles an hour drawn by a single horse, or impelled fifteen miles an hour by Blenkinsop's steam-engine. Such would have been a legitimate motive for overstepping the income of a nation, and the completion of so great and useful a work would have afforded rational ground for public triumph in general jubilee."

There was, however, as yet, no general recognition of the advantages either of railways or locomotives. The government of this country never leads in any work of public enterprise, and is usually rather a drag upon industrial operations than otherwise. As for the general public, it was enough for them that the Wandsworth and Croydon Railway did not pay.

Mr. Tredgold, in his "Practical Treatise on Railroads and Carriages," published in 1825, observes:

"Up to this period railways have been employed with success only in the conveyance of heavy mineral products, and for short distances where immense quantities were to be conveyed. In the few instances where they have been intended for the general purposes of trade, they have never answered the expectations of their projectors. But this seems to have arisen altogether from following too closely the models adopted for the conveyance of minerals, such modes of forming and using railways not being at all adapted for the general purposes of trade."

The ill success of railways was generally recognized. Joint-stock companies for all sorts of purposes were formed during the joint-stock mania of 1821, but few projectors were found daring enough to propose schemes so unpromising as railways. Hence nearly twenty years passed between the construction of the first and the second public railway in England; and this brings us to the projection of the Stockton and Darlington, which may be regarded as the parent public locomotive railway in the kingdom.

The district lying to the west of Darlington, in the county of Durham, is one of the richest mineral fields of the North. Vast stores of coal underlie the Bishop Auckland Valley, and from an early period it was felt to be an exceedingly desirable object to open up new communications to enable the article to be sent to market. But the district lay a long way from the sea, and, the Tees being unnavigable, there was next to no vend for the Bishop Auckland coal.

It is easy to understand, therefore, how the desire to obtain an outlet for this coal for land sale, as well as for its transport to London by sea, should have early occupied the attention of the coal-owners in the Bishop Auckland district. The first idea that found favor was the construction of a canal. About a century ago, in 1766, shortly after the Duke of Bridgewater's Canal had been opened between Worsley and Manchester, a movement was set on foot at Darlington with the view of having the country surveyed between that place and Stockton-on-Tees.

Brindley was requested to lay out the proposed line of canal; but he was engrossed at the time by the prosecution of the works on the Duke's Canal to Liverpool, and Whitworth, his pupil and assistant, was employed in his stead; George Dixon, grandfather of John Dixon, engineer of the future Stockton and Darlington Railway, taking an active part in the survey. In October, 1768, Whitworth presented his plan of the proposed canal from Stockton by Darlington to Winston, and in the following year, to give weight to the scheme, Brindley concurred with him in a joint report as to the plan and estimate.

Nothing was, however, done in the matter. Enterprise was slow to move. Stockton waited for Darlington, and Darlington waited for Stockton, but neither stirred until twenty years later, when Stockton began to consider the propriety of straightening the Tees below that town, and thereby shortening and improving the navigation. When it became known that some engineering scheme was afoot at Stockton, that indefatigable writer of prospectuses and drawer of plans, Ralph Dodd, the first projector of a tunnel under the Thames, the first projector of the Waterloo Bridge, and the first to bring a steam-boat from Glasgow into the Thames, addressed the Mayor and Corporation of Stockton in 1796 on the propriety of forming a line of internal navigation by Darlington and Staindrop to Winston. Still nothing was done. Four years later, another engineer, George Atkinson, reported in favor of a water-way to connect the then projected Great Trunk Canal, from about Boroughbridge to Piersebridge, with the Tees above Yarm.

At length, in 1808, the Tees Navigation Company, slow in their movements, obtained an act enabling them to make the short cut projected seventeen years before, and two years later the cut was opened, and celebrated by the inevitable dinner. The Stockton people, who adopted as the motto of their company "Meliora speramus," held a public meeting after the dinner to meditate upon and discuss the better things to come. They appointed a committee to inquire into the practicability and advantages of forming *a railway* or canal from Stockton by Darlington to Winston. Here, then, in 1810, we have the first glimpse of the railway; but it was long before the idea germinated and bore fruit. The collieries must be got at to make the new cut a success, but *how* for a long time remained the question.

Sixteen months passed, and the committee at Stockton went to sleep. But it came up again, and this time at Darlington, with Edward Pease as one of the members. The Darlington committee met and made their report, but they could not decide between the respective merits of a railroad and a canal. It was felt that either would be of great advantage. To settle the question, they determined to call the celebrated engineer, John Rennie, to their aid, and he was ready with his report in 1813. His report was not published, but it is understood that he was in favor of a canal on Brindley and Whitworth's line, though he afterward inclined to a tram-road. Still nothing was done. War was on foot in Europe, and enterprise was every where dormant. The scheme must therefore wait the advent of peace. At length peace came, and with it a revival of former projects.

At Newcastle, a plan was set on foot for connecting the Tyne with the Solway Frith by a canal. A county meeting was held on the subject in August, 1817, under the presidency of the high sheriff. Previous to this time, Sir John Swinburne had stood up for a railway in preference to a canal; but when the meeting took place, the opinion of those present was in favor of a canal —Mr. William Armstrong (father of the present Sir William) being one of the most zealous advocates of the water-road. Yet there were even then railroads in the immediate neighborhood of Newcastle, at Wylam and Killingworth, which had been successfully and economically worked by the locomotive for years past, but which the Northumbrians seem completely to have ignored.

The public head is usually very thick, and it is difficult to hammer a new idea into it. Canals were established methods of conveyance, and were every where recognized; whereas railways were new things, and were struggling hard to gain a footing. Besides, the only public railway in England, the Wandsworth, Croydon, and Merstham, had proved a commercial failure, and was held up as a warning to all speculators in tram-ways. But, though the Newcastle meeting approved of a canal in preference to a railway from the Tyne to the Solway, nothing was really done to promote the formation of either.

The movement in favor of a canal was again revived at Stockton. A requisition, very numerously signed by persons of influence in South Durham, was presented to the Mayor of Stockton in May, 1818, requesting him to convene a public meeting "to consider the expediency of forming a canal for the conveyance of coal, lime, etc., from Evenwood Bridge, near West Auckland, to the River Tees, upon a plan recently made by Mr. George Leatham, engineer." Among the names attached to the petition we find those of Edward, John, and Thomas Pease, and John Dixon, Darlington. They were doubtless willing to pull with any party that would open up a way, whether by rail or by water, between the Bishop Auckland coal-field and Stockton, whether the line passed through Darlington or not.

An enthusiastic meeting was held at Stockton, and a committee was appointed, by whom it was resolved to apply to Parliament for an act to make the intended canal "if funds are forthcoming." Never was there greater virtue in an *if.* Funds were *not* forthcoming; the project fell through, and a great blunder was prevented. When the Stockton men had discussed and resolved without any practical result, the leading men of Darlington took up the subject by themselves, determined, if possible, to bring it to some practical issue. In September, 1818, they met under the presidency of Thomas Meynell, Esq. Mr. Overton, who had laid down several coal railways in Wales, was consulted, and, after surveying the district between the Bishop Auckland coal-field and the Tees, sent in his report. Mr. Rennie also was again consulted. Both engineers gave their opinion in favor of a railway by Darlington in preference to a canal by Auckland, "whether taken as a line for the exportation of coal or as one for a local trade." The committee accordingly reported in favor of the railway.

It is curious now to look back at the modest estimate of traffic formed by the committee. They considered that the export trade in coal "might be taken, perhaps, at 10,000 tons a year, which is about one cargo a week!" It was intended to haul the coal by horse-power; a subsequent report stating "on undoubted authority" that one horse of moderate power could easily draw downward on the railway, between Darlington and Stockton, about ten tons, and upward about four tons of loading, exclusively of the empty wagons. No allusion was made to passengers in any of the reports; nor did the committee at first contemplate the accommodation of traffic of this description.

A survey of the line was then ordered, and steps were taken to apply to Parliament for the necessary powers to construct the railway. But the controversy was not yet at an end. Stockton stood by its favorite project of a canal, and would not subscribe a farthing toward the projected railway; but neither did it subscribe toward the canal. The landlords, the road trustees, the carriers, the proprietors of donkeys (by whom coals were principally carried for inland sale), were strenuously opposed to the new project; while the general public, stupid and skeptical, for the most part stood aloof, quoting old saws and keeping their money in their pockets.

Several energetic men, however, were now at the head of the Stockton and Darlington Railway project, and determined to persevere with it. Among these, the Peases were the most zealous. Edward Pease might be regarded as the back-bone of the concern. Opposition did not daunt him, nor failure discourage him. When apparently overthrown and prostrate, he would rise again like Antæus, stronger than before, and renew his efforts with increased vigor. He had in him the energy and perseverance of many men. One who knew him in 1818 said, "He was a man who could see a hundred years ahead." When the author last saw him in 1854, a few years before his death, Mr. Pease was in his eighty-eighth year; yet he still possessed the hopefulness and mental vigor of a man in his prime. Still sound in health, his eye had not lost its brilliancy, nor his cheek its color, and there was an elasticity in his step which younger men might have envied.

In getting up a company for surveying and forming a railway, Mr. Pease had great difficulties to encounter. The people of the

EDWARD PEASE.

neighborhood spoke of it as a ridiculous undertaking, and predicted that it would be ruinous to all concerned in it. Even those most interested in the opening up of new markets for the sale of their coal were indifferent, if not hostile. Mr. Pease nevertheless persevered in the formation of a company, and he induced many of his friends and relations to follow his example. The Richardsons and Backhouses, members, like himself, of the Society of Friends, influenced by his persuasion, united themselves with him; and so many of the same denomination (having confidence in these influential Darlington names) followed their example and subscribed for shares, that the railway obtained the designation, which it long retained, of "The Quakers' Line."

The Stockton and Darlington scheme had to run the gauntlet of a fierce opposition in three successive sessions of Parliament. The application of 1818 was defeated by the Duke of Cleveland, who afterward profited so largely by the railway. The ground of his opposition was that the line would interfere with one of his fox-covers, and it was mainly through his influence that the bill was thrown out, but only by a majority of thirteen, upward of one hundred members having voted for the bill. A nobleman said, when he heard of the division, "Well, if the Quakers in these times, when nobody knows any thing about railways, can raise such a phalanx in their support, I should recommend the country gentlemen to be very wary how they oppose them in future."

The next year, in 1819, an amended survey of the line was made, and, the duke's fox-cover being avoided, his opposition was thus averted; but, on Parliament becoming dissolved on the death of George III., the bill was necessarily suspended until another session.

In the mean time the local opposition to the measure revived, and now it was led by the road trustees, who spread it abroad that the mortgagees of the tolls arising from the turnpike-road leading from Darlington to West Auckland would be seriously injured by the formation of the proposed railway. On this, Edward Pease issued a printed notice, requesting any alarmed mortgagee to apply to the company's solicitors at Darlington, who were authorized to purchase their securities at the prices originally given for them. This notice had the effect of allaying the alarm spread abroad; and the bill, though still strongly opposed, passed both houses of Parliament in 1821.

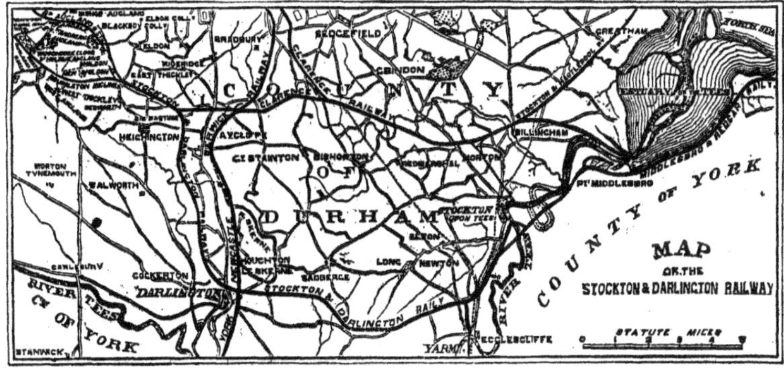

MAP OF STOCKTON AND DARLINGTON RAILWAY.

The preamble of the act sets forth the public utility of the proposed line for the conveyance of coal and other commodities from the interior of the county of Durham to Stockton and the northern parts of Yorkshire. Nothing was said about passengers, for passenger-traffic was not yet contemplated; and nothing was said about locomotives, as it was at first intended to work the line entirely by horse-power. The road was to be free to all persons who chose to place their wagons and horses upon it for the haulage of coal and merchandise, provided they paid the tolls fixed by the act.

The company were empowered to charge fourpence a ton per mile for all coal intended for land sale, but only a halfpenny a ton per mile for coal intended for shipment at Stockton. This latter proviso was inserted at the instance of Mr. Lambton, afterward Earl of Durham, for the express purpose of preventing the line being used in competition against his coal loaded at Sunderland; for it was not believed possible that coal could be carried at that low rate except at a heavy loss. As it was, however, the rate thus fixed by the act eventually proved the vital element of success in the working of the undertaking.

While the Stockton and Darlington Railway scheme was still before Parliament, we find Edward Pease writing letters to a York paper, urging the propriety of extending it southward into Yorkshire by a branch from Croft. It is curious now to look back upon the arguments by which Mr. Pease sought to influence public opinion in favor of railways, and to observe the very modest anticipations which even its most zealous advocate entertained as to their supposed utility and capabilities:

"The late improvements in the construction of railways," Mr. Pease wrote, "have rendered them much more perfect than when constructed after the old plan. To such a degree of utility have they now been brought that they may be regarded as *very little inferior to canals.*

"If we compare the railway with the best lines of common road, it may be fairly stated that in the case of a level railway the work will be increased in at least an eightfold degree. The best horse is sufficiently loaded with three quarters of a ton on a common road, from the undulating line of its draught, while on a railway it is calculated that a horse will easily draw a load of ten tons. At Lord Elgin's works, Mr. Stevenson, the celebrated engineer, states that he has actually seen a horse draw twenty-three tons thirteen cwt. upon a railway which was in some parts level, and at other parts presented a gentle declivity!

"The formation of a railway, if it creates no improvement in a country, certainly bars none, as all the former modes of communication remain unimpaired; and the public obtain, at the risk of the subscribers, another and better mode of carriage, which it will always be to the interest of the proprietors to make cheap and serviceable to the community.

"On undertakings of this kind, when compared with canals, the advantages of which (where an ascending or descending line can be obtained) are nearly equal, it may be remarked that public opinion is not easily changed on any subject. It requires the experience of many years, sometimes ages, to accomplish this, even in cases which by some may be deemed obvious. Such is the effect of habit, and such the aversion of mankind to any thing like innovation or change. Although this is often regretted, yet, if the principle be investigated in all its ramifications, it will perhaps be found to be one of the most fortunate dispositions of the human mind.

"The system of cast-iron railways is as yet to be considered but in its infancy. It will be found to be an immense improvement on the common road, and also on the wooden railway. It neither presents the friction of the tram-way, nor partakes of the perishable nature of the wooden railway, and, as regards utility, it may be considered as the medium between the navigable canal and the common road. We may therefore hope that as this system develops itself, our roads will be laid out as much as possible on *one level*, and in connection with the great lines of communication throughout the country."

Such were the modest anticipations of Edward Pease respecting railways in the year 1821. Ten years later, an age of progress, by comparison, had been effected.

Some time elapsed before any active steps were taken to proceed with the construction of the railway. Doubts were raised whether the line was the best that could be adopted for the district, and the subscribers generally were not so sanguine about the undertaking as to induce them to press it forward.

One day, about the end of the year 1821, two strangers knocked at the door of Mr. Pease's house in Darlington, and a message was brought to him that some persons from Killingworth wanted to speak with him. They were invited in, on which one of the visitors introduced himself as Nicholas Wood, viewer at Killingworth, and then turning to his companion, he introduced him as George Stephenson, engine-wright, of the same place.

Mr. Pease entered into conversation with his visitors, and was soon told their object. Stephenson had heard of the passing of the Stockton and Darlington Act, and desiring to increase his railway experience, and also to employ in some larger field the practical knowledge he had already acquired, he determined to visit the known projector of the undertaking, with the view of being employed to carry it out. He had brought with him his friend Wood for the purpose at the same time of relieving his diffidence and supporting his application.

Mr. Pease liked the appearance of his visitor: "there was," as he afterward remarked when speaking of Stephenson, "such an honest, sensible look about him, and he seemed so modest and unpretending. He spoke in the strong Northumbrian dialect of his district, and described himself as 'only the engine-wright at Killingworth; that's what he was.'"

Mr. Pease soon saw that our engineer was the very man for his purpose. The whole plans of the railway were still in an undetermined state, and Mr. Pease was therefore glad to have the opportunity of profiting by Stephenson's experience. In the course of their conversation, the latter strongly recommended a *railway* in preference to a tram-road. They also discussed the kind of tractive power to be employed, Mr. Pease stating that the company had based their whole calculations on the employment of *horse*-power. "I was so satisfied," said he afterward, "that a horse upon an iron road would draw ten tons for one ton on a common road, that I felt sure that before long the railway would become the king's highway."

But Mr. Pease was scarcely prepared for the bold assertion made by his visitor, that the locomotive engine with which he had been working the Killingworth Railway for many years past was worth fifty horses, and that engines made after a similar plan would yet entirely supersede all horse-power upon railroads. Stephenson was daily becoming more positive as to the superiority of his locomotive, and hence he strongly urged Mr. Pease to adopt it. "Come over to Killingworth," said he, "and see what my engines can do; seeing is believing, sir." Mr. Pease accordingly promised that on some early day he would go over to Killingworth, and take a look at the wonderful machine that was to supersede horses.

The result of the interview was, that Mr. Pease promised to bring Stephenson's application for the appointment of engineer before the directors, and to support it with his influence; whereon the two visitors prepared to take their leave, informing Mr. Pease that they intended to return to Newcastle "by nip;" that is, they expected to get a smuggled lift on the stage-coach by tipping Jehu—for in those days the stage-coachmen regarded all casual roadside passengers as their proper perquisites. They had, however, been so much engrossed by their conversation that the lapse of time was forgotten, and when Stephenson and his friend made inquiries about the return coach, they found the last had left, and they had to walk eighteen miles to Durham on their way back to Newcastle.

Mr. Pease having made farther inquiries respecting Stephenson's character and qualifications, and having received a very strong recommendation of him as the right man for the intended work, he brought the subject of his application before the directors of the Stockton and Darlington Company. They resolved to adopt his recommendation that a railway be formed instead of a tram-road; and they farther requested Mr. Pease to write to Stephenson, desiring him to undertake a resurvey of the line at the earliest practicable period.

A man was dispatched on a horse with the letter, and when he reached Killingworth he made diligent inquiry after the person named on the address, "George Stephenson, Esquire, Engineer." No such person was known in the village. It is said that the man was on the point of giving up all farther search, when the happy thought struck some of the colliers' wives who had gathered about him that it must be "Geordie the engine-wright" the man was in search of, and to Geordie's cottage he accordingly went, found him at home, and delivered the letter.

About the end of September Stephenson went carefully over the line of the proposed railway for the purpose of suggesting such improvements and deviations as he might consider desirable.

He was accompanied by an assistant and a chainman, his son Robert entering the figures while his father took the sights. After being engaged in the work at intervals for about six weeks, Stephenson reported the result of his survey to the Board of Directors, and showed that, by certain deviations, a line shorter by about three miles might be constructed at a considerable saving in expense, while at the same time more favorable gradients—an important consideration—would be secured.

It was, however, determined in the first place to proceed with the works at those parts of the line where no deviation was proposed, and the first rail of the Stockton and Darlington Railway was laid with considerable ceremony, near Stockton, on the 23d of May, 1822.

It is worthy of note that Stephenson, in making his first estimate of the cost of forming the railway according to the instructions of the directors, set down, as part of the cost, £6200 for stationary engines, not mentioning locomotives at all. It was the intention of the directors, in the first place, to employ only horses for the haulage of the coals, and fixed engines and ropes where horse-power was not applicable. The whole question of steam-locomotive power was, in the estimation of the public, as well as of practical and scientific men, as yet in doubt. The confident anticipations of George Stephenson as to the eventual success of locomotive engines were regarded as mere speculations; and when he gave utterance to his views, as he frequently took the opportunity of doing, it even had the effect of shaking the confidence of some of his friends in the solidity of his judgment and his practical qualities as an engineer.

When Mr. Pease discussed the question with Stephenson, his remark was, "Come over and see my engines at Killingworth, and satisfy yourself as to the efficiency of the locomotive. I will show you the colliery books, that you may ascertain for yourself the actual cost of working. And I must tell you that the economy of the locomotive engine is no longer a matter of theory, but a matter of fact." So confident was the tone in which Stephenson spoke of the success of his engines, and so important were the consequences involved in arriving at a correct conclusion on the subject, that Mr. Pease at length resolved on paying a visit to Killingworth in the summer of 1822, in company with his friend Thomas Richardson, a considerable subscriber to the Stockton and Darlington undertaking,* to inspect the wonderful new power so much vaunted by their engineer.

When Mr. Pease arrived at Killingworth village, he inquired for George Stephenson, and was told that he must go over to the West Moor, and seek for a cottage by the roadside with a dial over the door—"that was where George Stephenson lived." They soon found the house with the dial, and, on knocking, the door was opened by Mrs. Stephenson. In answer to Mr. Pease's inquiry for her husband, she said he was not in the house at present, but that she would send for him to the colliery. And in a short time Stephenson appeared before them in his working dress, just as he had come out of the pit.

He very soon had his locomotive brought up to the crossing close by the end of the cottage, made the gentlemen mount it, and showed them its paces. Harnessing it to a train of loaded wagons, he ran it along the railroad, and so thoroughly satisfied his visitors of its power and capabilities, that from that day Edward Pease was a declared supporter of the locomotive engine. In preparing the Amended Stockton and Darlington Act, at Stephenson's urgent request Mr. Pease had a clause inserted, taking power to work the railway by means of locomotive engines, and to employ them for the haulage of passengers as well as of merchandise.† The act was obtained in 1823, on which Stephenson was appointed the company's engineer, at a salary of £300 per annum; and it was determined that the line should be constructed and opened for traffic as soon as practicable.

He at once proceeded, accompanied by his assistants, with the working survey of the line, laying out every foot of the ground himself. Railway surveying was as yet in its infancy, and was slow and difficult work. It afterward became a separate branch of railway business, and was intrusted to a special staff. Indeed, on no subsequent line did George Stephenson take the sights through the spirit-level with his own hands and eyes as he did on this railway. He started very early—dressed in a blue tailed

* Mr. Richardson was founder of the afterward well-known discount-house of Richardson, Overend, and Gurney, Lombard Street, London.

† The first clause in any railway act empowering the employment of locomotive engines for the working of passenger traffic.

coat, breeches, and top-boots—and surveyed until dusk. He was not at any time particular as to his living; and, during the survey, he took his chance of getting a little milk and bread at some cottager's house along the line, or occasionally joined in a homely dinner at some neighboring farm-house. The country people were accustomed to give him a hearty welcome when he appeared at their door, for he was always full of cheery and homely talk, and, when there were children about the house, he had plenty of humorous chat for them as well as for their seniors.

After the day's work was over, George would drop in at Mr. Pease's to talk over the progress of the survey, and discuss various matters connected with the railway. Mr. Pease's daughters were usually present; and, on one occasion, finding the young ladies learning the art of embroidery, he volunteered to instruct them.* "I know all about it," said he, "and you will wonder how I learned it. I will tell you. When I was a brakesman at Killingworth, I learned the art of embroidery while working the pitmen's button-holes by the engine fire at nights." He was never ashamed, but, on the contrary, rather proud, of reminding his friends of these humble pursuits of his early life. Mr. Pease's family were greatly pleased with his conversation, which was always amusing and instructive; full of all sorts of experience, gathered in the oddest and most out-of-the-way places. Even at that early period, before he mixed in the society of educated persons, there was a dash of speculativeness in his remarks which gave a high degree of originality to his conversation; and he would sometimes, in a casual remark, throw a flash of light upon a subject which called up a train of pregnant suggestions.

One of the most important subjects of discussion at these meetings with Mr. Pease was the establishment of a manufactory at Newcastle for the building of locomotive engines. Up to this time all the locomotives constructed after Stephenson's designs had been made by ordinary mechanics working at the collieries in the North of England. But he had long felt that the accuracy and style of their workmanship admitted of great improvement, and that upon this the more perfect action of the locomo-

* This incident, communicated to the author by the late Edward Pease, has since been made the subject of a fine picture by Mr. A. Rankley, A.R.A., exhibited at the Royal Academy Exhibition of 1861.

tive engine, and its general adoption, in a great measure depended. One principal object that he had in view in establishing the proposed factory was to concentrate a number of good workmen for the purpose of carrying out the improvements in detail which he was from time to time making in his engine; for he felt hampered by the want of efficient help from skilled mechanics, who could work out in a practical form the ideas of which his busy mind was always so prolific. Doubtless, too, he believed that the manufactory would prove a remunerative investment, and that, on the general adoption of the railway system which he anticipated, he would derive solid advantages from the fact of his establishment being the only one of the kind for the special construction of locomotive engines.

Mr. Pease approved of his design, and strongly recommended him to carry it into effect. But there was the question of means; and Stephenson did not think he had capital enough for the purpose. He told Mr. Pease that he could advance £1000—the amount of the testimonial presented by the coal-owners for his safety-lamp invention, which he had still left untouched; but he did not think this sufficient for the purpose, and he thought that he should require at least another £1000. Mr. Pease had been very much struck with the successful performances of the Killingworth engine; and, being an accurate judge of character, he believed that he could not go far wrong in linking a portion of his fortune with the energy and industry of George Stephenson. He consulted his friend Thomas Richardson in the matter, and the two consented to advance £500 each for the purpose of establishing the engine factory at Newcastle. A piece of land was accordingly purchased in Forth Street, in August, 1823, on which a small building was erected—the nucleus of the gigantic establishment which was afterward formed around it; and active operations were begun early in 1824.

While the Stockton and Darlington Railway works were in progress, our engineer had many interesting discussions with Mr. Pease on points connected with its construction and working, the determination of which in a great measure affected the formation and working of future railways. The most important points were these: 1. The comparative merits of cast and wrought iron rails. 2. The gauge of the railway. 3. The employment of horse or engine power in working it when ready for traffic.

The kind of rails to be laid down to form the permanent road was a matter of considerable importance. A wooden tram-road had been contemplated when the first act was applied for; but Stephenson having advised that an iron road should be laid down, he was instructed to draw up a specification of the rails. He went before the directors to discuss with them the kind of material to be specified. He was himself interested in the patent for cast-iron rails, which he had taken out in conjunction with Mr. Losh in 1816, and, of course, it was to his interest that his articles should be used. But when requested to give his opinion on the subject, he frankly said to the directors, "Well, gentlemen, to tell you the truth, although it would put £500 in my pocket to specify my own patent rails, I can not do so after the experience I have had. If you take my advice, you will not lay down a single cast-iron rail." "Why?" asked the directors. "Because they will not stand the weight, and you will be at no end of expense for repairs and relays." "What kind of road, then," he was asked, "would you recommend?" "Malleable rails, certainly," said he; "and I can recommend them with the more confidence from the fact that at Killingworth we have had some Swedish bars laid down—nailed to wooden sleepers—for a period of fourteen years, the wagons passing over them daily, and there they are, in use yet, whereas the cast rails are constantly giving way."*

The price of malleable rails was, however, so high—being then worth about £12 per ton as compared with cast-iron rails at about £5 10*s.*—and the saving of expense was so important a consideration with the subscribers, that Stephenson was directed to provide in the specification that only one half of the rails required—or about 800 tons—should be of malleable iron, and the remainder of cast iron. The malleable rails were of the kind called "fish-bellied," and weighed 28 lbs. to the yard, being 2¼ inches

* Stephenson's recommendation of wrought-iron instead of cast-iron rails was the cause of a rupture between Mr. Losh and himself. Stephenson thought his duty was to give his employers the best advice; Losh thought his business was to push the patent cast-iron rails wherever he could. Stephenson regarded this view as sordid; and the two finally separated after a quarrel, in high dudgeon with each other.

broad at the top, with the upper flange ¾ inch thick. They were only 2 inches in depth at the points at which they rested on the chairs, and 3¼ inches in the middle or bellied part.

When forming the road, the proper gauge had also to be determined. What width was this to be? The gauge of the first tram-road laid down had virtually settled the point. The gauge of wheels of the common vehicles of the country—of the carts and wagons employed on common roads, which were first used on the tram-roads—was about 4 feet 8½ inches. And so the first tram-roads were laid down of this gauge. The tools and machinery for constructing coal-wagons and locomotives were formed with this gauge in view. The Wylam wagon-way, afterward the Wylam plate-way, the Killingworth railroad, and the Hetton railroad, were as nearly as possible on the same gauge. Some of the earth-wagons used to form the Stockton and Darlington road were brought from the Hetton Railway; and others which were specially constructed were formed of the same dimensions, these being intended to be afterward employed in the working of the traffic.

As the period drew near for the opening of the line, the question of the tractive power to be employed was anxiously discussed. At the Brusselton incline, fixed engines must necessarily be made use of; but with respect to the mode of working the railway generally, it was decided that horses were to be largely employed, and arrangements were made for their purchase.

Although locomotives had been regularly employed in hauling coal-wagons on the Middleton Colliery Railway, near Leeds, for more than twelve years, and on the Wylam and Killingworth Railways near Newcastle for more than ten years, great skepticism still prevailed as to the economy of employing them for the purpose in lieu of horses. In this case, it would appear that seeing was *not* believing. The popular skepticism was as great at Newcastle, where the opportunities for accurate observation were the greatest, as any where else. In 1824 the scheme of a canal between that town and Carlisle again came up, and, though a few timid voices were raised on behalf of a railway, the general opinion was still in favor of a canal. The example of the Hetton Railway, which had been successfully worked by Stephenson's locomotives for two years past, was pointed to in proof of the practicability of a locomotive line between the two places; but the voice of the press as well as of the public was decidedly against the "new-fangled roads."

"There has been some talk," wrote the "Whitehaven Gazette," "from a puff criticism in the 'Monthly Review,' of an improvement on the principle of railways; but we suspect that this improvement will turn out like the steam-carriages, of which we have been told so much, that were to supersede the use of horses entirely, and travel *at a rate almost equal to the speed of the fleetest horse!*" The idea was too chimerical to be entertained, and the suggested railway was accordingly rejected as impracticable.

The "Tyne Mercury" was equally decided against railways. "What person," asked the editor (November 16th, 1824), "would ever think of *paying any thing* to be conveyed from Hexham to Newcastle in something like a coal-wagon, upon a dreary wagon-way, and to be dragged for the greater part of the distance by a ROARING STEAM-ENGINE!" The very notion of such a thing was preposterous, ridiculous, and utterly absurd.

When such was the state of public opinion as to railway locomotion, some idea may be formed of the clearsightedness and moral courage of the Stockton and Darlington directors in ordering three of Stephenson's locomotive engines, at a cost of several thousand pounds, against the opening of the railway.

These were constructed after Stephenson's most matured designs, and embodied all the improvements which he had contrived up to that time. No. 1 engine, the "Locomotion," which was first delivered, weighed about eight tons. It had one large flue or tube through the boiler, by which the heated air passed direct from the furnace at one end, lined with fire-bricks, to the chimney at the other. The combustion in the furnace was quickened by the adoption of the steam-blast in the chimney. The heat raised was sometimes so great, and it was so imperfectly abstracted by the surrounding water, that the chimney became almost red-hot. Such engines, when put to their speed, were found capable of running at the rate of from twelve to sixteen miles an hour; but they were better adapted for the heavy work of hauling coal-trains at low speeds—for which, indeed, they were specially constructed—than for running at the higher speeds afterward adopted. Nor was it contemplated by the directors as possible, at the time when they were ordered, that locomotives could be made available for the purposes of passenger traveling. Besides, the Stockton and Darlington Railway did not run through a district in which passengers were supposed to be likely to constitute any considerable portion of the traffic.

We may easily imagine the anxiety felt by George Stephenson during the progress of the works toward completion, and his mingled hopes and doubts (though his doubts were but few) as to the issue of this great experiment. When the formation of the line near Stockton was well advanced, the engineer one day, accompanied by his son Robert and John Dixon, made a journey of inspection of the works. The party reached Stockton, and proceeded to dine at one of the inns there. After dinner, Stephenson ventured on the very unusual measure of ordering in a bottle of wine, to drink success to the railway. John Dixon relates with pride the utterance of the master on the occasion. "Now, lads," said he to the two young men, "I venture to tell you that I think you will live to see the day when railways will supersede almost all other methods of conveyance in this country—when mail-coaches will go by railway, and railroads will become the great highways for the king and all his subjects. The time is coming when it will be cheaper for a working man to travel on a railway than to walk on foot. I know there are great and almost insurmountable difficulties to be encountered, but what I have said will come to pass as sure as you now hear me. I only wish I may live to see the day, though that I can scarcely hope for, as I know how slow all human progress is, and with what difficulty I have been able to get the locomotive introduced thus far, notwithstanding my more than ten years' successful experiment at Killingworth." The result, however, outstripped even George Stephenson's most sanguine anticipations; and his son Robert, shortly after his return from America in 1827, saw his father's locomotive adopted as the tractive power on railways generally.

Tuesday, the 27th of September, 1825, was a great day for Darlington. The railway, after having been under construction for more than three years, was at length about to be opened. The project had been the talk of the neighborhood for so long that there were few people within a range of twenty miles who did not feel more or less interested about it. Was it to be a failure or a success? Opinions were pretty equally divided as to the railway, but as regarded the locomotive the general belief was that it would "never answer." However, there the locomotive was—"No. 1"—delivered on to the line, and ready to draw the first train of wagons on the opening day.

A great concourse of people assembled on the occasion. Some came from Newcastle and Durham, many from the Aucklands, while Darlington held a general holiday, and turned out all its population. To give *éclat* to the opening, the directors of the company issued a programme of the proceedings, intimating the times at which the procession of wagons would pass certain points along the line. The proprietors assembled as early as six in the morning at the Brusselton fixed engine, where the working of the inclined planes was successfully rehearsed. A train of wagons laden with coals and merchandise was drawn up the western incline by the fixed engine, a length of 1960 yards, in seven and a half minutes, and then lowered down the incline on the eastern side of the hill, 880 yards, in five minutes.

At the foot of the incline the procession of vehicles was formed, consisting of the locomotive engine No. 1, driven by George Stephenson himself; after it six wagons loaded with coals and flour, then a covered coach containing directors and proprietors, next twenty-one coal-wagons fitted up for passengers (with which they were crammed), and lastly six more wagons loaded with coals.

Strange to say, a man on a horse, carrying a flag, with the motto of the company inscribed on it, *Periculum privatum utilitas publica*, headed the procession! A lithographic view of the great event, published shortly after, duly exhibits the horseman and his flag. It was not thought so dangerous a place after all. The locomotive was only supposed to be able to go at the rate of from four to six miles an hour, and an ordinary horse could easily keep ahead of that.

Off started the procession, with the horseman at its head. A great concourse of people stood along the line. Many of them tried to accompany it by running, and some gentlemen on horseback galloped across the fields to keep up with the train. The railway descending with a gentle incline toward Darlington, the

PROCESSION AT THE OPENING OF THE STOCKTON AND DARLINGTON RAILWAY.
[Fac-simile of a local lithograph.]

rate of speed was consequently variable. At a favorable part of the road Stephenson determined to try the speed of the engine, and he called upon the horseman with the flag to get out of the way! Most probably, deeming it unnecessary to carry his *Periculum privatum* farther, the horseman turned aside, and Stephenson "put on the steam." The speed was at once raised to twelve miles an hour, and, at a favorable part of the road, to fifteen. The runners on foot, the gentlemen on horseback, and the horseman with the flag, were consequently soon left far behind. When the train reached Darlington, it was found that four hundred and fifty passengers occupied the wagons, and that the load of men, coals, and merchandise amounted to about ninety tons.

At Darlington the procession was rearranged. The six loaded coal-wagons were left behind, and other wagons were taken on with a hundred and fifty more passengers, together with a band of music. The train then started for Stockton—a distance of only twelve miles—which was reached in about three hours. The day was kept throughout the district as a holiday; and horses, gigs, carts, and other vehicles, filled with people, stood along the railway, as well as crowds of persons on foot, waiting to see the train pass. The whole population of Stockton turned out to receive the procession, and, after a walk through the streets, the inevitable dinner in the Town Hall wound up the day's proceedings.

All this, however, was but gala work. The serious business of the company began on the following day. Upon the result of the experiment now fairly initiated by the Stockton and Darlington Company the future of railways in a great measure depended. If it failed, like the Wandsworth, Croydon, and Merstham undertaking, then a great check would unquestionably be given to speculation in railways. If it succeeded, the Stockton and Darlington enterprise would mark the beginning of a new era, and issue in neither more nor less than a complete revolution of the means of communication in all civilized countries.

The circumstances were on the whole favorable, and boded success rather than failure. Prudent, careful, thoughtful men were at the head of the concern, interested in seeing it managed economically and efficiently; and they had the advantage of the assistance of an engineer possessed of large resources of mother wit, mechanical genius, and strong common sense. There was an almost unlimited quantity of coal to be carried, the principal difficulty being in accommodating it satisfactorily. Yet it was only after the line had been at work for some time that the extensive character of the coal traffic began to be appreciated. At first it was supposed that the chief trade would be in coal for land sale. But the clause inserted in the original act, at the instance of Mr. Lambton, by which the company were limited to ½*d.* per ton per mile for coal led to Stockton for shipment, led to the most unexpected consequences. It was estimated that only about 10,000 tons a year would be shipped, and that principally by way of ballast. Instead of which, in the course of a very few years, the coal carried on the line for export constituted the main bulk of the traffic, while that carried for land sale was merely subsidiary.*

* The rapid progress of the coal and merchandise traffic of the Stockton and Darlington line, of which Middlesbro' is the principal sea-port, may be inferred from the following brief statement of facts: The orginal estimate assumed that 165,488 tons of coal would be carried annually, and produce an income of £11,904. The revenue from other sources was taken at £4104. In 1827, the first year in which the coal and merchandise traffic was fully worked, the revenue from coal was £14,455; from lime, merchandise, and sundries, £3285; and from passengers (which had not been taken into account), £563. In 1860, when the original line of 25 miles had become ex-

The anticipations of the company as to passenger-traffic were in like manner more than realized. At first passengers were not thought of, and it was only while the works were in progress that the starting of a passenger-coach was seriously contemplated. Some eighty years since there was only one post-chaise in Darlington, which ran on three wheels. There are people still living who remember when a coach ran from Stockton three days in the week, passing through Darlington and Barnard Castle; but it was starved off the road for want of support. There was then very little intercourse between the towns, though they were so near to each other, and comparatively so populous; and it was not known whether people would trust themselves to the iron road. Nevertheless, it was determined to make trial of a railway coach, and George Stephenson was authorized to have one built at Newcastle at the cost of the company. This was done accordingly, and the first railway passenger-carriage was built after our engineer's design. It was, however, a very modest, and, indeed, a somewhat uncouth machine, more resembling a showman's caravan than a passenger-coach of any extant form. A row of seats ran along each side of the interior, and a long deal table was fixed in the centre, the access being by means of a door at the back end, in the manner of an omnibus. This coach arrived from Newcastle on the day before the opening, and formed part of the procession above described. Stephenson was consulted as to the name of the coach, and he at once suggested the "Experiment;" and by this name it was called. Such was the sole passenger-carrying stock of the Stockton and Darlington Company in the year 1825. But "The Experiment" proved the forerunner of a mighty traffic; and long time did not elapse before it was displaced, not only by improved coaches (still drawn by horses), but afterward by long trains of passenger-carriages drawn by locomotive engines.

The "Experiment" was fairly started as a passenger-coach on the 10th of October, 1825, a fortnight after the opening of the

tended to 125 miles, and the original capital of £150,000 had swelled to £3,800,000, the quantity of coal carried had increased to 3,045,596 tons in the year, besides 1,484,409 tons of ironstone and other minerals, producing a revenue of £280,375; while 1,484,409 tons of merchandise had been carried in the same year, producing £63,478, and 687,728 passengers, producing £45,398.

line. It was drawn by one horse, and performed a journey daily each way between the two towns, accomplishing the distance of twelve miles in about two hours. The fare charged was a shilling, without distinction of class; and each passenger was allowed fourteen pounds of luggage free. The "Experiment" was not, however, worked by the company, but was let to contractors, who worked it under an arrangement whereby toll was paid for the use of the line, rent of booking-cabins, etc.*

THE FIRST RAILWAY-COACH.

The speculation answered so well that several private coaching companies were shortly after got up by innkeepers at Darlington and Stockton for the purpose of running other coaches upon the railroad, and an active competition for passenger-traffic sprang up. The "Experiment," being found too heavy for one horse to

* The coaches were not allowed to be run upon the line without considerable opposition. We find Edward Pease writing to Joseph Sandars, of Liverpool, on the 18th of June, 1827: "Our railway coach proprietors have individually received notices of a process in the Exchequer for various fines, to the amount of £150, in penalties of £20 each, for neglecting to have the plates, with the numbers of their licenses, on the coach doors, agreeably to the provision of the Act 95 George IV. In looking into the nature of this proceeding and its consequences, it is clear, if the court shall confirm it by conviction, that we are undone as to the conveyance of passengers." Mr. Pease incidentally mentions the names of the several coach proprietors at the time—"Pickersgill and Co., Richard Scott, and Martha Hewson." The proceeding was eventually defeated, it being decided that the penalties only applied to coaches traveling on common or turnpike roads.

draw, besides being found an uncomfortable machine, was banished to the coal district. Its place was then supplied by other and better vehicles, though they were no other than old stage-coach bodies purchased by the company, each mounted on an under-frame with flange wheels. These were let on hire to the coaching companies, who horsed and managed them under an arrangement as to tolls, in like manner as the "Experiment" had been worked. Now began the distinction of inside and outside passengers, equivalent to first and second class, paying different fares. The competition with each other upon the railway, and with the ordinary stage-coaches upon the road, soon brought up the speed, which was increased to ten miles an hour—the mail-coach rate of traveling in those days, and considered very fast.

Mr. Clephan, a native of the district, has communicated to the author the following account of the competition between the rival coach companies:

"There were two separate coach companies in Stockton, and amusing collisions sometimes occurred between the drivers, who found on the rail a novel element for contention. Coaches can not pass each other on the rail as on the road, and, as the line was single, with four sidings in the mile, when two coaches met, or two trains, or coach and train, the question arose which of the drivers must go back. This was not always settled in silence. As to trains, it came to be a sort of understanding that empty should give way to loaded wagons; and as to trains and coaches, that passengers should have preference over coals; while coaches, when they met, must quarrel it out. At length, midway between sidings, a post was erected, and the rule was laid down that he who had passed the pillar must go on, and the 'coming man' go back. At the Goose Pool and Early Nook it was common for the coaches to stop, and there, as Jonathan would say, passengers and coachmen 'liquored.' One coach, introduced by an innkeeper, was a compound of two mourning-coaches—an approximation to the real railway-coach, which still adheres, with multiplying exceptions, to the stage-coach type. One Dixon, who drove the 'Experiment' between Darlington and Shildon, is the inventor of carriage-lighting on the rail. On a dark winter night, having compassion on his passengers, he would buy a penny candle, and place it lighted among them on the table of the 'Experiment'—the first railway-coach (which, by the way, ended its days at Shildon as a railway cabin), being also the first coach on the rail (first, second, and third class jammed all into one) that indulged its customers with light in darkness."

The traffic of all sorts increased so steadily and so rapidly that considerable difficulty was experienced in working it satisfactorily. It had been provided by the first Stockton and Darlington Act that the line should be free to all parties who chose to use it at certain prescribed rates, and that any person might put horses and wagons on the railway, and carry for himself. But this arrangement led to increasing confusion and difficulty, and could not continue in the face of a large and rapidly-increasing traffic. The goods trains got so long that the carriers found it necessary to call in the aid of the locomotive engine to help them on their way. Then mixed trains of passengers and merchandise began to run; and the result was that the Railway Company found it necessary to take the entire charge and working of the traffic. In course of time new coaches were specially built for the better accommodation of the public, until at length regular passenger-trains were run, drawn by the locomotive engine, though this was not until after the Liverpool and Manchester Company had established this as a distinct branch of their traffic.

The three Stephenson locomotives were from the first regularly employed to work the coal-trains, and their proved efficiency for this purpose led to the gradual increase of the locomotive power. The speed of the engine—slow though it seems now—was in those days regarded as something marvelous. A race actually came off between No. 1 engine, the "Locomotion," and one of the stage-coaches traveling from Darlington to Stockton by the ordinary road, and it was regarded as a great triumph of mechanical skill that the locomotive reached Stockton first, beating the stage-coach by about a hundred yards! The same engine continued in good working order in the year 1846, when it headed the railway procession on the opening of the Middlesborough and Redcar Railway, traveling at the rate of about fourteen miles an hour. This engine, the first that traveled on the first public locomotive railway, has recently been placed upon a pedestal in front of the railway station at Darlington.

For some years, however, the principal haulage of the line was performed by horses. The inclination of the gradients being to-

THE NO. 1 ENGINE AT DARLINGTON.

ward the sea, this was perhaps the cheapest mode of traction, so long as the traffic was not very large. The horse drew the train along the level road until, on reaching a descending gradient, down which the train ran by its own gravity, the animal was unharnessed, when, wheeling round to the other end of the wagons, to which a "dandy-cart" was attached, its bottom being only a few inches from the rail, and bringing his step into unison with the speed of the train, he leaped nimbly into his place in the hind car, which was usually fitted with a well-filled hay-rack.

The details of the working were gradually perfected by experience, the projectors of the line being scarcely conscious at first of the importance and significance of the work which they had taken in hand, and little thinking that they were laying the foundations of a system which was yet to revolutionize the internal communications of the world, and confer the greatest blessings on mankind. It is important to note that the commercial results of the enterprise were considered satisfactory from the opening of the railway. Besides conferring a great public benefit upon the inhabitants of the district, and throwing open entirely new markets for the almost boundless stores of coal found in the Bishop Auckland district, the profits derived from the traffic created by the railway enabled increasing dividends to be paid to those who had risked their capital in the undertaking, and thus held forth an encouragement to the projectors of railways generally, which was not without an important effect in stimulating the projection of similar enterprises in other districts. These results, as displayed in the annual dividends, must have been eminently encouraging to the astute commercial men of Liverpool and Manchester, who were then engaged in the prosecution of their railway. Indeed, the commercial success of the Stockton and Darlington Company may be justly characterized as the turning-point of the railway system. With that practical illustration daily in sight of the public, it was no longer possible for Parliament to have prevented its eventual extension.

Before leaving the subject of the Stockton and Darlington Railway, we can not avoid alluding to one of its most remarkable and direct results—the creation of the town of Middlesborough-on-Tees. When the railway was opened in 1825, the site of this future metropolis of Cleveland was occupied by one solitary farm-house and its out-buildings. All round was pasture-land or mud-banks; scarcely another house was within sight. The corporation of the town of Stockton being unwilling or unable to provide accommodation for the rapidly increasing coal traffic, Mr. Edward Pease, in 1829, joined by a few of his Quaker friends, bought about 500 or 600 acres of land five miles lower down the river—the site of the modern Middlesborough—for the purpose of there forming a new sea-port for the shipment of coals brought to the Tees by the railway. The line was accordingly extended thither; docks were excavated; a town sprang up; churches, chapels, and schools were built, with a custom-house, mechanics' institute, banks, ship-building yards, and iron factories, and in a few years the port of Middlesborough became one of the most thriving on the northeast coast of England. In ten years a busy population of some 6000 persons (since swelled to about 25,000) occupied the site of the original farm-house. More recently, the discovery of vast stores of ironstone in the Cleveland Hills, close adjoining Middlesborough, has tended still more rapidly to augment the population and increase the commercial importance of the place.

It is pleasing to relate, in connection with this great work—

the Stockton and Darlington Railway, projected by Edward Pease and executed by George Stephenson—that when Mr. Stephenson became a prosperous and a celebrated man, he did not forget the friend who had taken him by the hand, and helped him on in his early days. He continued to remember Mr. Pease with gratitude and affection, and that gentleman, to the close of his life, was proud to exhibit a handsome gold watch, received as a gift from his celebrated *protégé*, bearing these words—"Esteem and gratitude: from George Stephenson to Edward Pease."

MIDDLESBOROUGH-ON-TEES.]

CHAPTER IX.

THE LIVERPOOL AND MANCHESTER RAILWAY PROJECTED.

WHILE the coal proprietors of the Bishop Auckland district were taking steps to connect their collieries with the sea by means of an iron railroad, the merchants of Liverpool and Manchester were considering whether some better means could not be devised for bringing these important centres of commerce and manufacture into more direct connection.

There were canals as well as roads between the two places, but all routes were alike tedious and costly, especially as regarded the transit of heavy goods. The route by turnpike road was thirty-six miles, by the Duke of Bridgewater's Canal fifty miles, by the Mersey and Irwell navigation the same, and by the Leeds and Liverpool Canal fifty-six miles.

These were all overburdened with traffic. The roads were bad, the tolls heavy, and the haulage expensive. The journey by coach occupied from five to six hours, and by wagon nearly a day. But very few heavy goods went by road. The canals nearly monopolized this traffic, and, having contrived to keep up the rates, the canal companies charged what they liked. They conducted their business in a drowsy, sleepy, stupid manner. If the merchant complained of delay, he was told to do better if he could. If he objected to the rates, he was warned that if he did not pay them promptly his goods might not be carried at all.

The canal companies were in a position to dictate their own terms, and they did this in such a way as to disgust alike the senders and the receivers of goods, so that both Liverpool and Manchester were up in arms against them. Worse even than the heavy charges for goods was the occasional entire stoppage of the canals. Sometimes they were frozen up; sometimes they were blocked by the press of traffic, so that goods lay on the wharves unmoved for weeks together; and at some seasons it occupied a longer time to bring cotton from Liverpool to Manchester by canal-boat than it had done to bring it from New York to Liverpool by sailing ship.

Was there no way of remedying these great and admitted evils? Were the commercial public to continue to be bound hand and foot, and left at the mercy of the canal proprietors? Immense interests at Liverpool and Manchester were at stake. The Liverpool merchants wanted new facilities for sending raw material inland, and the Manchester manufacturers for sending the manufactured products back to Liverpool for shipment. Vast populations had become settled in the towns of South Lancashire, to whom it was of vital importance that the communication with the sea should be regular, constant, and economical.

These considerations early led to the discussion of some improved mode of transit from Liverpool into the interior for heavy goods, and one of the most favored plans was that of a tram-road. It was first suggested by the corn-merchants of Liverpool, who had experienced the great inconveniences resulting from the canal monopoly. One of the most zealous advocates of the tram-road was Mr. Joseph Sandars, who took considerable pains to ascertain the results of the working of the coal lines in the North, both by horse and engine power, and he satisfied himself that either method would, if adopted between Liverpool and Manchester, afford the desired relief to the commercial and manufacturing interests. The subject was ventilated by him in the local papers, and in the course of the year 1821 Mr. Sandars succeeded in getting together a committee of Liverpool gentlemen for the purpose of farther considering the subject, and, if found practicable, of starting a company with the object of forming a tram-road between the two towns.

While the project was still in embryo, the rumor of it reached the ears of Mr. William James, then of West Bromwich, an enthusiastic advocate of tram-roads and railways. As a land-surveyor and land-agent, as well as coal-owner, he had already laid down many private railroads. He had also laid out and superintended the execution and the working of canals, projected extensive schemes of drainage and inclosure, and, on the whole, was one of the most useful and active men of his time. But a series of unfortunate speculations in mines having seriously impaired his fortunes, he again reverted to his original profession of land-surveyor, and was so occupied in the neighborhood of Liverpool when he heard of the scheme set on foot for the construction of the proposed tram-road to Manchester.

He at once called upon Mr. Sandars and offered his services as its surveyor. We believe he at first offered to survey the line at his own expense, to which Mr. Sandars could not object; but his means were too limited to enable him to do this successfully, and Mr. Sandars and several of his friends agreed to pay him £300 for the survey, or at the rate of about £10 a mile. Mr. James's first interview with Mr. Sandars was in the beginning of July, 1821, when it was arranged that he should go over the ground and form a general opinion as to the practicability of a tramway.

A trial survey was then begun, but it was conducted with great difficulty, the inhabitants of the district entertaining much prejudice against the scheme. In some places Mr. James and his surveying party had even to encounter personal violence. At St. Helen's one of the chain-men was laid hold of by a mob of colliers, and threatened to be hurled down a coal-pit. A number of men, women, and children assembled, and ran after the surveyors wherever they made their appearance, bawling nicknames and throwing stones at them. As one of the chain-men was climbing over a gate one day, a laborer made at him with a pitchfork, and ran it through his clothes into his back; other watchers running up, the chain-man, who was more stunned than hurt, took to his heels and fled. But that mysterious-looking instrument—the theodolite—most excited the fury of the natives, who concentrated on the man who carried it their fiercest execrations and most offensive nicknames.

A powerful fellow, a noted bruiser, was hired by the surveyors to carry the instrument, with a view to its protection against all assailants; but one day an equally powerful fellow, a St. Helen's collier, cock of the walk in his neighborhood, made up to the theodolite bearer to wrest it from him by sheer force. A battle took place, the collier was soundly pommeled, but the natives poured in volleys of stones upon the surveyors and their instruments, and the theodolite was smashed in pieces.

Met by these and other obstructions, it turned out that the survey could not be completed in time for depositing the proper plans, and the intended application to Parliament in the next session could not be made. In the mean time, Mr. James proceeded to Killingworth to see Stephenson's locomotives at work. Stephenson was not at home at the time, but James saw his engines, and was very much struck by their power and efficiency. He saw at a glance the magnificent uses to which the locomotive might be applied. "Here," said he, "is an engine that will, before long, effect a complete revolution in society." Returning to Moreton-in-the-Marsh, he wrote to Mr. Losh (Stephenson's partner in the patent) expressing his admiration of the Killingworth engine. "It is," said he, "the greatest wonder of the age, and the

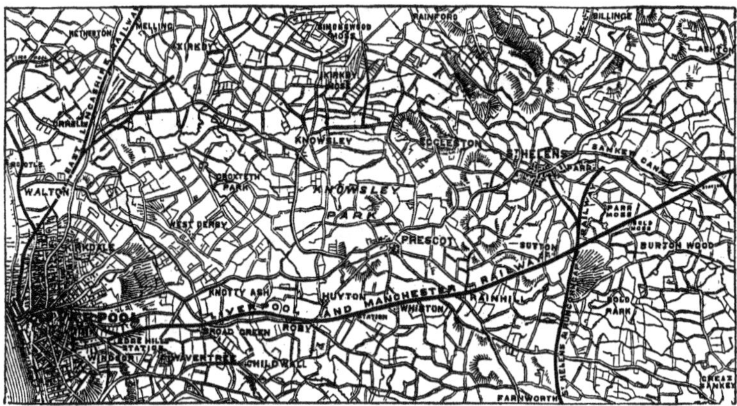

MAP OF LIVERPOOL AND MANCHESTER RAILWAY. [Western Part.]

forerunner, as I firmly believe, of the most important changes in the internal communications of the kingdom." Shortly after, Mr. James, accompanied by his two sons, made a second journey to Killingworth, where he met both Losh and Stephenson. The visitors were at once taken to where one of the locomotives was working, and invited to "jump up." The uncouth and extraordinary appearance of the machine, as it came snorting along, was somewhat alarming to the youths, who expressed their fears lest it should burst; and they were with some difficulty induced to mount.

The engine went through its usual performances, dragging a heavy load of coal-wagons at about six miles an hour with apparent ease, at which Mr. James expressed his extreme satisfaction, and declared to Mr. Losh his opinion that Stephenson "was the greatest practical genius of the age," and that, "if he developed the full powers of that engine (the locomotive), his fame in the world would rank equal with that of Watt." Mr. James informed Stephenson and Losh of his survey of the proposed tram-road between Liverpool and Manchester, and did not hesitate to state that he would thenceforward advocate the construction of a locomotive railroad instead of the tram-road which had originally been proposed.

Stephenson and Losh were naturally desirous of enlisting James's good services on behalf of their patent locomotive, for

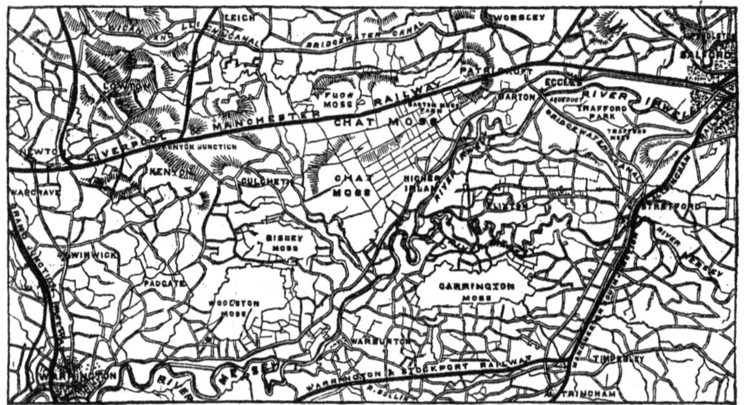

MAP OF LIVERPOOL AND MANCHESTER RAILWAY. [Eastern Part.]

as yet it had proved comparatively unproductive. They believed that he might be able so to advocate it in influential quarters as to insure its more extensive adoption, and with that object they proposed to give him an interest in the patent. Accordingly, they entered into an agreement by which they assigned to him one fourth of any profits which might be derived from the use of the patent locomotive on any railways constructed south of a line drawn across England from Liverpool to Hull. The arrangement, however, led to no beneficial results. Mr. James endeavored to introduce the engine on the Moreton-on-Marsh Railway, but it was opposed by the engineer of the line, and the attempt failed. He next urged that a locomotive should be sent for trial upon the Merstham tram-road; but, anxious though Stephenson was as to its extended employment, he was too cautious to risk an experiment which might bring discredit upon the engine; and the Merstham Road being only laid with cast-iron plates which would not bear its weight, the invitation was declined.

The first survey made of the Liverpool and Manchester line having been found very imperfect, it was determined to have a second and more complete one made in the following year. Robert Stephenson, though then a lad of only nineteen, had already obtained some practical knowledge of surveying, having been engaged on the preliminary survey of the Stockton and Darlington Railway in the previous year, and he was sent over to Liverpool by his father to give Mr. James such assistance as he could. Robert Stephenson was present with Mr. James on the occasion on which he tried to lay out the line across Chat Moss—a proceeding which was not only difficult, but dangerous. The Moss was very wet at the time, and only its edges could be ventured on. Mr. James was a heavy, thick-set man; and one day, when endeavoring to obtain a stand for his theodolite, he felt himself suddenly sinking. He immediately threw himself down, and rolled over and over until he reached firm ground again, in a sad mess. Other attempts which he subsequently made to advance into the Moss for the same purpose were abandoned for the same reason —the want of a solid stand for the theodolite.

As Mr. James proceeded with his survey, he found a host of opponents springing up in all directions, some of whom he conciliated by deviations, but others refused to be conciliated on any terms. Among these last were Lords Derby and Wilton, Mr. Bradshaw, and the Strafford family. The proposed line passed through their lands, and, regarding it as a nuisance, without the slightest compensating advantage to them, they determined to oppose it at every stage. Their agents drove the surveyors off their land; the farmers set men at the gates armed with pitchforks to resist their progress; and the survey proceeded with great difficulty. Mr. James endeavored to avoid Lord Derby's Knowsley estate, but as he had received instructions from Messrs. Ewart and Gladstone to lay out the line so as to enable it to be extended to the docks, he found it difficult to accomplish this object and at the same time avert the hostility of the noble lord. The only large land-owners who gave the scheme their support were

Mr. Legh and Mr. Wyrley Birch, who not only subscribed for shares, but attended several public meetings, and spoke in favor of the proposed railroad. Public opinion was, however, beginning to be roused, and the canal companies began at length to feel alarmed.

"At Manchester," Mr. James wrote to Mr. Sandars, "the subject engages all men's thoughts, and it is curious as well as amusing to hear their conjectures. The canal companies (southward) are alive to their danger. I have been the object of their persecution and hate; they would immolate me if they could; but if I can die the death of Samson, by pulling away the pillars, I am content to die with these Philistines. Be assured, my dear sir, that not a moment shall be lost, nor shall my attention for a day be diverted from this concern, which increases in importance every hour, as well as in the certainty of ultimate success."

Mr. James was one of the most enthusiastic of men, especially about railways and locomotives. He believed, with Thomas Gray, who brought out his book about this time, that railways were yet to become the great high roads of civilization. The speculative character of the man may be inferred from the following passage in one of his letters to Mr. Sandars, written from London:

"Every Parliamentary friend I have seen—and I have many of both houses—eulogizes our plan, and they are particularly anxious that engines should be introduced in the south. I am now negotiating about the Wandsworth Railroad. A fortune is to be made by buying the shares, and introducing the engine system upon it. I am confident capital will treble itself in two years. I do not choose to publish my views *here*, and I wish to God some of our Liverpool friends would take this advantage. I have bought some shares, but my capital is locked up in unproductive lands and mines."

As the survey of the Liverpool and Manchester line proceeded, Mr. James's funds fell short, and he was under the necessity of applying to Mr. Sandars and his friends from time to time for farther contributions. It was also necessary for him to attend to his business as a surveyor in other parts of the country, and he was at such times under the necessity of leaving the work to be done by his assistants. Thus the survey was necessarily imperfect, and when the time arrived for lodging the plans, it was found that they were practically worthless. Mr. James's pecuniary difficulties had also reached their climax. "The surveys and plans," he wrote to Mr. Sandars, "can't be completed, I see, till the end of the week. With illness, anguish of mind, and inexpressible distress, I perceive I must sink if I wait any longer; and, in short, I have so neglected the suit in Chancery I named to you, that if I do not put in an answer I shall be outlawed."

Mr. James's embarrassments increased, and he was unable to shake himself free from them. He was confined for many months in the Queen's Bench Prison, during which time this indefatigable railway propagandist wrote an essay illustrative of the advantages of direct inland communication by a line of engine railroad between London, Brighton, and Portsmouth. Meanwhile the Liverpool and Manchester scheme seemed to have fallen to the ground. But it only slept. When its promoters found that they could no longer rely on Mr. James's services, they determined to employ another engineer.

Mr. Sandars had by this time visited George Stephenson at Killingworth, and, like all who came within reach of his personal influence, was charmed with him at first sight. The energy which he had displayed in carrying on the works of the Stockton and Darlington Railway, now approaching completion; his readiness to face difficulties, and his practical ability in overcoming them; the enthusiasm which he displayed on the subject of railways and railway locomotion, concurred in satisfying Mr. Sandars that he was, of all men, the best calculated to help forward the undertaking at this juncture; and having, on his return to Liverpool, reported this opinion to the committee, they approved his recommendation, and George Stephenson was unanimously appointed engineer of the projected railway. On the 25th of May, 1824, Mr. Sandars wrote to Mr. James as follows:

"I think it right to inform you that the committee have engaged your friend George Stephenson. We expect him here in a few days. The subscription-list for £300,000 is filled, and the Manchester gentlemen have conceded to us the entire management. I very much regret that, by delays and promises, you have forfeited the confidence of the subscribers. I can not help it. I fear now that you will only have the fame of being connected with the commencement of this undertaking."

It will be observed that Mr. Sandars had held to his original purpose with great determination and perseverance, and he gradually succeeded in enlisting on his side an increasing number of influential merchants and manufacturers both at Liverpool and Manchester. Early in 1824 he published a pamphlet, in which he strongly urged the great losses and interruptions to the trade of the district by the delays in the forwarding of merchandise; and in the same year he had a Public Declaration drawn up, and signed by upward of 150 of the principal merchants of Liverpool, setting forth that they considered "the present establishments for the transport of goods quite inadequate, and that a new line of conveyance has become absolutely necessary to conduct the increasing trade of the country with speed, certainty, and economy."

A public meeting was then held to consider the best plan to be adopted, and resolutions were passed in favor of a railroad. A committee was appointed to take the necessary measures; but, as if reluctant to enter upon their arduous struggle with the "vested interests," they first waited on Mr. Bradshaw, the Duke of Bridgewater's canal agent, in the hope of persuading him to increase the means of conveyance, as well as to reduce the charges; but they were met by an unqualified refusal. He would not improve the existing means of conveyance; he would have nothing to do with the proposed railway; and, if persevered in, he would oppose it with all his power. The canal proprietors, confident in their imagined security, ridiculed the proposed railway as a chimera. It had been spoken about years before, and nothing had come of it then; it would be the same now.

In order to form a better opinion as to the practicability of the railroad, a deputation of gentlemen interested in the project proceeded to Killingworth to inspect the engines which had been so long in use there. They first went to Darlington, where they found the works of the Stockton line in progress, though still unfinished. Proceeding next to Killingworth with George Stephenson, they there witnessed the performances of his locomotive engines. The result of their visit was, on the whole, so satisfactory, that on their return to Liverpool it was determined to form a company of the proprietors for the construction of a double line of railway between Liverpool and Manchester.

The original promoters of the undertaking included men of the highest standing and local influence in Liverpool and Manchester, with Charles Lawrence as chairman, Lister Ellis, Robert Gladstone, John Moss, and Joseph Sandars as deputy chairmen; while among the ordinary members of the committee were Robert Benson, James Cropper, John Ewart, Wellwood Maxwell, and William Rathbone, of Liverpool, and the brothers Birley, Peter Ewart, William Garnett, John Kennedy, and William Potter, of Manchester.

The committee also included another important name—that of Henry Booth, then a corn-merchant of Liverpool, and afterward the secretary and manager of the Liverpool and Manchester Railway. Mr. Booth was a man of admirable business qualities, sagacious and far-seeing, shrewd and practical, of considerable literary ability, and he also possessed a knowledge of mechanics, which afterward proved of the greatest value to the railway interest; for to him we owe the suggestion of the multitubular boiler in the form in which it has since been employed upon all railways, and the coupling-screw, as well as other important mechanical appliances which have come into general use.

The first prospectus, issued in October, 1824, set forth in clear and vigorous language the objects of the company, the urgent need of additional means of communication between Liverpool and Manchester, and the advantages offered by the railway over all other proposed expedients. It was shown that the water-carriers not only exacted the most arbitrary terms from the public, but were positively unable to carry the traffic requiring accommodation. Against the indefinite continuance or recurrence of those evils, said the prospectus, the public have but one security: "It is competition that is wanted; and the proof of this assertion may be adduced from the fact that shares in the Old Quay Navigation, of which the original cost was £70, have been sold as high as £1250 each!" The advantages of the railway over the canals for the carriage of coals was also urged, and it was stated that the charge for transit would be very materially reduced.

"In the present state of trade and of commercial enterprise (the prospectus proceeded), dispatch is no less essential than economy. Merchandise is frequently brought across the Atlantic from New York to Liverpool in twenty-one days, while, owing to the various causes of delay above enumerated, goods have in some instances been longer on their passage from Liverpool to Manchester. But this reproach must not be perpetual. The advancement in mechanical science renders it unnecessary—the good sense of the community makes it impossible. Let it not, however, be imagined that, were England to be tardy, other countries would pause in the march of improvement. Application has been made, on behalf of the Emperor of Russia, for models of the locomotive engine; and other of the Continental governments have been duly apprised of the important schemes for the facilitating of inland traffic, now under discussion by the British public. In the United States of America, also, they are fully alive to the important results to be anticipated from the introduction of railroads; a gentleman from the United States having recently arrived in Liverpool, with whom it is a principal object to collect the necessary information in order to the establishment of a railway to connect the great rivers Potomac and Ohio."

It will be observed that the principal, indeed almost the sole, object contemplated by the projectors of the undertaking was the improved carriage of merchandise and coal, and that the conveyance of passengers was scarcely calculated on, the only paragraph in the prospectus relating to the subject being the following: "Moreover, as a cheap and expeditious means of conveyance for travelers, the railway holds out the fair prospect of a public accommodation, the magnitude and importance of which can not be immediately ascertained." The estimated expense of forming the line was set down at £400,000—a sum which was eventually found quite inadequate. The subscription list, when opened, was filled up without difficulty.

While the project was still under discussion, its promoters, desirous of removing the doubts which existed as to the employment of steam-power on the proposed railway, sent a second deputation to Killingworth for the purpose of again observing the action of Stephenson's engines. The cautious projectors of the railway were not yet quite satisfied, and a third journey was made to Killingworth in January, 1825, by several gentlemen of the committee, accompanied by practical engineers, for the purpose of being personal eye-witnesses of what steam-carriages were able to perform upon a railway. There they saw a train, consisting of a locomotive and loaded wagons, weighing in all 54 tons, traveling at the average rate of about 7 miles an hour, the greatest speed being about 9½ miles an hour. But when the engine was run with only one wagon attached containing twenty gentlemen, five of whom were engineers, the speed attained was from 10 to 12 miles an hour.

In the mean time the survey was proceeded with, in the face of great opposition on the part of the proprietors of the lands through which the railway was intended to pass. The prejudices of the farming and laboring classes were strongly excited against the persons employed upon the ground, and it was with the greatest difficulty that the levels could be taken. This opposition was especially manifested when the attempt was made to survey the line through the properties of Lords Derby and Sefton, and also where it crossed the Duke of Bridgewater's Canal. At Knowsley, Stephenson and his surveyors were driven off the ground by the keepers, and threatened with rough handling if found there again. Lord Derby's farmers also turned out their men to watch the surveying party, and prevent them entering on any lands where they had the power of driving them off. Afterward Stephenson suddenly and unexpectedly went upon the ground with a body of surveyors and their assistants who outnumbered Lord Derby's keepers and farmers, hastily collected to resist them, and this time they were only threatened with the legal consequences of their trespass.

The same sort of resistance was offered by Lord Sefton's keepers and farmers, with whom the following ruse was adopted. A minute was concocted, purporting to be a resolution of the Old Quay Canal Company to oppose the projected railroad by every possible means, and calling upon land-owners and others to afford every facility for making such a survey of the intended line as should enable the opponents to detect errors in the scheme of the promoters, and thereby insure its defeat. A copy of this minute, without any signature, was exhibited by the surveyors who went upon the ground, and the farmers, believing them to have the sanction of the landlords, permitted them to proceed with the hasty completion of their survey.

The principal opposition, however, was experienced from Mr. Bradshaw, the manager of the Duke of Bridgewater's canal property, who offered a vigorous and protracted resistance to the survey in all its stages. The duke's farmers obstinately refused permission to enter upon their fields, although Stephenson offered to pay for any damage that might be done. Mr. Bradshaw positively refused his sanction in any case; and being a strict preserver of game, with a large staff of keepers in his pay, he declared that he would order them to shoot or apprehend any persons attempting a survey over his property. But one moonlight night a survey was effected by the following ruse. Some men, under the orders of the surveying party, were set to fire off guns in a particular quarter, on which all the gamekeepers on the watch made off in that direction, and they were drawn away to such a distance in pursuit of the supposed poachers as to enable a rapid survey to be made during their absence. Describing before Parliament the difficulties which he encountered in making the survey, Stephenson said: "I was threatened to be ducked in the pond if I proceeded, and, of course, we had a great deal of the survey to take by stealth, at the time when the people were at dinner. We could not get it done by night; indeed, we were watched day and night, and guns were discharged over the grounds belonging to Captain Bradshaw to prevent us. I can state farther that I was myself twice turned off Mr. Bradshaw's grounds by his men, and they said if I did not go instantly they would take me up and carry me off to Worsley."

The same kind of opposition had to be encountered all along the line of the intended railway. Mr. Clay, one of the company's solicitors, wrote to Mr. Sandars from the Bridgewater Arms, Prescott, on the 31st of December, that the landlords, occupiers, trustees of turnpike roads, proprietors of bleach-works, carriers and carters, and even the coal-owners, were dead against the railroad. "In a word," said he, "the country is up in arms against us." There were only three considerable land-owners who remained doubtful; and "if these be against us," said Mr. Clay, "then *the whole* of the great proprietors along the whole line are dissentient, excepting only Mr. Trafford."

The cottagers and small proprietors were equally hostile. "The trouble we have with them," wrote Mr. Clay, "is beyond belief; and those patches of gardens at the end of Manchester bordering on the Irwell, and the tenants of Hulme Hall, who, though insignificant, must be seen, give us infinite trouble, all of which, as I have reason to believe, is by no means accidental." There was also the opposition of the great Bradshaw, the duke's agent. "I wrote you this morning," said Mr. Clay, in a wrathful letter of the same date, "since which we have been into Bradshaw's warehouse, now called the Knot Mill, and, after traversing two of the rooms, we got very *civilly* turned out, which, under all the circumstances, I thought very lucky, and more than we deserved. However, we have seen more than half of his d—d cottagers."

There were also the canal companies, who made common cause, formed a common purse, and determined to wage war to the knife against all railways. The following circular, issued by the Liverpool Railroad Company, with the name of Mr. Lawrence, the chairman, attached, will serve to show the resolute spirit in which the canal proprietors were preparing to resist the bill:

"Sir,—The Leeds and Liverpool, the Birmingham, the Grand Trunk, and other canal companies having issued circulars, calling upon 'every canal and navigation company in the kingdom' to oppose *in limine* and by a united effort the establishment of railroads wherever contemplated, I have most earnestly to solicit your active exertions on behalf of the Liverpool and Manchester Railroad Company, to counteract the avowed purpose of the canal proprietors, by exposing the misrepresentations of interested parties, by conciliating good will, and especially by making known, as far as you have opportunity, not only the general superiority of railroads over other modes of conveyance, but, in our peculiar case, the absolute necessity of a new and additional line of communication, in order to effect with economy and dispatch the transport of merchandise between this port and Manchester.

"(Signed) Charles Lawrence, Chairman."

Such was the state of affairs and such the threatenings of war on both sides immediately previous to the Parliamentary session of 1825.

When it became known that the promoters of the undertaking were determined—imperfect though the plans were believed to be, from the obstructions thrown in the way of the surveying parties—to proceed with the bill in the next session of Parliament, the canal companies appealed to the public through the press.

Pamphlets were published and newspapers hired to revile the railway. It was declared that its formation would prevent the cows grazing and hens laying, while the horses passing along the road would be driven distracted. The poisoned air from the locomotives would kill the birds that flew over them, and render the preservation of pheasants and foxes no longer possible. Householders adjoining the projected line were told that their houses would be burnt up by the fire thrown from the engine chimneys, while the air around would be polluted by clouds of smoke. There would no longer be any use for horses; and if railways extended, the species would become extinguished, and oats and hay be rendered unsalable commodities. Traveling by rail would be highly dangerous, and country inns would be ruined. Boilers would burst and blow passengers to atoms. But there was always this consolation to wind up with—that the weight of the locomotive would completely prevent its moving, and that railways, even if made, could *never* be worked by steam-power.

Although the press generally spoke of the Liverpool and Manchester project as a mere speculation—as only one of the many bubble schemes of the period*—there were other writers who entertained different views, and boldly and ably announced them. Among the most sagacious newspaper articles of the day, calling attention to the application of the locomotive engine to the purposes of rapid steam-traveling on railroads, was a series which appeared in 1824, in the "Scotsman" newspaper, then edited by Mr. Charles Maclaren. In those publications the wonderful powers of the locomotive were logically demonstrated, and the writer, arguing from the experiments on friction made more than half a century before by Vince and Coulomb, which scientific men seemed to have altogether lost sight of, clearly showed that, by the use of steam-power on railroads, the cheaper as well as more rapid transit of persons and merchandise might be confidently anticipated.

* "Many years ago I met in a public library with a bulky volume, consisting of the prospectuses of various projects bound up together, and labeled, 'Some of the Bubbles of 1825.' Among the projects thus described was one that has since been productive of the greatest and most rapid advance in the social condition of mankind effected since the first dawn of civilization: it was the plan of the company for constructing a railway between Liverpool and Manchester."—W. B. Hodge, in "Journal of the Institute of Actuaries," No. 40, July, 1860.

Not many years passed before the anticipations of the writer, sanguine and speculative though they were at that time regarded, were amply realized. Even Mr. Nicholas Wood, in 1825, speaking of the powers of the locomotive, and referring doubtless to the speculations of the "Scotsman" as well as of his equally sanguine friend Stephenson, observed: "It is far from my wish to promulgate to the world that the ridiculous expectations, or rather professions, of the enthusiastic speculist will be realized, and that we shall see engines traveling at the rate of twelve, sixteen, eighteen, or twenty miles an hour. Nothing could do more harm toward their general adoption and improvement than the promulgation of such nonsense."*

Among the papers left by Mr. Sandars we find a letter addressed to him by Sir John Barrow, of the Admiralty, as to the proper method of conducting the case in Parliament, which pretty accurately represents the state of public opinion as to the practicability of locomotive traveling on railroads at the time at which it was written, the 10th of January, 1825. Sir John strongly urged Mr. Sandars to keep the locomotive altogether in the background; to rely upon the proved inability of the canals and common roads to accommodate the existing traffic; and to be satisfied with proving the absolute necessity of a new line of conveyance; above all, he recommended him not even to hint at the intention of carrying passengers.

"You will at once," said he, "raise a host of enemies in the proprietors of coaches, post-chaises, innkeepers, etc., whose interests will be attacked, and who, I have no doubt, will be strongly supported, and for what? Some thousands of passengers, *you* say—but a few hundreds *I* should say—in the year."

He accordingly urged that *passengers* as well as *speed* should be kept entirely out of the act; but, if the latter were insisted on, then he recommended that it should be kept as low as possible—say at five miles an hour!

Indeed, when George Stephenson, at the interviews with counsel held previous to the Liverpool and Manchester Bill going into Committee of the House of Commons, confidently stated his expectation of being able to run his locomotive at the rate of twenty miles an hour, Mr. William Brougham, who was retained by

* "Wood on Railroads," ed. 1825, p. 290.

the promoters to conduct their case, frankly told him that if he did not moderate his views, and bring his engine within a *reasonable* speed, he would "inevitably damn the whole thing, and be himself regarded as a maniac fit only for Bedlam."

The idea thrown out by Stephenson of traveling at a rate of speed double that of the fastest mail-coach appeared at the time so preposterous that he was unable to find any engineer who would risk his reputation in supporting such "absurd views." Speaking of his isolation at the time, he subsequently observed at a public meeting of railway men in Manchester: "He remembered the time when he had very few supporters in bringing out the railway system—when he sought England over for an engineer to support him in his evidence before Parliament, and could find only one man, James Walker, but was afraid to call that gentleman, because he knew nothing about railways. He had then no one to tell his tale to but Mr. Sandars, of Liverpool, who did listen to him, and kept his spirits up; and his schemes had at length been carried out only by dint of sheer perseverance."

George Stephenson's idea was at that time regarded as but the dream of a chimerical projector. It stood before the public friendless, struggling hard to gain a footing, scarcely daring to lift itself into notice for fear of ridicule. The civil engineers generally rejected the notion of a Locomotive Railway; and when no leading man of the day could be found to stand forward in support of the Killingworth mechanic, its chances of success must indeed have been pronounced but small.

When such was the hostility of the civil engineers, no wonder the Reviewers were puzzled. The "Quarterly," in an able article in support of the projected Liverpool and Manchester Railway, while admitting its *absolute necessity*, and insisting that there was no choice left but a railroad, on which the journey between Liverpool and Manchester, whether performed by horses or engines, would always be accomplished "within the day," nevertheless scouted the idea of traveling at a greater speed than eight or nine miles an hour. Adverting to a project for forming a railway to Woolwich, by which passengers were to be drawn by locomotive engines moving with twice the velocity of ordinary coaches, the reviewer observed: "What can be more palpably absurd and ridiculous than the prospect held out of locomotives traveling *twice as fast* as stage-coaches! We would as soon expect the people of Woolwich to suffer themselves to be fired off upon one of Congreve's ricochet rockets, as trust themselves to the mercy of such a machine going at such a rate. We will back old Father Thames against the Woolwich Railway for any sum. We trust that Parliament will, in all railways it may sanction, limit the speed to *eight or nine miles an hour*, which we entirely agree with Mr. Sylvester is as great as can be ventured on with safety."

SURVEYING ON CHAT MOSS.

CHAPTER X.

PARLIAMENTARY CONTEST ON THE LIVERPOOL AND MANCHESTER BILL.

THE Liverpool and Manchester Bill went into Committee of the House of Commons on the 21st of March, 1825. There was an extraordinary array of legal talent on the occasion, but especially on the side of the opponents to the measure. Their wealth and influence enabled them to retain the ablest counsel at the bar; Mr. (afterward Baron) Alderson, Mr. Stephenson, Mr. (afterward Baron) Parke, Mr. Rose, Mr. Macdonnell, Mr. Harrison, Mr. Erle, and Mr. Cullen, appeared for various clients, who made common cause with each other in opposing the bill, the case for which was conducted by Mr. Adam, Mr. Sergeant Spankie, Mr. William Brougham, and Mr. Joy.

Evidence was taken at great length as to the difficulties and delays in forwarding raw goods of all kinds from Liverpool to Manchester, as also in the conveyance of manufactured articles from Manchester to Liverpool. The evidence adduced in support of the bill on these grounds was overwhelming. The utter inadequacy of the existing modes of conveyance to carry on satisfactorily the large and rapidly-growing trade between the two towns was fully proved. But then came the main difficulty of the promoters' case—that of proving the practicability of constructing a railroad to be worked by locomotive power. Mr. Adam, in his opening speech, referred to the cases of the Hetton and the Killingworth railroads, where heavy goods were safely and economically transported by means of locomotive engines. "None of the tremendous consequences," he observed, "have ensued from the use of steam in land carriage that have been stated. The horses have not started, nor the cows ceased to give their milk, nor have ladies miscarried at the sight of these things going forward at the rate of four miles and a half an hour." Notwithstanding the petition of two ladies alleging the great danger to be apprehended from the bursting of the locomotive boilers, he urged the safety of the high-pressure engine when the boilers were constructed of wrought iron; and as to the rate at which they could travel, he expressed his full conviction that such engines "could supply force to drive a carriage at the rate of five or six miles an hour."

The taking of the evidence as to the impediments thrown in the way of trade and commerce by the existing system extended over a month, and it was the 21st of April before the committee went into the engineering evidence, which was the vital part of the question.

On the 25th George Stephenson was called into the witness-box. It was his first appearance before a committee of the House of Commons, and he well knew what he had to expect. He was aware that the whole force of the opposition was to be directed against him; and if they could break down his evidence, the canal monopoly might yet be upheld for a time. Many years afterward, when looking back at his position on this trying occasion, he said: "When I went to Liverpool to plan a line from thence to Manchester, I pledged myself to the directors to attain a speed of ten miles an hour. I said I had no doubt the locomotive might be made to go much faster, but that we had better be moderate at the beginning. The directors said I was quite right; for that if, when they went to Parliament, I talked of going at a greater rate than ten miles an hour, I should put a cross upon the concern. It was not an easy task for me to keep the engine down to ten miles an hour, but it must be done, and I did my best. I had to place myself in that most unpleasant of all positions—the witness-box of a Parliamentary committee. I was not long in it before I began to wish for a hole to creep out at! I could not find words to satisfy either the committee or myself. I was subjected to the cross-examination of eight or ten barristers, purposely, as far as possible, to bewilder me. Some member of the committee asked *if I was a foreigner*,* and another

* George's Northumberland "burr" was so strong that it rendered him almost unintelligible to persons who were unfamiliar with it; and he had even thoughts of going to school again, for the purpose, if possible, of getting rid of it. In the year 1823, when Stephenson was forty-two years of age, we find his friend Thomas Richardson, of Lombard Street, writing to Samuel Thoroughgood, a schoolmaster at Peckham, as follows: "DEAR FRIEND,—My friend George Stephenson, a man

hinted that *I was mad*. But I put up with every rebuff, and went on with my plans, determined not to be put down."

George Stephenson stood before the committee to prove what the public opinion of that day held to be impossible. The self-taught mechanic had to demonstrate the practicability of accomplishing that which the most distinguished engineers of the time regarded as impracticable. Clear though the subject was to himself, and familiar as he was with the powers of the locomotive, it was no easy task for him to bring home his convictions, or even to convey his meaning, to the less informed minds of his hearers. In his strong Northumbrian dialect, he struggled for utterance, in the face of the sneers, interruptions, and ridicule of the opponents of the measure, and even of the committee, some of whom shook their heads and whispered doubts as to his sanity when he energetically avowed that he could make the locomotive go at the rate of twelve miles an hour! It was so grossly in the teeth of all the experience of honorable members, that the man "must certainly be laboring under a delusion!"

And yet his large experience of railways and locomotives, as described by himself to the committee, entitled this "untaught, inarticulate genius," as he has been described, to speak with confidence on the subject. Beginning with his experience as a brakesman at Killingworth in 1803, he went on to state that he was appointed to take the entire charge of the steam-engines in 1813, and had superintended the railroads connected with the numerous collieries of the Grand Allies from that time downward. He had laid down or superintended the railways at Burradon, Mount Moor, Springwell, Bedlington, Hetton, and Darlington, besides improving those at Killingworth, South Moor, and Derwent Crook. He had constructed fifty-five steam-engines, of which sixteen were locomotives. Some of these had been sent to France. The engines constructed by him for the working of the Killingworth Railroad, eleven years before, had continued steadily at work ever since, and fulfilled his most san-

of first-rate abilities as an engineer, but of little or no education, wants to consult thee or some other person to see if he can not improve himself—he has so much Northumberland dialect, etc. He will be at my house on sixth day next, about five o'clock, if thou could make it convenient to see him. Thy assured friend, THOS. RICHARDSON."

guine expectations. He was prepared to prove the safety of working high-pressure locomotives on a railroad, and the superiority of this mode of transporting goods over all others. As to speed, he said he had recommended eight miles an hour with twenty tons, and four miles an hour with forty tons; but he was quite confident that much more might be done. Indeed, he had no doubt they might go at the rate of twelve miles. As to the charge that locomotives on a railroad would so terrify the horses in the neighborhood that to travel on horseback or to plow the adjoining fields would be rendered highly dangerous, the witness said that horses learned to take no notice of them, though there *were* horses that would shy at a wheelbarrow. A mail-coach was likely to be more shied at by horses than a locomotive. In the neighborhood of Killingworth, the cattle in the fields went on grazing while the engines passed them, and the farmers made no complaints.

Mr. Alderson, who had carefully studied the subject, and was well skilled in practical science, subjected the witness to a protracted and severe cross-examination as to the speed and power of the locomotive, the stroke of the piston, the slipping of the wheels upon the rails, and various other points of detail. Stephenson insisted that no slipping took place, as attempted to be extorted from him by the counsel. He said, "It is impossible for slipping to take place so long as the adhesive weight of the wheel upon the rail is greater than the weight to be dragged after it." There was a good deal of interruption to the witness's answers by Mr. Alderson, to which Mr. Joy more than once objected. As to accidents, Stephenson knew of none that had occurred with his engines. There had been one, he was told, at the Middleton Colliery, near Leeds, with a Blenkinsop engine. The driver had been in liquor, and put a considerable load on the safety-valve, so that upon going forward the engine blew up and the man was killed. But he added, if proper precautions had been used with that boiler, the accident could not have happened. The following cross-examination occurred in reference to the question of speed:

"Of course," he was asked, "when a body is moving upon a road, the greater the velocity the greater the momentum that is generated?" "Certainly." "What would be the momentum of forty tons moving at the rate of twelve miles an hour?" "It would be very great." "Have you seen a railroad that would stand that?" "Yes." "Where?" "Any railroad that would bear going four miles an hour: I mean to say, that if it would bear the weight at four miles an hour, it would bear it at twelve." "Taking it at four miles an hour, do you mean to say that it would not require a stronger railway to carry the same weight twelve miles an hour?" "I will give an answer to that. I dare say every person has been over ice when skating, or seen persons go over, and they know that it would bear them better at a greater velocity than it would if they went slower; when they go quick, the weight in a measure ceases." "Is not than upon the hypothesis that the railroad is perfect?" "It is; and I mean to make it perfect."

It is not necessary to state that to have passed through his severe ordeal scatheless needed no small amount of courage, intelligence, and ready shrewdness on the part of the witness. Nicholas Wood, who was present on the occasion, has since stated that the point on which Stephenson was hardest pressed was that of speed. "I believe," he says, "that it would have lost the company their bill if he had gone beyond eight or nine miles an hour. If he had stated his intention of going twelve or fifteen miles an hour, not a single person would have believed it to be practicable." Mr. Alderson had, indeed, so pressed the point of "twelve miles an hour," and the promoters were so alarmed lest it should appear in evidence that they contemplated any such extravagant rate of speed, that immediately on Mr. Alderson sitting down, Mr. Joy proceeded to re-examine Stephenson, with the view of removing from the minds of the committee an impression so unfavorable, and, as they supposed, so damaging to their case. "With regard," asked Mr. Joy, "to all those hypothetical questions of my learned friend, they have been all put on the supposition of going twelve miles an hour: now that is not the rate at which, I believe, any of the engines of which you have spoken have traveled?" "No," replied Stephenson, "except as an experiment for a short distance." "But what they have gone has been three, five, or six miles an hour?" "Yes." "So that those hypothetical cases of twelve miles an hour do not fall within your general experience?" "They do not."

The committee also seem to have entertained some alarm as to the high rate of speed which had been spoken of, and proceeded to examine the witness farther on the subject. They supposed the case of the engine being upset when going at nine miles an hour, and asked what, in such a case, would become of the cargo astern. To which the witness replied that it would not be upset. One of the members of the committee pressed the witness a little farther. He put the following case: "Suppose, now, one of these engines to be going along a railroad at the rate of nine or ten miles an hour, and that a cow were to stray upon the line and get in the way of the engine; would not that, think you, be a very awkward circumstance?" "Yes," replied the witness, with a twinkle in his eye, "very awkward—*for the coo!*" The honorable member did not proceed farther with his cross-examination; to use a railway phrase, he was "shunted." Another asked if animals would not be very much frightened by the engine passing at night, especially by the glare of the red-hot chimney? "But how would they know that it wasn't painted?" said the witness.

On the following day (the 26th of April) the engineer was subjected to a most severe examination. On that part of the scheme with which he was most practically conversant, his evidence was clear and conclusive. Now, he had to give evidence on the plans made by his surveyors, and the estimates which had been founded on those plans. So long as he was confined to locomotive engines and iron railroads, with the minutest details of which he was more familiar than any man living, he felt at home and in his element. But when the designs of bridges and the cost of constructing them had to be gone into, the subject being comparatively new to him, his evidence was much less satisfactory.

He was cross-examined as to the practicability of forming a road on so unstable a foundation as Chat Moss.

"'Now, with respect to your evidence upon Chat Moss,' asked Mr. Alderson, 'did you ever walk on Chat Moss on the proposed line of the railway?' 'The greater part of it, I have.'

"'Was it not extremely boggy?' 'In parts it was.'

"'How deep did you sink in?' 'I could have gone with shoes; I do not know whether I had boots on.'

"'If the depth of the Moss should prove to be 40 feet instead of 20, would not this plan of the railway over this Moss be impracticable?' 'No, it would not. If the gentleman will allow me, I will refer to a railroad belonging to the Duke of Portland, made over a moss; there are no levels to drain it properly, such as we have at Chat Moss, and it is made by an embankment over the moss, which is worse than making a cutting, for there is the weight of the embankment to press upon the moss.'

"'Still, you must go to the bottom of the moss?' 'It is not necessary; the deeper you get, the more consolidated it is.'

"'Would you put some hard materials on it before you commenced?' 'Yes, perhaps I should.'

"'What?' 'Brushwood, perhaps.'

"'And you, then, are of opinion that it would be a solid embankment?' 'It would have a tremulous motion for a time, but would not give way, like clay.'"

Mr. Alderson also cross-examined him at great length on the plans of the bridges, the tunnels, the crossings of the roads and streets, and the details of the survey, which, it soon appeared, were in some respects seriously at fault. It seems that, after the plans had been deposited, Stephenson found that a much more favorable line might be laid out, and he made his estimates accordingly, supposing that Parliament would not confine the company to the precise plan which had been deposited. This was felt to be a serious blot in the Parliamentary case, and one very difficult to get over.

For three entire days was our engineer subjected to cross-examination by Mr. Alderson, Mr. Cullen, and the other leading counsel for the opposition. He held his ground bravely, and defended the plans and estimates with remarkable ability and skill, but it was clear they were imperfect, and the result was, on the whole, damaging to the bill. Mr. (afterward Sir William) Cubitt was called by the promoters, Mr. Adam stating that he proposed by this witness to correct some of the levels as given by Stephenson. It seems a singular course to have been taken by the promoters of the measure, for Mr. Cubitt's evidence went to upset the statements made by Stephenson as to the survey. This adverse evidence was, of course, made the most of by the opponents of the scheme.

Mr. Sergeant Spankie then summed up for the bill on the 2d

of May, in a speech of great length, and the case of the opponents was next gone into, Mr. Harrison opening with a long and eloquent speech on behalf of his clients, Mrs. Atherton and others. He indulged in strong vituperation against the witnesses for the bill, and especially dwelt upon the manner in which Mr. Cubitt, for the promoters, had proved that Stephenson's levels were wrong.

"They got a person," said he, "whose character and skill I do not dispute, though I do not exactly know that I should have gone to the inventor of the treadmill as the fittest man to take the levels of Knowsley Moss and Chat Moss, which shook almost as much as a treadmill, as you recollect, for he (Mr. Cubitt) said Chat Moss trembled so much under his feet that he could not take his observations accurately...... In fact, Mr. Cubitt did not go on to Chat Moss, because he knew that it was an immense mass of pulp, and nothing else. It actually rises in height, from the rain swelling it like a sponge, and sinks again in dry weather; and if a boring instrument is put into it, it sinks immediately by its own weight. The making of an embankment out of this pulpy, wet moss is no very easy task. Who but Mr. Stephenson would have thought of entering into Chat Moss, carrying it out almost like wet dung? It is ignorance almost inconceivable. It is perfect madness, in a person called upon to speak on a scientific subject, to propose such a plan...... Every part of the scheme shows that this man has applied himself to a subject of which he has no knowledge, and to which he has no science to apply."

Then, adverting to the proposal to work the intended line by means of locomotives, the learned gentleman proceeded:

"When we set out with the original prospectus, we were to gallop I know not at what rate—I believe it was at the rate of twelve miles an hour. My learned friend, Mr. Adam, contemplated—possibly alluding to Ireland—that some of the Irish members would arrive in the wagons to a division. My learned friend says that they would go at the rate of twelve miles an hour with the aid of the devil in the form of a locomotive sitting as postillion on the fore horse, and an honorable member sitting behind him to stir up the fire, and keep it at full speed. But the speed at which these locomotive engines are to go has slackened: Mr. Adam does not go faster now than five miles an hour. The learned sergeant (Spankie) says he should like to have seven, but he would be content to go six. I will show he can not go six; and probably, for any practical purposes, I may be able to show that I can keep up with him *by the canal*. . . . Locomotive engines are liable to be operated upon by the weather. You are told they are affected by rain, and an attempt has been made to cover them; but the wind will affect them; and any gale of wind which would affect the traffic on the Mersey would render it *impossible* to set off a locomotive engine, either by poking of the fire, or keeping up the pressure of the steam till the boiler was ready to burst."

How amusing it now is to read these extraordinary views as to the formation of a railway over Chat Moss, and the impossibility of starting a locomotive engine in the face of a gale of wind?

Evidence was called to show that the house property passed by the proposed railway would be greatly deteriorated—in some places almost destroyed; that the locomotive engines would be terrible nuisances, in consequence of the fire and smoke vomited forth by them; and that the value of land in the neighborhood of Manchester alone would be deteriorated by no less than £20,000! Evidence was also given at great length showing the utter impossibility of forming a road of any kind upon Chat Moss. A Manchester builder, who was examined, could not imagine the feat possible, unless by arching it across in the manner of a viaduct from one side to the other. It was the old story of "nothing like leather." But the opposition mainly relied upon the evidence of the leading engineers—not, like Stephenson, self-taught men, but regular professionals. Mr. Francis Giles, C.E., was their great card. He had been twenty-two years an engineer, and could speak with some authority. His testimony was mainly directed to the utter impossibility of forming a railway over Chat Moss. "*No engineer in his senses*," said he, "would go through Chat Moss if he wanted to make a railroad from Liverpool to Manchester. In my judgment, *a railroad certainly can not be safely made over Chat Moss without going to the bottom of the Moss*." The following may be taken as a specimen of Mr. Giles's evidence:

"'Tell us whether, in your judgment, a railroad can be safely made over Chat Moss without going to the bottom of the bog?' 'I say, *certainly not*.'

"'Will it be necessary, therefore, in making a permanent railroad, to take out the whole of the moss to the bottom, along the whole line of road?' 'Undoubtedly.'

"'Will that make it necessary to cut down the thirty-three or thirty-four feet of which you have been speaking?' 'Yes.'

"'And afterward to fill it up with other soil?' 'To such height as the railway is to be carried; other soil mixed with a portion of the moss.'

"'But suppose they were to work upon this stuff, could they get their carriages to this place?' '*No carriage can stand on the moss short of the bottom.*'

"'What could they do to make it stand—laying planks, or something of that sort?' 'Nothing would support it.'

"'So that, if you would carry a railroad over this fluid stuff—if you could do it, it would still take a great number of men and a great sum of money. Could it be done, in your opinion, for £6000?' 'I should say £200,000 would not get through it.'

"'My learned friend wishes to know what it would cost to lay it with diamonds?'"

Mr. H. R. Palmer, C.E., gave evidence to prove that resistance to a moving body going under four and a quarter miles an hour was *less* upon a canal than upon a railroad; and that, when going against a strong wind, the progress of a locomotive was retarded "very much." Mr. George Leather, C.E., the engineer of the Croydon and Wandsworth Railway, on which he said the wagons went at from two and a half to three miles an hour, also testified against the practicability of Stephenson's plan. He considered his estimate a "very wild" one. He had no confidence in locomotive power. The Weardale Railway, of which he was engineer, had given up the use of locomotive engines. He supposed that, when used, they traveled at three and a half to four miles an hour, because they were considered to be then more effective than at a higher speed.

When these distinguished engineers had given their evidence, Mr. Alderson summed up in a speech which extended over two days. He declared Stephenson's plan to be "the most absurd scheme that ever entered into the head of man to conceive:"

"My learned friends," said he, "almost endeavored to stop my examination; they wished me to put in the plan, but I had rather have the exhibition of Mr. Stephenson in that box. I say he never had one—I believe he never had one—I do not believe he is capable of making one. His is a mind perpetually fluctuating between opposite difficulties: he neither knows whether he is to make bridges over roads or rivers of one size or of another, or to make embankments, or cuttings, or inclined planes, or in what way the thing is to be carried into effect. Whenever a difficulty is pressed, as in the case of a tunnel, he gets out of it at one end, and when you try to catch him at that, he gets out at the other."

Mr. Alderson proceeded to declaim against the gross ignorance of this so-called engineer, who proposed to make "impossible ditches by the side of an impossible railway" over Chat Moss; and he contrasted with his evidence that given "by that most respectable gentleman we have called before you, I mean Mr. Giles, who has executed a vast number of works," etc. Then Mr. Giles's evidence as to the impossibility of making any railway over the Moss that would stand short of the bottom was emphatically dwelt upon; and Mr. Alderson proceeded:

"Having now, sir, gone through Chat Moss, and having shown that Mr. Giles is right in his principle when he adopts a solid railway—and I care not whether Mr. Giles is right or wrong in his estimate, for whether it be effected by means of piers raised up all the way for four miles through Chat Moss, whether they are to support it on beams of wood or by erecting masonry, or whether Mr. Giles shall put a solid bank of earth through it—in all these schemes there is not one found like that of Mr. Stephenson's, namely, to cut impossible drains on the side of this road; and it is sufficient for me to suggest, and to show, that this scheme of Mr. Stephenson's is impossible or impracticable, and that no other scheme, if they proceed upon this line, can be suggested which will not produce enormous expense. I think that has been irrefragably made out. Every one knows Chat Moss—every one knows that Mr. Giles speaks correctly when he says the iron sinks immediately on its being put upon the surface. I have heard of culverts which have been put upon the Moss, which, after having been surveyed the day before, have the next morning disappeared; and that a house (a poet's house, who may be supposed in the habit of building castles even in the air), story after story, as fast as one is added, the lower one sinks! There is nothing, it appears, except long sedgy grass, and a little soil, to prevent its sinking into the shades of eternal night. I have now done, sir, with Chat Moss, and there I leave this railroad."

Mr. Alderson, of course, called upon the committee to reject the bill; and he protested "against the despotism of the Exchange at Liverpool striding across the land of this country. I do protest," he concluded, "against a measure like this, supported as it is by such evidence, and founded upon such calculations."

The case of the other numerous petitioners against the bill still remained to be gone into. Witnesses were called to prove the residential injury which would be caused by the "intolerable nuisance" of the smoke and fire from the locomotives, and others to prove that the price of coals and iron would "infallibly" be greatly raised throughout the country. This was part of the case of the Duke of Bridgewater's trustees, whose witnesses "proved" many very extraordinary things. The Leeds and Liverpool Canal Company were so fortunate as to pick up a witness from Hetton who was ready to furnish some damaging evidence as to the use of Stephenson's locomotives on that railway. This was Mr. Thomas Wood, one of the Hetton Company's clerks, whose evidence was to the effect that the locomotives, having been found ineffective, were about to be discontinued in favor of fixed engines. The evidence of this witness, incompetent though he was to give an opinion on the subject, and exaggerated as his statements were afterward proved to be, was made the most of by Mr. Harrison when summing up the case of the canal companies.

"At length," he said, "we have come to this—having first set out at twelve miles an hour, the speed of these locomotives is reduced to six, and now comes down to two or two and a half. They must be content to be pulled along by horses and donkeys; and all those fine promises of galloping along at the rate of twelve miles an hour are melted down to a total failure; the foundation on which their case stood is cut from under them completely; for the Act of Parliament, the committee will recollect, prohibits any person using any animal power, of any sort, kind, or description, except the projectors of the railway themselves; therefore I say that the whole foundation on which this project exists is gone."

After farther personal abuse of Mr. Stephenson, whose evidence he spoke of as "trash and confusion," Mr. Harrison closed the case of the canal companies on the 30th of May. Mr. Adam replied for the promoters, recapitulating the principal points of their case, and vindicating Mr. Stephenson and the evidence which he had given before the committee.

The committee then divided on the preamble, which was carried by a majority of only *one*—thirty-seven voting for it, and thirty-six against it. The clauses were next considered, and on a division, the first clause, empowering the company to make the railway, was lost by a majority of nineteen to thirteen. In like manner, the next clause, empowering the company to take land, was lost; on which Mr. Adam, on the part of the promoters, withdrew the bill.

Thus ended this memorable contest, which had extended over two months—carried on throughout with great pertinacity and skill, especially on the part of the opposition, who left no stone unturned to defeat the measure. The want of a new line of communication between Liverpool and Manchester had been clearly proved; but the engineering evidence in support of the proposed railway having been thrown almost entirely upon George Stephenson, who fought this, the most important part of the battle, single-handed, was not brought out so clearly as it would have been had he secured more efficient engineering assistance, which he was not able to do, as all the engineers of eminence of that day were against the locomotive railway. The obstacles thrown in the way of the survey by the land-owners and canal companies, by which the plans were rendered exceedingly imperfect, also tended in a great measure to defeat the bill.

Mr. Gooch says the rejection of the scheme was probably the most severe trial George Stephenson underwent in the whole course of his life. The circumstances connected with the defeat of the bill, the errors in the levels, his severe cross-examination, followed by the fact of his being superseded by another engineer, all told fearfully upon him, and for some time he was as terribly weighed down as if a personal calamity of the most serious kind had befallen him. It is also right to add that he was badly served by his surveyors, who were unpracticed and incompetent. On the 27th of September, 1824, we find him writing to Mr. Sandars: "I am quite shocked with Auty's conduct; we must throw him aside as soon as possible. Indeed, I have begun to fear that he has been fee'd by some of the canal proprietors to make a botch of the job. I have a letter from Steele,* whose views of Auty's conduct quite agree with yours."

* Hugh Steele and Elijah Galloway afterward proceeded with the survey at one part of the line, and Messrs. Oliver and Blackett at another. The former couple

The result of this first application to Parliament was so far discouraging. Stephenson had been so terribly abused by the leading counsel for the opposition in the course of the proceedings before the committee—stigmatized by them as an ignoramus, a fool, and a maniac—that even his friends seem for a time to have lost faith in him and in the locomotive system, whose efficiency he continued to uphold. Things never looked blacker for the success of the railway system than at the close of this great Parliamentary struggle. And yet it was on the very eve of its triumph.

The Committee of Directors appointed to watch the measure in Parliament were so determined to press on the project of a railway, even though it should have to be worked merely by horse-power, that the bill had scarcely been defeated ere they met in London to consider their next step. They called their Parliamentary friends together to consult as to their future proceedings. Among those who attended the meeting of gentlemen with this object in the Royal Hotel, St. James's Street, on the 4th of June, were Mr. Huskisson, Mr. Spring Rice, and General Gascoyne. Mr. Huskisson urged the promoters to renew their application to Parliament. They had secured the first step by the passing of their preamble; the measure was of great public importance; and, whatever temporary opposition it might meet with, he conceived that Parliament must ultimately give its sanction to the undertaking. Similar views were expressed by other speakers; and the deputation went back to Liverpool determined to renew their application to Parliament in the ensuing season.

It was not considered desirable to employ George Stephenson in making the new survey. He had not as yet established his reputation beyond the boundaries of his own district, and the promoters of the bill had doubtless felt the disadvantages of this in the course of their Parliamentary struggle. They therefore resolved now to employ engineers of the highest established reputation, as well as the best surveyors that could be obtained. In

seem to have made some grievous blunder in the levels on Chat Moss, and the circumstance weighed so heavily on Steele's mind that, shortly after hearing of the rejection of the bill, he committed suicide in Stephenson's office at Newcastle. Mr. Gooch informs us that this unhappy affair served to impress upon the minds of Stephenson's other pupils the necessity of insuring greater accuracy and attention in future, and that the lesson, though sad, was not lost upon them.

accordance with these views, they engaged Messrs. George and John Rennie to be the engineers of the railway; and Mr. Charles Vignolles, on their behalf, was appointed to prepare the plans and sections. The line which was eventually adopted differed somewhat from that surveyed by Stephenson, entirely avoiding Lord Sefton's property, and passing through only a few detached fields of Lord Derby's at a considerable distance from the Knowsley domain. The principal parks and game preserves of the district were also carefully avoided. The promoters thus hoped to get rid of the opposition of the most influential of the resident land-owners. The crossing of certain of the streets of Liverpool was also avoided, and the entrance contrived by means of a tunnel and an inclined plane. The new line stopped short of the River Irwell at the Manchester end, and thus, in some measure, removed the objections grounded on an anticipated interruption to the canal or river traffic. And, with reference to the use of the locomotive engine, the promoters, remembering with what effect the objections to it had been urged by the opponents of the measure, intimated, in their second prospectus, that, "as a guarantee of their good faith toward the public, they will not require any clause empowering them to use it; or they will submit to such restrictions in the employment of it as Parliament may impose, for the satisfaction and ample protection both of proprietors on the line of road and of the public at large."

It was found that the capital required to form the line of railway, as laid out by the Messrs. Rennie, was considerably beyond the amount of Stephenson's estimate, and it became a question with the committee in what way the new capital should be raised. A proposal was made to the Marquis of Stafford, who was principally interested in the Duke of Bridgewater's Canal, to become a shareholder in the undertaking. A similar proposal had at an earlier period been made to Mr. Bradshaw, the trustee for the property; but his answer was "all or none," and the negotiation was broken off. The Marquis of Stafford, however, now met the projectors of the railway in a more conciliatory spirit, and it was ultimately agreed that he should become a subscriber to the extent of a thousand shares.

The survey of the new line having been completed, the plans were deposited, the standing orders duly complied with, and the bill went before Parliament. The same counsel appeared for the promoters, but the examination of witnesses was not nearly so protracted as on the former occasion. Mr. Erle and Mr. Harrison led the case of the opposition. The bill went into committee on the 6th of March, and on the 16th the preamble was declared proved by a majority of forty-three to eighteen. On the third reading in the House of Commons, an animated, and what now appears a very amusing discussion, took place. The Hon. Edward Stanley (since Earl of Derby, and prime minister) moved that the bill be read that day six months. In the course of his speech he undertook to prove that the railway trains would take *ten hours* on the journey, and that they could only be worked by horses; and he called upon the House to stop the bill, "and prevent this mad and extravagant speculation from being carried into effect." Sir Isaac Coffin seconded the motion, and in doing so denounced the project as a most flagrant imposition. He would not consent to see widows' premises and their strawberry-beds invaded; and "what, he would like to know, was to be done with all those who had advanced money in making and repairing turnpike roads? What with those who may still wish to travel in their own or hired carriages, after the fashion of their forefathers? What was to become of coach-makers and harness-makers, coach-masters and coachmen, innkeepers, horse-breeders, and horse-dealers? Was the House aware of the smoke and the noise, the hiss and the whirl, which locomotive engines, passing at the rate of ten or twelve miles an hour, would occasion? Neither the cattle plowing in the fields or grazing in the meadows could behold them without dismay. Iron would be raised in price 100 per cent., or more probably exhausted altogether! It would be the greatest nuisance, the most complete disturbance of quiet and comfort in all parts of the kingdom that the ingenuity of man could invent!"

Mr. Huskisson and other speakers, though unable to reply to such arguments as these, strongly supported the bill, and it was carried on the third reading by a majority of eighty-eight to forty-one. The bill passed the House of Lords almost unanimously, its only opponents being the Earl of Derby and his relative the Earl of Wilton. The cost of obtaining the act amounted to the enormous sum of £27,000.

CHAPTER XI.

CHAT MOSS—CONSTRUCTION OF THE RAILWAY.

THE appointment of principal engineer of the railway was taken into consideration at the first meeting of the directors held at Liverpool subsequent to the passing of the act of incorporation. The magnitude of the proposed works, and the vast consequences involved in the experiment, were deeply impressed on their minds, and they resolved to secure the services of a resident engineer of proved experience and ability. Their attention was naturally directed to George Stephenson; at the same time, they desired to have the benefit of the Messrs. Rennie's professional assistance in superintending the works. Mr. George Rennie had an interview with the board on the subject, at which he proposed to undertake the chief superintendence, making six visits in each year, and stipulating that he should have the appointment of the resident engineer. But the responsibility attaching to the direction in the matter of the efficient carrying on of the works would not admit of their being influenced by ordinary punctilios on the occasion, and they accordingly declined Mr. Rennie's proposal, and proceeded to appoint George Stephenson principal engineer at a salary of £1000 per annum.

He at once removed his residence to Liverpool, and made arrangements to commence the works. He began with the "impossible thing"—to do that which some of the principal engineers of the day had declared that "no man in his senses would undertake to do"—namely, to make the road over Chat Moss! It was, indeed, a most formidable undertaking, and the project of carrying a railway along, under, or over such a material as that of which it consisted would certainly never have occurred to an ordinary mind. Michael Drayton supposed the Moss to have had its origin at the Deluge. Nothing more impassable could have been imagined than that dreary waste; and Mr. Giles only spoke the popular feeling of the day when he declared that no carriage could stand on it "short of the bottom." In this bog, singular to say, Mr. Roscoe, the accomplished historian of the Medicis, buried his fortune in the hopeless attempt to cultivate a portion of it which he had bought.

Chat Moss is an immense peat-bog of about twelve square miles in extent. Unlike the bogs or swamps of Cambridge and Lincolnshire, which consist principally of soft mud or silt, this bog is a vast mass of spongy vegetable pulp, the result of the growth and decay of ages. Spagni, or bog-mosses, cover the entire area; one year's growth rising over another, the older growths not entirely decaying, but remaining partially preserved by the antiseptic properties peculiar to peat. Hence the remarkable fact that, though a semifluid mass, the surface of Chat Moss rises above the level of the surrounding country. Like a turtle's back, it declines from the summit in every direction, having from thirty to forty feet gradual slope to the solid land on all sides. From the remains of trees, chiefly alder and birch, which have been dug out of it, and which must have previously flourished on the surface of the soil now deeply submerged, it is probable that the sand and clay base on which the bog rests is saucer-shaped, and so retains the entire mass in position. In rainy weather, such is its capacity for water that it sensibly swells, and rises in those parts where the moss is the deepest. This occurs through the capillary attraction of the fibres of the submerged moss, which is from twenty to thirty feet in depth, while the growing plants effectually check evaporation from the surface. This peculiar character of the Moss has presented an insuperable difficulty in the way of draining on any extensive system—such as by sinking shafts in its substance, and pumping up the water by steam-power, as has been proposed by some engineers. For, supposing a shaft of thirty feet deep to be sunk, it has been calculated that this would only be effectual for draining a circle of about one hundred yards, the water running down an incline of about 5 to 1; indeed, it was found, in the course of draining the bog, that a ditch three feet deep only served to drain a space of less than five yards on either side, and two ditches of this depth, ten feet apart, left a portion of the Moss between them scarcely affected by the drains.

The three resident engineers selected by Mr. Stephenson to superintend the construction of the line were Mr. Joseph Locke, Mr. Allcard, and Mr. John Dixon. The last was appointed to that portion which included the proposed road across the Moss, the other two being any thing but desirous of exchanging posts with him. On Mr. Dixon's arrival, about the month of July, 1826, Mr. Locke proceeded to show him over the length he was to take charge of, and to instal him in office. When they reached Chat Moss, Mr. Dixon found that the line had already been staked out and the levels taken in detail by the aid of planks laid upon the bog. The cutting of the drains along each side of the proposed road had also been commenced, but the soft pulpy stuff had up to this time flowed into the drains and filled them up as fast as they were cut. Proceeding across the Moss on his first day's inspection, the new resident, when about half way over, slipped off the plank on which he walked, and sank to his knees in the bog. Struggling only sent him the deeper, and he might have disappeared altogether but for the workmen, who hastened to his assistance upon planks, and rescued him from his perilous position. Much disheartened, he desired to return, and even for the moment thought of giving up the job; but Mr. Locke assured him that the worst part was now past; so the new resident plucked up heart again, and both floundered on until they reached the farther edge of the Moss, wet and plastered over with bog sludge. Mr. Dixon's assistants endeavored to comfort him by the assurance that he might in future avoid similar perils by walking upon "pattens," or boards fastened to the soles of his feet, as they had done when taking the levels, and as the workmen did when engaged in making drains in the softest parts of the Moss. Still the resident engineer could not help being puzzled by the problem of how to construct a road for a heavy locomotive, with a train of passengers or goods, upon a bog which he had found to be incapable of supporting his own individual weight!

Stephenson's idea was that such a road might be made to *float* upon the bog simply by means of a sufficient extension of the bearing surface. As a ship, or a raft capable of sustaining heavy loads, floated in water, so, in his opinion, might a light road be floated upon a bog which was of considerably greater consistency than water. Long before the railway was thought of, Mr. Roscoe had adopted the remarkable expedient of fitting his plow-horses with flat wooden soles or pattens, to enable them to walk upon the Moss land which he had brought into cultivation. These pattens were fitted on by means of a screw apparatus, which met in front of the foot and was easily fastened. The mode by which these pattens served to sustain the horse is capable of easy explanation, and it will be observed that the *rationale* alike explains the floating of a railway. The foot of an ordinary farm-horse presents a base of about five inches diameter, but if this base be enlarged to seven inches—the circles being to each other as the squares of the diameters—it will be found that, by this slight enlargement of the base, a circle of nearly double the area has been secured, and consequently the pressure of the foot upon every unit of ground on which the horse stands has been reduced one half. In fact, this contrivance has an effect tantamount to setting the horse upon eight feet instead of four.

Apply the same reasoning to the ponderous locomotive, and it will be found that even such a machine may be made to stand upon a bog by means of a similar extension of the bearing surface. Suppose the engine to be twenty feet long and five feet wide, thus covering a surface of a hundred square feet, and, provided the bearing has been extended by means of cross sleepers supported upon a matting of heath and branches of trees covered with a few inches of gravel, the pressure of an engine of twenty tons will be only equal to about three pounds per inch over the whole surface on which it stands. Such was George Stephenson's idea in contriving his floating road—something like an elongated raft—across the Moss; and we shall see that he steadily kept it in view in carrying the work into execution.

The first thing done was to form a footpath of ling or heather along the proposed road, on which a man might walk without risk of sinking. A single line of temporary railway was then laid down, formed of ordinary cross-bars about three feet long and an inch square, with holes punched through them at the end and nailed down to temporary sleepers. Along this way ran the wagons in which were conveyed the materials requisite to form the permanent road. These wagons carried about a ton each, and they were propelled by boys running behind them along the narrow bar of iron. The boys became so expert that they would run the four miles across at the rate of seven or eight miles an hour without missing a step; if they had done so, they would have sunk in many places up to their middle.* The slight extension of the bearing surface was sufficient to enable the bog to bear this temporary line, and the circumstance was a source of increased confidence and hope to our engineer in proceeding with the formation of the permanent road alongside.

The digging of drains had been proceeding for some time along each side of the intended railway, but they filled up almost as soon as dug, the sides flowing in and the bottom rising up, and it was only in some of the drier parts of the bog that a depth of three or four feet could be reached. The surface-ground between the drains, containing the intertwined roots of heather and long grass, was left untouched, and upon this were spread branches of trees and hedge-cuttings; in the softest places rude gates or hurdles, some eight or nine feet long by four feet wide, interwoven with heather, were laid in double thicknesses, their ends overlapping each other; and upon this floating bed was spread a thin layer of gravel, on which the sleepers, chairs, and rails were laid in the usual manner. Such was the mode in which the road was formed upon the Moss.

It was found, however, after the permanent road had been thus laid, that there was a tendency to sinking at those parts where the bog was the softest. In ordinary cases, where a bank subsides, the sleepers are packed up with ballast or gravel, but in this case the ballast was dug away and removed in order to lighten the road, and the sleepers were packed instead with cakes of dry turf or bundles of heath. By these expedients the subsided parts were again floated up to the level, and an approach was made toward a satisfactory road. But the most formidable difficulties were encountered at the centre and toward the edges of the Moss, and it required no small degree of ingenuity and perseverance on the part of the engineer successfully to overcome them.

The Moss, as has been already observed, was highest in the

* When the Liverpool directors went to inspect the works in progress on the Moss, they were run along the temporary rails in the little three-feet gauge wagons used for forming the road. They were being thus impelled one day at considerable speed when the wagon suddenly ran off the road, and Mr. Moss, one of the directors, was thrown out in a soft place, from which, however, he was speedily extricated, not without leaving a deep mark. George used afterward laughingly to refer to the circumstance as "the meeting of the Mosses."

centre, and it there presented a sort of hunchback with a rising and falling gradient. At that point it was found necessary to cut deeper drains in order to consolidate the ground between them on which the road was to be formed. But, as at other parts of the Moss, the deeper the cutting the more rapid was the flow of fluid bog into the drain, the bottom rising up almost as fast as it was removed. To meet this emergency, a quantity of empty tar-barrels was brought from Liverpool, and, as soon as a few yards of drain were dug, the barrels were laid down end to end, firmly fixed to each other by strong slabs laid over the joints, and nailed; they were then covered over with clay, and thus formed an underground sewer of wood instead of bricks. This expedient was found to answer the purpose intended, and the road across the centre of the Moss having thus been prepared, it was then laid with the permanent materials.

The greatest difficulty was, however, experienced in forming an embankment on the edge of the bog at the Manchester end. Moss, as dry as it could be cut, was brought up in small wagons by men and boys, and emptied so as to form an embankment; but the bank had scarcely been raised three or four feet in height when the stuff broke through the heathery surface of the bog and sunk overhead. More moss was brought up and emptied in with no better result, and for many weeks the filling was continued without any visible embankment having been made. It was the duty of the resident engineer to proceed to Liverpool every fortnight to obtain the wages for the workmen employed under him, and on these occasions he was required to color up, on a section drawn to a working scale suspended against the wall of the directors' room, the amount of excavation, embankment, etc., executed from time to time. But on many of these occasions Mr. Dixon had no progress whatever to show for the money expended on the Chat Moss embankment. Sometimes, indeed, the visible work done was *less* than it had appeared a fortnight or a month before!

The directors now became seriously alarmed, and feared that the evil prognostications of the eminent engineers were about to be fulfilled. The resident himself was greatly disheartened, and he was even called upon to supply the directors with an estimate of the cost of filling up the Moss with solid stuff from the bottom, as also the cost of piling the roadway, and, in effect, constructing a four-mile viaduct of timber across the Moss, from twenty to thirty feet high. But the expense appalled the directors, and the question then arose whether the work was to be proceeded with or *abandoned!*

Stephenson himself afterward described the alarming position of affairs at a public dinner given at Birmingham on the 23d of December, 1837, on the occasion of a piece of plate being presented to his son after the completion of the London and Birmingham Railway. He related the anecdote, he said, for the purpose of impressing upon the minds of those who heard him the necessity of perseverance.

"After working for weeks and weeks," said he, "in filling in materials to form the road, there did not yet appear to be the least sign of our being able to raise the solid embankment one single inch; in short, we went on filling in without the slightest apparent effect. Even my assistants began to feel uneasy, and to doubt of the success of the scheme. The directors, too, spoke of it as a hopeless task; and at length they became seriously alarmed, so much so, indeed, that a board meeting was held on Chat Moss to decide whether I should proceed any farther. They had previously taken the opinion of other engineers, who reported unfavorably. There was no help for it, however, but to go on. An immense outlay had been incurred, and great loss would have been occasioned had the scheme been then abandoned, and the line taken by another route. So the directors were *compelled* to allow me to go on with my plans, of the ultimate success of which I myself never for one moment doubted."

During the progress of this part of the works, the Worsley and Trafford men, who lived near the Moss, and plumed themselves upon their practical knowledge of bog-work, declared the completion of the road to be utterly impracticable. "If you knew as much about Chat Moss as we do," they said, "you would never have entered on so rash an undertaking; and depend upon it, all you have done and are doing will prove abortive. You must give up altogether the idea of a floating railway, and either fill the Moss up with hard material from the bottom, or else deviate the line so as to avoid it altogether." Such were the conclusions of science and experience.

In the midst of all these alarms and prophecies of failure, Stephenson never lost heart, but held to his purpose. His motto was "Persevere!" "You must go on filling in," he said; "there is no other help for it. The stuff emptied in is doing its work out of sight, and if you will but have patience, it will soon begin to show." And so the filling in went on; several hundreds of men and boys were employed to skin the Moss all round for many thousand yards, by means of sharp spades, called by the turf-cutters "tommy-spades;" and the dried cakes of turf were afterward used to form the embankment, until at length, as the stuff sank and rested upon the bottom, the bank gradually rose above the surface, and slowly advanced onward, declining in height and consequently in weight, until it became joined to the floating road already laid upon the Moss. In the course of forming the embankment, the pressure of the bog turf tipped out of the wagons caused a copious stream of bog-water to flow from the end of it, in color resembling Barclay's double stout; and when completed, the bank looked like a long ridge of tightly-pressed tobacco-leaf. The compression of the turf may be understood from the fact that 670,000 cubic yards of raw moss formed only 277,000 cubic yards of embankment at the completion of the work.

At the western, or Liverpool end of the Chat Moss, there was a like embankment; but, as the ground there was solid, little difficulty was experienced in forming it, beyond the loss of substance caused by the oozing out of the water held by the moss-earth.

At another part of the Liverpool and Manchester line, Parr Moss was crossed by an embankment about a mile and a half in extent. In the immediate neighborhood was found a large excess of cutting, which it would have been necessary to "put out in spoil-banks" (according to the technical phrase) but for the convenience of Parr Moss, into which the surplus clay, stone, and shale were tipped, wagon after wagon, until a solid but congealed embankment, from fifteen to twenty feet high, was formed, although to the eye it appears to be laid upon the level of the adjoining surface, as at Chat Moss.

The road across Chat Moss was finished by the 1st of January, 1830, when the first experimental train of passengers passed over it, drawn by the "Rocket;" and it turned out that, instead of being the most expensive part of the line, it was about the cheapest. The total cost of forming the line over the Moss was £28,000, whereas Mr. Giles's estimate was £270,000! It also proved to be one of the best portions of the railway. Being a floating road, it was as smooth and easy to run upon as Dr. Arnott's water-bed is soft and easy to lie upon—the pressure being equal at all points. There was, and still is, a sort of springiness in the road over the Moss, such as is felt when passing along a suspended bridge; and those who looked along the Moss as a train passed over it said they could observe a waviness, such as precedes and follows a skater upon ice.

During the progress of the works the most ridiculous rumors were set afloat. The drivers of the stage-coaches, who feared for their calling, brought the alarming intelligence into Manchester from time to time that "Chat Moss was blown up!" "Hundreds of men and horses had sunk in the bog; and the works were completely abandoned!" The engineer himself was declared to have been swallowed up in the Serbonian bog; and "railways were at an end forever!"

In the construction of the railway, George Stephenson's capacity for organizing and directing the labors of a large number of workmen of all kinds eminently displayed itself. A vast quantity of ballast-wagons had to be constructed for the purposes of the work, and implements and materials had to be collected, before the mass of labor to be employed could be efficiently set in motion at the various points of the line. There were not at that time, as there are now, large contractors, possessed of railway plant, capable of executing earthworks on a large scale. Our engineer had, therefore, not only to contrive the plant, but to organize the labor, and direct it in person. The very laborers themselves had to be trained to their work by him; and it was on the Liverpool and Manchester line that Mr. Stephenson organized the staff of that formidable band of railway navvies, whose handiworks will be the wonder and admiration of succeeding generations. Looking at their gigantic traces, the men of some future age may be found to declare, of the engineer and of his workmen, that "there were giants in those days."

Although the works of the Liverpool and Manchester Railway

are of a much less formidable character than those of many lines that have since been constructed, they were then regarded as of a stupendous kind. Indeed, few works of such magnitude had before been executed in England. It had been the engineer's original intention to carry the railway from the north end of Liverpool round the red sandstone ridge on which the upper part of the town is built, and also round the higher rise of the coal formation at Rainhill, by following the natural levels to the north of Knowsley. But the opposition of the land-owners having forced the line more to the south, it was rendered necessary to cut through the hills, and go over the high grounds instead of round them. The first consequence of this alteration in the plans was the necessity for constructing a tunnel under the town of Liverpool a mile and a half in length, from the docks at Wapping to the top of Edgehill; the second was the necessity for forming a long and deep cutting through the red sandstone rock at Olive Mount; and the third and worst of all was the necessity for ascending and descending the Whiston and Sutton hills by means of inclined planes of 1 in 96. The line was also, by the same forced deviation, prevented passing through the Lancashire coal-field, and the engineer was compelled to carry the works across the Sankey valley at a point where the waters of the brook had dug out an excessively deep channel through the marl-beds of the district.

The principal difficulty was experienced in pushing on the works connected with the formation of the tunnel under Liverpool, 2200 yards in length. The blasting and hewing of the rock were vigorously carried on night and day; and the engineer's practical experience in the collieries here proved of great use to him. Many obstacles had to be encountered and overcome in the formation of the tunnel, the rock varying in hardness and texture at different parts. In some places the miners were deluged by water, which surged from the soft blue shale found at the lowest level of the tunnel. In other places beds of wet sand were cut through, and there careful propping and pinning were necessary to prevent the roof from tumbling in until the masonry to support it could be erected. On one occasion, while Stephenson was absent from Liverpool, a mass of loose moss-earth and sand fell from the roof, which had been insufficiently propped. The miners withdrew from the work; and on the engineer's return he found them in a refractory state, refusing to re-enter the tunnel. He induced them, however, by his example, to return to their labors; and when the roof had been secured, the work went on again as before. When there was danger, he was always ready to share it with the men; and, gathering confidence from his fearlessness, they proceeded vigorously with the undertaking, boring and mining their way toward the light.

The Olive Mount cutting was the first extensive stone cutting

OLIVE MOUNT CUTTING. [By Percival Skelton.]

executed on any railway, and to this day it is one of the most formidable. It is about two miles long, and in some parts more than a hundred feet deep. It is a narrow ravine or defile cut out of the solid rock, and not less than four hundred and eighty thousand cubic yards of stone were removed from it. Mr. Vignolles, afterward describing it, said it looked as if it had been dug out by giants.

The crossing of so many roads and streams involved the necessity for constructing an unusual number of bridges. There were not fewer than sixty-three, under or over the railway, on the thirty miles between Liverpool and Manchester. Up to this time bridges had been applied generally to high roads, where inclined approaches were of comparatively small importance, and in de-

SANKEY VIADUCT. [By Percival Skelton.]

termining the rise of his arch the engineer selected any headway he thought proper. Every consideration was indeed made subsidiary to constructing the bridge itself, and the completion of one large structure of this sort was regarded as an epoch in engineering history. Yet here, in the course of a few years, no fewer than sixty-three bridges were constructed on one line of railway! Mr. Stephenson early found that the ordinary arch was inapplicable in certain cases, where the headway was limited, and yet the level of the railway must be preserved. In such cases he employed simple cast-iron beams, by which he safely bridged gaps of moderate width, economizing headway, and introducing the use of a new material of the greatest possible value to the engineer. The bridges of masonry upon the line were of many kinds; several of them were skew bridges, while others, such as those at Newton and over the Irwell at Manchester, were straight and of considerable dimensions. But the principal piece of masonry on the line was the Sankey viaduct.

This fine work is principally of brick, with stone facings. It consists of nine arches of fifty feet span each. The massive piers are supported on two hundred piles driven deep into the soil; and they rise to a great height—the coping of the parapet being seventy feet above the level of the valley, in which flow the Sankey brook and Canal. Its total cost was about £45,000.

By the end of 1828 the directors found they had expended £460,000 on the works, and that they were still far from completion. They looked at the loss of interest on this large investment, and began to grumble at the delay. They desired to see their capital becoming productive; and in the spring of 1829 they urged the engineer to push on the works with increased vigor. Mr. Cropper, one of the directors, who took an active interest in their progress, said to Stephenson one day, "Now, George, thou must get on with the railway, and have it finished without farther delay: thou must really have it ready for opening by the first day of January next." "Consider the heavy character of the works, sir, and how much we have been delayed by the want of money, not to speak of the wetness of the weather: it is impossible." "Impossible!" rejoined Cropper; "I wish I could get Napoleon to thee—he would tell thee there is no such word as 'impossible' in the vocabulary." "Tush!" exclaimed Stephenson, with warmth, "don't speak to me about Napoleon! Give me men, money, and materials, and I will do what Napoleon couldn't do—drive a railroad from Liverpool to Manchester over Chat Moss!" And truly the formation of a high road over that bottomless bog was apparently a more difficult task than the making even of Napoleon's far-famed road across the Simplon.

The directors had more than once been embarrassed by want of funds to meet the heavy expenditure. The country had scarcely yet recovered from the general panic and crash of 1825, and it was with difficulty that the calls could be raised from the shareholders. A loan of £100,000 was obtained from the Exchequer Loan Commissioners in 1826; and in 1829 an act was passed enabling the company to raise farther capital, to provide working plant for the railway. Two acts were also obtained during the progress of the undertaking, enabling deviations and alterations to be made; one to improve the curves and shorten the line near Rainhill, and the other to carry the line across the Irwell into the town of Manchester. Thanks to the energy of the engineer, the industry of his laborers, and the improved supply of money by the directors, the railway made rapid progress in the course of the year 1829. Double sets of laborers were employed on Chat Moss and at other places in carrying on the works by night and day, the night shifts working by torch and fire light; and at length, the work advancing at all points, the directors saw their way to the satisfactory completion of the undertaking.

It may well be supposed that Stephenson's time was fully occupied in superintending the extensive and for the most part novel works connected with the railway, and that even his extraordinary powers of labor and endurance were taxed to the utmost during the four years that they were in progress. Almost every detail in the plans was directed and arranged by himself. Every bridge, from the simplest to the most complicated, including the then novel structure of the "skew bridge," iron girders, siphons, fixed engines, and the machinery for working the tunnel at the Liverpool end, had all to be thought out by his own head, and reduced to definite plans under his own eyes. Besides all this, he had to design the working plant in anticipation of the opening of the railway. He must be prepared with wagons, trucks, and carriages, himself superintending their manufacture. The permanent road, turn-tables, switches, and crossings — in short, the entire structure and machinery of the line, from the turning of the first sod to the running of the first train of carriages on the railway, went on under his immediate supervision. And it was in the midst of this vast accumulation of work and responsibility that the battle of the locomotive engine had to be fought — a battle not merely against material difficulties, but against the still more trying obstructions of deeply-rooted mistrust and prejudice on the part of a considerable minority of the directors.

He had no staff of experienced assistants—not even a staff of draughtsmen in his office—but only a few pupils learning their business, and he was frequently without even their help. The time of his engineering inspectors was fully occupied in the actual superintendence of the works at different parts of the line, and he took care to direct all their important operations in person. The principal draughtsman was Mr. Thomas Gooch, a pupil he had brought with him from Newcastle. "I may say," writes Mr. Gooch, "that nearly the whole of the working and other drawings, as well as the various land-plans for the railway, were drawn by my own hand. They were done at the company's office in Clayton Square during the day, from instructions supplied in the evenings by Mr. Stephenson, either by word of mouth, or by little rough hand sketches on letter-paper. The evenings were also generally devoted to my duties as secretary, in writing (mostly from his own dictation) his letters and reports, or in making calculations and estimates. The mornings before breakfast were not unfrequently spent by me in visiting and lending a helping hand in the tunnel and other works near Liverpool—the untiring zeal and perseverance of George Stephenson never for an instant flagging, and inspiring with a like enthusiasm all who were engaged under him in carrying forward the works."*

The usual routine of his life at this time—if routine it could be called—was to rise early, by sunrise in summer and before it in winter, and "break the back of the day's work" by midday. While the tunnel under Liverpool was in progress, one of his first duties in the morning before breakfast was to go over the various shafts, clothed in a suitable dress, and inspect the progress of the

* Mr. Gooch's letter to the author, December 13th, 1861. Referring to the preparation of the plans and drawings, Mr. Gooch adds, "When we consider the extensive sets of drawings which most engineers have since found it right to adopt in carrying out similar works, it is not the least surprising feature in George Stephenson's early professional career that he should have been able to confine himself to so limited a number as that which could be supplied by the hands of one person in carrying out the construction of the Liverpool and Manchester Railway; and this may still be said, after full allowance is made for the alteration of system involved by the adoption of the large contract system."

work at different points; on other days he would visit the extensive workshops at Edgehill, where most of the "plant" for the line was manufactured. Then, returning to his house in Upper Parliament Street, Windsor, after a hurried breakfast, he would ride along the works to inspect their progress, and push them on with greater energy where needful. On other days he would prepare for the much less congenial engagement of meeting the board, which was often a cause of great anxiety and pain to him; for it was difficult to satisfy men of all tempers, some of which were not of the most generous kind. On such occasions he might be seen with his right-hand thumb thrust through the topmost button-hole of his coat-breast, vehemently hitching his right shoulder, as was his habit when laboring under any considerable excitement. Occasionally he would take an early ride before breakfast, to inspect the progress of the Sankey viaduct. He

STEPHENSON'S BAITING-PLACE AT SANKEY.

had a favorite horse, brought by him from Newcastle, called "Bobby"—so tractable that, with his rider on his back, he would walk up to a locomotive with the steam blowing off, and put his nose against it without shying. "Bobby," saddled and bridled, was brought to Stephenson's door betimes in the morning, and, mounting him, he would ride the fifteen miles to Sankey, putting up at a little public house which then stood upon the banks of the canal. There he had his breakfast of "crowdie," which he made with his own hands. It consisted of oatmeal stirred into a basin of hot water—a sort of porridge—which was supped with cold sweet milk. After this frugal breakfast he would go upon the works, and remain there, riding from point to point for the greater part of the day. If he returned home before midday it would be to examine the pay-sheets in the different departments sent in by the assistant engineers, or by the foremen of the workshops; all this he did himself with the greatest care, requiring a full explanation of every item.

After a late dinner, which occupied very short time and was always of a plain and frugal description,* he would proceed to dispose of his correspondence, or prepare sketches of drawings, and give instructions as to their completion. He would occasionally refresh himself for this evening work by a short doze, which, however, he would never admit had exceeded the limits of "winking," to use his own term. Mr. Frederick Swanwick, who officiated as his secretary after the appointment of Mr. Gooch as resident engineer to the Bolton and Leigh Railway, has informed us that he then remarked—what in after years he could better appreciate—the clear, terse, and vigorous style of Stephenson's dictation; there was nothing superfluous in it, but it was close, direct, and to the point—in short, thoroughly business-like. And if, in passing through the pen of the amanuensis, his meaning happened in any way to be distorted or modified, it did not fail to escape his detection, though he was always tolerant of any liberties taken with his own form of expression, so long as the words written down conveyed his real meaning. His strong natural acumen showed itself even in such matters as grammar and composition—a department of knowledge in which, it might be supposed, he

* While at Liverpool Stephenson had very little time for "company;" but on one particular occasion he invited his friend Mr. Sandars to dinner, and, as that gentleman was a connoisseur in port wine, his host determined to give him a special treat of that drink. Stephenson accordingly went to the small merchant with whom he usually dealt, and ordered "half a dozen of his very best port wine," which was promised of first-rate quality. After dinner the wine was produced; and when Mr. Sandars had sipped a glass, George, after waiting a little for the expected eulogium, at length asked, "Well, Sandars, how d'ye like the port?" "Poor stuff!" said the guest, "poor stuff!" George was very much shocked, and with difficulty recovered his good humor. But he lived to be able to treat Mr. Sandars to a better article at Tapton House, when he used to laugh over his first futile attempt at Liverpool to gain a reputation for his port.

could scarcely have had either time or opportunity to acquire much information. But here, as in all other things, his shrewd common sense came to his help, and his simple, vigorous English might almost be cited as a model of composition.

His letters and reports written, and his sketches of drawings made and explained, the remainder of the evening was usually devoted to conversation with his wife and those of his pupils who lived under his roof, and constituted, as it were, part of the family. He then delighted to test the knowledge of his young companions, and to question them upon the principles of mechanics. If they were not quite "up to the mark" on any point, there was no escaping detection by evasive or specious explanations on their part. These always met with the verdict of, "Ah! you know naught about it now; but think it over again, and tell me the answer when you understand it." If there was even partial success in the reply, it would at once be acknowledged, and a full explanation was given, to which the master would add illustrative examples for the purpose of impressing the principle more deeply upon the pupil's mind.

It was not so much his object and purpose to "cram" the minds of the young men committed to his charge with the *results* of knowledge as to stimulate them to educate themselves—to induce them to develop their mental and moral powers by the exercise of their own free energies, and thus acquire that habit of self-thinking and self-reliance which is the spring of all true manly action. In a word, he sought to bring out and invigorate the *character* of his pupils. He felt that he himself had been made stronger and better through his encounters with difficulty, and he would not have the road of knowledge made too smooth and easy for them. "Learn for yourselves—think for yourselves," he would say: "make yourselves masters of principles—persevere—be industrious—and there is then no fear of you." And not the least emphatic proof of the soundness of this system of education, as conducted by George Stephenson, was afforded by the after history of the pupils themselves. There was not one of those trained under his eye who did not rise to eminent usefulness and distinction as an engineer. He sent them forth into the world braced with the spirit of self-help—inspired by his own noble example; and they repeated in their after career the lessons of earnest effort and persistent industry which his daily life had taught them.

Mr. Stephenson's evenings at home were not, however, exclusively devoted either to business or to the graver exercises above referred to. He would often indulge in cheerful conversation and anecdote, falling back from time to time upon the struggles and difficulties of his early life. The not unfrequent winding up of his story, addressed to those about him, was, "Ah! ye young fellows don't know what *wark* is in these days!" Mr. Swanwick delights recalling to mind how seldom, if ever, a cross or captious word, or an angry look, marred the enjoyment of those evenings. The presence of Mrs. Stephenson gave them an additional charm: amiable, kind-hearted, and intelligent, she shared quietly in the pleasure of the party; and the atmosphere of comfort which always pervaded her home contributed in no small degree to render it a centre of cheerful, hopeful intercourse, and of earnest, honest industry.

CHAT MOSS—WORKS IN PROGRESS.

When Stephenson retired for the night, it was not always that he permitted himself to sink into slumber. Like Brindley, he worked out many a difficult problem in bed; and for hours he would turn over in his mind and study how to overcome some obstacle, or to mature some project, on which his thoughts were bent. Some remark inadvertently dropped by him at the breakfast-table in the morning served to show that he had been stealing some hours from the night in reflection and study. Yet he would rise at his accustomed early hour, and there was no abatement of his usual energy in carrying on the business of the day.

CHAPTER XII.

ROBERT STEPHENSON'S RESIDENCE IN COLOMBIA, AND RETURN—THE BATTLE OF THE LOCOMOTIVE—"THE ROCKET."

WE return to the career of Robert Stephenson, who was absent from England during the construction of the Liverpool Railway, but was now about to rejoin his father and take part in "the battle of the locomotive" which was impending.

We have seen that, on his return from Edinburg College at the end of 1821, he had assisted in superintending the works of the Hetton Railway until its opening in 1822, after which he proceeded to Liverpool to take part with Mr. James in surveying the proposed railway there. In the following year we found him assisting his father in the working survey of the Stockton and Darlington Railway; and when the Locomotive Engine Works were started in Forth Street, Newcastle, he took an active part in that concern. "The factory," he says, "was in active operation in 1824; I left England for Colombia in June of that year, having finished drawing the designs of the Brusselton stationary engines for the Stockton and Darlington Railway before I left."*

Speculation was very rife at the time, and among the most promising adventures were the companies organized for the purpose of working the gold and silver mines of South America. Great difficulty was experienced in finding mining engineers capable of carrying out those projects, and young men of even the most moderate experience were eagerly sought after. The Colombian Mining Association of London offered an engagement to young Stephenson to go out to Mariquita and take charge of the engineering operations of that company. Robert was himself desirous of accepting it, but his father said it would first be necessary to ascertain whether the proposed change would be for his good. His health had been very delicate for some time, partly occasioned by his rapid growth, but principally because of

* Letter to the author.

his close application to work and study. Father and son proceeded together to call upon Dr. Headlam, the eminent physician of Newcastle, to consult him on the subject. During the examination which ensued, Robert afterward used to say that he felt as if he were upon trial for life or death. To his great relief, the doctor pronounced that a temporary residence in a warm climate was the very thing likely to be most beneficial to him. The appointment was accordingly accepted, and, before many weeks had passed, Robert Stephenson had set sail for South America.

After a tolerably prosperous voyage he landed at La Guayra, on the north coast of Venezuela, on the 23d of July, from thence proceeding to Caraccas, the capital of the district, about fifteen miles inland. There he remained for two months, unable to proceed in consequence of the wretched state of the roads in the interior. He contrived, however, to make occasional excursions in the neighborhood with an eye to the mining business on which he had come. About the beginning of October he set out for Bogotá, the capital of Colombia or New Granada. The distance was about twelve hundred miles, through a very difficult region, and it was performed entirely upon mule-back, after the fashion of the country.

In the course of the journey Robert visited many of the districts reported to be rich in minerals, but he met with few traces except of copper, iron, and coal, with occasional indications of gold and silver. He found the people ready to furnish information, which, however, when tested, usually proved worthless. A guide, whom he employed for weeks, kept him buoyed up with the hope of finding richer mining places than he had yet seen; but when he professed to be able to show him mines of "brass, steel, alcohol, and pinchbeck," Stephenson discovered him to be an incorrigible rogue, and immediately dismissed him. At length our traveler reached Bogotá, and after an interview with Mr. Illingworth, the commercial manager of the Mining Company, he proceeded to Honda, crossed the Magdalena, and shortly after reached the site of his intended operations on the eastern slope of the Andes.

Mr. Stephenson used afterward to speak in glowing terms of this his first mule-journey in South America. Every thing was entirely new to him. The variety and beauty of the indigenous plants, the luxurious tropical vegetation, the appearance, manners, and dress of the people, and the mode of traveling, were altogether different from every thing he had before seen. His own traveling garb also must have been strange even to himself. "My hat," he says, "was of plaited grass, with a crown nine inches in height, surrounded by a brim of six inches; a white cotton suit; and a *ruana* of blue and crimson plaid, with a hole in the centre for the head to pass through. This cloak is admirably adapted for the purpose, amply covering the rider and mule, and at night answering the purpose of a blanket in the net-hammock, which is made from the fibres of the aloe, and which every traveler carries before him on his mule, and suspends to the trees or in houses, as occasion may require."

The part of the journey which seems to have made the most lasting impression on his mind was that between Bogotá and the mining district in the neighborhood of Mariquita. As he ascended the slopes of the mountain range, and reached the first step of the table-land, he was struck beyond expression with the noble view of the valley of Magdalena behind him, so vast that he failed in attempting to define the point at which the course of the river blended with the horizon. Like all travelers in the district, he noted the remarkable changes of climate and vegetation as he rose from the burning plains toward the fresh breath of the mountains. From an atmosphere as hot as that of an oven he passed into delicious cool air, until, in his onward and upward journey, a still more temperate region was reached, the very perfection of climate. Before him rose the majestic Cordilleras, forming a rampart against the western sky, and at certain times of the day looking black, sharp, and even at their summit almost like a wall.

Our engineer took up his abode for a time at Mariquita, a fine old city, though then greatly fallen into decay. During the period of the Spanish dominion it was an important place, most of the gold and silver convoys passing through it on their way to Cartagena, there to be shipped in galleons for Europe. The mountainous country to the west was rich in silver, gold, and other metals, and it was Mr. Stephenson's object to select the best site for commencing operations for the company. With this object he "prospected" about in all directions, visiting long-abandoned mines, and analyzing specimens obtained from many quarters. The mines eventually fixed upon as the scene of his operations were those of La Manta and Santa Anna, long before worked by the Spaniards, though, in consequence of the luxuriance and rapidity of the vegetation, all traces of the old workings had become completely overgrown and lost. Every thing had to be begun anew. Roads had to be cut to open a way to the mines, machinery had to be erected, and the ground opened up, when some of the old adits were eventually hit upon. The native peons or laborers were not accustomed to work, and they usually contrived to desert when they were not watched, so that very little progress could be made until the arrival of the expected band of miners from England. The authorities were by no means helpful, and the engineer was driven to an old expedient with the object of overcoming this difficulty. "We endeavor all we can," he says, in one of his letters, "to make ourselves popular, and this we find most effectually accomplished by 'regaling the venal beasts.'" He also gave a ball at Mariquita, which passed off with éclat, the governor from Honda, with a host of friends, honoring it with their presence. It was, indeed, necessary to "make a party" in this way, as other schemers were already trying to undermine the Colombian Company in influential directions. The engineer did not exaggerate when he said, "The uncertainty of transacting business in this country is perplexing beyond description." In the mean time laborers had been attracted to Santa Anna, which became, the engineer wrote, "like an English fair on Sundays: people flock to it from all quarters to buy beef and chat with their friends. Sometimes three or four torros are slaughtered in a day. The people now eat more beef in a week than they did in two months before, and they are consequently getting fat."*

At last Stephenson's party of miners arrived from England, but they gave him even more trouble than the peons had done. They were rough, drunken, and sometimes ungovernable. He

* Letter to Mr. Illingworth, September 25th, 1825. The reports made to the directors and officers of the company, which we have seen, contain the details of the operations carried on at the mines, but they are as dry and uninteresting as such reports usually are, and furnish no materials calculated to illustrate the subject of the text.

set them to work at the Santa Anna mine without delay, and at the same time took up his abode among them, "to keep them," he said, "if possible, from indulging in the detestable vice of drunkenness, which, if not put a stop to, will eventually destroy themselves, and involve the mining association in ruin." To add to his troubles, the captain of the miners displayed a very hostile and insubordinate spirit, quarreled and fought with the men, and was insolent to the engineer himself. The captain and his gang, being Cornishmen, told Robert to his face that because he was a North-country man, and not brought up in Cornwall, it was impossible that he should know any thing of mining. Disease also fell upon him—first fever, and then visceral derangement, followed by a return of his "old complaint, a feeling of oppression in the breast." No wonder that in the midst of these troubles he should longingly speak of returning to his native land. But he stuck to his post and his duty, kept up his courage, and by a mixture of mildness and firmness, and the display of great coolness and judgment, he contrived to keep the men to their work, and gradually to carry forward the enterprise which he had undertaken. By the beginning of July, 1826, quietness and order had been restored, and the works were proceeding more satisfactorily, though the yield of silver was not as yet very promising, the engineer being of opinion that at least three years' diligent and costly operations would be necessary to render the mines productive.

In the mean time he removed to the dwelling which had been erected for his accommodation at Santa Anna. It was a structure speedily raised after the fashion of the country. The walls were of split and flattened bamboo, tied together with the long fibres of a dried climbing plant; the roof was of palm-leaves, and the ceiling of reeds. When an earthquake shook the district—for earthquakes were frequent—the inmates of such a fabric merely felt as if shaken in a basket, without sustaining any harm. In front of the cottage lay a woody ravine, extending almost to the base of the Andes, gorgeously clothed in primeval vegetation—magnolias, palms, bamboos, tree-ferns, acacias, cedars; and towering over all were the great almendrons, with their smooth, silvery stems, bearing aloft noble clusters of pure white blossom. The forest was haunted by myriads of gay insects, butterflies with wings of dazzling lustre, birds of brilliant plumage, humming-birds, golden orioles, toucans, and a host of solitary warblers. But the glorious sunsets seen from his cottage-porch more than all astonished and delighted the young engineer, and he was accustomed to say that, after having witnessed them, he was reluctant to accuse the ancient Peruvians of idolatry.

ROBERT STEPHENSON'S COTTAGE AT SANTA ANNA.

But all these natural beauties failed to reconcile him to the harassing difficulties of his position, which continued to increase rather than diminish. He was hampered by the action of the board at home, who gave ear to hostile criticisms on his reports; and although they afterward made handsome acknowledgment of his services, he felt his position to be altogether unsatisfactory. He therefore determined to leave at the expiry of his three years' engagement, and communicated his decision to the directors accordingly.*

* In a letter to Mr. Illingworth, then resident at Bogotá, dated the 24th of March, 1826, Robert wrote as follows: "Nothing but the fullest consent of my partners in England could induce me to stay in this country, and the assurance that no absolute necessity existed to call me home. I must also have the consent of my father. I

On receiving his letter, the board, through Mr. Richardson, of Lombard Street, one of the directors, communicated with his father at Newcastle, representing that if he would allow his son to remain in Colombia the company would make it "worth his while." To this the father gave a decided negative, and intimated that he himself urgently needed his son's assistance, and that he must return at the expiry of his three years' term—a decision, Robert wrote, "at which I feel much gratified, as it is clear that he is as anxious to have me back in England as I am to get there."

At the same time, Edward Pease, a principal partner in the Newcastle firm, privately wrote Robert to the following effect, urging his return home: "I can assure thee that the business at Newcastle, as well as thy father's engineering, have suffered very much from thy absence, and, unless thou soon return, the former will be given up, as Mr. Longridge is not able to give it that attention it requires; and what *is* done is not done with credit to the house." The idea of the manufactory being given up, which Robert had labored so hard to establish before leaving England, was painful to him in the extreme, and he wrote to Mr. Illingworth, strongly urging that arrangements should be made for enabling him to leave without delay. In the mean time he was laid prostrate by another violent attack of aguish fever; and when able to write, in June, 1827, he expressed himself as "completely wearied and worn down with vexation."

At length, when he was sufficiently recovered from his attack and able to travel, he set out on his voyage homeward in the beginning of August. At Mompox, on his way down the River Magdalena, he met Mr. Bodmer, his successor, with a fresh party

know that he must have suffered severely from my absence, but that having been extended so far beyond the period he was led to expect, may have induced him to curtail his plans, which, had they been accomplished, as they would have been by my assistance, would have placed us both in a situation far superior to any thing that I can hope for as the servant of an association however wealthy and liberal. What I might do in England is perhaps known to myself only; it is difficult, therefore, for the association to calculate upon rewarding me to the full extent of my prospects at home. My prosperity is involved in that of my father, whose property was sacrificed in laying the foundations of an establishment for me; his capital being invested in a concern which requires the greatest attention, and which, with our personal superintendence, could not fail to secure that independence which forms so principally the object of all our toil."

of miners from England, on their way up the country to the quarters which he had just quitted. Next day, six hours after leaving Mompox, a steam-boat was met ascending the river, with Bolivar the Liberator on board, on his way to St. Bogotá; and it was a mortification to our engineer that he had only a passing sight of that distinguished person. It was his intention, on leaving Mariquita, to visit the Isthmus of Panamá on his way home, for the purpose of inquiring into the practicability of cutting a canal to unite the Atlantic and Pacific—a project which then formed the subject of considerable public discussion; but Mr. Bodmer having informed him at Mompox that such a visit would be inconsistent with the statements made to the London Board that his presence was so anxiously desired at home, he determined to embrace the first opportunity of proceeding to New York.

Arrived at the port of Cartagena, he found himself under the necessity of waiting some time for a ship. The delay was very irksome to him, the more so as the place was then desolated by the ravages of the yellow fever. While sitting one day in the large, bare, comfortless public room of the miserable hotel at which he put up, he observed two strangers, whom he at once perceived to be English. One of the strangers was a tall, gaunt man, shrunken and hollow-looking, shabbily dressed, and apparently poverty-stricken. On making inquiry, he found it was Trevithick, the builder of the first railroad locomotive! He was returning home from the gold mines of Peru penniless. Robert Stephenson lent him £50 to enable him to reach England; and though he was afterward heard of as an inventor there, he had no farther part in the ultimate triumph of the locomotive.

But Trevithick's misadventures on this occasion had not yet ended, for before he reached New York he was wrecked, and Robert Stephenson with him. The following is the account of the voyage, "big with adventures," as given by the latter in a letter to his friend Illingworth:

"At first we had very little foul weather, and, indeed, were for several days becalmed among the islands, which was so far fortunate, for a few degrees farther north the most tremendous gales were blowing, and they appear (from our future information) to have wrecked every vessel exposed to their violence. We had two examples of the effects of the hurricane; for, as we sailed north, we took on board the remains of two crews found floating about on dismantled hulls. The one had been nine days without food of any kind except the carcasses of two of their companions who had died a day or two previously from fatigue and hunger. The other crew had been driven about for six days, and were not so dejected, but reduced to such a weak state that they were obliged to be drawn on board our vessel by ropes. A brig bound for Havana took part of the men, and we took the remainder. To attempt any description of my feelings on witnessing such scenes would be in vain. You will not be surprised to learn that I felt somewhat uneasy at the thought that we were so far from England, and that I also might possibly suffer similar shipwreck; but I consoled myself with the hope that fate would be more kind to us. It was not so much so, however, as I had flattered myself; for on voyaging toward New York, after we had made the land, we ran aground about midnight. The vessel soon filled with water, and, being surrounded by the breaking surf, the ship shortly split up, and before morning our situation became perilous. Masts and all were cut away to prevent the hull rocking, but all we could do was of no avail. About eight o'clock on the following morning, after a most miserable night, we were taken off the wreck, and were so fortunate as to reach the shore. I saved my minerals, but Empson lost part of his botanical collection. Upon the whole, we got off well; and, had I not been on the American side of the Atlantic, I 'guess' I would not have gone to sea again."

After a short tour in the United States and Canada, Robert Stephenson and his friend took ship for Liverpool, where they arrived at the end of November, and at once proceeded to Newcastle. The factory, we have seen, was by no means in a prosperous state. During the time Robert had been in America it had been carried on at a considerable loss; and Edward Pease, very much disheartened, wished to retire from it, but George Stephenson being unable to raise the requisite money to buy him out, the establishment was of necessity carried on by its then partners until the locomotive could be established in public estimation as a practicable and economical working power. Robert Stephenson immediately instituted a rigid inquiry into the working of the concern, unraveled the accounts, which had been allowed to fall into confusion during his father's absence at Liverpool, and very shortly succeeded in placing the affairs of the factory in a more healthy condition. In all this he had the hearty support of his father, as well as of the other partners.

The works of the Liverpool and Manchester Railway were now approaching completion. But, strange to say, the directors had not yet decided as to the tractive power to be employed in working the line when opened for traffic. The differences of opinion among them were so great as apparently to be irreconcilable. It was necessary, however, that they should come to some decision without farther loss of time, and many board meetings were accordingly held to discuss the subject. The old-fashioned and well-tried system of horse-haulage was not without its advocates; but, looking at the large amount of traffic which there was to be conveyed, and at the probable delay in the transit from station to station if this method were adopted, the directors, after a visit made by them to the Northumberland and Durham railways in 1828, came to the conclusion that the employment of horse-power was inadmissible.

Fixed engines had many advocates; the locomotive very few: it stood as yet almost in a minority of one—George Stephenson. The prejudice against the employment of the latter power had even increased since the Liverpool and Manchester Bill underwent its first ordeal in the House of Commons. In proof of this, it may be mentioned that the Newcastle and Carlisle Railway Act was conceded in 1829 on the express condition that it should *not* be worked by locomotives, but by horses only.

Grave doubts still existed as to the practicability of working a large traffic by means of traveling engines. The most celebrated engineers offered no opinion on the subject. They did not believe in the locomotive, and would scarcely take the trouble to examine it. The ridicule with which George Stephenson had been assailed by the barristers before the Parliamentary Committee had not been altogether distasteful to them. Perhaps they did not relish the idea of a man who had picked up his experience in Newcastle coal-pits appearing in the capacity of a leading engineer before Parliament, and attempting to establish a new system of internal communication in the country.

The directors could not disregard the adverse and conflicting views of the professional men whom they consulted. But Stephenson had so repeatedly and earnestly urged upon them the propriety of making a trial of the locomotive before coming to any decision against it, that they at length authorized him to proceed with the construction of one of his engines by way of experiment. In their report to the proprietors at their annual meeting on the 27th of March, 1828, they state that they had, after due consideration, authorized the engineer "to prepare a locomotive engine, which, from the nature of its construction and from the experiments already made, he is of opinion will be effective for the purposes of the company, without proving an annoyance to the public." The locomotive thus ordered was placed upon the line in 1829, and was found of great service in drawing the wagons full of marl from the two great cuttings.

In the mean time the discussion proceeded as to the kind of power to be permanently employed for the working of the railway. The directors were inundated with schemes of all sorts for facilitating locomotion. The projectors of England, France, and America seemed to be let loose upon them. There were plans for working the wagons along the line by water-power. Some proposed hydrogen, and others carbonic acid gas. Atmospheric pressure had its eager advocates. And various kinds of fixed and locomotive steam-power were suggested. Thomas Gray urged his plan of a greased road with cog-rails; and Messrs. Vignolles and Ericsson recommended the adoption of a central friction-rail, against which two horizontal rollers under the locomotive, pressing upon the sides of this rail, were to afford the means of ascending the inclined planes.

The directors felt themselves quite unable to choose from amid this multitude of projects. Their engineer expressed himself as decidedly as heretofore in favor of smooth rails and locomotive engines, which, he was confident, would be found the most economical and by far the most convenient moving power that could be employed. The Stockton and Darlington Railway being now at work, another deputation went down personally to inspect the fixed and locomotive engines on that line, as well as at Hetton and Killingworth. They returned to Liverpool with much information; but their testimony as to the relative merits of the two kinds of engines was so contradictory, that the directors were as far from a decision as ever.

They then resolved to call to their aid two professional engineers of high standing, who should visit the Darlington and Newcastle railways, carefully examine both modes of working—the fixed and the locomotive—and report to them fully on the subject. The gentlemen selected were Mr. Walker, of Limehouse, and Mr. Rastrick, of Stourbridge. After carefully examining the working of the Northern lines, they made their report to the directors in the spring of 1829. They concurred in the opinion that the cost of an establishment of fixed engines would be somewhat greater than that of locomotives to do the same work, but they thought the annual charge would be less if the former were adopted. They calculated that the cost of moving a ton of goods thirty miles by fixed engines would be 6·40*d.*, and by locomotives, 8·36*d.*, assuming a profitable traffic to be obtained both ways. At the same time, it was admitted that there appeared more grounds for expecting improvements in the construction and working of locomotives than of stationary engines. "On the whole, however, and looking especially at the computed annual charge of working the road on the two systems on a large scale, Messrs. Walker and Rastrick were of opinion that fixed engines were preferable, and accordingly recommended their adoption to the directors."* And in order to carry the system recommended by them into effect, they proposed to divide the railroad between Liverpool and Manchester into nineteen stages of about a mile and a half each, with twenty-one engines fixed at the different points to work the trains forward.

Such was the result, so far, of George Stephenson's labors.

* Mr. Booth's Account, p. 70–1. While concurring with Mr. Rastrick in recommending "the stationary reciprocating system as the best" if it was the directors' intention to make the line complete at once, so as to accommodate the traffic expected by them, or a quantity approaching to it (*i. e.*, 3750 tons of goods and passengers from Liverpool toward Manchester, and 3950 tons from Manchester toward Liverpool), Mr. Walker added, "but if any circumstances should induce the directors to proceed by degrees, and to proportion the power of conveyance to the demand, then we recommend locomotive engines upon the line generally; and two fixed engines upon Rainhill and Sutton planes, to draw up the locomotive engines as well as the goods and carriages;" and "if on any occasion the trade should get beyond the supply of locomotives, the horse might form a temporary substitute." As, however, it was the directors' determination, with a view to the success of their experiment, to open the line complete for working, they felt that it would be unadvisable to adopt this partial experiment; and it was still left for them to decide whether they would adopt or not the substantial recommendation of the reporting engineers in favor of the stationary-engine system for the complete accommodation of the expected traffic.

The two best practical engineers of the day concurred in reporting substantially in favor of the employment of fixed engines. Not a single professional man of eminence could be found to coincide with the engineer of the railway in his preference for locomotive over fixed engine power. He had scarcely a supporter, and the locomotive system seemed on the eve of being abandoned. Still he did not despair. With the profession against him, and public opinion against him—for the most frightful stories went abroad respecting the dangers, the unsightliness, and the nuisance which the locomotive would create—Stephenson held to his purpose. Even in this, apparently the darkest hour of the locomotive, he did not hesitate to declare that locomotive railroads would, before many years had passed, be "the great highways of the world."

He urged his views upon the directors in all ways, in season, and, as some of them thought, out of season. He pointed out the greater convenience of locomotive power for the purposes of a public highway, likening it to a series of short unconnected chains, any one of which could be removed and another substituted without interruption to the traffic; whereas the fixed-engine system might be regarded in the light of a continuous chain extending between the two termini, the failure of any link of which would derange the whole.* But the fixed-engine party were very strong at the board, and, led by Mr. Cropper, they urged the propriety of forthwith adopting the report of Messrs. Walker and Rastrick. Mr. Sandars and Mr. William Rathbone, on the other hand, desired that a fair trial should be given to the locomotive; and they with reason objected to the expenditure of the large capital necessary to construct the proposed engine-houses, with their fixed engines, ropes, and machinery, until they had tested the powers of the locomotive as recommended by their

* The arguments used by Mr. Stephenson with the directors in favor of the locomotive engine were afterward collected and published in 1830 by Robert Stephenson and Joseph Locke, as "compiled from the Reports of Mr. George Stephenson." The pamphlet was entitled "Observations on the Comparative Merits of Locomotive and Fixed Engines." Robert Stephenson, speaking of the authorship many years after, said, "I believe I furnished the facts and the arguments, and Locke put them into shape. Locke was a very flowery writer, whereas my style was rather bald and unattractive; so he was the editor of the pamphlet, which excited a good deal of attention among engineers at the time."

own engineer. George Stephenson continued to urge upon them that the locomotive was yet capable of great improvements, if proper inducements were held out to inventors and machinists to make them; and he pledged himself that, if time were given him, he would construct an engine that should satisfy their requirements, and prove itself capable of working heavy loads along the railway with speed, regularity, and safety. At length, influenced by his persistent earnestness not less than by his arguments, the directors, at the suggestion of Mr. Harrison, determined to offer a prize of £500 for the best locomotive engine, which, on a certain day, should be produced on the railway, and perform certain specified conditions in the most satisfactory manner.*

The requirements of the directors as to speed were not excessive. All that they asked for was that ten miles an hour should be maintained. Perhaps they had in mind the animadversions of the "Quarterly Reviewer" on the absurdity of traveling at a greater velocity, and also the remarks published by Mr. Nicholas

* The conditions were these:

1. The engine must effectually consume its own smoke.

2. The engine, if of six tons' weight, must be able to draw after it, day by day, twenty tons' weight (including the tender and water-tank) at *ten miles* an hour, with a pressure of steam on the boiler not exceeding fifty pounds to the square inch.

3. The boiler must have two safety valves, neither of which must be fastened down, and one of them be completely out of the control of the engine-man.

4. The engine and boiler must be supported on springs, and rest on six wheels, the height of the whole not exceeding fifteen feet to the top of the chimney.

5. The engine, with water, must not weigh more than six tons; but an engine of less weight would be preferred on its drawing a proportionate load behind it; if of only four and a half tons, then it might be put on only four wheels. The company to be at liberty to test the boiler, etc., by a pressure of one hundred and fifty pounds to the square inch.

6. A mercurial gauge must be affixed to the machine, showing the steam pressure above forty-five pounds per square inch.

7. The engine must be delivered, complete and ready for trial, at the Liverpool end of the railway, not later than the 1st of October, 1829.

8. The price of the engine must not exceed £550.

Many persons of influence declared the conditions published by the directors of the railway chimerical in the extreme. One gentleman of some eminence in Liverpool, Mr. P. Ewart, who afterward filled the office of Government Inspector of Post-office Steam Packets, declared that only a parcel of charlatans would ever have issued such a set of conditions; that it had been *proved* to be impossible to make a locomotive engine go at ten miles an hour; but if it ever was done, he would undertake to eat a stewed engine-wheel for his breakfast!

Wood, whom they selected to be one of the judges of the competition, in conjunction with Mr. Rastrick, of Stourbridge, and Mr. Kennedy, of Manchester.

It was now felt that the fate of railways in a great measure depended upon the issue of this appeal to the mechanical genius of England. When the advertisement of the prize for the best locomotive was published, scientific men began more particularly to direct their attention to the new power which was thus struggling into existence. In the mean time public opinion on the subject of railway working remained suspended, and the progress of the undertaking was watched with intense interest.

During the progress of this important controversy with reference to the kind of power to be employed in working the railway, George Stephenson was in constant communication with his son Robert, who made frequent visits to Liverpool for the purpose of assisting his father in the preparation of his reports to the board on the subject. Mr. Swanwick remembers the vivid interest of the evening discussions which then took place between father and son as to the best mode of increasing the powers and perfecting the mechanism of the locomotive. He wondered at their quick perception and rapid judgment on each other's suggestions; at the mechanical difficulties which they anticipated and provided for in the practical arrangement of the machine; and he speaks of these evenings as most interesting displays of two actively ingenious and able minds stimulating each other to feats of mechanical invention, by which it was ordained that the locomotive engine should become what it now is. These discussions became more frequent, and still more interesting, after the public prize had been offered for the best locomotive by the directors of the railway, and the working plans of the engine which they proposed to construct had to be settled.

One of the most important considerations in the new engine was the arrangement of the boiler and the extension of its heating surface to enable steam enough to be raised rapidly and continuously for the purpose of maintaining high rates of speed—the effect of high-pressure engines being ascertained to depend mainly upon the quantity of steam which the boiler can generate, and upon its degree of elasticity when produced. The quantity of steam so generated, it will be obvious, must chiefly depend upon the quantity of fuel consumed in the furnace, and, by necessary consequence, upon the high rate of temperature maintained there.

It will be remembered that in Stephenson's first Killingworth engines he invited and applied the ingenious method of stimulating combustion in the furnace by throwing the waste steam into the chimney after performing its office in the cylinders, thereby accelerating the ascent of the current of air, greatly increasing the draught, and consequently the temperature of the fire. This plan was adopted by him, as we have seen, as early as 1815, and it was so successful that he himself attributed to it the greater economy of the locomotive as compared with horse-power. Hence the continuance of its use upon the Killingworth Railway.

Though the adoption of the steam-blast greatly quickened combustion and contributed to the rapid production of high-pressure steam, the limited amount of heating surface presented to the fire was still felt to be an obstacle to the complete success of the locomotive engine. Mr. Stephenson endeavored to overcome this by lengthening the boilers and increasing the surface presented by the flue-tubes. The "Lancashire Witch," which he built for the Bolton and Leigh Railway, and used in forming the Liverpool and Manchester Railway embankments, was constructed with a double tube, each of which contained a fire, and passed longitudinally through the boiler. But this arrangement necessarily led to a considerable increase in the weight of those engines, which amounted to about twelve tons each; and as six tons was the limit allowed for engines admitted to the Liverpool competition, it was clear that the time was come when the Killingworth engine must undergo a farther important modification.

For many years previous to this period, ingenious mechanics had been engaged in attempting to solve the problem of the best and most economical boiler for the production of high-pressure steam.

The use of tubes in boilers for increasing the heating surface had long been known. As early as 1780, Matthew Boulton employed copper tubes longitudinally in the boiler of the Wheal Busy engine in Cornwall—the fire passing *through* the tubes—and it was found that the production of steam was thereby considerably increased.* The use of tubular boilers afterward became common in Cornwall. In 1803, Woolf, the Cornish engineer, patented a boiler with tubes, with the same object of increasing the heating surface. The water was *inside* the tubes, and the fire of the boiler outside. Similar expedients were proposed by other inventors. In 1815 Trevithick invented his light high-pressure boiler for portable purposes, in which, to "expose a large surface to the fire," he constructed the boiler of a number of small perpendicular tubes "opening into a common reservoir at the top." In 1823 W. H. James contrived a boiler composed of a series of annular wrought-iron tubes, placed side by side and bolted together, so as to form by their union a long cylindrical boiler, in the centre of which, at the end, the fireplace was situated. The fire played round the tubes, which contained the water. In 1826 James Neville took out a patent for a boiler with vertical tubes surrounded by the water, through which the heated air of the furnace passed, explaining also in his specification that the tubes might be horizontal or inclined, according to circumstances. Mr. Goldsworthy Gurney, the persevering adaptor of steam-carriages to traveling on common roads, applied the tubular principle in the boiler of his engine, in which the steam was generated *within* the tubes; while the boiler invented by Messrs. Summers and Ogle for their turnpike-road steam-carriage consisted of a series of tubes placed vertically over the furnace, through which the heated air passed before reaching the chimney.

About the same time George Stephenson was trying the effect of introducing small tubes in the boilers of his locomotives, with the object of increasing their evaporative power. Thus, in 1829, he sent to France two engines constructed at the Newcastle works for the Lyons and St. Etienne Railway, in the boilers of which tubes were placed containing water. The heating surface was thus considerably increased; but the expedient was not successful, for the tubes, becoming furred with deposit, shortly burned out and were removed. It was then that M. Seguin, the engineer

* Some correspondence took place between Boulton and Watt on the subject, when the latter was scheming the application of the steam-engine to locomotive purposes. In a letter to Boulton, dated the 27th of August, 1784, Watt said, "Perhaps some means may be hit upon to make the boiler cylindrical *with a number of tubes passing through*, like the organ-pipe condenser, whereby it might be thinner and lighter; but," he added, "I fear this would be too subject to accidents."

of the railway, pursuing the same idea, is said to have adopted his plan of employing horizontal tubes through which the heated air passed in streamlets, and for which he took out a French patent.

In the mean time Mr. Henry Booth, secretary to the Liverpool and Manchester Railway, whose attention had been directed to the subject on the prize being offered for the best locomotive to work that line, proposed the same method, which, unknown to him, Matthew Boulton had employed, but not patented, in 1780, and James Neville had patented, but not employed, in 1826; and it was carried into effect by Robert Stephenson in the construction of the "Rocket," which won the prize at Rainhill in October, 1829. The following is Mr. Booth's account in a letter to the author:

"I was in almost daily communication with Mr. Stephenson at the time, and I was not aware that he had any intention of competing for the prize till I communicated to him my scheme of a multitubular boiler. This new plan of boiler comprised the introduction of numerous small tubes, two or three inches in diameter, and less than one eighth of an inch thick, through which to carry the fire, instead of a single tube or flue eighteen inches in diameter, and about half an inch thick, by which plan we not only obtain a very much larger heating surface, but the heating surface is much more effective, as there intervenes between the fire and the water only a thin sheet of copper or brass, not an eighth of an inch thick, instead of a plate of iron of four times the substance, as well as an inferior conductor of heat.

"When the conditions of trial were published, I communicated my multitubular plan to Mr. Stephenson, and proposed to him that we should jointly construct an engine and compete for the prize. Mr. Stephenson approved the plan, and agreed to my proposal. He settled the mode in which the fire-box and tubes were to be mutually arranged and connected, and the engine was constructed at the works of Messrs. Robert Stephenson and Co., Newcastle-on-Tyne.

"I am ignorant of M. Seguin's proceedings in France, but I claim to be the inventor in England, and feel warranted in stating, without reservation, that until I named my plan to Mr. Stephenson, with a view to compete for the prize at Rainhill, it had not been tried, and was not known in this country."

From the well-known high character of Mr. Booth, we believe

his statement to be made in perfect good faith, and that he was as much in ignorance of the plan patented by Neville as he was of that of Seguin. As we have seen, from the many plans of tubular boilers invented during the preceding thirty years, the idea was not by any means new; and we believe Mr. Booth to be entitled to the merit of inventing the method by which the multitubular principle was so effectually applied in the construction of the famous "Rocket" engine.

The principal circumstances connected with the construction of the "Rocket," as described by Robert Stephenson to the author, may be briefly stated. The tubular principle was adopted in a more complete manner than had yet been attempted. Twenty-five copper tubes, each three inches in diameter, extended from one end of the boiler to the other, the heated air passing through them on its way to the chimney; and the tubes being surrounded by the water of the boiler, it will be obvious that a large extension of the heating surface was thus effectually secured. The principal difficulty was in fitting the copper tubes in the boiler-ends so as to prevent leakage. They were manufactured by a Newcastle coppersmith, and soldered to brass screws which were screwed into the boiler-ends, standing out in great knobs. When the tubes were thus fitted, and the boiler was filled with water, hydraulic pressure was applied; but the water squirted out at every joint, and the factory floor was soon flooded. Robert went home in despair; and in the first moment of grief he wrote to his father that the whole thing was a failure. By return of post came a letter from his father, telling him that despair was not to be thought of—that he must "try again;" and he suggested a mode of overcoming the difficulty, which his son had already anticipated and proceeded to adopt. It was, to bore clean holes in the boiler-ends, fit in the smooth copper tubes as tightly as possible, solder up, and then raise the steam. This plan succeeded perfectly, the expansion of the copper tubes completely filling up all interstices, and producing a perfectly water-tight boiler, capable of withstanding extreme external pressure.

The mode of employing the steam-blast for the purpose of increasing the draught in the chimney was also the subject of numerous experiments. When the engine was first tried, it was thought that the blast in the chimney was not sufficiently strong for the purpose of keeping up the intensity of the fire in the furnace, so as to produce high-pressure steam with the required velocity. The expedient was therefore adopted of hammering the copper tubes at the point at which they entered the chimney, whereby the blast was considerably sharpened; and on a farther trial it was found that the draught was increased to such an extent as to enable abundance of steam to be raised. The rationale of the blast may be simply explained by referring to the effect of contracting the pipe of a water-hose, by which the force of the jet of water is proportionately increased. Widen the nozzle of the pipe, and the jet is in like manner diminished. So is it with the steam-blast in the chimney of the locomotive.

Doubts were, however, expressed whether the greater draught obtained by the contraction of the blast-pipe was not counterbalanced in some degree by the negative pressure upon the piston. Hence a series of experiments was made with pipes of different diameters, and their efficiency was tested by the amount of vacuum that was produced in the smoke-box. The degree of rarefaction was determined by a glass tube fixed to the bottom of the smoke-box, and descending into a bucket of water, the tube being open at both ends. As the rarefaction took place, the water would of course rise in the tube, and the height to which it rose above the surface of the water in the bucket was made the measure of the amount of rarefaction. These experiments proved that a considerable increase of draught was obtained by the contraction of the orifice; accordingly, the two blast-pipes opening from the cylinders into either side of the "Rocket" chimney, and turned up within it, were contracted slightly below the area of the steam-ports; and before the engine left the factory, the water rose in the glass tube three inches above the water in the bucket.

The other arrangements of the "Rocket" were briefly these: the boiler was cylindrical, with flat ends, six feet in length, and three feet four inches in diameter. The upper half of the boiler was used as a reservoir for the steam, the lower half being filled with water. Through the lower part the copper tubes extended, being open to the fire-box at one end, and to the chimney at the other. The fire-box, or furnace, two feet wide and three feet high, was attached immediately behind the boiler, and was also surrounded with water. The cylinders of the engine were placed on each side of the boiler, in an oblique position, one end being nearly level with the top of the boiler at its after end, and the other pointing toward the centre of the foremost or driving pair of wheels, with which the connection was directly made from the piston-rod to a pin on the outside of the wheel. The engine, together with its load of water, weighed only four tons and a quarter; and it was supported on four wheels, not coupled. The tender was four-wheeled, and similar in shape to a wagon—the foremost part holding the fuel, and the hind part a water-cask.

When the "Rocket" was finished, it was placed upon the Killingworth Railway for the purpose of experiment. The new boiler arrangement was found perfectly successful. The steam

THE "ROCKET."

was raised rapidly and continuously, and in a quantity which then appeared marvelous. The same evening Robert dispatched a letter to his father at Liverpool, informing him, to his great joy, that the "Rocket" was "all right," and would be in complete working trim by the day of trial. The engine was shortly after sent by wagon to Carlisle, and thence shipped for Liverpool.

The time so much longed for by George Stephenson had now arrived, when the merits of the passenger locomotive were about to be put to the test. He had fought the battle for it until now almost single-handed. Engrossed by his daily labors and anxieties, and harassed by difficulties and discouragements which would have crushed the spirit of a less resolute man, he had held firmly to his purpose through good and through evil report. The hostility which he experienced from some of the directors opposed to the adoption of the locomotive was the circumstance that caused him the greatest grief of all; for where he had looked for encouragement, he found only carping and opposition. But his pluck never failed him; and now the "Rocket" was upon the ground to prove, to use his own words, "whether he was a man of his word or not."

Great interest was felt at Liverpool, as well as throughout the country, in the approaching competition. Engineers, scientific men, and mechanics arrived from all quarters to witness the novel display of mechanical ingenuity on which such great results depended. The public generally were no indifferent spectators either. The populations of Liverpool, Manchester, and the adjacent towns felt that the successful issue of the experiment would confer upon them individual benefits and local advantages almost incalculable, while populations at a distance waited for the result with almost equal interest.

On the day appointed for the great competition of locomotives at Rainhill the following engines were entered for the prize:

1. Messrs. Braithwaite and Ericsson's* "Novelty."
2. Mr. Timothy Hackworth's "Sanspareil."
3. Messrs. R. Stephenson and Co.'s "Rocket."
4. Mr. Burstall's "Perseverance."

Another engine was entered by Mr. Brandreth, of Liverpool—the "Cycloped," weighing three tons, worked by a horse in a frame, but it could not be admitted to the competition. The above were the only four exhibited, out of a considerable number of engines constructed in different parts of the country in an-

* The inventor of this engine was a Swede, who afterward proceeded to the United States, and there achieved considerable distinction as an engineer. His caloric engine has so far proved a failure, but his iron cupola vessel, the "Monitor," must be admitted to have been a remarkable success in its way.

ticipation of this contest, many of which could not be satisfactorily completed by the day of trial.

The ground on which the engines were to be tried was a level piece of railroad, about two miles in length. Each was required to make twenty trips, or equal to a journey of seventy miles, in the course of the day, and the average rate of traveling was to be not under ten miles an hour. It was determined that, to avoid confusion, each engine should be tried separately, and on different days.

The day fixed for the competition was the 1st of October, but, to allow sufficient time to get the locomotives into good working order, the directors extended it to the 6th. On the morning of the 6th the ground at Rainhill presented a lively appearance, and there was as much excitement as if the St. Leger were about to be run. Many thousand spectators looked on, among whom were some of the first engineers and mechanicians of the day. A stand was provided for the ladies; the "beauty and fashion" of the neighborhood were present, and the side of the railroad was lined with carriages of all descriptions.

It was quite characteristic of the Stephensons that, although their engine did not stand first on the list for trial, it was the first that was ready, and it was accordingly ordered out by the judges for an experimental trip. Yet the "Rocket" was by no means the "favorite" with either the judges or the spectators. Nicholas Wood has since stated that the majority of the judges were strongly predisposed in favor of the "Novelty," and that "nine tenths, if not ten tenths, of the persons present were against the 'Rocket' because of its appearance."* Nearly every person favored some other engine, so that there was nothing for the "Rocket" but the practical test. The first trip made by it was quite successful. It ran about twelve miles, without interruption, in about fifty-three minutes.

The "Novelty" was next called out. It was a light engine, very compact in appearance, carrying the water and fuel upon the same wheels as the engine. The weight of the whole was only three tons and one hundred weight. A peculiarity of this engine was that the air was driven or *forced* through the fire by means of bellows. The day being now far advanced, and some dispute

* Mr. Wood's speech at Newcastle, 26th of October, 1858.

having arisen as to the method of assigning the proper load for the "Novelty," no particular experiment was made farther than that the engine traversed the line by way of exhibition, occasionally moving at the rate of twenty-four miles an hour. The "Sanspareil," constructed by Mr. Timothy Hackworth, was next exhibited, but no particular experiment was made with it on this day. This engine differed but little in its construction from the locomotive last supplied by the Stephensons to the Stockton and Darlington Railway, of which Mr. Hackworth was the locomotive foreman.

The contest was postponed until the following day; but, before the judges arrived on the ground, the bellows for creating the blast in the "Novelty" gave way, and it was found incapable of

LOCOMOTIVE COMPETITION AT RAINHILL.

going through its performance. A defect was also detected in the boiler of the "Sanspareil," and some farther time was allowed to get it repaired. The large number of spectators who had assembled to witness the contest were greatly disappointed at this postponement; but, to lessen it, Stephenson again brought out the "Rocket," and, attaching to it a coach containing thirty persons, he ran them along the line at the rate of from twenty-four to thirty miles an hour, much to their gratification and amazement. Before separating, the judges ordered the engine to be in readiness by eight o'clock on the following morning, to go through its definitive trial according to the prescribed conditions.

On the morning of the 8th of October the "Rocket" was again ready for the contest. The engine was taken to the extremity of the stage, the fire-box was filled with coke, the fire lighted, and the steam raised until it lifted the safety-valve loaded to a pressure of fifty pounds to the square inch. This proceeding occupied fifty-seven minutes. The engine then started on its journey, dragging after it about thirteen tons' weight in wagons, and made the first ten trips backward and forward along the two miles of road, running the thirty-five miles, including stoppages, in an hour and forty-eight minutes. The second ten trips were in like manner performed in two hours and three minutes. The maximum velocity attained during the trial trip was twenty-nine miles an hour, or about three times the speed that one of the judges of the competition had declared to be the limit of possibility. The average speed at which the whole of the journeys were performed was fifteen miles an hour, or five miles beyond the rate specified in the conditions published by the company. The entire performance excited the greatest astonishment among the assembled spectators; the directors felt confident that their enterprise was now on the eve of success; and George Stephenson rejoiced to think that, in spite of all false prophets and fickle counselors, the locomotive system was now safe. When the "Rocket," having performed all the conditions of the contest, arrived at the "grand stand" at the close of its day's successful run, Mr. Cropper—one of the directors favorable to the fixed engine system—lifted up his hands, and exclaimed, "Now has George Stephenson at last delivered himself."

Neither the "Novelty" nor the "Sanspareil" was ready for trial until the 10th, on the morning of which day an advertisement appeared, stating that the former engine was to be tried on that day, when it would perform more work than any engine on the ground. The weight of the carriages attached to it was only about seven tons. The engine passed the first post in good style; but, in returning, the pipe from the forcing-pump burst and put an end to the trial. The pipe was afterward repaired, and the engine made several trips by itself, in which it was said to have gone at the rate of from twenty-four to twenty-eight miles an hour.

The "Sanspareil" was not ready until the 13th; and when its boiler and tender were filled with water, it was found to weigh four hundred weight beyond the weight specified in the published conditions as the limit of four-wheeled engines; nevertheless, the judges allowed it to run on the same footing as the other engines, to enable them to ascertain whether its merits entitled it to favorable consideration. It traveled at the average speed of about fourteen miles an hour, with its load attached; but at the eighth trip the cold-water pump got wrong, and the engine could proceed no farther.

It was determined to award the premium to the successful engine on the following day, the 14th, on which occasion there was an unusual assemblage of spectators. The owners of the "Novelty" pleaded for another trial, and it was conceded. But again it broke down. Then Mr. Hackworth requested the opportunity for making another trial of his "Sanspareil." But the judges had now had enough of failures, and they declined, on the ground that not only was the engine above the stipulated weight, but that it was constructed on a plan which they could not recommend for adoption by the directors of the company. One of the principal practical objections to this locomotive was the enormous quantity of coke consumed or wasted by it—about 692 lbs. per hour when traveling—caused by the sharpness of the steam-blast in the chimney, which blew a large proportion of the burning coke into the air.

The "Perseverance" of Mr. Burstall was found unable to move at more than five or six miles an hour, and it was withdrawn from the contest at an early period. The "Rocket" was thus the only engine that had performed, and more than performed, all the stipulated conditions, and it was declared to be entitled to the prize of £500, which was awarded to the Messrs. Stephenson and Booth accordingly. And farther to show that the engine had been working quite within its powers, George Stephenson ordered it to be brought upon the ground and detached from all incumbrances, when, in making two trips, it was found to travel at the astonishing rate of thirty-five miles an hour.

The "Rocket" had thus eclipsed the performances of all locomotive engines that had yet been constructed, and outstripped even the sanguine expectations of its constructors. It satisfactorily answered the report of Messrs. Walker and Rastrick, and established the efficiency of the locomotive for working the Liverpool and Manchester Railway, and, indeed, all future railways.

The "Rocket" showed that a new power had been born into the world, full of activity and strength, with boundless capability of work. It was the simple but admirable contrivance of the steam-blast, and its combination with the multitubular boiler, that at once gave locomotion a vigorous life, and secured the triumph of the railway system.* As has been well observed, this wonderful ability to increase and multiply its powers of performance with the emergency that demands them has made this giant engine the noblest creation of human wit, the very lion among machines. The success of the Rainhill experiment, as judged by the public, may be inferred from the fact that the shares of the company immediately rose ten per cent., and nothing farther was heard of the proposed twenty-one fixed engines, engine-houses, ropes, etc. All this cumbersome apparatus was thenceforward effectually disposed of.

Very different now was the tone of those directors who had distinguished themselves by the persistency of their opposition to George Stephenson's plans. Coolness gave way to eulogy, and hostility to unbounded offers of friendship, after the manner of many men who run to the help of the strong. Deeply though the engineer had felt aggrieved by the conduct exhibited toward him during this eventful struggle by some from whom forbearance was to have been expected, he never entertained toward them in after life any angry feelings; on the contrary, he forgave all. But, though the directors afterward passed unanimous resolutions eulogizing "the great skill and unwearied energy" of

* When heavier and more powerful engines were brought upon the road, the old "Rocket," becoming regarded as a thing of no value, was sold in 1837. It was purchased by Mr. Thompson, of Kirkhouse, the lessee of the Earl of Carlisle's coal and lime works, near Carlisle. He worked the engine on the Midgeholme Railway for five or six years, during which it hauled coals from the pits to the town. There was wonderful vitality in the old engine, as the following circumstance proves. When the great contest for the representation of East Cumberland took place, and Sir James Graham was superseded by Major Aglionby, the "Rocket" was employed to convey the Alston express with the state of the poll from Midgeholme to Kirkhouse. On that occasion the engine was driven by Mr. Mark Thompson, and it ran the distance of upward of four miles in four and a half minutes, thus reaching a speed of nearly sixty miles an hour, proving its still admirable qualities as an engine. But again it was superseded by heavier engines; for it only weighed about four tons, whereas the new engines were at least three times that weight. The "Rocket" was consequently laid up in ordinary in the yard at Kirkhouse, from whence it has since been transferred to the Museum of Patents at Kensington, where it is still to be seen.

their engineer, he himself, when speaking confidentially to those with whom he was most intimate, could not help pointing out the difference between his "foul-weather and fair-weather friends." Mr. Gooch says that, though naturally most cheerful and kind-hearted in disposition, the anxiety and pressure which weighed upon his mind during the construction of the railway had the effect of making him occasionally impatient and irritable, like a spirited horse touched by the spur, though his original good nature from time to time shone through it all. When the line had been brought to a successful completion, a very marked change in him became visible. The irritability passed away, and when difficulties and vexations arose they were treated by him as matters of course, and with perfect composure and cheerfulness.

RAILWAY *versus* ROAD.

CHAPTER XIII.

OPENING OF THE LIVERPOOL AND MANCHESTER RAILWAY, AND EXTENSION OF THE RAILWAY SYSTEM.

THE directors of the railway now began to see daylight, and they derived encouragement from the skillful manner in which their engineer had overcome the principal difficulties of the undertaking. He had formed a solid road over Chat Moss, and thus achieved one "impossibility;" and he had constructed a locomotive that could run at a speed of thirty miles an hour, thus vanquishing a still more formidable difficulty.

A single line of way was completed over Chat Moss by the 1st of January, 1830, and on that day the "Rocket," with a carriage full of directors, engineers, and their friends, passed along the greater part of the road between Liverpool and Manchester. Mr. Stephenson continued to direct his close attention to the improvement of the details of the locomotive, every successive trial of which proved more satisfactory. In this department he had the benefit of the able and unremitting assistance of his son, who, in the workshops at Newcastle, directly superintended the construction of the engines required for the public working of the railway. He did not by any means rest satisfied with the success, decided though it was, which had been achieved by the "Rocket." He regarded it but in the light of a successful experiment; and every successive engine placed upon the railway exhibited some improvement on its predecessors. The arrangement of the parts, and the weight and proportion of the engines, were altered as the experience of each successive day, or week, or month suggested; and it was soon found that the performances of the "Rocket" on the day of trial had been greatly within the powers of the improved locomotive.

The first entire trip between Liverpool and Manchester was performed on the 14th of June, 1830, on the occasion of a board meeting being held at the latter town. The train was on this occasion drawn by the "Arrow," one of the new locomotives, in which the most recent improvements had been adopted. George Stephenson himself drove the engine, and Captain Scoresby, the circumpolar navigator, stood beside him on the foot-plate, and minuted the speed of the train. A great concourse of people assembled at both termini, as well as along the line, to witness the novel spectacle of a train of carriages drawn by an engine at the speed of seventeen miles an hour. On the return journey to Liverpool in the evening, the "Arrow" crossed Chat Moss at a speed of nearly twenty-seven miles an hour, reaching its destination in about an hour and a half.

In the mean time Mr. Stephenson and his assistant, Mr. Gooch, were diligently occupied in making the necessary preliminary arrangements for the conduct of the traffic against the time when the line should be ready for opening. The experiments made with the object of carrying on the passenger traffic at quick velocities were of an especially harassing and anxious character. Every week, for nearly three months before the opening, trial trips were made to Newton and back, generally with two or three trains following each other, and carrying altogether from two to three hundred persons. These trips were usually made on Saturday afternoons, when the works could be more cenveniently stopped and the line cleared for the occasion. In these experiments Mr. Stephenson had the able assistance of Mr. Henry Booth, the secretary of the company, who contrived many of the arrangements in the passenger carriages, not the least valuable of which was his invention of the coupling screw, still in use on all passenger railways.

At length the line was finished and ready for the public opening, which took place on the 15th of September, 1830, and attracted a vast number of spectators from all parts of the country. The completion of the railway was justly regarded as an important national event, and the ceremony of its opening was celebrated accordingly. The Duke of Wellington, then prime minister, Sir Robert Peel, Secretary of State, Mr. Huskisson, one of the members for Liverpool and an earnest supporter of the project from its commencement, were among the number of distinguished public personages present.

Eight locomotive engines, constructed at the Stephenson works, had been delivered and placed upon the line, the whole of which had been tried and tested, weeks before, with perfect success. The several trains of carriages accommodated in all about six hundred persons. The "Northumbrian" engine, driven by George Stephenson himself, headed the line of trains; then followed the "Phœnix," driven by Robert Stephenson; the "North Star," by Robert Stephenson senior (brother of George); the "Rocket," by Joseph Locke; the "Dart," by Thomas L. Gooch; the "Comet," by William Allcard; the "Arrow," by Frederick Swanwick; and the "Meteor," by Anthony Harding. The procession was cheered in its progress by thousands of spectators—through the deep ravine of Olive Mount; up the Sutton incline; over the great Sankey viaduct, beneath which a multitude of persons had assembled—carriages filling the narrow lanes, and barges crowding the river; the people below gazing with wonder and admiration at the trains which sped along the line, far above their heads, at the rate of some twenty-four miles an hour.

At Parkside, about seventeen miles from Liverpool, the engines stopped to take in water. Here a deplorable accident occurred to one of the illustrious visitors, which threw a deep shadow over the subsequent proceedings of the day. The "Northumbrian" engine, with the carriage containing the Duke of Wellington, was drawn up on one line, in order that the whole of the trains on the other line might pass in review before him and his party. Mr. Huskisson had alighted from the carriage, and was standing on the opposite road, along which the "Rocket" was observed rapidly coming up. At this moment the Duke of Wellington, between whom and Mr. Huskisson some coolness had existed, made a sign of recognition, and held out his hand. A hurried but friendly grasp was given; and before it was loosened there was a general cry from the by-standers of "Get in, get in!" Flurried and confused, Mr. Huskisson endeavored to get round the open door of the carriage, which projected over the opposite rail, but in so doing he was struck down by the "Rocket," and falling with his leg doubled across the rail, the limb was instantly crushed. His first words, on being raised, were, "I have met my death," which unhappily proved true, for he expired that same evening in the parsonage of Eccles. It was cited at the time as a remarkable fact that the "Northumbrian" engine, driven by George Stephenson himself, conveyed the wounded body of the unfortunate gentleman a distance of about fifteen miles in twenty-five minutes, or at the rate of thirty-six miles an hour. This incredible speed burst upon the world with the effect of a new and unlooked-for phenomenon.

The accident threw a gloom over the rest of the day's proceedings. The Duke of Wellington and Sir Robert Peel expressed a wish that the procession should return to Liverpool. It was, however, represented to them that a vast concourse of people had assembled at Manchester to witness the arrival of the trains; that report would exaggerate the mischief if they did not complete the journey; and that a false panic on that day might seriously affect future railway traveling and the value of the company's property. The party consented accordingly to proceed to Manchester, but on the understanding that they should return as soon as possible, and refrain from farther festivity.

As the trains approached Manchester, crowds of people were found covering the banks, the slopes of the cuttings, and even the railway itself. The multitude, become impatient and excited by the rumors which reached them, had outflanked the military, and all order was at an end. The people clambered about the carriages, holding on by the door-handles, and many were tumbled over; but, happily, no fatal accident occurred. At the Manchester station the political element began to display itself; placards about "Peterloo," etc., were exhibited, and brickbats were thrown at the carriage containing the duke. On the trains coming to a stand in the Manchester station, the duke did not descend, but remained seated, shaking hands with the women and children who were pushed forward by the crowd. Shortly after, the trains returned to Liverpool, which they reached, after considerable delays, late at night.

On the following morning the railway was opened for public traffic. The first train of 140 passengers was booked and sent on to Manchester, reaching it in the allotted time of two hours; and from that time the traffic has regularly proceeded from day to day until now.

It is scarcely necessary that we should speak at any length of the commercial results of the Liverpool and Manchester Railway. Suffice it to say that its success was complete and decisive. The anticipations of its projectors were, however, in many respects at fault. They had based their calculations almost entirely on the heavy merchandise traffic—such as coal, cotton, and timber—relying little upon passengers; whereas the receipts derived from the conveyance of passengers far exceeded those derived from merchandise of all kinds, which for a time continued a subordinate branch of the traffic. In the evidence given before the Committee of the House of Commons, the promoters stated their expectation of obtaining about one half of the whole number of passengers which the coaches then running could carry, or about 400 a day. But the railway was scarcely opened before it carried on an average about 1200 passengers daily; and five years after the opening, it carried nearly half a million of persons yearly. So successful, indeed, was the passenger traffic, that it engrossed the whole of the company's small stock of engines.

For some time after the public opening of the line, Mr. Stephenson's ingenuity continued to be employed in devising improved methods for securing the safety and comfort of the traveling public. Few are aware of the thousand minute details which have to be arranged—the forethought and contrivance that have to be exercised—to enable the traveler by railway to accomplish his journey in safety. After the difficulties of constructing a level road over bogs, across valleys, and through deep cuttings have been overcome, the maintenance of the way has to be provided for with continuous care. Every rail, with its fastenings, must be complete, to prevent risk of accident, and the road must be kept regularly ballasted up to the level to diminish the jolting of vehicles passing over it at high speeds. Then the stations must be protected by signals observable from such a distance as to enable the train to be stopped in event of an obstacle, such as a stopping or shunting train being in the way. For some years the signals employed on the Liverpool Railway were entirely given by men with flags of different colors stationed along the line; there were no fixed signals nor electric telegraphs; but the traffic was nevertheless worked quite as safely as under the more elaborate and complicated system of telegraphing which has since been established.

From an early period it became obvious that the iron road, as originally laid down, was quite insufficient for the heavy traffic which it had to carry. The line was in the first place laid with fish-bellied rails of only thirty-five pounds to the yard, calculated only for horse-traffic, or, at most, for engines like the "Rocket," of very light weight. But as the power and the weight of the locomotives were increased, it was found that such rails were quite insufficient for the safe conduct of the traffic, and it therefore became necessary to relay the road with heavier and stronger rails at considerable expense.

The details of the carrying stock had in like manner to be settled by experience. Every thing had, as it were, to be begun from the beginning. The coal-wagon, it is true, served in some degree as a model for the railway-truck; but the railway passenger-carriage was an entirely novel structure. It had to be mounted upon strong framing, of a peculiar kind, supported on springs to prevent jolting. Then there was the necessity for contriving some method of preventing hard bumping of the carriage-ends when the train was pulled up, and hence the contrivance of buffer-springs and spring-frames. For the purpose of stopping the train, brakes on an improved plan were also contrived, with new modes of lubricating the carriage-axles, on which the wheels revolved at an unusually high velocity. In all these contrivances Mr. Stephenson's inventiveness was kept constantly on the stretch; and though many improvements in detail have been effected since his time, the foundations were then laid by him of the present system of conducting railway traffic. As a curious illustration of the inventive ingenuity which he displayed in contriving the working of the Liverpool line, we may mention his invention of the Self-acting Brake. He early entertained the idea that the momentum of the running train might itself be made available for the purpose of checking its speed. He proposed to fit each carriage with a brake which should be called into action immediately on the locomotive at the head of the train being pulled up. The impetus of the carriages carrying them forward, the buffer-springs would be driven home, and, at the same time, by a simple arrangement of the mechanism, the brakes would be called into simultaneous action; thus the wheels would be brought into a state of sledge, and the train speedily stopped. This plan was adopted by Mr. Stephenson before he left the Liverpool and Manchester Railway, though it was afterward discontinued; and it is a remarkable fact, that this identical plan, with the addition of a centrifugal apparatus, was recently revived by M. Guérin, a French engineer, and extensively employed on foreign railways.

Finally, Mr. Stephenson had to attend to the improvement of the power and speed of the locomotive—always the grand object of his study—with a view to economy as well as regularity in the working of the railway. In the "Planet" engine, delivered upon the line immediately subsequent to the public opening, all the improvements which had up to this time been contrived by him and his son were introduced in combination—the blast-pipe, the tubular boiler, horizontal cylinders inside the smoke-box, the cranked axle, and the fire-box firmly fixed to the boiler. The first load of goods conveyed from Liverpool to Manchester by the "Planet" was eighty tons in weight, and the engine performed the journey against a strong head wind in two hours and a half. On another occasion, the same engine brought up a cargo of voters from Manchester to Liverpool, during a contested election, within a space of sixty minutes. The "Samson," delivered in the following year, exhibited still farther improvements, the most important of which was that of *coupling* the fore and hind wheels of the engine. By this means the adhesion of the wheels on the rails was more effectually secured, and thus the full hauling power of the locomotive was made available. The "Samson," shortly after it was placed upon the line, dragged after it a train of wagons weighing a hundred and fifty tons at a speed of about twenty miles an hour, the consumption of coke being reduced to only about a third of a pound per ton per mile.

The rapid progress thus made will show that the inventive faculties of Mr. Stephenson and his son were kept fully on the stretch; but their labors were amply repaid by the result. They were, doubtless, to some extent stimulated by the number of competitors who about the same time appeared as improvers of the locomotive engine. But the superiority of Stephenson's locomotives over all others that had yet been tried induced the directors of the railway to require that the engines supplied to them by other builders should be constructed after the same model. Mr. Stephenson himself always had the greatest faith in the superiority of his own engines over all others, and did not hesitate strongly to declare it. When it was once proposed to introduce the engines of another maker on the Manchester and Leeds line, he said, "Very well; I have no objection; but put them to this fair test. Hang one of ——'s engines on to one of mine, back to back. Then let them go at it; and whichever walks away with the other, *that's the engine.*"

The engineer had also to seek out the proper men to maintain and watch the road, and more especially to work the locomotive engines. Steadiness, sobriety, common sense, and practical experience were the qualities which he especially valued in those selected by him for that purpose. But where were the men of experience to be found? Very few railways were yet at work, and these were almost exclusively confined to the northern coal counties; hence a considerable proportion of the drivers and firemen employed on the Liverpool line were brought from the neighborhood of Newcastle. But he could not always find skilled workmen enough for the important and responsible duties to be performed. It was a saying of his that "he could engineer matter very well, and make it bend to his purpose, but his greatest difficulty was in engineering *men.*" He often wished that he could contrive heads and hands on which he might rely, as easily as he could construct railways and manufacture locomotives. As it was, Stephenson's mechanics were in request all over England—the Newcastle workshops continuing for many years to perform the part of a training-school for engineers, and to supply locomotive superintendents and drivers, not only for England, but for nearly every country in Europe—preference being given to them by the directors of railways, in consequence of their previous training and experience, as well as because of their generally excellent qualities as steady and industrious workmen.

The success of the Liverpool and Manchester experiment naturally excited great interest. People flocked to Lancashire from all quarters to see the steam-coach running upon a railway at three times the speed of a mail-coach, and to enjoy the excitement of actually traveling in the wake of an engine at that incredible velocity. The travelers returned to their respective districts full of the wonders of the locomotive, considering it to be the greatest marvel of the age. Railways are familiar enough objects now, and our children who grow up in their midst may think little of them; but thirty years since it was an event in one's life to see a locomotive, and to travel for the first time upon a public railroad.

In remote districts, however, the stories told about the benefits conferred by the Liverpool Railway were received with considerable incredulity, and the proposal to extend such roads in all directions throughout the country caused great alarm. In the districts through which stage-coaches ran, giving employment to large numbers of persons, it was apprehended that, if railways were established, the turnpike roads would become deserted and grown over with grass, country inns and their buxom landladies would be ruined, the race of coach-drivers and hostlers would become extinct, and the breed of horses be entirely destroyed. But there was hope for the coaching interest in the fact that the government were employing their engineers to improve the public high roads so as to render railways unnecessary. It was announced in the papers that a saving of thirty miles would be effected by the new road between London and Holyhead, and an equal saving between London and Edinburg. And to show what the speed of horses could accomplish, we find it set forth as an extraordinary fact that the "Patent Tally-ho Coach," in the year 1830 (when the Birmingham line had been projected), performed the entire journey of 109 miles between London and Birmingham—breakfast included—in seven hours and fifty minutes! Great speed was also recorded on the Brighton road, the "Red Rover" doing the distance between London and Brighton in four hours and a half. These speeds were not, however, secured without accidents, for there was scarcely a newspaper of the period that did not contain one or more paragraphs headed "Another dreadful coach accident."

The practicability of railway locomotion being now proved, and its great social and commercial advantages ascertained, the extension of the system was merely a question of time, money, and labor. A fine opportunity presented itself for the wise and judicious action of the government in the matter, the improvement of the internal communications of a country being really one of its most important functions. But the government of the day, though ready enough to spend money in improving the old turnpike roads, regarded the railroads with hostility, and met them with obstructions of all kinds. They seemed to think it their duty to protect the turnpike trusts, disregarding the paramount interest of the public. This may possibly account for the singular circumstance that, at the very time they were manifesting indifference or aversion to the locomotive on the railroad, they were giving every encouragement to the locomotive on turnpike roads. In 1831, we find a Committee of the House of Commons appointed to inquire into and report upon—not the railway system, but—the applicability of the steam-carriage to common roads; and, after investigation, the committee were so satisfied with the evidence taken, that they reported decidedly in favor of the road locomotive system. Though they ignored the railway, they recognized the steam-carriage.

But even a Report of the House of Commons, powerful though it be, can not alter the laws of gravity and friction; and the road locomotive remained, what it ever will be, an impracticable machine. Not that it is impossible to work a locomotive upon a common road, but to work it to any profit at all as compared with the locomotive upon a railway. Numerous trials of steam-carriages were made at the time by Sir Charles Dance, Mr. Hancock, Mr. Gurney, Sir James Anderson, and other distinguished gentlemen of influence. Journalists extolled their utility, compared with "the much-boasted application on railroads."* But, notwithstanding all this, and the House of Commons' Report in its favor, Stephenson's first verdict, pronounced on the road locomotive many years before, when he was only an engine-wright at Killingworth, was fully borne out by the result, and it became day by day clearer that the attempt to introduce the engine into general use upon turnpike roads could only prove a delusion and a snare.

Although the Legislature took no initiative step in the direction of railway extension, the public spirit and enterprise of the country did not fail it at this juncture. The English people, though they may be defective in their capacity for organization, are strong in individualism, and not improbably their admirable qualities in the latter respect detract from their efficiency in the former. Thus, in all times, their greatest national enterprises have not been planned by officialism and carried out upon any

* Letter of Mr. John Herapath in "Mechanics' Magazine," vol. xv., p. 123.

regular system, but have sprung, like their Constitution, their laws, and their entire industrial arrangements, from the force of circumstances and the individual energies of the people. Hence railway extension, like so many other great English enterprises, was now left to be carried out by the genius of English engineers, backed by the energy of the British public.

The mode of action was characteristic and national. The execution of the new lines was undertaken entirely by joint-stock associations of proprietors, after the manner of the Stockton and Darlington, and Liverpool and Manchester companies. These associations are conformable to our national habits, and fit well into our system of laws. They combine the power of vast resources with individual watchfulness and motives of self-interest; and by their means gigantic undertakings, which elsewhere would be impossible to any but kings and emperors with great national resources at command, were carried out by the co-operation of private persons. And the results of this combination of means and of enterprise have been truly marvelous. Within the life of the present generation, the private citizens of England engaged in railway extension have, in the face of government obstructions, and without taking a penny from the public purse, executed a system of communications involving works of the most gigantic kind, which, in their total mass, their cost, and their public utility, far exceed the most famous national undertakings of any age or country.

Mr. Stephenson was, of course, actively engaged in the construction of the numerous railways now projected by the joint-stock companies. During the formation of the Manchester and Liverpool line he had been consulted respecting many projects of a similar kind. One of these was a short railway between Canterbury and Whitstable, about six miles in length. He was too much occupied with the works at Liverpool to give this scheme much of his personal attention; but he sent his assistant, Mr. John Dixon, to survey the line, and afterward Mr. Locke to superintend the execution of the works. The act was obtained in 1826, and the line was opened for traffic in 1830. It was partly worked by fixed engine-power, and partly by Stephenson's locomotives, similar to the engines used upon the Stockton and Darlington Railway.

But the desire for railway extension principally pervaded the manufacturing districts, especially after the successful opening of the Liverpool and Manchester line. The commercial classes of the larger towns soon became eager for a participation in the good which they had so recently derided. Railway projects were set on foot in great numbers, and Manchester became a centre from which main lines and branches were started in all directions. The interest, however, which attaches to these later schemes is of a much less absorbing kind than that which belongs to the early history of the railway and the steps by which it was mainly established. We naturally sympathize more with the early struggles of a great principle, its trials and its difficulties, than with its after stages of success; and, however gratified and astonished we may be at its results, the interest is in a great measure gone when its triumph has become a matter of certainty.

The commercial results of the Liverpool and Manchester line were so satisfactory, and, indeed, so greatly exceeded the expectations of its projectors, that many of the abandoned projects of the speculative year 1825 were forthwith revived. An abundant crop of engineers sprang up, ready to execute railways of any extent. Now that the Liverpool and Manchester line had been made, and the practicability of working it by locomotive power had been proved, it was as easy for engineers to make railways and to work them as it was for navigators to find America after Columbus had made the first voyage. Mr. Francis Giles himself took the field as a locomotive railway engineer, attaching himself to the Newcastle and Carlisle and London and Southampton projects. Mr. Brunel appeared, in like manner, as the engineer of the line projected between London and Bristol; and Mr. Braithwaite, the builder of the "Novelty" engine, as the engineer of a line from London to Colchester.

The first lines, however, which were actually constructed subsequent to the opening of the Liverpool and Manchester Railway were in connection with it, and principally in the county of Lancaster. Thus a branch was formed from Bolton to Leigh, and another from Leigh to Kenyon, where it formed a junction with the main line between Liverpool and Manchester. Branches to Wigan on the north, and to Runcorn Gap and Warrington on the south of the same line, were also formed; and a continuation of the latter, as far south as Birmingham, was shortly after projected, under the name of the Grand Junction Railway.

The last-mentioned line was projected as early as the year 1824, when the Liverpool and Manchester scheme was under discussion, and Mr. Stephenson then published a report on the subject. The plans were deposited, but the bill was thrown out on the opposition of the land-owners and canal proprietors. When engaged in making the survey, Stephenson called upon some of the land-owners in the neighborhood of Nantwich to obtain their assent, and was greatly disgusted to learn that the agents of the canal companies had been before him, and described the locomotive to the farmers as a most frightful machine, emitting a breath as poisonous as the fabled dragon of old; and telling them that if a bird flew over the district when one of these engines passed, it would inevitably drop down dead!. The application for the bill was renewed in 1826, and again failed; and at length it was determined to wait the issue of the Liverpool and Manchester experiment. The act was eventually obtained in 1833, by which time the projectors of railways had learned the art of "conciliating" the landlords—and a very expensive process it proved. But it was the only mode of avoiding a still more expensive Parliamentary opposition.

When it was proposed to extend the advantages of railways to the population of the midland and southern counties of England, an immense amount of alarm was created in the minds of the country gentlemen. They did not relish the idea of private individuals, principally residents in the manufacturing districts, invading their domains, and they every where rose up in arms against the "new-fangled roads." Colonel Sibthorpe openly declared his hatred of the "infernal railroads," and said that he "would rather meet a highwayman, or see a burglar on his premises, than an engineer!" Mr. Berkeley, the member for Cheltenham, at a public meeting in that town, re-echoed Colonel Sibthorpe's sentiments, and "wished that the concoctors of every such scheme, with their solicitors and engineers, were at rest in Paradise!" The impression prevailed among the rural classes that fox-covers and game-preserves would be seriously prejudiced by the formation of railroads; that agricultural communications would be destroyed, land thrown out of cultivation, land-owners and farmers reduced to beggary, the poor-rates increased through the number of persons thrown out of employment by the railways, and all this in order that Liverpool, Manchester, and Birmingham shop-keepers and manufacturers might establish a monstrous monopoly in railway traffic.

The inhabitants of even some of the large towns were thrown into a state of consternation by the proposal to provide them with the accommodation of a railway. The line from London to Birmingham would naturally have passed close to the handsome town of Northampton, and was so projected. But the inhabitants of the place, urged on by the local press, and excited by men of influence and education, opposed the project, and succeeded in forcing the promoters, in their survey of the line, to pass the town at a distance. The necessity was thus involved of distorting the line, by which the enormous expense of constructing the Kilsby Tunnel was incurred. Not many years elapsed before the inhabitants of Northampton became clamorous for railway accommodation, and a special branch was constructed for them. The additional cost involved by this forced deviation of the line could not have amounted to less than half a million sterling; the loss falling, not upon the shareholders only, but upon the public.

Other towns in the south followed the example of Northampton in howling down the railways. When the first railway through Kent was projected, the line was laid out so as to pass by Maidstone, the county town. But it had not a single supporter among the townspeople, while the land-owners for many miles round continued to oppose it. A few years later the Maidstone burgesses, like those of Northampton, became clamorous for a railway, and a branch was formed for their accommodation. In like manner, the London and Bristol (afterward the Great Western) Railway was vehemently opposed by the people of the towns through which the line was projected to pass; and when the bill was thrown out by the Lords—after £30,000 had been expended by the promoters—the inhabitants of Eton assembled, under the presidency of the Marquis of Chandos, to rejoice and congratulate themselves and the country upon its defeat. Eton, however, has now the convenience of two railways to the metropolis.

During the time that the works of the Liverpool and Manchester line were in progress, our engineer was consulted respecting a short railway proposed to be formed between Leicester and Swannington, for the purpose of opening up a communication between the town of Leicester and the coal-fields in the western part of the county. Mr. Ellis, the projector of this undertaking, had some difficulty in getting the requisite capital subscribed for, the Leicester townspeople who had money being for the most part interested in canals. George Stephenson was invited to come upon the ground and survey the line. He did so, and then the projector told him of the difficulty he had in finding subscribers to the concern. "Give me a sheet," said Stephenson, "and I will raise the money for you in Liverpool." The engineer was as good as his word, and in a short time the sheet was returned with the subscription complete. Mr. Stephenson was then asked to undertake the office of engineer for the line, but his answer was that he had thirty miles of railway in hand, which was enough for any engineer to attend to properly. Was there any person he could recommend? "Well," said he, "I think my son Robert is competent to undertake the thing." Would Mr. Stephenson be answerable for him? "Oh yes, certainly." And Robert Stephenson, at twenty-seven years of age, was installed engineer of the line accordingly.

MAP OF THE LEICESTER AND SWANNINGTON RAILWAY.

The requisite Parliamentary powers having been obtained, Robert Stephenson proceeded with the construction of the railway, about sixteen miles in length, toward the end of 1830. The works were comparatively easy, excepting at the Leicester end, where the young engineer encountered his first stiff bit of tunneling. The line passed under ground for a mile and three quarters, and 500 yards of its course lay through loose running sand. The presence of this material rendered it necessary for the engineer, in the first place, to construct a wooden tunnel to support the soil while the brick-work was being executed. This measure proved sufficient, and the whole was brought to a successful termination within a reasonable time. While the works were in progress, Robert kept up a regular correspondence with his father at Liverpool, consulting him on all points in which his greater experience was likely to be of service. Like his father, Robert was very observant, and always ready to seize opportunity by the forelock. It happened that the estate of Snibston, near Ashby-de-la-Zouch, was advertised for sale, and the young engineer's experience as a coal-viewer and practical geologist suggested to his mind that coal was most probably to be found underneath. He communicated his views to his father on the subject. The estate lay in the immediate neighborhood of the railway; and if the conjecture proved correct, the finding of the coal must necessarily prove a most fortunate circumstance for the purchasers of the land. He accordingly requested his father to come over to Snibston and look at the property, which he did; and after a careful inspection of the ground, he arrived at the same conclusion as his son.

The large manufacturing town of Leicester, about fourteen miles distant, had up to that time been exclusively supplied with coal brought by canal from Derbyshire, and the Stephensons saw that the railway under construction from Swannington to Leicester would furnish a ready market for any coals which might be found at Snibston. Having induced two of his Liverpool friends to join him in the venture, the Snibston estate was purchased in 1831, and shortly after Stephenson removed his home from Liverpool to Alton Grange, for the purpose of superintending the sinking of the pit.

Sinking operations were immediately begun, and proceeded satisfactorily until the old enemy, water, burst in upon the workmen, and threatened to drown them out. But by means of efficient pumping-engines, and the skillful casing of the shaft with segments of cast iron—a process called "tubbing,"* which Ste-

* Tubbing is now adopted in many cases as a substitute for brick-walling. The tubbing consists of short portions of cast-iron cylinder fixed in segments. Each

phenson was the first to adopt in the Midland Counties—it was eventually made water-tight, and the sinking proceeded. When a depth of 166 feet had been reached, a still more formidable difficulty presented itself—one which had baffled former sinkers in the neighborhood, and deterred them from farther operations. This was a remarkable bed of whinstone or greenstone, which had originally been poured out as a sheet of burning lava over the denuded surface of the coal measures; indeed, it was afterward found that it had turned to cinders one part of the seam of coal with which it had come in contact. The appearance of this bed of solid rock was so unusual a circumstance in coal-mining that some experienced sinkers urged Stephenson to proceed no farther, believing the occurrence of the dike at that point to be altogether fatal to his enterprise. But, with his faith still firm in the existence of coal underneath, he fell back on his old motto of "Persevere!" He determined to go on boring; and down through the solid rock he went until, twenty-two feet lower, he came upon the coal measures. In the mean time, however, lest the boring at that point should prove unsuccessful, he had commenced sinking another pair of shafts about a quarter of a mile west of the "fault," and, after about nine months' labor, he reached the principal seam, called the "main coal."

The works were then opened out on a large scale, and George Stephenson had the pleasure and good fortune to send the first train of main coal to Leicester by railway. The price was immediately reduced there to about 8*s.* a ton, effecting a pecuniary saving to the inhabitants of the town of about £40,000 per annum, or equivalent to the whole amount then collected in government taxes and local rates, besides giving an impetus to the manufacturing prosperity of the place, which has continued to the present day. The correct principles upon which the mining operations at Snibston were conducted offered a salutary example to the neighboring colliery owners. The numerous improvements there introduced were freely exhibited to all, and they were afterward reproduced in many forms all over the Midland Counties, greatly to the advantage of the mining interest.

weighs about 4½ cwt., is about three or four feet long, and about three eighths of an inch thick. These pieces are fitted closely together, length under length, and form an impermeable wall along the sides of the pit.

Nor was Mr. Stephenson less attentive to the comfort and well-being of those immediately dependent upon him—the work-people of the Snibston Colliery and their families. Unlike many of those large employers who have "sprung from the ranks," he was one of the kindest and most indulgent of masters. He would have a fair day's work for a fair day's wages, but he never forgot that the employer had his duties as well as his rights. First of all, he attended to the proper home accommodation of his work-people. He erected a village of comfortable cottages, each provided with a snug little garden. He was also instrumental in erecting a church adjacent to the works, as well as Church schools for the education of the colliers' children; and with that broad catholicity of sentiment which distinguished him, he farther provided a chapel and a school-house for the use of the Dissenting portion of the colliers and their families—an example of benevolent liberality which was not without a salutary influence upon the neighboring employers.

STEPHENSON'S HOUSE AT ALTON GRANGE.

Robert Stephenson.

Engraved by [illegible] after a photograph by [illegible]

NEW YORK, HARPER & BROTHERS.

CHAPTER XIV.

ROBERT STEPHENSON CONSTRUCTS THE LONDON AND BIRMINGHAM RAILWAY.

OF the numerous extensive projects which followed close upon the completion of the Liverpool and Manchester line and the locomotive triumph at Rainhill, that of a railway between London and Birmingham was the most important. The scheme originated at the latter place in 1830. Two committees were formed, and two plans were proposed. One was of a line to London by way of Oxford, and the other by way of Coventry. The object of the promoters of both schemes being to secure the advantages of railway communication with the metropolis, they wisely determined to combine their strength to secure it. They resolved to call George Stephenson to their aid, and requested him to advise them as to the two schemes which were before them. After a careful examination of the country, Stephenson reported in favor of the Coventry route. The Lancashire gentlemen, who were the principal subscribers to the project, having confidence in his judgment, supported his decision, and the line recommended by him was adopted accordingly.

At the meeting of gentlemen held at Birmingham to determine upon the appointment of the engineer for the railway, there was a strong party in favor of associating with Stephenson a gentleman with whom he had been brought into serious collision in the course of the Liverpool and Manchester undertaking. When the offer was made to him that he should be joint engineer with the other, he requested leave to retire and consider the proposal with his son. The two walked into St. Philip's church-yard, which adjoined the place of meeting, and debated the proposal. The father was in favor of accepting it. His struggle heretofore had been so hard that he could not bear the idea of missing so promising an opportunity of professional advancement. But the son, foreseeing the jealousies and heartburnings which the joint engineership would most probably create, recommended his father to decline the connection. George adopted the suggestion, and, returning to the committee, announced to them his decision, on which the promoters decided to appoint him the engineer of the undertaking in conjunction with his son.

This line, like the Liverpool and Manchester, was very strongly opposed, especially by the land-owners. Numerous pamphlets were published, calling on the public to "beware of the bubbles," and holding up the promoters of railways to ridicule. They were compared to St. John Long and similar quacks, and pronounced fitter for Bedlam than to be left at large. The canal proprietors, land-owners, and road trustees made common cause against them. The failure of railways was confidently predicted —indeed, it was elaborately attempted to be proved that they had failed; and it was industriously spread abroad that the locomotive engines, having been found useless and highly dangerous on the Liverpool and Manchester line, were immediately to be abandoned in favor of horses—a rumor which the directors of the company thought it necessary publicly to contradict.

Public meetings were held in all the counties through which the line would pass between London and Birmingham, at which the project was denounced, and strong resolutions against it were passed. The attempt was made to conciliate the landlords by explanations, but all such efforts proved futile, the owners of nearly seven eighths of the land being returned as dissentients. "I remember," said Robert Stephenson, describing the opposition, "that we called one day on Sir Astley Cooper, the eminent surgeon, in the hope of overcoming his aversion to the railway. He was one of our most inveterate and influential opponents. His country house at Berkhampstead was situated near the intended line, which passed through part of his property. We found a courtly, fine-looking old gentleman, of very stately manners, who received us kindly, and heard all we had to say in favor of the project. But he was quite inflexible in his opposition to it. No deviation or improvement that we could suggest had any effect in conciliating him. He was opposed to railways generally, and to this in particular. 'Your scheme,' said he, 'is preposterous in the extreme. It is of so extravagant a character as to be positively absurd. Then look at the recklessness of your proceedings! You are proposing to cut up our estates in all directions for the purpose of making an unnecessary road. Do you think for one moment of the destruction of property involved by it? Why, gentlemen, if this sort of thing be permitted to go on, you will in a very few years *destroy the noblesse!*' We left the honorable baronet without having produced the slightest effect upon him, excepting perhaps, it might be, increased exasperation against our scheme. I could not help observing to my companions as we left the house, 'Well, it is really provoking to find one who has been made a "Sir" for cutting that wen out of George the Fourth's neck, charging us with contemplating the destruction of the *noblesse* because we propose to confer upon him the benefits of a railroad.'"

Such being the opposition of the owners of land, it was with the greatest difficulty that an accurate survey of the line could be made. At one point the vigilance of the land-owners and their servants was such that the surveyors were effectually prevented taking the levels by the light of day, and it was only at length accomplished at night by means of dark lanterns. There was one clergyman, who made such alarming demonstrations of his opposition, that the extraordinary expedient was resorted to of surveying his property during the time he was engaged in the pulpit. This was managed by having a strong force of surveyors in readiness to commence their operations, who entered the clergyman's grounds on one side the moment they saw him fairly off them on the other. By a well-organized and systematic arrangement, each man concluded his allotted task just as the reverend gentleman concluded his sermon; so that, before he left the church, the deed was done, and the sinners had all decamped. Similar opposition was offered at many other points, but ineffectually. The laborious application of Robert Stephenson was such that, in examining the country to ascertain the best line, he walked the whole distance between London and Birmingham upward of twenty times.

When the bill went before the committee of the Commons in 1832, a formidable array of evidence was produced. All the railway experience of the day was brought to bear in support of the measure, and all that interested opposition could do was set in motion against it. The necessity for an improved mode of communication between London and Birmingham was clearly demonstrated, and the engineering evidence was regarded as quite satisfactory. Not a single fact was proved against the utility of the measure, and the bill passed the committee, and afterward the third reading in the Commons, by large majorities.

It was then sent to the Lords, and went into committee, when a similar mass of testimony was again gone through. But scarcely had the proceedings been opened when it became clear that the fate of the bill had been determined before a word of the evidence had been heard. At that time the committees were open to all peers; and the promoters of the measure found, to their dismay, many of the lords who were avowed opponents of the measure as land-owners, sitting as judges to decide its fate. Their principal object seemed to be to bring the proceedings to a termination as quickly as possible. An attempt at negotiation was made in the course of the proceedings in committee, but failed, and the bill was thrown out on the motion of Earl Brownlow, one of Lady Bridgewater's trustees; but, though carried by a large majority, the vote was far from unanimous.

As the result had been foreseen, measures were taken to neutralize the effect of this decision as regarded future operations. Not less than £32,000 had been expended in preliminary and Parliamentary expenses up to this stage; but the promoters determined not to look back, and forthwith made arrangements for prosecuting the bill in a future session. A meeting of the friends of the measure was held in London, attended by members of both houses of Parliament and by leading bankers and merchants, when a series of resolutions was passed, declaring their conviction of the necessity for the railway, and deprecating the opposition by which it had been encountered. Lord Wharncliffe, who had acted as the chairman of the Lords' Committee, attributed the failure of the bill entirely to the land-owners; and Mr. Glyn subsequently declared that they had tried to smother it by the high price which they demanded for their property. It was determined to reintroduce the bill in the following session (1833), and measures were taken to prosecute it vigorously. Strange to say, the bill on this occasion passed both houses silently and almost without opposition. The mystery was afterward solved by the appearance of a circular issued by the directors of the company, in which it was stated that they had opened negotiations with the most influential of their opponents; that "these measures had been successful to a greater extent than they had ventured to anticipate; and the most active and formidable had been conciliated." An instructive commentary on the mode by which these noble lords and influential landed proprietors had been "conciliated" was found in the simple fact that the estimate for land was nearly trebled, and that the owners were paid about £750,000 for what had been originally estimated at £250,000. The total expenses of carrying the bill through Parliament amounted to the enormous sum of £72,868.

The land-owners having been thus "conciliated," the promoters of the measure were at length permitted to proceed with the formation of their great highway. Robert Stephenson was, with his father's sanction, appointed engineer-in-chief of the line, at a salary of £1500 a year. He was now a married man, having become united to Miss Frances Sanderson in 1829, since which his home had been at Newcastle, near to the works there; but, on receiving his new appointment, he removed with his wife to London, to a house on Haverstock Hill, where he resided during the execution of the Birmingham Railway.

Steps were at once taken to proceed with the working survey, to prepare the working drawings, and arrange for the prosecution of the undertaking. Eighty miles of the line were shortly under construction; the works were let (within the estimates) to contractors, who were necessarily, for the most part, new to such work. The business of railway construction was not then well understood. There were no leviathans among contractors as now, able to undertake the formation of a line of railway hundreds of miles in length; they were, for the most part, men of small capital and slender experience. Their tools and machinery were imperfect; they did not understand the economy of time and piece labor; the workmen, as well as their masters, had still to learn their trade; and every movement of an engineer was attended with outlays, which were the inevitable result of a new system of things, but which each succeeding day's experience tended to diminish.

The difficulties encountered in the construction of this railway were thus very great, the most formidable of them originating in the character of the works themselves. Extensive tunnels had to be driven through unknown strata, and miles of underground excavation had to be carried out in order to form a level road from valley to valley under the intervening ridges. This kind of work was the newest of all to the contractors of that day. Robert Stephenson's experience in the collieries of the North rendered him well fitted to grapple with such difficulties; yet even he, with all his practical knowledge, could scarcely have foreseen the serious obstacles which he was called upon to encounter in executing the formidable cuttings, embankments, and tunnels of the London and Birmingham Railway. It would be an uninteresting, as it would be a fruitless task, to attempt to describe these works in detail; but a general outline of their extraordinary character and extent may not be out of place.

The length of railway to be constructed between London and Birmingham was 112½ miles. The line crossed a series of low-lying districts, separated from each other by considerable ridges of hills, and it was the object of the engineer to cross the valleys at as high an elevation, and the hills at as low a one as possible. The high ground was therefore cut down, and the "stuff" led into embankments, in some places of great height and extent, so as to form a road upon as level a plane as was considered practicable for the working of the locomotive engine. In some places the high grounds were passed in open cuttings, while in others it was necessary to bore through them in tunnels with deep cuttings at either end.

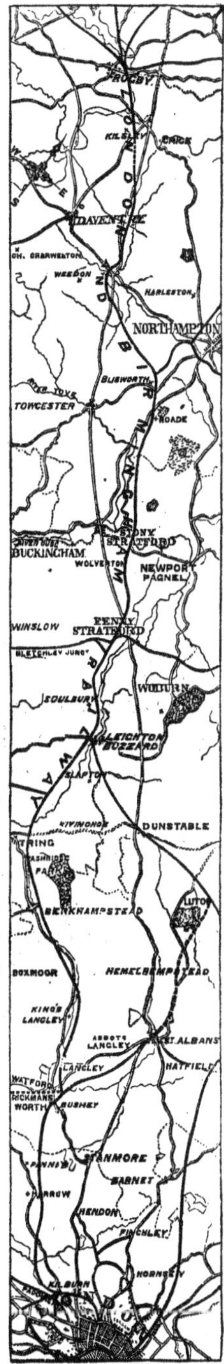

The most formidable excavations on the line are those at Tring, Denbigh Hall, and

Blisworth. The Tring cutting is an immense chasm across the great chalk ridge of Ivinghoe. It is two miles and a half long, and for a quarter of a mile is fifty-seven feet deep. A million and a half cubic yards of chalk and earth were taken out of this cutting by means of horse-runs, and deposited in spoil-banks, besides the immense quantity run into the embankment north of the cutting, forming a solid mound nearly six miles long and about thirty feet high. Passing over the Denbigh Hall cutting, and the Wolverton embankment of a mile and a half in length across the valley of the Ouse, we come to the excavation at Blisworth, a brief description of which will give the reader an idea of one of the most formidable kinds of railway work.

The Blisworth Cutting is a mile and a half long, in some places

BLISWORTH CUTTING. [By Percival Skelton.]

sixty-five feet deep, passing through earth, stiff clay, and hard rock. Not less than a million cubic yards of these materials were dug, quarried, and blasted out of it. One third of the cutting was stone, and beneath the stone lay a thick bed of clay, under which were found beds of loose shale so full of water that almost constant pumping was necessary at many points to enable the works to proceed. For a year and a half the contractor went on fruitlessly contending with these difficulties, and at length he was compelled to abandon the adventure. The engineer then took the works in hand for the company, and they were vigorously proceeded with. Steam-engines were set to work to pump out the water; two locomotives were put on, one at either end of the cutting, to drag away the excavated rock and clay; and eight hundred men and boys were employed along the work, in digging, wheeling, and blasting, besides a large number of horses. Some idea of the extent of the blasting operations may be formed from the fact that twenty-five barrels of gunpowder were exploded weekly, the total quantity used in forming this one excavation being about three thousand barrels. Considerable difficulty was experienced in supporting the bed of rock cut through, which overlaid the clay and shale along either side of the cutting. It was found necessary to hold it up by strong retaining walls, to prevent the clay bed from bulging out, and these walls were farther supported by a strong invert—that is, an arch placed in an inverted position under the road—thus binding together the walls on both sides. Behind the retaining walls, a drift or horizontal drain was run to enable the water to escape, and occasional openings were left in the walls themselves for the same purpose. The work was at length brought to a successful completion, but the extraordinary difficulties encountered in executing the undertaking had the effect of greatly increasing the cost of this portion of the railway.

The Tunnels on the line are eight in number, their total length being 7336 yards. The first high ground encountered was Primrose Hill, where the stiff London clay was passed through for a distance of about 1164 yards. The clay was close, compact, and dry, more difficult to work than stone itself. It was entirely free from water; but the absorbing properties of the clay were such that when exposed to the air it swelled out rapidly. Hence an unusual thickness of brick lining was found necessary; and the engineer afterward informed the author that for some time he entertained an apprehension lest the pressure should force in the brick-work altogether, as afterward happened in the case of the short Preston Brook tunnel upon the Grand Junction Railway, constructed by his father. The pressure behind the brick-work was so great that it made the face of the bricks to fly off in minute chips, which covered his clothes while he was inspecting the work. The materials used in the building were, however, of excellent quality, and the work was happily brought to a completion without accident.

At Watford the chalk ridge was penetrated by a tunnel about 1800 yards long, and at Northchurch, Lindslade, and Stowe Hill there were other tunnels of minor extent. But the chief difficulty of the undertaking was the execution of that under the Kilsby ridge. Though not the largest, this is in many respects one of the most interesting works of the kind. It is about two thousand four hundred yards long, and runs at an average depth of about a hundred and sixty feet below the surface. The ridge under which it extends is of considerable extent, the famous battle of Naseby having been fought upon one of the spurs of the same high ground, about seven miles to the eastward.

Previous to the letting of the contract, the character of the underground soil was fairly tested by trial shafts, which indicated that it consisted of shale of the lower oolite, and the works were

LINE OF THE SHAFTS OVER KILSBY TUNNEL. [By Percival Skelton.]

let accordingly. But they had scarcely been commenced when it was discovered that, at an interval between the two trial-shafts, which had been sunk about two hundred yards from the south end of the tunnel, there existed an extensive quicksand under a bed of clay forty feet thick, which the borings had escaped in the most singular manner. At the bottom of one of these shafts, the excavation and building of the tunnel were proceeding, when the roof at one part suddenly gave way, a deluge of water burst in, and the party of workmen with the utmost difficulty escaped with their lives. They were only saved by means of a raft, on which they were towed by one of the engineers swimming with the rope in his mouth to the lower end of the shaft, out of which they were safely lifted to the daylight.

The works were of course at that point immediately stopped. The contractor who had undertaken the construction of the tunnel was so overwhelmed by the calamity that, though he was relieved by the company from his engagement, he took to his bed and shortly after died. Pumping-engines were erected for the purpose of draining off the water, but for a long time it prevailed, and sometimes even rose in the shaft. The question arose whether, in the face of so formidable a difficulty, the works should be proceeded with or abandoned. Robert Stephenson sent over to Alton Grange for his father, and the two took serious counsel together. George was in favor of pumping out the water from the top by powerful engines erected over each shaft, until the water was fairly mastered. Robert concurred in that view, and, although other engineers who were consulted pronounced strongly against the practicability of the scheme and advised the abandonment of the enterprise, the directors authorized him to proceed, and powerful steam-engines were ordered to be constructed and delivered without loss of time.

In the mean time Robert suggested to his father the expediency of running a drift along the heading from the south end of the tunnel, with the view of draining off the water in that way. George said he thought it would scarcely answer, but that it was worth a trial, at all events until the pumping-engines were got ready. Robert accordingly gave orders for the drift to be proceeded with. The excavators were immediately set to work, and they had nearly reached the quicksand, when one day, while the engineer, his assistants, and the workmen were clustered about the open entrance of the drift-way, they heard a sudden roar as of distant thunder. It was hoped that the water had burst in—for all the workmen were out of the drift—and that the sand-bed would now drain itself off in a natural way. Instead of which, very little water made its appearance, and on examining the inner end of the drift, it was found that the loud noise had been caused by the sudden discharge into it of an immense mass of sand, which had completely choked up the passage, and thus prevented the water from draining off.

The engineer now found that nothing remained but to sink numerous additional shafts over the line of the tunnel at the points at which it crossed the quicksand, and endeavor to master the water by sheer force of engines and pumps. The engines, which were shortly erected, possessed an aggregate power of 160 horses; and they went on pumping for eight months, emptying out an almost incredible quantity of water. It was found that the water, with which the bed of sand extending over many miles was charged, was in a great degree held back by the particles of the sand itself, and that it could only percolate through at a certain average rate. It appeared in its flow to take a slanting direction to the suction of the pumps, the angle of inclination depending upon the coarseness or fineness of the sand, and regulating the time of the flow. Hence the distribution of the pumping power at short intervals along the line of the tunnel had a much greater effect than the concentration of that power at any one place. It soon appeared that the water had found its master. Protected by the pumps, which cleared a space for engineering operations—carried on, as it were, amid two almost perpendicular walls of water and sand on either side—the workmen proceeded with the building of the tunnel at numerous points. Every exertion was used to wall in the dangerous parts as quickly as possible, the excavators and bricklayers laboring night and day until the work was finished. Even while under the protection of the immense pumping power above described, it often happened that the bricks were scarcely covered with cement ready for the setting ere they were washed quite clean by the streams of water which poured from overhead. The men were accordingly under the necessity of holding over their work large whisks of straw and other appliances to protect the bricks and cement at the moment of setting.

The quantity of water pumped out of the sand-bed during eight months of this incessant pumping averaged two thousand gallons per minute, raised from an average depth of 120 feet. It is difficult to form an adequate idea of the bulk of water thus raised, but it may be stated that if allowed to flow for three hours only, it would fill a lake one acre square to the depth of one foot, and if allowed to flow for an entire day it would fill the lake to over eight feet in depth, or sufficient to float a vessel of a hundred tons' burden. The water pumped out of the tunnel while the work was in progress would be nearly equivalent to the contents of the Thames at high water between London and Woolwich. It is a curious circumstance, that notwithstanding the quantity of water thus removed, the level of the surface in the tunnel was only lowered about two and a half to three inches per week, showing the vast area of the quicksand, which probably extended along the entire ridge of land under which the railway passed.

The cost of the line was greatly increased by the difficulties thus encountered at Kilsby. The original estimate for the tunnel was only £99,000; but by the time it was finished it had cost about £100 per lineal yard forward, or a total of nearly £300,000. The expenditure on the other parts of the line also greatly exceeded the amount first set down by the engineer, and, before the railway was complete, it had been more than doubled. The land cost three times more than the estimate, and the claims for compensation were enormous. Although the contracts were let within the estimates, very few of the contractors were able to finish them without the assistance of the company, and many became bankrupt. Speaking of the difficulties encountered during the construction of the line, Robert Stephenson subsequently observed to us: "After the works were let, wages rose, the prices of materials of all kinds rose, and the contractors, many of whom were men of comparatively small capital, were thrown on their beam-ends. Their calculations as to expenses and profits were completely upset. Let me just go over the list. There was Jackson, who took the Primrose Hill contract—he failed. Then there was the next length—Nowells; then Copeland and Harding;

north of them Townsend, who had the Tring cutting; next Norris, who had Stoke Hammond; then Soars; then Hughes: I think all of these broke down, or at least were helped through by the directors. Then there was that terrible contract of the Kilsby Tunnel, which broke the Nowells, and killed one of them. The contractors to the north of Kilsby were more fortunate, though some of them pulled through only with the greatest difficulty. Of the eighteen contracts in which the line was originally let, only seven were completed by the original contractors. Eleven firms were ruined by their contracts, which were relet to others at advanced prices, or were carried on and finished by the company. The principal cause of increase in the expense, however, was the enlargement of the stations. It appeared that we had greatly under-estimated the traffic, and it accordingly became necessary to spend more and more money for its accommodation, until I think I am within the mark when I say that the expenditure on this account alone exceeded by eight or ten fold the amount of the Parliamentary estimate."

The magnitude of the works, which were unprecedented in England, was one of the most remarkable features in the undertaking. The following striking comparison has been made between this railway and one of the greatest works of ancient times. The great Pyramid of Egypt was, according to Diodorus Siculus, constructed by three hundred thousand—according to Herodotus, by one hundred thousand—men. It required for its execution twenty years, and the labor expended upon it has been estimated as equivalent to lifting 15,733,000,000 of cubic feet of stone one foot high; whereas, if the labor expended in constructing the London and Birmingham Railway be in like manner reduced to one common denomination, the result is 25,000,000,000 of cubic feet *more* than was lifted for the Great Pyramid; and yet the English work was performed by about 20,000 men in less than five years. And while the Egyptian work was executed by a powerful monarch concentrating upon it the labor and capital of a great nation, the English railway was constructed, in the face of every conceivable obstruction and difficulty, by a company of private individuals out of their own resources, without the aid of government or the contribution of one farthing of public money.

The laborers who executed these formidable works were in

many respects a remarkable class. The "railway navvies,"* as they were called, were men drawn by the attraction of good wages from all parts of the kingdom; and they were ready for any sort of hard work. Many of the laborers employed on the Liverpool line were Irish; others were from the Northumberland and Durham railways, where they had been accustomed to similar work; and some of the best came from the fen districts of Lincoln and Cambridge, where they had been trained to execute works of excavation and embankment. These old practitioners formed a nucleus of skilled manipulation and aptitude which rendered them of indispensable utility in the immense undertakings of the period. Their expertness in all sorts of earth-work, in embanking, boring, and well-sinking—their practical knowledge of the nature of soils and rocks, the tenacity of clays, and the porosity of certain stratifications—were very great; and, rough-looking as they were, many of them were as important in their own department as the contractor or the engineer.

During the railway-making period the navvy wandered about from one public work to another, apparently belonging to no country and having no home. He usually wore a white felt hat with the brim turned up, a velveteen or jean square-tailed coat, a scarlet plush waistcoat with little black spots, and a bright-colored kerchief round his Herculean neck, when, as often happened, it was not left entirely bare. His corduroy breeches were retained in position by a leathern strap round the waist, and were tied and buttoned at the knee, displaying beneath a solid calf and foot incased in strong high-laced boots. Joining together in a "butty gang," some ten or twelve of these men would take a contract to cut out and remove so much "dirt"—as they denominated earth-cutting—fixing their price according to the character of the "stuff," and the distance to which it had to be wheeled and tipped. The contract taken, every man put himself to his mettle; if any was found skulking, or not putting forth his full working power, he was ejected from the gang. Their powers of endurance were extraordinary. In times of emergency they would work for twelve and even sixteen hours, with only short

* The word "navvie," or "navigator," is supposed to have originated in the fact of many of these laborers having been originally employed in making the navigations, or canals, the construction of which immediately preceded the railway era.

intervals for meals. The quantity of flesh-meat which they consumed was something enormous; but it was to their bones and muscles what coke is to the locomotive—the means of keeping up the steam. They displayed great pluck, and seemed to disregard peril. Indeed, the most dangerous sort of labor—such as working horse-barrow runs, in which accidents are of constant occurrence—has always been most in request among them, the danger seeming to be one of its chief recommendations.

KILSBY TUNNEL. [North End.]

Working together, eating, drinking, and sleeping together, and daily exposed to the same influences, these railway laborers soon presented a distinct and well-defined character, strongly marking them from the population of the districts in which they labored. Reckless alike of their lives as of their earnings, the navvies worked hard and lived hard. For their lodging, a hut of turf would content them; and, in their hours of leisure, the meanest public house would serve for their parlor. Unburdened, as they usually were, by domestic ties, unsoftened by family affection, and without much moral or religious training, the navvies came to be distinguished by a sort of savage manners, which contrasted strangely with those of the surrounding population. Yet, ignorant and violent though they might be, they were usually good-hearted fellows in the main—frank and open-handed with their comrades, and ready to share their last penny with those in distress. Their pay-nights were often a saturnalia of riot and disorder, dreaded by the inhabitants of the villages along the line of works. The irruption of such men into the quiet hamlet of Kilsby must, indeed, have produced a very startling effect on the recluse inhabitants of the place. Robert Stephenson used to tell a story of the clergyman of the parish waiting upon the foreman of one of the gangs to expostulate with him as to the shocking impropriety of his men working during Sunday. But the head navvy merely hitched up his trowsers and said, "Why, Soondays hain't cropt out here yet!" In short, the navvies were little better than heathens, and the village of Kilsby was not restored to its wonted quiet until the tunnel-works were finished, and the engines and scaffolding removed, leaving only the immense masses of *débris* around the line of shafts which extend along the top of the tunnel.

CHAPTER XV.

MANCHESTER AND LEEDS, AND MIDLAND RAILWAYS — STEPHENSON'S LIFE AT ALTON — VISIT TO BELGIUM — GENERAL EXTENSION OF RAILWAYS AND THEIR RESULTS.

THE rapidity with which railways were carried out, when the spirit of the country became roused, was indeed remarkable. This was doubtless in some measure owing to the increased force of the current of speculation at the time, but chiefly to the desire which the public began to entertain for the general extension of the system. It was even proposed to fill up the canals and convert them into railways. The new roads became the topic of conversation in all circles; they were felt to give a new value to time; their vast capabilities for "business" peculiarly recommended them to the trading classes, while the friends of "progress" dilated on the great benefits they would eventually confer upon mankind at large. It began to be seen that Edward Pease had not been exaggerating when he said, "Let the country but make the railroads, and the railroads will make the country!" They also came to be regarded as inviting objects of investment to the thrifty, and a safe outlet for the accumulations of inert men of capital. Thus new avenues of iron road were soon in course of formation, branching in all directions, so that the country promised in a wonderfully short space of time to become wrapped in one vast network of iron.

In 1836 the Grand Junction Railway was under construction between Warrington and Birmingham—the northern part by Mr. Stephenson, and the southern by Mr. Rastrick. The works on that line embraced heavy cuttings, long embankments, and numerous viaducts; but none of these are worthy of any special description. Perhaps the finest piece of masonry on the railway is the Dutton Viaduct across the valley of the Weaver. It consists of 20 arches of 60 feet span, springing 16 feet from the perpendicular shaft of each pier, and 60 feet in height from the crown of the arches to the level of the river. The foundations of the piers were built on piles driven 20 feet deep. The structure has a solid and majestic appearance, and is perhaps the finest of George Stephenson's viaducts.

THE DUTTON VIADUCT.

The Manchester and Leeds line was in progress at the same time — an important railway connecting Yorkshire and Lancashire, passing through a district full of manufacturing towns and villages, the hives of population, industry, and enterprise. An attempt was made to obtain the act as early as the year 1831; but its promoters were defeated by the powerful opposition of the land-owners, aided by the canal companies, and the project was not revived for several years. The act authorizing the construction of the line was obtained in 1836; it was amended in the following year, and the first ground was broken on the 18th of August, 1837.

An incident occurred while the second Manchester and Leeds Bill was before the Committee of the Lords which is worthy of passing notice in this place, as illustrative of George Stephenson's character. The line which was authorized by Parliament in 1836 had been hastily surveyed within a period of less than six weeks, but before it received the royal assent the engineer became convinced that many important improvements might be made in it, and he communicated his views to the directors. They determined, however, to obtain the act, although conscious at the time that they would have to go for a second and improved line in the following year. The second bill passed the Commons in 1837 without difficulty, and was expected in like manner to pass the Lords' Committee. Quite unexpectedly, however, Lord Wharncliffe, who was interested in the Manchester and Sheffield line, which passed through his colliery property in the south of Yorkshire, conceiving that the new Manchester and Leeds line might have some damaging effect upon it, appeared as an opponent of the bill. Himself a member of the committee, he adopted the unusual course of rising to his feet, and making a set speech against the measure while the engineer was under examination. He alleged that the act obtained in the preceding session was one that the promoters had no intention of carrying out, that they had only secured it for the purpose of obtaining possession of the ground and reducing the number of the opponents to their present application, and that, in fact, they had been practicing a deception upon the House. Then, turning full round upon the witness, he said, "I ask you, sir, do you call that conduct *honest?*" Stephenson, his voice trembling with emotion, replied, "Yes, my lord, I *do* call it honest. And I will ask your lordship, whom I served for many years as your engine-wright at the Killingworth collieries, did you ever know me to do any thing that was not strictly honorable? You know what the collieries were when I went there, and you know what they were when I left them. Did you ever hear that I was found wanting when honest services were wanted, or when duty called me? Let your lordship but fairly consider the circumstances of the case, and I feel persuaded you will admit that my conduct has been equally honest throughout in this matter." He then briefly but clearly stated the history of the application to Parliament for the act, which was so satisfactory to the committee that they passed the preamble of the bill without farther objection; and Lord Wharncliffe requested that the committee would permit his observations to be erased from the record of the evidence, which, as an acknowledgment of his error, was allowed. Lord Kenyon and several other members of the committee afterward came up to Mr. Stephenson, shook him by the hand, and congratulated him on the manly way in which he had vindicated himself from the aspersions attempted to be cast upon him.

In conducting this project to an issue, the engineer had the usual opposition and prejudices to encounter. Predictions were confidently made in many quarters that the line could never succeed. It was declared that the utmost engineering skill could not construct a railway through such a country of hills and hard rocks; and it was maintained that, even if the railway were practicable, it could only be made at a cost altogether ruinous.

During the progress of the works, as the Summit Tunnel near Littleborough was approaching completion, the rumor was spread

ENTRANCE TO THE SUMMIT TUNNEL, LITTLEBOROUGH. [By Percival Skelton.]

abroad in Manchester that the tunnel had fallen in and buried a number of the workmen. The last arch had been keyed in, and the work was all but finished, when a slight accident occurred which was thus exaggerated by the lying tongue of rumor. An invert had given way through the irregular pressure of the surrounding earth and rock at a part of the tunnel where a "fault" had occurred in the strata.

A party of the directors accompanied the engineer to inspect the scene of the accident. They entered the tunnel mouth preceded by upward of fifty navvies, each bearing a torch. After walking a distance of about half a mile, the inspecting party arrived at the scene of the "frightful accident," about which so much alarm had been spread abroad. All that was visible was a certain unevenness of the ground, which had been forced up by the invert under it giving way; thus the ballast had been loosened, the drain running along the centre of the road had been displaced, and small pools of water stood about. But the whole of the walls and the roof were as perfect as at any other part of the tunnel. The engineer explained the cause of the accident; the blue shale,

THE LITTLEBOROUGH TUNNEL. [The Walsden End.]

he said, through which the excavation passed at that point, was considered so hard and firm as to render it unnecessary to build the invert very strong there. But shale is always a deceptive material. Subjected to the influence of the atmosphere, it gives but a treacherous support. In this case, falling away like quicklime, it had left the lip of the invert alone to support the pressure of the arch above, and hence its springing inward and upward. Stephenson then directed the attention of the visitors to the completeness of the arch overhead, where not the slightest fracture or yielding could be detected. Speaking of the work in the course of the same day, he said, "I will stake my character, my head, if that tunnel ever give way, so as to cause danger to any of the public passing through it. Taking it as a whole, I don't think there is another such a piece of work in the world. It is the greatest work that has yet been done of this kind, and there has been less repairing than is usual—though an engineer might well be beaten in his calculations, for he can not beforehand see into those little fractured parts of the earth he may meet with." As Stephenson had promised, the invert was put in, and the tunnel was made perfectly safe.

The construction of this subterranean road employed the labor of above a thousand men for nearly four years. Besides excavating the arch out of the solid rock, they used 23,000,000 of bricks and 8000 tons of Roman cement in the building of the tunnel. Thirteen stationary engines, and about 100 horses, were also employed in drawing the earth and stone out of the shafts. Its entire length is 2869 yards, or nearly a mile and three quarters, exceeding the famous Kilsby Tunnel by 471 yards.

The Midland Railway was a favorite line of Mr. Stephenson's for several reasons. It passed through a rich mining district, in which it opened up many valuable coal-fields, and it formed part of the great main line of communication between London and Edinburg. The line was originally projected by gentlemen interested in the London and Birmingham Railway. Their intention

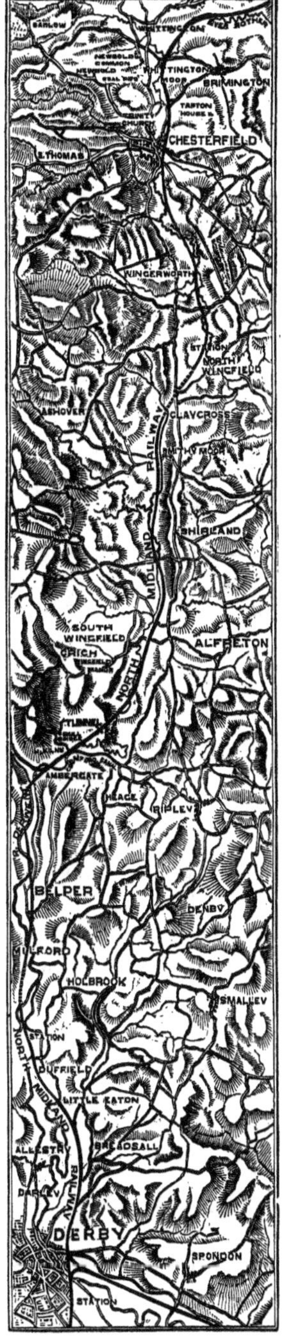

was to extend that line from Rugby to Leeds; but, finding themselves anticipated in part by the projection of the Midland Counties Railway from Rugby to Derby, they confined themselves to the district between Derby and Leeds, and in 1835 a company was formed to construct the North Midland line, with George Stephenson for its engineer. The act was obtained in 1836, and the first ground was broken in February, 1837.

Although the Midland Railway was only one of the many great works of the same kind executed at that time, it was almost enough of itself to be the achievement of a life. Compare it, for example, with Napoleon's military road over the Simplon, and it will at once be seen how greatly it excels that work, not only in the constructive skill displayed in it, but also in its cost and magnitude, and the amount of labor employed in its formation. The road of the Simplon is 45 miles in length; the North Midland Railway 72½ miles. The former has 50 bridges and 5 tunnels, measuring together 1338 feet in length; the latter has 200 bridges and 7 tunnels, measuring together 11,400 feet, or about 2¼ miles. The former cost about £720,000 sterling, the latter above £3,000,000. Napoleon's grand military road was constructed in six years, at the public cost of the two great kingdoms of France and Italy, while Stephenson's railway was formed in about three years by a company of private merchants and capitalists out of their own funds and under their own superintendence.

It is scarcely necessary that we should give any account in detail of the North Midland works. The making of one tunnel so much resembles the making of another—the building of bridges and viaducts, no matter how extensive, so much resembles the building of others—the cutting out of "dirt," the blasting of rocks, and the wheeling of excavation into embankments, is so much matter of mere time and hard work, that it is quite unnecessary to detain the reader by any attempt at their description. Of course there were the usual difficulties to encounter and overcome, but the railway engineer regarded these as mere matters of course, and would probably have been disappointed if they had not presented themselves.

On the Midland, as on other lines, water was the great enemy to be fought against—water in the Clay-cross and other tunnels—

water in the boggy or sandy foundations of bridges—and water in cuttings and embankments. As an illustration of the difficulties of bridge building, we may mention the case of the five-arch bridge over the Derwent, where it took two years' work, night and day, to get in the foundations of the piers alone. Another curious illustration of the mischief done by water in cuttings may be briefly mentioned. At a part of the North Midland line, near Ambergate, it was necessary to pass along a hill-side in a cutting a few yards deep. As the cutting proceeded, a seam of shale was cut across, lying at an inclination of 6 to 1; and shortly after, the water getting behind it, the whole mass of earth along the hill above began to move down across the line of excavation. The accident completely upset the estimates of the contractor, who, instead of fifty thousand cubic yards, found that he had about five hundred thousand to remove, the execution of this part of the railway occupying fifteen months instead of two.

LAND-SLIP ON NORTH MIDLAND LINE, NEAR AMBERGATE.

The Oakenshaw cutting near Wakefield was also of a very formidable character. About six hundred thousand yards of rock shale and bind were quarried out of it, and led to form the adjoining Oakenshaw embankment. The Normanton cutting was almost as heavy, requiring the removal of four hundred thousand yards of the same kind of excavation into embankment and spoil. But the progress of the works on the line was so rapid during 1839 that no less than 450,000 cubic yards of excavation were accomplished per month.

BULL BRIDGE, NEAR AMBERGATE.

As a curiosity in construction, we may also mention a very delicate piece of work executed on the same railway at Bull Bridge in Derbyshire, where the line at the same point passes *over* a bridge which here spans the River Amber, and *under* the bed of the Cromford Canal. Water, bridge, railway, and canal were thus piled one above the other, four stories high. In order to prevent the possibility of the waters of the canal breaking in upon the railway works, Stephenson had an iron trough made, 150 feet long, of the width of the canal, and exactly fitting the bottom. It was brought to the spot in three pieces, which were firmly welded together, and the trough was then floated into its place and sunk, the whole operation being completed without in the least interfering with the navigation of the canal. The railway works underneath were then proceeded with and finished.

Another line of the same series, constructed by George Stephenson, was the York and North Midland, extending from Normanton—a point on the Midland Railway—to York; but it was a line of easy formation, traversing a comparatively level country. The inhabitants of Whitby, as well as York, were projecting a railway to connect these towns as early as 1832, and in the year following Whitby succeeded in obtaining a horse line of twenty-four miles, connecting it with the small market-town of Pickering. The York citizens were more ambitious, and agitated the question of a locomotive line to connect them with the town of Leeds. Stephenson recommended them to connect their line with the Midland at Normanton, and they adopted his advice. The company was formed, the shares were at once subscribed for, the act was obtained in the following year, and the works were constructed without difficulty.

As the best proof of his conviction that the York and North Midland would prove a good investment, Stephenson invested in it a considerable portion of his savings, being a subscriber for 420 shares. The interest taken in this line by the engineer was on more than one occasion specially mentioned by Mr. Hudson, then Lord-mayor of York, as an inducement to other persons of capital to join the undertaking; and had it not been afterward encumbered and overlaid by comparatively useless and profitless branches, in the projection of which Stephenson had no part, the sanguine expectations which he early formed of the paying qualities of that railway would have been more than realized.

There was one branch, however, of the York and North Midland Line in which he took an anxious interest, and of which he may be said to have been the projector—the branch to Scarborough, which proved one of the most profitable parts of the railway. He was so satisfied of its value, that, at a meeting of the York and North Midland proprietors, he volunteered his gratuitous services as engineer until the company was formed, in addition to subscribing largely to the undertaking. At that meeting he took an opportunity of referring to the charges brought against engineers of so greatly exceeding the estimates: "He had had a good deal to do with making out the estimate of the North Midland Railway, and he believed there never was a more honest one. He had always endeavored to state the truth as far as was in his power. He had known a contractor who, when he (Mr. Stephenson) had sent in an estimate, came forward and said, 'I can do it for half the money.' The contractor's estimate went into Parliament, but it came out his. He could go through the whole list of the undertakings in which he had been engaged, and show that he had never had any thing to do with stock-jobbing concerns. He would say that he would not be concerned in any scheme unless he was satisfied that it would pay the proprietors; and in bringing forward the proposed line to Scarborough, he was satisfied that it would pay, or he would have had nothing to do with it."

During the time that our engineer was engaged in superintending the execution of these undertakings, he was occupied upon other projected railways in various parts of the country. He surveyed several lines in the neighborhood of Glasgow, and afterward alternate routes along the east coast from Newcastle to Edinburg, with the view of completing the main line of communication with London. When out on foot in the field on these occasions, he was ever foremost in the march, and he delighted to test the prowess of his companions by a good jump at any hedge or ditch that lay in their way. His companions used to remark his singular quickness of observation. Nothing escaped his attention — the trees, the crops, the birds, or the farmer's stock; and he was usually full of lively conversation, every thing in nature affording him an opportunity for making some striking remark or propounding some ingenious theory. When taking a flying survey of a new line, his keen observation proved very useful, for he rapidly noted the general configuration of the country, and inferred its geological structure. He afterward remarked to a friend, "I have planned many a railway traveling along in a post-chaise, and following the natural line of the country." And it was remarkable that his first impressions of the direction to be taken almost invariably proved correct; and there are few of the lines surveyed and recommended by him which have not been executed, either during his lifetime or since. As an illustration of his quick and shrewd observation on such occasions, we may mention that when employed to lay out a line to connect Manchester, through Macclesfield, with the Potteries, the gentleman who accompanied him on the journey of inspection cautioned him to provide large accommodation for carrying off the water, observing, "You must not judge by the appearance of the brooks; for after heavy rains these hills pour down volumes of water, of which you can have no conception." "Pooh! pooh! *don't I see your bridges?*" replied the engineer. He had noted the details of each as he passed along.

Among the other projects which occupied his attention about the same time were the projected lines between Chester and Holyhead, between Leeds and Bradford, and between Lancaster and Maryport by the west coast. This latter was intended to form part of a western line to Scotland; Stephenson favoring it partly because of the flatness of the gradients, and because it could be formed at comparatively small cost, while it would open out a valuable iron-mining district, from which a large traffic in ironstone was expected. One of its collateral advantages, in the engineer's opinion, was that, by forming the railway directly across Morecambe Bay, on the northwest coast of Lancashire, a large tract of valuable land might be reclaimed from the sea, the sale of which would considerably reduce the cost of the works. He estimated that, by means of a solid embankment across the bay, not less than 40,000 acres of rich alluvial land would be gained. He proposed to carry the road across the ten miles of sands which lie between Poulton, near Lancaster, and Humphrey Head on the opposite coast, forming the line in a segment of a circle of five miles' radius. His plan was to drive in piles across the entire length, forming a solid fence of stone blocks on the land side for the purpose of retaining the sand and silt brought down by the rivers from the interior. The embankment would then be raised from time to time as the deposit accumulated, until the land was filled up to high-water mark; provision being made, by means of sufficient arches, for the flow of the river waters into the bay. The execution of the railway after this plan would, however, have occupied more years than the promoters of the West Coast line were disposed to wait, and eventually Mr. Locke's more direct but less level line by Shap Fell was adopted. A railway has, however, since been carried across the head of the bay, in a modified form, by the Ulverstone and Lancaster Railway Company; and it is not improbable that Stephenson's larger scheme of reclaiming the vast tract of land now left bare at every receding tide may yet be carried out.

While occupied in carrying out the great railway undertakings which we have above so briefly described, George Stephenson's home continued, for the greater part of the time, to be at Alton Grange, near Leicester. But he was so much occupied in traveling about from one committee of directors to another—one week in England, another in Scotland, and probably the next in Ireland, that he often did not see his home for weeks together. He had also to make frequent inspections of the various important and difficult works in progress, especially on the Midland and Manchester and Leeds lines, besides occasionally going to Newcastle to see how the locomotive works were going on there. During the three years ending 1837—perhaps the busiest years of his life*—he traveled by post-chaise alone upward of 20,000 miles, and yet not less than six months out of the three years were spent in London. Hence there is comparatively little to record of Mr. Stephenson's private life at this period, during which he had scarcely a moment that he could call his own.

To give an idea of the number of projects which at this time occupied our engineer's attention, and of the extent and rapidity of his journeys, we subjoin from his private secretary's journal the following epitome of one of them, on which he entered immediately after the conclusion of the heavy Parliamentary session of 1836.

"August 9th. From Alton Grange to Derby and Matlock, and forward by mail to Manchester, to meet the committee of the South Union Railway. August 10th. Manchester to Stockport, to meet committee of the Manchester and Leeds Railway; thence to meet directors of the Chester and Birkenhead, and Chester and Crewe Railways. August 11th. Liverpool to Woodside, to meet committee of the Chester and Birkenhead line; journey with them along the proposed railway to Chester; then back to Liverpool. August 12th. Liverpool to Manchester, to meet directors of the Manchester and Leeds Railway, and traveling with them over the works in progress. August 13th. Continued journey over the works, and arrival at Wakefield; thence to York. August 14th. Meeting with Mr. Hudson at York, and journey from York to Newcastle. August 15th. At Newcastle, working up arrears of correspondence. August 16th. Meeting with Mr. Brandling as to the station for the

* During this period he was engaged on the North Midland, extending from Derby to Leeds; the York and North Midland, from Normanton to York; the Manchester and Leeds; the Birmingham and Derby, and the Sheffield and Rotherham Railways; the whole of these, of which he was principal engineer, having been authorized in 1836. In that session alone, powers were obtained for the construction of 214 miles of new railways under his direction, at an expenditure of upward of five millions sterling.

Brandling Junction at Gateshead, and stations at other parts of the line. August 17th. Carlisle to Wigton and Maryport, examining the railway. August 19th. Maryport to Carlisle, continuing the inspection. August 20th. At Carlisle, examining the ground for a station; and working up correspondence. August 21st. Carlisle to Dumfries by mail; forward to Ayr by chaise, proceeding up the valley of the Nith, through Thornhill, Sanquhar, and Cumnock. August 22d. Meeting with promoters of the Glasgow, Kilmarnock, and Ayr Railway, and journey along the proposed line; meeting with the magistrates of Kilmarnock at Beith, and journey with them over Mr. Gale's proposed line to Kilmarnock. August 23d. From Kilmarnock along Mr. Miller's proposed line to Beith, Paisley, and Glasgow. August 24th. Examination of site of proposed station at Glasgow; meeting with the directors; then from Glasgow, by Falkirk and Linlithgow, to Edinburg, meeting there with Mr. Grainger, engineer, and several of the committee of the proposed Edinburg and Dunbar Railway. August 25th. Examining the site of the proposed station at Edinburg; then to Dunbar, by Portobello and Haddington, examining the proposed line of railway. August 26th. Dunbar to Tommy Grant's, to examine the summit of the country toward Berwick, with a view to a through line to Newcastle; then return to Edinburg. August 27th. At Edinburg, meeting the provisional committee of the proposed Edinburg and Dunbar Railway. August 28th. Journey from Edinburg, through Melrose and Jedburg, to Horsley, along the route of Mr. Richardson's proposed railway across Carter Fell. August 29th. From Horsley to Mr. Brandling's, then on to Newcastle; engaged on the Brandling Junction Railway. August 30th. Engaged with Mr. Brandling; after which, meeting a deputation from Maryport. August 31st. Meeting with Mr. Brandling and others as to the direction of the Brandling Junction in connection with the Great North of England line, and the course of the railway through Newcastle; then on to York. September 1st. At York; meeting with York and North Midland directors; then journeying over Lord Howden's property, to arrange for a deviation; examining the proposed site of the station at York. September 2d. At York, giving instructions as to the survey; then to Manchester by Leeds. September 3d. At Manchester; journey to Stockport, with Mr. Bidder and Mr. Bourne, examining the line to Stockport, and fixing the crossing of the river there; attending to the surveys; then journey back to Manchester, to meet the directors of the Manchester and Leeds Railway. September 4th. Sunday at Manchester. September 5th.

Journey along part of the Manchester and Leeds Railway. September 6th. At Manchester, examining and laying down the section of the South Union line to Stockport; afterward engaged on the Manchester and Leeds working plans, in endeavoring to give a greater radius to the curves; seeing Mr. Seddon about the Liverpool, Manchester, and Leeds Junction Railway. September 7th. Journey along the Manchester and Leeds line, then on to Derby. September 8th. At Derby; seeing Mr. Carter and Mr. Beale about the Tamworth deviation; then home to Alton Grange. September 10th. At Alton Grange, preparing report to the committee of the Edinburg and Dunbar Railway."

Such is a specimen of the enormous amount of physical and mental labor undergone by the engineer during the busy years above referred to. He was no sooner home than he was called away again by some other railway or business engagement. Thus, in four days after his arrival at Alton Grange from the above journey into Scotland, we find him going over the whole of the North Midland line as far as Leeds; then by Halifax to Manchester, where he staid for several days on the business of the South Union line; then to Birmingham and London; back to Alton Grange, and next day to Congleton and Leek; thence to Leeds and Goole, and home again by the Sheffield and Rotherham and the Midland works. And early in the following month (October) he was engaged in the north of Ireland, examining the line, and reporting upon the plans of the projected Ulster Railway. He was also called upon to inspect and report upon colliery works, salt works, brass and copper works, and such like, in addition to his own colliery and railway business. He usually also staked out himself the lines laid out by him, which involved a good deal of labor since undertaken by assistants. And occasionally he would run up to London, attending in person to the preparation and depositing of the plans and sections of the projected undertakings for which he was engaged as engineer.

His correspondence increased so much that he found it necessary to engage a private secretary, who accompanied him on his journeys. He was himself exceedingly averse to writing letters. The comparatively advanced age at which he learned the art of writing, and the nature of his duties while engaged at the Killingworth Colliery, precluded that facility in correspondence which only constant practice can give. He gradually, however, acquired great facility in dictation, and had also the power of laboring continuously at this work, the gentleman who acted as his secretary in the year 1835 having informed us that during his busy season he one day dictated no fewer than thirty-seven letters, several of them embodying the results of much close thinking and calculation. On another occasion he dictated reports and letters for twelve continuous hours, until his secretary was ready to drop off his chair from sheer exhaustion, and at length pleaded for a suspension of the labor. This great mass of correspondence, though closely bearing on the subjects under discussion, was not, however, of a kind to supply the biographer with matter for quotation, or to give that insight into the life and character of the writer which the letters of literary men so often furnish. They were, for the most part, letters of mere business, relating to works in progress, Parliamentary contests, new surveys, estimates of cost, and railway policy—curt, and to the point; in short, the letters of a man every moment of whose time was precious.

Fortunately, George Stephenson possessed a facility of sleeping, which enabled him to pass through this enormous amount of fatigue and labor without injury to his health. He had been trained in a hard school, and could bear with ease conditions which, to men more softly nurtured, would have been the extreme of physical discomfort. Many, many nights he snatched his sleep while traveling in his chaise; and at break of day he would be at work, surveying until dark, and this for weeks in succession. His whole powers seemed to be under the control of his will, for he could wake at any hour, and go to work at once. It was difficult for secretaries and assistants to keep up with such a man.

It is pleasant to record that in the midst of these engrossing occupations his heart remained as soft and loving as ever. In spring-time he would not be debarred of his boyish amusement of bird-nesting, but would go rambling along the hedges spying for nests. In the autumn he went nutting, and when he could snatch a few minutes he indulged in his old love of gardening. His uniform kindness and good temper, and his communicative, intelligent disposition, made him a great favorite with the neighboring farmers, to whom he would volunteer much valuable advice on agricultural operations, drainage, plowing, and labor-saving processes. Sometimes he took a long rural ride on his favorite "Bobby," now growing old, but as fond of his master as ever. Toward the end of his life "Bobby" lived in clover, his master's pet, doing no work; and he died at Tapton in 1845, more than twenty years old.

During one of George's brief sojourns at the Grange he found time to write to his son a touching account of a pair of robins that had built their nest within one of the empty upper chambers of the house. One day he observed a robin fluttering outside the windows, and beating its wings against the panes, as if eager to gain admission. He went up stairs, and there found, in a retired part of one of the rooms, a robin's nest, with one of the parent birds sitting over three or four young—all dead. The excluded bird outside still beat against the panes; and on the window being let down, it flew into the room, but was so exhausted that it dropped upon the floor. Stephenson took up the bird, carried it down stairs, and had it warmed and fed. The poor robin revived, and for a time was one of his pets. But it shortly died too, as if unable to recover from the privations it had endured during its three days' fluttering and beating at the windows. It appeared that the room had been unoccupied, and the sash having been let down, the robins had taken the opportunity of building their nest within it; but the servant having closed the window again, the calamity befell the birds which so strongly excited the engineer's sympathies. An incident such as this, trifling though it may seem, gives a true key to the heart of a man.

The amount of his Parliamentary business having greatly increased with the projection of new lines of railway, the Stephensons found it necessary to set up an office in London in 1836. George's first office was at No. 9 Duke Street, Westminster, from whence he removed in the following year to 30½ Great George Street. That office was the busy scene of railway politics for several years. There consultations were held, schemes were matured, deputations were received, and many projectors called upon our engineer for the purpose of submitting to him their plans of railways and railway working. His private secretary at the time has informed us that at the end of the first Parliamentary session in which he had been engaged as engineer for more companies than one, it became necessary for him to give instructions as to the preparation of the accounts to be rendered to the several companies. In the simplicity of his heart, he directed Mr. Binns to take his full time at the rate of ten guineas a day, and charge the railway companies in the proportion in which he had actually been employed in their respective business during each day. When Robert heard of this instruction, he went directly to his father and expostulated with him against this unprofessional course; and, other influences being brought to bear upon him, George at length reluctantly consented to charge as other engineers did, an entire day's fee to each of the companies for which he was concerned while their business was going forward; but he cut down the number of days charged for, and reduced the daily amount from ten to seven guineas.

Besides his journeys at home, George Stephenson was on more than one occasion called abroad on railway business. Thus, at the desire of King Leopold, he made several visits to Belgium to assist the Belgian engineers in laying out the national lines of the kingdom. That enlightened monarch at an early period discerned the powerful instrumentality of railways in developing a country's resources, and he determined at the earliest possible period to adopt them as the great high roads of the nation. The country, being rich in coals and minerals, had great manufacturing capabilities. It had good ports, fine navigable rivers, abundant canals, and a teeming, industrious population. Leopold perceived that railways were eminently calculated to bring the industry of the country into full play, and to render the riches of the provinces available to the rest of the kingdom. He therefore openly declared himself the promoter of public railways throughout Belgium. A system of lines was projected at his instance, connecting Brussels with the chief towns and cities of the state, extending from Ostend eastward to the Prussian frontier, and from Antwerp southward to the French frontier.

Mr. Stephenson and his son, as the leading railway engineers of England, were consulted by the king, in 1835, as to the best mode of carrying out his intentions. In the course of that year they visited Belgium, and had several interesting conferences with Leopold and his ministers on the subject of the proposed railways. The king then appointed George Stephenson by royal ordinance a Knight of the Order of Leopold. At the invitation of the monarch, Mr. Stephenson made a second visit to Belgium in 1837, on the occasion of the public opening of the line from Brussels to Ghent. At Brussels there was a public procession, and another at Ghent on the arrival of the train. Stephenson and his party accompanied it to the Public Hall, there to dine with the chief ministers of state, the municipal authorities, and about five hundred of the principal inhabitants of the city; the English embassador being also present. After the king's health and a few others had been drunk, that of Mr. Stephenson was proposed; on which the whole assembly rose up, amid great excitement and loud applause, and made their way to where he sat, in order to "jingle glasses" with him, greatly to his own amazement. On the day following, our engineer dined with the king and queen at their own table at Laaken, by special invitation, afterward accompanying his majesty and suite to a public ball, given by the municipality of Brussels in honor of the opening of the line to Ghent, as well as of their distinguished English guests. On entering the room, the general and excited inquiry was, "Which is Stephenson?" The English engineer had not before imagined that he was esteemed to be so great a man.

The London and Birmingham Railway having been completed in September, 1838, after being about five years in progress, the great main system of railway communication between London, Liverpool, and Manchester was then opened to the public. For some months previously the line had been partially open, coaches performing the journey between Denbigh Hall (near Wolverton) and Rugby—the works of the Kilsby tunnel being still incomplete. It was already amusing to hear the complaints of the travelers about the slowness of the coaches as compared with the railway, though the coaches traveled at a speed of eleven miles an hour. The comparison of comfort was also greatly to the disparagement of the coaches. Then the railway train could accommodate any quantity, whereas the road conveyances were limited; and when a press of travelers occurred—as on the occasion of the queen's coronation—the greatest inconvenience was experienced, as much as £10 having been paid for a seat on a donkey-chaise between Rugby and Denbigh. On the opening of the railway throughout, of course all this inconvenience and delay was brought to an end.

Numerous other openings of railways constructed by George Stephenson took place about the same time. The Birmingham and Derby line was opened for traffic in August, 1839; the Sheffield and Rotherham in November, 1839; and in the course of the following year, the Midland, the York and North Midland, the Chester and Crewe, the Chester and Birkenhead, the Manchester and Birmingham, the Manchester and Leeds, and the Maryport and Carlisle railways, were all publicly opened in whole or in part. Thus 321 miles of railway (exclusive of the London and Birmingham), constructed under Mr. Stephenson's superintendence, at a cost of upward of eleven millions sterling, were, in the course of about two years, added to the traffic accommodation of the country.

The ceremonies which accompanied the public opening of these lines were often of an interesting character. The adjoining population held general holiday; bands played, banners waved, and assembled thousands cheered the passing trains amid the occasional booming of cannon. The proceedings were usually wound up by a public dinner; and in the course of his speech which followed, Mr. Stephenson would revert to his favorite topic—the difficulties which he had early encountered in the promotion of the railway system, and in establishing the superiority of the locomotive. On such occasions he always took great pleasure in alluding to the services rendered to himself and the public by the young men brought up under his eye—his pupils at first, and afterward his assistants. No great master ever possessed a more devoted band of assistants and fellow-workers than he did; and it was one of the most marked evidences of his admirable tact and judgment that he selected, with such undeviating correctness, the men best fitted to carry out his plans. Indeed, the ability to accomplish great things, to carry grand ideas into practical effect, depends in no small measure on that intuitive knowledge of character which our engineer possessed in so remarkable a degree.

At the dinner at York, which followed the partial opening of the York and North Midland Railway, Mr. Stephenson said "he was sure they would appreciate his feelings when he told them that, when he first began railway business, his hair was black, although it was now gray; and that he began his life's labor as but a poor plowboy. About thirty years since he had applied himself to the study of how to generate high velocities by mechanical means. He thought he had solved that problem; and they had for themselves seen, that day, what perseverance had brought him to. He was, on that occasion, only too happy to have an opportunity of acknowledging that he had, in the latter portion of his career, received much most valuable assistance particularly from young men brought up in his manufactory. Whenever talent showed itself in a young man, he had always given that talent encouragement where he could, and he would continue to do so."

That this was no exaggerated statement is amply proved by many facts which redound to Stephenson's credit. He was no niggard of encouragement and praise when he saw honest industry struggling for a footing. Many were the young men whom, in the course of his career, he took by the hand and led steadily up to honor and emolument, simply because he had noted their zeal, diligence, and integrity. One youth excited his interest while working as a common carpenter on the Liverpool and Manchester line; and before many years had passed he was recognized as an engineer of distinction. Another young man he found industriously working away at his by-hours, and, admiring his diligence, he engaged him as his private secretary, the gentleman shortly after rising to a position of eminent influence and usefulness. Indeed, nothing gave the engineer greater pleasure than in this way to help on any deserving youth who came under his observation, and, in his own expressive phrase, to "make a man of him."

The openings of the great main lines of railroad communication shortly proved the fallaciousness of the numerous rash prophecies which had been promulgated by the opponents of railways. The proprietors of the canals were astounded by the fact that, notwithstanding the immense traffic conveyed by rail, their own traffic and receipts continued to increase; and that, in common with other interests, they fully shared in the expansion of trade and commerce which had been so effectually promoted by the extension of the railway system. The cattle-owners were equally amazed to find the price of horseflesh increasing with the extension of railways, and that the number of coaches running to and from the new railway stations gave employment to a greater number of horses than under the old stage-coach system. Those who had prophesied the decay of the metropolis, and the ruin of the suburban cabbage-growers, in consequence of the approach of railways to London, were disappointed; for, while the new roads let citizens out of London, they also let country-people in. Their action, in this respect, was centripetal as well as centrifugal. Tens of thousands who had never seen the metropolis could now visit it expeditiously and cheaply; and Londoners who had never visited the country, or but rarely, were enabled, at little cost of time or money, to see green fields and clear blue skies far from the smoke and bustle of town. If the dear suburban-grown cabbages became depreciated in value, there were truck-loads of fresh-grown country cabbages to make amends for the loss: in this case, the "partial evil" was a far more general good. The food of the metropolis became rapidly improved, especially in the supply of wholesome meat and vegetables. And then the price of coals—an article which, in this country, is as indispensable as daily food to all classes—was greatly reduced. What a blessing to the metropolitan poor is described in this single fact!

The prophecies of ruin and disaster to landlords and farmers were equally confounded by the openings of the railways. The agricultural communications, so far from being "destroyed," as had been predicted, were immensely improved. The farmers were enabled to buy their coals, lime, and manure for less money, while they obtained a readier access to the best markets for their stock and farm-produce. Notwithstanding the predictions to the contrary, their cows gave milk as before, the sheep fed and fattened, and even skittish horses ceased to shy at the passing trains. The smoke of the engines did not obscure the sky, nor were farmyards burnt up by the fire thrown from the locomotives. The farming classes were not reduced to beggary; on the contrary, they soon felt that, so far from having any thing to dread, they had very much good to expect from the extension of railways.

Landlords also found that they could get higher rent for farms situated near a railway than at a distance from one. Hence they became clamorous for "sidings." They felt it to be a grievance to be placed at a distance from a station. After a railway had been once opened, not a landlord would consent to have the line taken from him. Owners who had fought the promoters before Parliament, and compelled them to pass their domains at a distance, at a vastly increased expense in tunnels and deviations, now petitioned for branches and nearer station-accommodation. Those who held property near towns, and had extorted large sums as compensation for the anticipated deterioration in the value of their building land, found a new demand for it springing up at greatly advanced prices. Land was now advertised for sale with the attraction of being "near a railway station."

The prediction that, even if railways were made, the public would not use them, was also completely falsified by the results. The ordinary mode of fast traveling for the middle classes had heretofore been by mail-coach and stage-coach. Those who could not afford to pay the high prices charged by such conveyances went by wagon, and the poorer classes trudged on foot. George Stephenson was wont to say that he hoped to see the day when it would be cheaper for a poor man to travel by railway than to walk, and not many years passed before his expectation was fulfilled. In no country in the world is time worth more money than in England; and by saving time—the criterion of distance—the railway proved a great benefactor to men of industry in all classes.

Many deplored the inevitable downfall of the old stage-coach system. There was to be an end of that delightful variety of incident usually attendant on a journey by road. The rapid scamper across a fine country on the outside of the four-horse "Express" or "Highflyer;" the seat on the box beside Jehu, or the equally coveted place near the facetious guard behind; the journey amid open green fields, through smiling villages and fine old towns, where the stage stopped to change horses and the passengers to dine, was all very delightful in its way, and many regretted that this old-fashioned and pleasant style of traveling was about to pass away. But it had its dark side also. Any one who remembers the journey by stage from London to Manchester or York will associate it with recollections and sensations of not unmixed delight. To be perched for twenty-four hours, exposed to all weathers, on the outside of a coach, trying in vain to find a soft seat—sitting now with the face to the wind, rain, or sun, and now with the back—without any shelter such as the commonest penny-a-mile Parliamentary train now daily provides—was a miserable undertaking, looked forward to with horror by many whose business required them to travel frequently between the provinces and the metropolis. Nor were the inside passengers more agreeably accommodated. To be closely packed in a little, inconvenient, straight-backed vehicle, where the cramped limbs could not be in the least extended, nor the wearied frame indulge in any change of posture, was felt by many to be a terrible thing. Then there were the constantly-recurring demands, not always couched in the politest terms, for an allowance to the driver every two or three stages, and to the guard every six or eight; and if the gratuity did not equal their expectations, growling and open abuse were not unusual. These *désagrémens*, together with the exactions practiced on travelers by innkeepers, seriously detracted from the romance of stage-coach traveling, and there was a general disposition on the part of the public to change the system for a better.

The avidity with which the public at once availed themselves of the railways proved that this better system had been discovered. Notwithstanding the reduction of the coach-fares on many of the roads to one third of their previous rate, the public preferred traveling by the railway. They saved in time, and they saved in money, taking the whole expenses into account. In point of comfort there could be no doubt as to the infinite superiority of the locomotive train. But there remained the question of safety, which had been a great bugbear with the early opponents of railways, and was made the most of by the coach-proprietors to deter the public from using them. It was predicted that trains of passengers would be blown to pieces, and that none but fools would intrust their persons to the conduct of an explosive machine such as the locomotive. It appeared, however, that during the first eight years not fewer than five millions of passengers had been conveyed along the Liverpool and Manchester Railway, and of this vast number only two persons had lost their lives by accident. During the same period, the loss of life by the upsetting of stage-coaches had been immensely greater in proportion. The public were not slow, therefore, to detect the fact that traveling by railways was greatly safer than traveling by common roads, and in all districts penetrated by railways the coaches were very shortly taken off for want of support.

George Stephenson himself had a narrow escape in one of the stage-coach accidents so common thirty years since, but which are already almost forgotten. While the Birmingham line was under construction, he had occasion to travel from Ashby-de-la-Zouch to London by coach. He was an inside passenger with several others, and the outsides were pretty numerous. When within ten miles of Dunstable, he felt, from the rolling of the coach, that one of the linchpins securing the wheels had given way, and that the vehicle must upset. He endeavored to fix himself in his seat, holding on firmly by the arm-straps, so that he might save himself on whichever side the coach fell. The coach soon toppled over, and fell crash upon the road, amid the shrieks of his fellow-passengers and the smashing of glass. He immediately pulled himself up by the arm-strap above him, let down the coach-window, and climbed out. The coachman and passengers lay scattered about on the road, stunned, and some of them bleeding, while the horses were plunging in their harness. Taking out his pocket-knife, he at once cut the traces and set the horses free. He then went to the help of the passengers, who were all more or less hurt. The guard had his arm broken, and the driver was seriously cut and contused. A scream from one of his fellow-passenger "insides" here attracted his attention: it proceeded from an elderly lady, whom he had before observed to be decorated with one of the enormous bonnets in fashion at the time. Opening the coach-door, he lifted the lady out, and her principal lamentation was that her large bonnet had been crushed beyond remedy! Stephenson then proceeded to the nearest village for help, and saw the passengers provided with proper assistance before he himself went forward on his journey.

It was some time before the more opulent classes, who could afford to post to town in aristocratic style, became reconciled to the railway train. It put an end to that gradation of rank in traveling which was one of the few things left by which the nobleman could be distinguished from the Manchester manufacturer and bagman. But to younger sons of noble families the convenience and cheapness of the railway did not fail to com-mend itself. One of these, whose eldest brother had just succeeded to an earldom, said to a railway manager, "I like railways—they just suit young fellows like me, with 'nothing per annum paid quarterly.' You know, we can't afford to post, and it used to be deuced annoying to me, as I was jogging along on the box-seat of the stage-coach, to see the little earl go by, drawn by his four posters, and just look up at me and give me a nod. But now, with railways, it's different. It's true, he may take a first-class ticket, while I can only afford a second-class one, but *we both go the same pace.*"

For a time, however, many of the old families sent forward their servants and luggage by railroad, and condemned themselves to jog along the old highway in the accustomed family chariot, dragged by country post-horses. But the superior comfort of the railway shortly recommended itself to even the oldest families; posting went out of date; post-horses were with difficulty to be had along even the great high roads; and nobles and servants, manufacturers and peasants, alike shared in the comfort, the convenience, and the dispatch of railway traveling. The late Dr. Arnold, of Rugby, regarded the opening of the London and Birmingham line as another great step accomplished in the march of civilization. "I rejoice to see it," he said, as he stood on one of the bridges over the railway, and watched the train flashing along under him, and away through the distant hedgerows—"I rejoice to see it, and to think that feudality is gone forever: it is so great a blessing to think that any one evil is really extinct."

It was long before the late Duke of Wellington would trust himself behind a locomotive. The fatal accident to Mr. Huskisson, which had happened before his eyes, contributed to prejudice him strongly against railways, and it was not until the year 1843 that he performed his first trip on the Southwestern Railway, in attendance upon her majesty. Prince Albert had for some time been accustomed to travel by railway alone, but in 1842 the queen began to make use of the same mode of conveyance between Windsor and London. Even Colonel Sibthorpe was eventually compelled to acknowledge its utility. For a time he continued to post to and from the country as before. Then he compromised the matter by taking a railway ticket for the long journey, and posting only a stage or two nearest town; until, at length, he undisguisedly committed himself, like other people, to the express train, and performed the journey throughout upon what he had formerly denounced as "the infernal railroad."

COALVILLE AND SNIBSTON COLLIERY.

TAPTON HOUSE. [By Percival Skelton.]

CHAPTER XVI.

GEORGE STEPHENSON'S COAL-MINES—APPEARS AT MECHANICS' INSTITUTES—HIS OPINION ON RAILWAY SPEEDS—ATMOSPHERIC SYSTEM—RAILWAY MANIA—VISITS TO BELGIUM AND SPAIN.

WHILE George Stephenson was engaged in carrying on the works of the Midland Railway in the neighborhood of Chesterfield, several seams of coal were cut through in the Claycross Tunnel, when it occurred to him that if mines were opened out there, the railway would provide the means of a ready sale for the article in the midland counties, and even as far south as the metropolis itself.

At a time when every body else was skeptical as to the possibility of coals being carried from the midland counties to London, and sold there at a price to compete with those which were sea-borne, he declared his firm conviction that the time was fast approaching when the London market would be regularly supplied with North-country coals led by railway. One of the great advantages of railways, in his opinion, was that they would bring iron and coal, the staple products of the country, to the doors of all England. "The strength of Britain," he would say, "lies in her iron and coal beds, and the locomotive is destined, above all other agencies, to bring it forth. The lord chancellor now sits upon a bag of wool; but wool has long since ceased to be emblematical of the staple commodity of England. He ought rather to sit upon a bag of coals, though it might not prove quite so comfortable a seat. Then think of the lord chancellor being addressed as the noble and learned lord *on the coal-sack!* I am afraid it wouldn't answer, after all."

To one gentleman he said: "We want from the coal-mining, the iron-producing and manufacturing districts, a great railway for the carriage of these valuable products. We want, if I may so say, a stream of steam running directly through the country from the North to London. Speed is not so much an object as utility and cheapness. It will not do to mix up the heavy merchandise and coal-trains with the passenger-trains. Coal and most kinds of goods can wait, but passengers will not. A less perfect road and less expensive works will do well enough for coal-trains, if run at a low speed; and if the line be flat, it is not of much consequence whether it be direct or not. Whenever you put passenger-trains on a line, all the other trains must be run at high speeds to keep out of their way. But coal-trains run at high speeds pull the road to pieces, besides causing large expenditure in locomotive power; and I doubt very much whether they will pay, after all; but a succession of long coal-trains, if run at from ten to fourteen miles an hour, would pay very well. Thus the Stockton and Darlington Company made a larger profit when running coal at low speeds at a halfpenny a ton per mile, than they have been able to do since they put on their fast passenger-trains, when every thing must needs be run faster, and a much larger proportion of the gross receipts is consequently absorbed by working expenses."

In advocating these views, George Stephenson was considerably ahead of his time; and although he did not live to see his anticipations fully realized as to the supply of the London coal-market, he was nevertheless the first to point it out, and to some extent to prove, the practicability of establishing a profitable coal-trade by railway between the northern counties and the metropolis. So long, however, as the traffic was conducted on main passenger-lines at comparatively high speeds, it was found that the expenditure on tear and wear of road and locomotive power —not to mention the increased risk of carrying on the first-class passenger traffic with which it was mixed up—necessarily left a very small margin of profit, and hence our engineer was in the habit of urging the propriety of constructing a railway which should be exclusively devoted to goods and mineral traffic run at low speeds as the only condition on which a large railway traffic of that sort could be profitably conducted.

Having induced some of his Liverpool friends to join him in a coal-mining adventure at Chesterfield, a lease was taken of the Claycross estate, then for sale, and operations were shortly after begun. At a subsequent period Stephenson extended his coal-mining operations in the same neighborhood, and in 1841 he himself entered into a contract with owners of land in the townships of Tapton, Brimington, and Newbold for the working of the coal thereunder, and pits were opened on the Tapton estate on an extensive scale. About the same time he erected great lime-works, close to the Ambergate station of the Midland Railway, from which, when in full operation, he was able to turn out upward of two hundred tons a day. The limestone was brought on a tramway from the village of Crich, about two or three miles distant from the kilns, the coal being supplied from his adjoining Claycross Colliery. The works were on a scale such as had not be-

LIME-WORKS AT AMBERGATE. [By Percival Skelton.]

fore been attempted by any private individual engaged in a similar trade, and we believe they proved very successful.

Tapton House was included in the lease of one of the collieries, and as it was conveniently situated—being, as it were, a central point on the Midland Railway, from which the engineer could readily proceed north or south on his journeys of inspection of the various lines then under construction in the midland and northern counties—he took up his residence there, and it continued his home until the close of his life.

Tapton House is a large, roomy brick mansion, beautifully situated amid woods, upon a commanding eminence, about a mile to the northeast of the town of Chesterfield. Green fields dotted with fine trees slope away from the house in all directions. The surrounding country is undulating and highly picturesque. North and south the eye ranges over a vast extent of lovely scenery; and on the west, looking over the town of Chesterfield, with its church and crooked spire, the extensive range of the Derbyshire hills bounds the distance. The Midland Railway skirts the western edge of the park in a deep rock cutting, and the locomotive's shrill whistle sounds near at hand as the trains speed past. The gardens and pleasure-grounds adjoining the house were in a very neglected state when Mr. Stephenson first went to Tapton, and he promised himself, when he had secured rest and leisure from business, that he would put a new face upon both. The first improvement he made was in cutting a woodland footpath up the hill-side, by which he at the same time added a beautiful feature to the park, and secured a shorter road to the Chesterfield station; but it was some years before he found time to carry into effect his contemplated improvements in the adjoining gardens and pleasure-grounds. He had so long been accustomed to laborious pursuits, and felt himself still so full of work, that he could not at once settle down into the habit of quietly enjoying the fruits of his industry.

He had no difficulty in usefully employing his time. Besides directing the mining operations at Claycross, the establishment of the lime-kilns at Ambergate, and the construction of the extensive railways still in progress, he occasionally paid visits to Newcastle, where his locomotive manufactory was now in full work, and the proprietors were reaping the advantages of his early foresight in an abundant measure of prosperity. One of his most interesting visits to the place was in 1838, on the occasion of the meeting of the British Association there, when he acted as one of the Vice-Presidents in the section of Mechanical Science. Extraordinary changes had taken place in his own fortunes, as well as in the face of the country, since he had first appeared before a scientific body in Newcastle—the members of the Literary and Philosophical Institute—to submit his safety-lamp for their examination. Twenty-three years had passed over his head, full of honest work, of manful struggle, and the humble "colliery engine-wright of the name of Stephenson" had

FORTH-STREET WORKS, NEWCASTLE.

achieved an almost world-wide reputation as a public benefactor. His fellow-townsmen, therefore, could not hesitate to recognize his merits and do honor to his presence. During the sittings of the Association, the engineer took the opportunity of paying a visit to Killingworth, accompanied by some of the distinguished savans whom he numbered among his friends. He there pointed out to them, with a degree of honest pride, the cottage in which he had lived for so many years, showing what parts of it had been his handiwork, and told them the story of the sun-dial over the door, describing the study and the labor it had cost him and his son to calculate its dimensions and fix it in its place. The dial had been serenely numbering the hours through the busy years that had elapsed since that humble dwelling had been his home, during which the Killingworth locomotive had become a great working power, and its contriver had established the railway system, which was now rapidly becoming extended in all parts of the civilized world.

About the same time, his services were very much in request at the meetings of Mechanics' Institutes held throughout the northern counties. From a very early period in his history he had taken an active interest in these valuable institutions. While residing at Newcastle in 1824, shortly after his locomotive foundery had been started in Forth Street, he presided at a public meeting held in that town for the purpose of establishing a Mechanics' Institute. The meeting was held; but, as George Stephenson was a man comparatively unknown even in Newcastle at that time, his name failed to secure "an influential attendance." Among those who addressed the meeting on the occasion was Joseph Locke, then his pupil, and afterward his rival as an engineer. The local papers scarcely noticed the proceedings, yet the Mechanics' Instititute was founded and struggled into existence. Years passed, and it was felt to be an honor to secure Mr. Stephenson's presence at any public meetings held for the promotion of popular education. Among the Mechanics' Institutes in his immediate neighborhood at Tapton were those of Belper and Chesterfield, and at their soirées he was a frequent and a welcome visitor. On these occasions he loved to tell his auditors of the difficulties which had early beset him through want of knowledge, and of the means by which he had overcome them. His grand text was—PERSEVERE; and there was manhood in the word.

On more than one occasion the author had the pleasure of listening to George Stephenson's homely but forcible addresses at the annual soirées of the Leeds Mechanics' Institute. He was always an immense favorite with his audiences there. His personal appearance was greatly in his favor. A handsome, ruddy, expressive face, lit up by bright dark blue eyes, prepared one for his earnest words when he stood up to speak, and the cheers had subsided which invariably hailed his rising. He was not glib, but he was very impressive. And who, so well as he, could serve as a guide to the working-man in his endeavors after higher knowledge? His early life had been all struggle — encounter with difficulty—groping in the dark after greater light, but always earnestly and perseveringly. His words were therefore all the more weighty, since he spoke from the fullness of his own experience.

Nor did he remain a mere inactive spectator of the improvements in railway working which increasing experience from day to day suggested. He continued to contrive improvements in the locomotive, and to mature his invention of the carriage-brake. When examined before the Select Committee on Railways in 1841, his mind seems to have been impressed with the necessity which existed for adopting a system of self-acting brakes, stating that, in his opinion, this was the most important arrangement that could be provided for increasing the safety of railway traveling. "I believe," he said, "that if self-acting brakes were put upon every carriage, scarcely any accident could take place." His plan consisted in employing the momentum of the running train to throw his proposed brakes into action immediately on the moving power of the engine being checked. He would also have these brakes under the control of the guard, by means of a connecting line running along the whole length of the train, by which they should at once be thrown out of gear when necessary. At the same time he suggested, as an additional means of safety, that the signals of the line should be self-acting, and worked by the locomotives as they passed along the railway. He considered the adoption of this plan of so much importance that, with a view to the public safety, he would even have it enforced upon railway companies by the Legislature. He was also of opinion that it was the interest of the companies themselves to adopt the plan, as it would save great tear and wear of engines, carriages, tenders, and brake-vans, besides greatly diminishing the risk of accidents upon railways.

While before the same committee, he took the opportunity of stating his views with reference to railway speeds, about which wild ideas were then afloat, one gentleman of celebrity having publicly expressed the opinion that a speed of a hundred miles an hour was practicable in railway traveling! Not many years had passed since Mr. Stephenson had been pronounced *insane* for stating his conviction that twelve miles an hour could be performed by the locomotive; but, now that he had established the fact, and greatly exceeded that speed, he was thought behind the age because he recommended it to be limited to forty miles an hour. He said: "I do not like either forty or fifty miles an hour upon any line—I think it is an unnecessary speed; and if there is danger upon a railway, it is high velocity that creates it. I should say no railway ought to exceed forty miles an hour on the most favorable gradient; but upon a curved line the speed ought not to exceed twenty-four or twenty-five miles an hour." He had, indeed, constructed for the Great Western Railway an engine capable of running fifty miles an hour with a load, and eighty miles without one. But he never was in favor of a hurricane speed of this sort, believing it could only be accomplished at an unnecessary increase both of danger and expense.

"It is true," he observed on other occasions,* "I have said the locomotive engine *might* be made to travel a hundred miles an hour, but I always put a qualification on this, namely, as to what speed would best suit the public. The public may, however, be unreasonable; and fifty or sixty miles an hour *is* an unreasonable speed. Long before railway traveling became general, I said to my friends that there was no limit to the speed of the locomotive, *provided the works could be made to stand.* But there are limits to the strength of iron, whether it be manufactured into rails or locomotives, and there is a point at which both rails and tires must break. Every increase of speed, by increasing the strain upon the road and the rolling stock, brings us nearer to that point. At thirty miles a slighter road will do, and less perfect rolling stock may be run upon it with safety. But if you increase the speed by say ten miles, then every thing must be greatly strengthened. You must have heavier engines, heavier and better-fastened rails, and all your working expenses will be immensely increased. I think I know enough of mechanics to know where to stop. I know that a pound will weigh a pound, and that more should not be put upon an iron rail than it will bear. If you could insure perfect iron, perfect rails, and perfect locomotives, I grant fifty miles an hour or more might be run with safety on a level railway. But then you must not forget

* It may be mentioned that these views were communicated to the author by Robert Stephenson, and noted down in his presence.

that iron, even the best, will 'tire,' and with constant use will become more and more liable to break at the weakest point—perhaps where there is a secret flaw that the eye can not detect. Then look at the rubbishy rails now manufactured on the contract system—some of them little better than cast metal: indeed, I have seen rails break merely on being thrown from the truck on to the ground. How is it possible for such rails to stand a twenty or thirty ton engine dashing over them at the speed of fifty miles an hour? No, no," he would conclude, "I am in favor of low speeds because they are safe, and because they are economical; and you may rely upon it that, beyond a certain point, with every increase of speed there is a certain increase in the element of danger."

When railways became the subject of popular discussion, many new and unsound theories were started with reference to them, which Stephenson opposed as calculated, in his opinion, to bring discredit on the locomotive system. One of these was with reference to what were called "undulating lines." Dr. Lardner, who at an earlier period was skeptical as to the powers of the locomotive, now promulgated the idea that a railway constructed with rising and falling gradients would be practically as easy to work as a line perfectly level. Mr. Badnell went even beyond him, for he held that an undulating railway was much better than a level one for purposes of working.* For a time this theory found favor, and the "undulating system" was extensively adopted; but George Stephenson never ceased to inveigh against it, and experience has proved that his judgment was correct. His practice, from the beginning of his career until the end of it, was to secure a road as nearly as possible on a level, following the course of the valleys and the natural line of the country; preferring to go round a hill rather than to tunnel under it or carry his railway over it, and often making a considerable circuit to secure good workable gradients. He studied to lay out his lines so that long trains of minerals and merchandise, as well as passengers, might be hauled along them at the least possible expenditure of locomotive power. He had long before ascertained, by careful experiments at Killingworth, that the engine expends half its power in overcoming a rising gradient of 1 in 260, which

* "Treatise on Railway Improvements." By Mr. Richard Badnell, C.E.

is about 20 feet in the mile; and that when the gradient is so steep as 1 in 100, not less than three fourths of its power is sacrificed in ascending the acclivity. He never forgot the valuable practical lessons taught him by these early trials, which he had made and registered long before the advantages of railways had become recognized. He saw clearly that the longer flat line must eventually prove superior to the shorter line of steep gradients as respected its paying qualities. He urged that, after all, the power of the locomotive was but limited; and, although he and his son had done more than any other men to increase its working capacity, it provoked him to find that every improvement made in it was neutralized by the steep gradients which the new school of engineers were setting it to overcome. On one occasion, when Robert Stephenson stated before a Parliamentary committee that every successive improvement in the locomotive was being rendered virtually nugatory by the difficult and almost impracticable gradients proposed on many of the new lines, his father, on his leaving the witness-box, went up to him, and said, "Robert, you never spoke truer words than those in all your life."

To this it must be added, that in urging these views George Stephenson was strongly influenced by commercial considerations. He had no desire to build up his reputation at the expense of railway shareholders, nor to obtain engineering *éclat* by making "ducks and drakes" of their money. He was persuaded that, in order to secure the practical success of railways, they must be so laid out as not only to prove of decided public utility, but also to be worked economically and to the advantage of their proprietors. They were not government roads, but private ventures—in fact, commercial speculations. He therefore endeavored to render them financially profitable; and he repeatedly declared that if he did not believe they could be "made to pay," he would have nothing to do with them.* Nor was he influenced by the sordid

* He often refused to act as engineer for lines which he thought would not prove remunerative, or when he considered the estimates too low. Thus, when giving evidence on the Great Western Bill, Stephenson said, "I made out an estimate for the Hartlepool Railway, which they returned on account of its being too high, but I declined going to Parliament with a lower estimate. Another engineer was employed. Then, again, I was consulted about a line from Edinburg to Glasgow. The directors chalked out a line and sent it to me, and I told them I could not support it in that

consideration merely of what he could *make* out of any company that employed him, but in many cases he voluntarily gave up his claim to remuneration where the promoters of schemes which he thought praiseworthy had suffered serious loss. Thus, when the first application was made to Parliament for the Chester and Birkenhead Railway Bill, the promoters were defeated. They repeated their application on the understanding that in event of their succeeding the engineer and surveyor were to be paid their costs in respect of the defeated measure. The bill was successful, and to several parties their costs were paid. Stephenson's amounted to £800, and he very nobly said, "You have had an expensive career in Parliament; you have had a great struggle; you are a young company; you can not afford to pay me this amount of money; I will reduce it to £200, and I will not ask you for the £200 until your shares are at £20 premium; for, whatever may be the reverses you have to go through, I am satisfied I shall live to see the day when your shares will be at £20 premium, and when I can legally and honorably claim that £200."* We may add that the shares did eventually rise to the premium specified, and the engineer was no loser by his generous conduct in the transaction.

Another novelty of the time with which George Stephenson had to contend was the proposed substitution of atmospheric pressure for locomotive steam-power in the working of railways. The idea of obtaining motion by means of atmospheric pressure originated with Denis Papin more than a century and a half ago; but it slept until revived in 1810 by Mr. Medhurst, who published a pamphlet to prove the practicability of carrying letters and goods by air. In 1824, Mr. Vallance, of Brighton, took out a patent for projecting passengers through a tube large enough to contain a train of carriages, the tube ahead of the carriages being previously exhausted of its atmospheric air. The same idea was afterward taken up, in 1835, by Mr. Pinkus, an ingenious American. Several scientific gentlemen, Dr. Lardner and Mr. Clegg among others, advocated the plan, and an association was

case." Hence the employment of another engineer to carry out the line which Stephenson could not conscientiously advocate.

* Speech of Wm. Jackson, Esq., M.P., at the meeting of the Chester and Birkenhead Railway Company, held at Liverpool, October, 1845.

formed to carry it into effect. Shares were created, and £18,000 raised; and a model apparatus was exhibited in London. Mr. Vignolles took Mr. Stephenson to see the model; and after carefully examining it, he observed emphatically, "*It won't do:* it is only the fixed engines and ropes over again, in another form; and, to tell you the truth, I don't think this rope of wind will answer so well as the rope of wire did." He did not think the principle would stand the test of practice, and he objected to the mode of applying the principle. The stationary-engine system was open to serious objections in whatever form applied; and every day's experience showed that the fixed engines could not compete with locomotives in point of efficiency and economy. Stephenson stood by the locomotive engine, and subsequent experience proved that he was right.

Messrs. Clegg and Samuda afterward, in 1840, patented their plan of an atmospheric railway, and they publicly tested its working on a portion of the West London Railway. The results of the experiment were considered so satisfactory, that the directors of the Dublin and Kingstown line adopted it between Kingstown and Dalkey. The London and Croydon Company also adopted the atmospheric principle; and their line was opened in 1845. The ordinary mode of applying the power was to lay between the line of rails a pipe, in which a large piston was inserted, and attached by a shaft to the framework of a carriage. The propelling power was the ordinary pressure of the atmosphere acting against the piston in the tube on one side, a vacuum being created in the tube on the other side of the piston by the working of a stationary engine. Great was the popularity of the atmospheric system; and still George Stephenson said, "It won't do; it's but a gimcrack." Engineers of distinction said he was prejudiced, and that he looked upon the locomotive as a pet child of his own. "Wait a little," he replied, "and you will see that I am right." It was generally supposed that the locomotive system was about to be snuffed out. "Not so fast," said Stephenson. "Let us wait to see if it will pay." He never believed it would. It was ingenious, clever, scientific, and all that; but railways were commercial enterprises, not toys; and if the atmospheric railway could not work to a profit, it would not do. Considered in this light, he even went so far as to call it "a great humbug."

No one can say that the atmospheric railway had not a fair trial. The government engineer, General Pasley, did for it what had never been done for the locomotive—he reported in its favor, whereas a former government engineer had inferentially reported against the use of locomotive power on railways. The House of Commons had also reported in favor of the use of the steam-engine on common roads; yet the railway locomotive had vitality enough in it to live through all. "Nothing will beat it," said George Stephenson, "for efficiency in all weathers, for economy in drawing loads of average weight, and for power and speed as occasion may require."

The atmospheric system was fairly and fully tried, and it was found wanting. It was admitted to be an exceedingly elegant mode of applying power; its devices were very skillful, and its mechanism was most ingenious. But it was costly, irregular in action, and, in particular kinds of weather, not to be depended upon. At best, it was but a modification of the stationary-engine system, and experience proved it to be so expensive that it was shortly after entirely abandoned in favor of locomotive power.*

One of the remarkable results of the system of railway locomotion which George Stephenson had by his persevering labors mainly contributed to establish was the outbreak of the railway mania toward the close of his professional career. The success of the first main lines of railway naturally led to their extension into many new districts; but a strongly speculative tendency soon began to display itself, which contained in it the elements of great danger.

The extension of railways had, up to the year 1844, been mainly effected by men of the commercial classes, and the shareholders in them principally belonged to the manufacturing districts—the capitalists of the metropolis as yet holding aloof, and prophesying disaster to all concerned in railway projects. The Stock Exchange looked askance upon them, and it was with difficulty

* The question of the specific merits of the atmospheric as compared with the fixed engine and locomotive systems will be found fully discussed in Robert Stephenson's able "Report on the Atmospheric Railway System, 1844, in which he gave the result of numerous observations and experiments made by him on the Kingstown Atmospheric Railway, with the object of ascertaining whether the new power would be applicable for the working of the Chester and Holyhead Railway then under construction. His opinion was decidedly against the atmospheric system.

that respectable brokers could be found to do business in the shares. But when the lugubrious anticipations of the City men were found to be so entirely falsified by the results—when, after the lapse of years, it was ascertained that railway traffic rapidly increased and dividends steadily improved—a change came over the spirit of the London capitalists. They then invested largely in railways, the shares in which became a leading branch of business on the Stock Exchange, and the prices of some rose to nearly double their original value.

A stimulus was thus given to the projection of farther lines, the shares in most of which came out at a premium, and became the subject of immediate traffic. A reckless spirit of gambling set in, which completely changed the character and objects of railway enterprise. The public outside the Stock Exchange became also infected, and many persons utterly ignorant of railways, but hungering and thirsting after premiums, rushed eagerly into the vortex. They applied for allotments, and subscribed for shares in lines, of the engineering character or probable traffic of which they knew nothing. Provided they could but obtain allotments which they could sell at a premium, and put the profit—in many cases the only capital they possessed*—into their pockets, it was enough for them. The mania was not confined to the precincts of the Stock Exchange, but infected all ranks. It embraced merchants and manufacturers, gentry and shop-keepers, clerks in public offices, and loungers at the clubs. Noble lords were pointed at as "stags;" there were even clergymen who were characterized as "bulls," and amiable ladies who had the reputation of "bears," in the share-markets. The few quiet men who remained uninfluenced by the speculation of the time were, in not a few cases, even reproached for doing injustice to their families in declining to help themselves from the stores of wealth that were poured out on all sides.

Folly and knavery were for a time in the ascendant. The sharpers of society were let loose, and jobbers and schemers became more and more plentiful. They threw out railway schemes

* The Marquis of Clanricarde brought under the notice of the House of Lords, in 1845, that one Charles Guernsey, the son of a charwoman and a clerk in a broker's office at 12*s.* a week, had his name down as a subscriber for shares in the London and York line for £52,000.

as lures to catch the unwary. They fed the mania with a constant succession of new projects. The railway papers became loaded with their advertisements. The post-office was scarcely able to distribute the multitude of prospectuses and circulars which they issued. For a time their popularity was immense. They rose like froth into the upper heights of society, and the flunkey Fitz Plushe, by virtue of his supposed wealth, sat among peers and was idolized. Then was the harvest-time for scheming lawyers, Parliamentary agents, engineers, surveyors, and traffic-takers, who were ready to take up any railway scheme however desperate, and to prove any amount of traffic even where none existed. The traffic in the credulity of their dupes was, however, the great fact that mainly concerned them, and of the profitable character of which there could be no doubt.

Parliament, whose previous conduct in connection with railway legislation was so open to reprehension, interposed no check —attempted no remedy. On the contrary, it helped to intensify the evils arising from this unseemly state of things. Many of its members were themselves involved in the mania, and as much interested in its continuance as the vulgar herd of money-grubbers. The railway prospectuses now issued—unlike the original Liverpool and Manchester, and London and Birmingham schemes —were headed by peers, baronets, landed proprietors, and strings of M.P's. Thus it was found in 1845 that no fewer than 157 members of Parliament were on the lists of new companies as subscribers for sums ranging from £291,000 downward! The projectors of new lines even came to boast of their Parliamentary strength, and of the number of votes which they could command in "the House." At all events, it is matter of fact, that many utterly ruinous branches and extensions projected during the mania, calculated only to benefit the inhabitants of a few miserable boroughs accidentally omitted from Schedule A, were authorized in the memorable sessions of 1844 and 1845.

George Stephenson was anxiously entreated to lend his name to prospectuses during the railway mania, but he invariably refused. He held aloof from the headlong folly of the hour, and endeavored to check it, but in vain. Had he been less scrupulous, and given his countenance to the numerous projects about which he was consulted, he might, without any trouble, have thus secured enormous gains; but he had no desire to accumulate a fortune without labor and without honor. He himself never speculated in shares. When he was satisfied as to the merits of an undertaking, he would sometimes subscribe for a certain amount of capital in it, when he held on, neither buying nor selling. At a dinner of the Leeds and Bradford directors at Ben Rydding in October, 1844, before the mania had reached its height, he warned those present against the prevalent disposition toward railway speculation. It was, he said, like walking upon a piece of ice with shallows and deeps; the shallows were frozen over, and they would carry, but it required great caution to get over the deeps. He was satisfied that in the course of the next year many would step on to places not strong enough to carry them, and would get into the deeps; they would be taking shares, and afterward be unable to pay the calls upon them. Yorkshiremen were reckoned clever men, and his advice to them was to stick together and promote communication in their own neighborhood—not to go abroad with their speculations. If any had done so, he advised them to get their money back as fast as they could, for if they did not they would not get it at all. He informed the company, at the same time, of his earliest holding of railway shares; it was in the Stockton and Darlington Railway, and the number he held was *three*—"a very large capital for him to possess at the time." But a Stockton friend was anxious to possess a share, and he sold him *one* at a premium of 33*s.*; he supposed he had been about the first man in England to sell a railway share at a premium.

During 1845, his son's office in Great George Street, Westminster, was crowded with persons of various conditions seeking interviews, presenting very much the appearance of the levee of a minister of state. The burly figure of Mr. Hudson, the "Railway King," surrounded by an admiring group of followers, was often to be seen there; and a still more interesting person, in the estimation of many, was George Stephenson, dressed in black, his coat of somewhat old-fashioned cut, with square pockets in the tails. He wore a white neckcloth, and a large bunch of seals was suspended from his watch-ribbon. Altogether, he presented an appearance of health, intelligence, and good humor, that it gladdened one to look upon in that sordid, selfish, and eventually ruinous saturnalia of railway speculation.

Being still the consulting engineer of several of the older companies, he necessarily appeared before Parliament in support of their branches and extensions. In 1845 his name was associated with that of his son as the engineer of the Southport and Preston Junction. In the same session he gave evidence in favor of the Syston and Peterborough branch of the Midland Railway; but his principal attention was confined to the promotion of the line from Newcastle to Berwick, in which he had never ceased to take the deepest interest.

Powers were granted by Parliament in 1845 to construct not less than 2883 miles of new railways in Britain, at an expenditure of about forty-four millions sterling! Yet the mania was not appeased; for in the following session of 1846, applications were made to Parliament for powers to raise £389,000,000 sterling for the construction of farther lines; and they were actually conceded to the extent of 4790 miles (including 60 miles of tunnels), at a cost of about £120,000,000 sterling.* During this session Mr. Stephenson appeared as engineer for only one new line—the Buxton, Macclesfield, Congleton, and Crewe Railway—a line in which, as a coal-owner, he was personally interested; and of three branch lines in connection with existing companies for which he had long acted as engineer. At the same period all the leading professional men were fully occupied, some of them appearing as consulting engineers for upward of thirty lines each!

One of the features of this mania was the rage for "direct lines" which every where displayed itself. There were "Direct Manchester," "Direct Exeter," "Direct York," and, indeed, new direct lines between most of the large towns. The Marquis of Bristol, speaking in favor of the "Direct Norwich and London" project at a public meeting at Haverhill, said, "If necessary, they might *make a tunnel beneath his very drawing-room* rather than be defeated in their undertaking!" And the Rev. F. Litchfield, at a meeting in Banbury on the subject of a line to that town, said, "He had laid down for himself a limit to his approbation

* On the 17th of November, 1845, Mr. Spackman published a list of the lines *projected* (many of which were not afterward prosecuted), from which it appeared that there were then 620 new railway projects before the public, requiring a capital of £563,203,000.

of railways—at least of such as approached the neighborhood with which he was connected—and that limit was, that he did not wish them to approach any nearer to him than *to run through his bedroom, with the bedposts for a station!*" How different was the spirit which influenced these noble lords and gentlemen but a few years before!

The course adopted by Parliament in dealing with the multitude of railway bills applied for during the prevalence of the mania was as irrational as it proved unfortunate. The want of foresight displayed by both houses in obstructing the railway system so long as it was based upon sound commercial principles was only equaled by the fatal facility with which they now granted railway projects based upon the wildest speculation. Parliament interposed no check, laid down no principle, furnished no guidance, for the conduct of railway projectors, but left every company to select its own locality, determine its own line, and fix its own gauge. No regard was paid to the claims of existing companies, which had already expended so large an amount in the formation of useful railways; and speculators were left at liberty to project and carry out lines almost parallel with theirs.

The House of Commons became thoroughly influenced by the prevailing excitement. Even the Board of Trade began to favor the views of the new and reckless school of engineers. In their "Report on the Lines projected in the Manchester and Leeds District," they promulgated some remarkable views respecting gradients, declaring themselves in favor of the "undulating system." They there stated that lines of an undulating character "which gave gradients of 1 in 70 or 1 in 80 distributed over them in short lengths, may be positively *better* lines, *i. e., more susceptible of cheap and expeditious working*, than others which have nothing steeper than 1 in 100 or 1 in 120!" They concluded by reporting in favor of the line which exhibited the worst gradients and the sharpest curves, chiefly on the ground that it could be constructed for less money

Sir Robert Peel took occasion, when speaking in favor of the continuance of the Railways Department of the Board of Trade, to advert to this report in the House of Commons on the 4th of March following, as containing "a novel and highly important view on the subject of gradients, which, he was certain, never could have been taken by any committee of the House of Commons, however intelligent;" and he might have added, that the more intelligent, the less likely would they be to arrive at any such conclusion. When George Stephenson saw this report of the premier's speech in the newspapers of the following morning, he went forthwith to his son, and asked him to write a letter to Sir Robert Peel on the subject. He saw clearly that if such views were adopted, the utility and economy of railways would be seriously curtailed. "These members of Parliament," said he, "are now as much disposed to exaggerate the powers of the locomotive as they were to underestimate them but a few years ago." Robert accordingly wrote a letter for his father's signature, embodying the views which he so strongly entertained as to the importance of flat gradients, and referring to the experiments conducted by him many years before in proof of the great loss of working power which was incurred on a line of steep as compared with easy gradients. It was clear, from the tone of Sir Robert Peel's speech in a subsequent debate, that he had carefully read and considered Mr. Stephenson's practical observations on the subject, though it did not appear that he had come to any definite conclusion thereon farther than that he strongly approved of the Trent Valley Railway, by which Tamworth would be placed upon a direct main line of communication.

The result of the labors of Parliament was a tisue of legislative bungling, involving enormous loss to the nation. Railway bills were granted in heaps. Two hundred and seventy-two additional acts were passed in 1846. Some authorized the construction of lines running almost parallel with existing railways, in order to afford the public "the benefits of unrestricted competition." Locomotive and atmospheric lines, broad-gauge and narrow-gauge lines, were granted without hesitation. Committees decided without judgment and without discrimination; and in the scramble for bills, the most unscrupulous were usually the most successful. As an illustration of the legislative folly of the period, Robert Stephenson, speaking at Toronto, in Upper Canada, some years later, adduced the following instances:

"There was one district through which it was proposed to run two lines, and there was no other difficulty between them than the simple rivalry that, if one got a charter, the other might also. But here, where the committee might have given both, they gave neither. In another instance, two lines were projected through a barren country, and the committee gave the one which afforded the least accommodation to the public. In another, where two lines were projected to run, merely to shorten the time by a few minutes, leading through a mountainous country, the committee gave both. So that, where the committee might have given both, they gave neither, and where they should have given neither, they gave both."

Among the many ill effects of the mania, one of the worst was that it introduced a low tone of morality into railway transactions. The bad spirit which had been evoked by it unhappily extended to the commercial classes, and many of the most flagrant swindles of recent times had their origin in the year 1845. Those who had suddenly gained large sums without labor, and also without honor, were too ready to enter upon courses of the wildest extravagance; and a false style of living arose, the poisonous influence of which extended through all classes. Men began to look upon railways as instruments to job with. Persons sometimes possessing information respecting railways, but more frequently possessing none, got upon boards for the purpose of promoting their individual objects, often in a very unscrupulous manner; land-owners, to promote branch lines through their property; speculators in shares, to trade upon the exclusive information which they obtained; while some directors were appointed through the influence mainly of solicitors, contractors, or engineers, who used them as tools to serve their own ends. In this way the unfortunate proprietors were in many cases betrayed, and their property was shamefully squandered, much to the discredit of the railway system.

One of the most prominent celebrities of the mania was George Hudson, of York. He was a man of some local repute in that city when the line between Leeds and York was projected. His views as to railways were then extremely moderate, and his main object in joining the undertaking was to secure for York the advantages of the best railway communication. The company was not very prosperous at first, and during the years 1840 and 1841 the shares had greatly sunk in value. Mr. Alderman Meek, the first chairman, having retired, Mr. Hudson was elected in his stead, and he very shortly contrived to pay improved dividends to the proprietors, who asked no questions. Desiring to extend the field of his operations, he proceeded to lease the Leeds and Selby Railway at five per cent. That line had hitherto been a losing concern; so its owners readily struck a bargain with Mr. Hudson, and sounded his praises in all directions. He increased the dividends on the York and North Midland shares to ten per cent., and began to be cited as the model of a railway chairman.

He next interested himself in the North Midland Railway, where he appeared in the character of a reformer of abuses. The North Midland shares also had gone to a heavy discount, and the shareholders were accordingly desirous of securing his services. They elected him a director. His bustling, pushing, persevering character gave him an influential position at the board, and he soon pushed the old members from their stools. He labored hard, at much personal inconvenience, to help the concern out of its difficulties, and he succeeded. The new directors, recognizing his power, elected him their chairman.

Railways revived in 1842, and public confidence in them as profitable investments was gradually increasing. Mr. Hudson had the benefit of this growing prosperity. The dividends in his lines improved, and the shares rose in value. The Lord-mayor of York began to be quoted as one of the most capable of railway directors. Stimulated by his success and encouraged by his followers, he struck out or supported many new projects—a line to Scarborough, a line to Bradford, lines in the Midland districts, and lines to connect York with Newcastle and Edinburg. He was elected chairman of the Newcastle and Darlington Railway; and when—in order to complete the continuity of the main line of communication—it was found necessary to secure the Durham junction, which was an important link in the chain, he and George Stephenson boldly purchased that railway between them, at the price of £88,500. It was an exceedingly fortunate purchase for the company, to whom it was worth double the money. The act, though not strictly legal, proved successful in the issue, and was much lauded. Thus encouraged, Mr. Hudson proceeded to buy the Brandling Junction line for £500,000 in his own name—an operation at the time regarded as equally favorable, though he was afterward charged with appropriating 1600 of the shares created for the purchase, when worth £21 premium each. The

Great North of England line being completed, Mr. Hudson had thus secured the entire line of communication from York to Newcastle, and the route was opened to the public in June, 1844. On that occasion Newcastle eulogized Mr. Hudson in its choicest local eloquence, and he was pronounced to be the greatest benefactor the district had ever known.

The adulation which followed Mr. Hudson would have intoxicated a stronger and more self-denying man. He was pronounced the man of the age, and hailed as "the Railway King." The highest test by which the shareholders judged him was the dividends that he paid, though subsequent events proved that these dividends were in many cases delusive, intended only "to make things pleasant." The policy, however, had its effect. The shares in all the lines of which he was chairman went to a premium, and then arose the temptation to create new shares in branch and extension lines, often worthless, which were issued at a premium also. Thus he shortly found himself chairman of nearly 600 miles of railway, extending from Rugby to Newcastle, and at the head of numerous new projects, by means of which paper-wealth could be created as it were at pleasure. He held in his own hands almost the entire administrative power of the companies over which he presided: he was chairman, board, manager, and all. His admirers for the time, inspired sometimes by gratitude for past favors, but oftener by the expectation of favors to come, supported him in all his measures. At the meetings of the companies, if any suspicious shareholder ventured to put a question about the accounts, he was snubbed by the chair and hissed by the proprietors. The Railway King was voted praises, testimonials, and surplus shares alike liberally, and scarcely a word against him could find a hearing. He was equally popular outside the circle of railway proprietors. His entertainments at Albert Gate were crowded by sycophants, many of them titled; and he went his rounds of visits among the peerage like a prince.

Of course Mr. Hudson was a great authority on railway questions in Parliament, to which the burgesses of Sunderland had sent him. His experience of railways, still little understood, though the subject of so much legislation, gave value and weight to his opinions, and in many respects he was a useful member. During the first years of his membership he was chiefly occupied in passing the railway bills in which he was more particularly interested; and in the session of 1845, when he was at the height of his power, it was triumphantly said of him that "he walked quietly through Parliament with some sixteen railway bills under his arm."

One of these bills, however, was the subject of a severe contest—we mean that empowering the construction of the railway from Newcastle to Berwick. It was almost the only bill in which George Stephenson was concerned that year. Mr. Hudson displayed great energy in supporting the measure, and he worked hard to insure its success both in and out of Parliament; but he himself attributed the chief merit to Stephenson. He accordingly suggested to the shareholders that they should present the engineer with some fitting testimonial in recognition of his services. Indeed, a Stephenson Testimonial had long been spoken of, and a committee was formed for raising subscriptions for the purpose as early as the year 1839. Mr. Hudson now revived the subject, and appealed to the Newcastle and Darlington, the Midland, and the York and North Midland Companies, who unanimously adopted the resolutions which he proposed to them amid "loud applause," but there the matter ended.

The Hudson Testimonial was a much more taking thing, for Hudson had it in his power to allot shares (selling at a premium) to his adulators. But Stephenson pretended to fill no man's pocket with premiums; he was no creator of shares, and could not therefore work upon shareholders' gratitude for "favors to come." The proposed testimonial to him accordingly ended with resolutions and speeches. The York, Newcastle, and Berwick Board — in other words, Mr. Hudson — did indeed mark their sense of the "great obligations" which they were under to George Stephenson for helping to carry their bill through Parliament by making him an allotment of thirty of the new shares authorized by the act. But, as afterward appeared, the chairman had at the same time appropriated to himself not fewer than 10,894 of the same shares, the premiums on which were then worth, in the market, about £145,000. This shabby manner of acknowledging the gratitude of the company to their engineer was strongly resented by Stephenson at the time, and a coolness took place between him and Hudson which was never wholly removed, though they afterward shook hands, and Stephenson declared that all was forgotten.

Mr. Hudson's brief reign drew to a close. The saturnalia of 1845 was followed by the usual reaction. Shares went down faster than they had gone up; the holders of them hastened to sell in order to avoid payment of the calls, and many found themselves ruined. Then came repentance, and a sudden return to virtue. The betting man, who, temporarily abandoning the turf for the share-market, had played his heaviest stake and lost; the merchant who had left his business, and the doctor who had neglected his patients, to gamble in railway stock and been ruined; the penniless knaves and schemers who had speculated so recklessly and gained so little; the titled and fashionable people, who had bowed themselves so low before the idol of the day, and found themselves deceived and "done;" the credulous small capitalists, who, dazzled by premiums, had invested their all in railway shares, and now saw themselves stripped of every thing, were grievously enraged, and looked about them for a victim. In this temper were shareholders when, at a railway meeting in York, some pertinent questions were put to the Railway King. His replies were not satisfactory, and the questions were pushed home. Mr. Hudson became confused. Angry voices rose in the meeting. A committee of investigation was appointed. The golden calf was found to be of brass, and hurled down, Hudson's own toadies and sycophants eagerly joining the chorus of popular indignation. Similar proceedings shortly after followed at the meetings of other companies, and the bubbles having by that time burst, the Railway Mania thus came to an ignominious end.

While the mania was at its height in England, railways were also being extended abroad, and George Stephenson continued to be invited to give the directors of foreign undertakings the benefit of his advice. One of the most agreeable of his excursions with that object was his third visit to Belgium in 1845. His special purpose was to examine the proposed line of the Sambre and Meuse Railway, for which a concession had been granted by the Belgian Legislature. Arrived on the ground, he went carefully over the entire length of the proposed line, by Couvins, through the Forest of Ardennes, to Rocroi, across the French frontier, examining the bearing of the coal-field, the slate and marble quarries, and the numerous iron-mines in existence between the Sambre and the Meuse, as well as carefully exploring the ravines which extended through the district, in order to satisfy himself that the best possible route had been selected. Stephenson was delighted with the novelty of the journey, the beauty of the scenery, and the industry of the population. His companions were entertained by his ample and varied stores of practical information on all subjects, and his conversation was full of reminiscences of his youth, on which he always delighted to dwell when in the society of his more intimate friends. The journey was varied by a visit to the coal-mines near Jemappe, where Stephenson examined with interest the mode adopted by the Belgian miners of draining the pits, inspecting their engines and brakeing machines, so familiar to him in early life.

The engineers of Belgium took the opportunity of the engineer's visit to invite him to a magnificent banquet at Brussels. The Public Hall, in which they entertained him, was gayly decorated with flags, prominent among which was the Union Jack, in honor of their distinguished guest. A handsome marble pedestal, ornamented with his bust crowned with laurels, stood at one end of the room. The chair was occupied by M. Massui, the Chief Director of the National Railways of Belgium; and the most eminent scientific men of the kingdom were present. Their reception of the "father of railways" was of the most enthusiastic description. Stephenson was greatly pleased with the entertainment. Not the least interesting incident of the evening was his observing, when the dinner was about half over, the model of a locomotive engine placed upon the centre table, under a triumphal arch. Turning suddenly to his friend Sopwith, he exclaimed, "Do you see the 'Rocket?'" It was, indeed, the model of that celebrated locomotive; and the engineer prized the delicate compliment thus paid him perhaps more than all the encomiums of the evening.

The next day (April 5th) King Leopold invited him to a private interview at the palace. Accompanied by Mr. Sopwith, he proceeded to Laaken, and was cordially received by his majesty. The king immediately entered into familiar conversation with him, discussing first the railway project which had been the object of his visit to Belgium, and then the structure of the Belgian coal-fields, his majesty expressing his sense of the great importance of economy in a fuel which had become indispensable to the comfort and well-being of society, which was the basis of all manufactures, and the vital power of railway locomotion. The subject was always a favorite one with George Stephenson, and, encouraged by the king, he proceeded to explain to him the geological structure of Belgium, the original formation of coal, its subsequent elevation by volcanic forces, and the vast amount of denudation. In describing the coal-beds he used his hat as a sort of model to illustrate his meaning, and the eyes of the king were fixed upon it as he proceeded with his description. The conversation then passed to the rise and progress of trade and manufactures, Stephenson pointing out how closely they every where followed the coal, being mainly dependent upon it, as it were, for their very existence.

The king seemed greatly pleased with the interview, and at its close expressed himself as obliged by the interesting information which the engineer had communicated. Shaking hands cordially with both the gentlemen, and wishing them success in their important undertakings, he bade them adieu. As they were leaving the palace, Stephenson, bethinking him of the model by which he had just been illustrating the Belgian coal-fields, said to his friend, "By-the-by, Sopwith, I was afraid the king would see the inside of my hat; it's a shocking bad one!"

George Stephenson paid a farther visit to Belgium in the course of the same year, on the business of the West Flanders Railway, and he had scarcely returned from it ere he was requested to proceed to Spain, for the purpose of examining and reporting upon a scheme then on foot for constructing "the Royal North of Spain Railway." A concession had been made by the Spanish government of a line of railway from Madrid to the Bay of Biscay, and a numerous staff of engineers was engaged in surveying the proposed line. The directors of the company had declined making the necessary deposits until more favorable terms had been secured; and Sir Joshua Walmsley, on their part, was about to visit Spain and press the government on the subject. George Stephenson, whom he consulted, was alive to the difficulties of the office which Sir Joshua was induced to undertake, and offered to be his companion and adviser on the occasion, declining to receive any recompense beyond the simple expenses of the journey. He could only arrange to be absent for six weeks, and he set out from England about the middle of September, 1845.

The party was joined at Paris by Mr. Mackenzie, the contractor for the Orleans and Tours Railway, then in course of construction, who took them over the works and accompanied them as far as Tours. They soon reached the great chain of the Pyrenees, and crossed over into Spain. It was on a Sunday evening, after a long day's toilsome journey through the mountains, that the party suddenly found themselves in one of those beautiful secluded valleys lying amid the Western Pyrenees. A small hamlet lay before them, consisting of some thirty or forty houses and a fine old church. The sun was low on the horizon, and under the wide porch, beneath the shadow of the church, were seated nearly all the inhabitants of the place. They were dressed in their holiday attire. The bright bits of red and amber color in the dresses of the women, and the gay sashes of the men, formed a striking picture, on which the travelers gazed in silent admiration. It was something entirely novel and unexpected. Beside the villagers sat two venerable old men, whose canonical hats indicated their quality as village pastors. Two groups of young women and children were dancing outside the porch to the accompaniment of a simple pipe, and within a hundred yards of them some of the youths of the village were disporting themselves in athletic exercises, the whole being carried on beneath the fostering care of the old church, and with the sanction of its ministers. It was a beautiful scene, and deeply moved the travelers as they approached the principal group. The villagers greeted them courteously, supplied their present wants, and pressed upon them some fine melons, brought from their adjoining gardens. George Stephenson used afterward to look back upon that simple scene, and speak of it as one of the most charming pastorals he had ever witnessed.

They shortly reached the site of the proposed railway, passing through Irun, St. Sebastian, St. Andero, and Bilbao, at which places they met deputations of the principal inhabitants who were interested in the object of their journey. At Raynosa Stephenson carefully examined the mountain passes and ravines through which a railway could be made. He rose at break of day, and surveyed until the darkness set in, and frequently his resting-place at night was the floor of some miserable hovel. He was thus laboriously occupied for ten days, after which he proceeded across the province of Old Castile toward Madrid, surveying as he went. The proposed plan included the purchase of the Castile Canal, and that property was also examined. He next proceeded to El Escorial, situated at the foot of the Guadarama Mountains, through which he found it would be necessary to construct two formidable tunnels; added to which, he ascertained that the country between El Escorial and Madrid was of a very difficult and expensive character to work through. Taking these circumstances into account, and looking at the expected traffic on the proposed line, Sir Joshua Walmsley, acting under the advice of Mr. Stephenson, offered to construct the line from Madrid to the Bay of Biscay on condition that the requisite land was given to the company for the purpose; that they should be allowed every facility for cutting such timber belonging to the crown as might be required for the purposes of the railway; and also that the materials required from abroad for the construction of the line should be admitted free of duty. In return for these concessions the company offered to clothe and feed several thousand convicts while engaged in the execution of the earthworks. General Narvaez, afterward Duke of Valencia, received Sir Joshua Walmsley and Mr. Stephenson on the subject of their proposition, and expressed his willingness to close with them; but it was necessary that other influential parties should give their concurrence before the scheme could be carried into effect. The deputation waited ten days to receive the answer of the Spanish government, but no answer of any kind was vouchsafed. The authorities, indeed, invited them to be present at a Spanish bull-fight, but that was not quite the business Stephenson had gone all the way to Spain to transact, and the offer was politely declined. The result was that Stephenson dissuaded his friend from making the necessary deposit at Madrid. Besides, he had by this time formed an unfavorable opinion of the entire project, and considered that the traffic would not amount to one eighth of the estimate.

Mr. Stephenson was now anxious to be in England. During the journey from Madrid he often spoke with affection of friends and relatives, and when apparently absorbed by other matters he would revert to what he thought might then be passing at home.

Few incidents worthy of notice occurred on the journey homeward, but one may be mentioned. While traveling in an open conveyance between Madrid and Vittoria, the driver urged his mules down hill at a dangerous pace. He was requested to slacken speed; but, suspecting his passengers to be afraid, he only flogged the brutes into a still more furious gallop. Observing this, Stephenson coolly said, "Let us try him on the other tack; tell him to show us the fastest pace at which Spanish mules can go." The rogue of a driver, when he found his tricks of no avail, pulled up and proceeded at a more moderate speed for the rest of the journey.

Urgent business required Mr. Stephenson's presence in London on the last day of November. They traveled, therefore, almost continuously, day and night, and the fatigue consequent on the journey, added to the privations endured by the engineer while carrying on the survey among the Spanish mountains, began to tell seriously on his health. By the time he reached Paris he was evidently ill, but he nevertheless determined on proceeding. He reached Havre in time for the Southampton boat, but when on board pleurisy developed itself, and it was necessary to bleed him freely. After a few weeks' rest at home, however, he gradually recovered, though his health remained severely shaken.

CLAYCROSS WORKS.

NEWCASTLE, FROM THE HIGH-LEVEL BRIDGE. [By R. P. Leitch.]

CHAPTER XVII.

ROBERT STEPHENSON'S CAREER—THE STEPHENSONS AND BRUNEL—EAST COAST ROUTE TO SCOTLAND—ROYAL BORDER BRIDGE, BERWICK—HIGH-LEVEL BRIDGE, NEWCASTLE.

THE career of George Stephenson was drawing to a close. He had for some time been gradually retiring from the more active pursuit of railway engineering, and confining himself to the promotion of only a few undertakings, in which he took a more than ordinary personal interest. In 1840, when the extensive main lines in the Midland districts had been finished and opened for traffic, he publicly expressed his intention of withdrawing from the profession. He had reached sixty, and, having spent the greater part of his life in very hard work, he naturally desired rest and retirement in his old age. There was the less necessity for his continuing "in harness," as Robert Stephenson was now in full career as a leading railway engineer, and his father had pleasure in handing over to him, with the sanction of the companies concerned, nearly all the railway appointments which he held.

Robert Stephenson amply repaid his father's care. The sound education of which he had laid the foundations at school, improved by his subsequent culture, but more than all by his father's example of application, industry, and thoroughness in all that he undertook, told powerfully in the formation of his character not less than in the discipline of his intellect. His father had early implanted in him habits of mental activity, familiarized him with the laws of mechanics, and carefully trained and stimulated his inventive faculties, the first great fruits of which, as we have seen, were exhibited in the triumph of the "Rocket" at Rainhill. "I am fully conscious in my own mind," said the son at a meeting of the Mechanical Engineers at Newcastle in 1858, "how greatly my civil engineering has been regulated and influenced by the mechanical knowledge which I derived directly from my father; and the more my experience has advanced, the more convinced I have become that it is necessary to educate an engineer in the workshop. That is, emphatically, the education which will render the engineer most intelligent, most useful, and the fullest of resources in times of difficulty."

Robert Stephenson was but twenty-six years old when the performances of the "Rocket" established the practicability of steam locomotion on railways. He was shortly after appointed engineer of the Leicester and Swannington Railway; after which, at his father's request, he was made joint engineer with himself in laying out the London and Birmingham Railway, and the execution of that line was afterward intrusted to him as sole engineer. The stability and excellence of the works of that railway, the difficulties which had been successfully overcome in the course of its construction, and the judgment which was displayed by Robert Stephenson throughout the whole conduct of the undertaking to its completion, established his reputation as an engineer, and his father could now look with confidence and pride upon his son's achievements. From that time forward, father and son worked together cordially, each jealous of the other's honor; and on the father's retirement it was generally recognized that, in the sphere of railways, Robert Stephenson was the foremost man, the safest guide, and the most active worker.

Robert Stephenson was subsequently appointed engineer of the Eastern Counties, the Northern and Eastern, and the Blackwall Railways, besides many lines in the midland and southern districts. When the speculation of 1844 set in, his services were, of course, greatly in request. Thus, in one session, we find him engaged as engineer for not fewer than thirty-three new schemes.

Projectors thought themselves fortunate who could secure his name, and he had only to propose his terms to obtain them. The work which he performed at this period of his life was indeed enormous, and his income was large beyond any previous instance of engineering gain. But much of the labor done was mere hackwork of a very uninteresting character. During the sittings of the committees of Parliament, much time was also occupied in consultations, and in preparing evidence or in giving it.

The crowded, low-roofed committee-rooms of the old houses of Parliament were altogether inadequate to accommodate the press of perspiring projectors of bills, and even the lobbies were sometimes choked with them. To have borne that noisome atmosphere and heat would have tested the constitutions of salamanders, and engineers were only human. With brains kept in a state of excitement during the entire day, no wonder their nervous systems became unstrung. Their only chance of refreshment was during an occasional rush to the bun and sandwich stand in the lobby, though sometimes even that resource failed them. Then, with mind and body jaded—probably after undergoing a series of consultations upon many bills after the rising of the committees—the exhausted engineers would seek to stimulate nature by a late, perhaps a heavy dinner. What chance had any ordinary constitution of surviving such an ordeal? The consequence was, that stomach, brain, and liver were alike injured, and hence the men who bore the heat and brunt of those struggles—Stephenson, Brunel, Locke, and Errington—have already all died, comparatively young men.

In mentioning the name of Brunel, we are reminded of him as the principal rival and competitor of Robert Stephenson. Both were the sons of distinguished men, and both inherited the fame and followed in the footsteps of their fathers. The Stephensons were inventive, practical, and sagacious; the Brunels ingenious, imaginative, and daring. The former were as thoroughly English in their characteristics as the latter perhaps were as thoroughly French. The fathers and the sons were alike successful in their works, though not in the same degree. Measured by practical and profitable results, the Stephensons were unquestionably the safer men to follow.

Robert Stephenson and Isambard Kingdom Brunel were destined often to come into collision in the course of their professional life. Their respective railway districts "marched" with each other, and it became their business to invade or defend those districts, according as the policy of their respective boards might direct. The gauge of 7 feet fixed by Brunel for the Great Western Railway, so entirely different from that of 4 feet 8½ inches adopted by the Stephensons on the Northern and Midland lines,* was from the first a great cause of contention. But Brunel had always an aversion to follow any man's lead; and that another engineer had fixed the gauge of a railway, or built a bridge, or designed an engine in one way, was of itself often a sufficient reason with him for adopting an altogether different course. Robert Stephenson, on his part, though less bold, was more practical, preferring to follow the old routes, and to tread in the safe steps of his father.

Mr. Brunel, however, determined that the Great Western should be a giant's road, and that traveling should be conducted upon it at double speed. His ambition was to make the *best* road that imagination could devise, whereas the main object of the Ste-

* The original width of the coal tram-roads in the North virtually determined the British gauge. It was the width of the ordinary road-track—not fixed after any scientific theory, but adopted simply because its use had already been established. George Stephenson introduced it without alteration on the Liverpool and Manchester Railway, and the lines subsequently formed in that district were laid down of the same width. Stephenson from the first anticipated the general extension of railways throughout England, and one of the ideas with which he started was the essential importance of preserving such a uniformity as would admit of perfect communication between them. When consulted about the gauge of the Canterbury and Whitstable, and Leicester and Swannington Railways, he said, "Make them of the same width: though they may be a long way apart now, depend upon it they will be joined together some day." All the railways, therefore, laid down by himself and his assistants in the neighborhood of Manchester, extending from thence to London on the south, and to Leeds on the east, were constructed on the Liverpool and Manchester, or narrow gauge. Besides the Great Western Railway, where the gauge adopted was seven feet, the only other line on which a broader gauge than four feet eight and a half inches was adopted was the Eastern Counties, where it was five feet, Mr. Braithwaite, the engineer, being of opinion that an increase of three and a half inches in the width of the line would afford better space for the machinery of the locomotive. But when the northern and eastern extension of the same line was formed, which was to work into the narrow-gauge system of the Midland Railway, Robert Stephenson, its new engineer, strongly recommended the directors of the Eastern Counties Line to alter their gauge accordingly, for the purpose of securing uniformity, and they adopted his recommendation.

phensons, both father and son, was to make a road that would *pay*. Although, tried by the Stephenson test, Brunel's magnificent road was a failure so far as the shareholders in the Great Western Company were concerned, the stimulus which his ambitious designs gave to mechanical invention at the time proved a general good. The narrow-gauge engineers exerted themselves to quicken their locomotives to the utmost. They improved and reimproved them. The machinery was simplified and perfected. Outside cylinders gave place to inside; the steadier and more rapid and effective action of the engine was secured, and in a few years the highest speed on railways went up from thirty to about fifty miles an hour. For this rapidity in progress we are in no small degree indebted to the stimulus imparted to the narrow-gauge engineers by Mr. Brunel.

It was one of the characteristics of Brunel to *believe* in the success of the schemes for which he was professionally engaged as engineer, and he proved this by investing his savings largely in the Great Western Railway, in the South Devon Atmospherical line, and in the Great Eastern steam-ship, with what results are well known. Robert Stephenson, on the contrary, with characteristic caution, toward the latter years of his life avoided holding unguaranteed railway shares; and though he might execute magnificent structures, such as the Victoria Bridge across the St. Lawrence, he was careful not to embark any portion of his own fortune in the ordinary capital of these concerns. In 1845 he shrewdly foresaw the inevitable crash that was about to succeed the mania of that year, and while shares were still at a premium he took the opportunity of selling out all that he held. He urged his father to do the same thing, but George's reply was characteristic. "No," said he, "I took my shares for an investment, and not to speculate with, and I am not going to sell them now because people have gone mad about railways." The consequence was, that he continued to hold the £60,000 which he had invested in the shares of various railways until his death, when they were at once sold out by his son, though at a great depreciation on their original cost.

One of the hardest battles fought between the Stephensons and Brunel was for the railway between Newcastle and Berwick, forming part of the great East Coast route to Scotland. As early as 1836 George Stephenson had surveyed two lines to connect Edinburg with Newcastle: one by Berwick and Dunbar along the coast, and the other, more inland, by Carter Fell, up the vale of the Gala, to the northern capital. Two years later he made a farther examination of the intervening country, and reported in favor of the coast line. The inland route, however, was not without its advocates. But both projects lay dormant for several years longer, until the completion of the Midland and other main lines as far north as Newcastle had the effect of again reviving the subject of the extension of the route as far as Edinburg.

On the 18th of June, 1844, the Newcastle and Darlington line —an important link of the great main highway to the north— was completed and publicly opened, thus connecting the Thames and the Tyne by a continuous line of railway. On that day George Stephenson and a distinguished party of railway men traveled by express train from London to Newcastle in about nine hours. It was a great event, and was worthily celebrated. The population of Newcastle held holiday; and a banquet given in the Assembly Rooms the same evening assumed the form of an ovation to Mr. Stephenson and his son.

After the opening of this railway, the project of the East Coast line from Newcastle to Berwick was revived, and George Stephenson, who had already identified himself with the question, and was intimately acquainted with every foot of the ground, was again called upon to assist the promoters with his judgment and experience. He again recommended as strongly as before the line he had previously surveyed; and on its being adopted by the local committee, the necessary steps were taken to have the scheme brought before Parliament in the ensuing session. The East Coast line was not, however, to be allowed to pass without a fight. On the contrary, it had to encounter as stout an opposition as Stephenson had ever experienced.

We have already stated that about this time the plan of substituting atmospheric pressure for locomotive steam-power in the working of railways had become very popular. Many eminent engineers avowedly supported atmospheric in preference to locomotive lines; and many members of Parliament, headed by the prime ministers, were strongly disposed in their favor. Mr. Brunel warmly espoused the atmospheric principle, and his persuasive manner, as well as his admitted scientific ability, unquestionably exercised considerable influence in determining the views of many leading members of both houses. Among others, Lord Howick, one of the members for Northumberland, advocated the new principle, and, possessing great local influence, he succeeded in forming a powerful confederacy of the landed gentry in favor of Brunel's atmospheric railway through the country.

George Stephenson could not brook the idea of seeing the locomotive, for which he had fought so many stout battles, pushed to one side, and that in the very county in which its great powers had been first developed. Nor did he relish the appearance of Mr. Brunel as the engineer of Lord Howick's scheme, in opposition to the line which had occupied his thoughts and been the object of his strenuous advocacy for so many years. When Stephenson first met Brunel in Newcastle, he good-naturedly shook him by the collar, and asked "what business he had north of the Tyne?" George gave him to understand that they were to have a fair stand-up fight for the ground, and shaking hands before the battle like Englishmen, they parted in good-humor. A public meeting was held at Newcastle in the following December, when, after a full discussion of the merits of the respective plans, Stephenson's line was almost unanimously adopted as the best.

The rival projects went before Parliament in 1845, and a severe contest ensued. The display of ability and tactics on both sides was great. Robert Stephenson was examined at great length as to the merits of the locomotive line, and Brunel at equally great length as to the merits of the atmospheric. Mr. Brunel, in his evidence, said that, after numerous experiments, he had arrived at the conclusion that the mechanical contrivance of the atmospheric system was perfectly applicable, and he believed that it would likewise be more economical in most cases than locomotive power. "In short," said he, "rapidity, comfort, safety, and economy are its chief recommendations."

Notwithstanding the promise of Mr. Sergeant Wrangham, the counsel for Lord Howick's scheme, that the Northumberland atmospheric was to be "a *respectable* line, and not one that was to be converted into a road for the accommodation of the coal-owners of the district," the locomotive again triumphed. The Stephenson Coast line secured the approval of Parliament, and the shareholders in the Atmospheric Company were happily prevented investing their capital in what would unquestionably have proved a gigantic blunder. For, less than three years later, the whole of the atmospheric tubes which had been laid down on other lines were pulled up and the materials sold, including Mr. Brunel's immense tube on the South Devon Railway*—to make way for the working of the locomotive engine. George Stephenson's first verdict of "It won't do" was thus conclusively confirmed.

Robert Stephenson used afterward to describe with gusto an interview which took place between Lord Howick and his father, at his office in Great George Street, during the progress of the bill in Parliament. His father was in the outer office, where he used to spend a good deal of his spare time, occasionally taking a quiet wrestle with a friend when nothing else was stirring.† On the day in question, George was standing with his back to the fire, when Lord Howick called to see Robert. Oh! thought George, he has come to try and talk Robert over about that atmospheric gimcrack; but I'll tackle his lordship. "Come in, my lord," said he; "Robert's busy; but I'll answer your purpose quite as well; sit down here, if you please." George began, "Now, my lord, I know very well what you have come about: it's that atmospheric line in the North; I will show you in less than five minutes that it can never answer." "If Mr. Robert Stephenson is not at liberty, I can call again," said his lordship.

* The atmospheric lines had for some time been working very irregularly and very expensively. Robert Stephenson, in a letter to Mr. T. Sopwith, F.R.S., dated the 8th of January, 1846, wrote: "Since my return [from Italy] I have learned that your atmospheric friends are very sickly. A slow typhus has followed the high fever I left them in about three months ago. I don't anticipate, however, that the patient will expire suddenly. There is every appearance of the case being a protracted one, though a fatal termination is inevitable. When the pipes are sold by auction, I intend to buy one and present it to the British Museum." During the last half year of the atmospheric experiment on the South Devon line in 1848, the expenditure exceeded the gross income (£26,782) by £2487, or about 9¾ per cent. excess of working expenses beyond the gross receipts.

† "When my father came about the office," said Robert, "he sometimes did not well know what to do with himself. So he used to invite Bidder to have a quiet wrestle with him, for old acquaintance sake. And the two wrestled together so often, and had so many 'falls' (sometimes I thought they would bring the house down between them), that they broke half the chairs in my outer office. I remember once sending my father in a joiner's bill of about £2 10*s*. for the mending of broken chairs."

"He's certainly occupied on important business just at present," was George's answer, "but I can tell you far better than he can what nonsense the atmospheric system is: Robert's good-natured, you see, and if your lordship were to get alongside of him you might talk him over; so you have been quite lucky in meeting with me. Now just look at the question of expense," and then he proceeded in his strong Doric to explain his views in detail, until Lord Howick could stand it no longer, and he rose and walked toward the door. George followed him down stairs to finish his demolition of the atmospheric system, and his parting words were, "You may take my word for it, my lord, it will never answer." George afterward told his son with glee of "the settler" he had given Lord Howick.

So closely were the Stephensons identified with this measure, and so great was the personal interest which they were both known to take in its success, that, on the news of the passing of the bill reaching Newcastle, a sort of general holiday took place, and the workmen belonging to the Stephenson Locomotive Factory, upward of eight hundred in number, walked in procession through the principal streets of the town, accompanied by music and banners.

It is unnecessary to enter into any description of the works of the Newcastle and Berwick Railway. There are no fewer than a hundred and ten bridges of all sorts on the line—some under and some over it—the viaducts over the Ouseburn, the Wansbeck, and the Coquet being of considerable importance. But by far the most formidable piece of masonry work on this railway is at its northern extremity, where it passes across the Tweed into Scotland, immediately opposite the formerly redoubtable castle of Berwick. Not many centuries had passed since the district amid which this bridge stands was the scene of almost constant warfare. Berwick was regarded as the key of Scotland, and was fiercely fought for, being sometimes held by a Scotch and sometimes by an English garrison. Though strongly fortified, it was repeatedly taken by assault. On its capture by Edward I., Boetius says, 17,000 persons were slain, so that its streets "ran with blood like a river." Within sight of the ramparts, a little to the west, is Halidon Hill, where a famous victory was gained by Edward III. over the Scottish army under Douglas; and there is

ROYAL BORDER BRIDGE, BERWICK. [By R. P. Leitch, after his original Drawing.]

scarcely a foot of ground in the neighborhood but has been the scene of contention in days long past. In the reigns of James I. and Charles I., a bridge of fifteen arches was built across the Tweed at Berwick; and now a railway bridge of twenty-eight arches was built a little above the old one, but at a much higher level. The bridge built by the kings out of the national resources cost £15,000, and occupied twenty-four years and four months in the building; the bridge built by the Railway Company, with funds drawn from private resources, cost £120,000, and was finished in three years and four months from the day of laying the foundation stone.

This important viaduct, built after the designs of Robert Stephenson, consists of a series of twenty-eight semicircular arches, each 61 feet 6 inches in span, the greatest height above the bed of the river being 126 feet. The whole is built of ashlar, with a hearting of rubble, excepting the river parts of the arches, which are constructed with bricks laid in cement. The total length of the work is 2160 feet. The foundations of the piers were got in by coffer-dams in the ordinary way, Nasmyth's steam-hammer being extensively used in driving the piles. The bearing piles, from which the foundations of the piers were built up, were each capable of carrying 70 tons.

Another bridge, of still greater importance, necessary to complete the continuity of the East Coast route, was the master-work erected by Robert Stephenson between the north and south banks of the Tyne, at Newcastle, commonly known as the High-Level Bridge. Mr. R. W. Brandling, George Stephenson's early friend, is entitled to the merit of originating the idea of this bridge, as it was eventually carried out, with a central terminus for the northern railways in the Castle Garth. The plan was first promulgated by him in 1841; and in the following year it was resolved that George Stephenson should be consulted as to the most advisable site for the proposed structure. A prospectus of a High-Level Bridge Company was issued in 1843, the names of George Stephenson and George Hudson appearing on the committee of management, Robert Stephenson being the consulting engineer. The project was eventually taken up by the Newcastle and Darlington Railway Company, and an act for the construction of the bridge was obtained in 1845.

The rapid extension of railways had given an extraordinary stimulus to the art of bridge-building; the number of such structures erected in Great Britain alone, since 1830, having been above thirty thousand, or far more than all that previously existed in the country. Instead of the erection of a single large bridge constituting, as formerly, an epoch in engineering, hundreds of extensive bridges of novel design were simultaneously constructed. The necessity which existed for carrying rigid roads, capable of bearing heavy railway trains at high speed, over extensive gaps free of support, rendered it apparent that the methods which had up to that time been employed for bridging space were altogether insufficient. The railway engineer could not, like the ordinary road engineer, divert his road, and make choice of the best point for crossing a river or a valley. He must take such ground as lay in the line of his railway, be it bog, or mud, or shifting sand. Navigable rivers and crowded thoroughfares had to be crossed without interruption to the existing traffic, sometimes by bridges at right angles to the river or road, sometimes by arches more or less oblique. In many cases great difficulty arose from the limited nature of the headway; but, as the level of the original road must generally be preserved, and that of the railway was in a measure fixed and determined, it was necessary to modify the form and structure of the bridge in almost every case, in order to comply with the public requirements. Novel conditions were met by fresh inventions, and difficulties of an unusual character were one after another successfully surmounted. In executing these extraordinary works, iron has been throughout the sheet-anchor of the engineer. In the various forms of cast and wrought iron it offered a valuable resource where rapidity of execution, great strength and cheapness of construction in the first instance were elements of prime importance, and by its skillful use the railway architect was enabled to achieve results which thirty years since would scarcely have been thought possible.

In many of the early cast-iron bridges the old form of the arch was adopted, the stability of the structure depending wholly on compression, the only novel feature consisting in the use of iron instead of stone. But in a large proportion of cases, the arch, with the railroad over it, was found inapplicable in consequence of the limited headway which it provided. Hence it early occurred to George Stephenson, when constructing the Liverpool and Manchester Railway, to adopt the simple cast-iron beam for the crossing of several roads and canals along that line—this beam resembling in some measure the lintel of the early temples—the pressure on the abutments being purely vertical. One of the earliest instances of this kind of bridge was that erected over Water Street, Manchester, in 1829; after which, cast-iron girders, with their lower webs considerably larger than their upper, were ordinarily employed where the span was moderate, and wrought-iron tie-rods below were added to give increased strength where the span was greater.

The next step was the contrivance of arched beams or bow-string girders, firmly held together by horizontal ties to resist the thrust, instead of abutments. Numerous excellent specimens of this description of bridge were erected by Robert Stephenson on the original London and Birmingham Railway; but by far the grandest work of the kind—perfect as a specimen of modern constructive skill—was the High-Level Bridge, which we owe to the genius of the same engineer.

The problem was to throw a railway bridge across the deep ravine which lies between the towns of Newcastle and Gateshead, at the bottom of which flows the navigable river Tyne. Along and up the sides of the valley—on the Newcastle bank especially—run streets of old-fashioned houses, clustered together in the strange forms peculiar to the older cities. The ravine is of great depth—so deep and gloomy-looking toward dusk, that local tradition records that when the Duke of Cumberland arrived late in the evening, at the brow of the hill overlooking the Tyne, on his way to Culloden, he exclaimed to his attendants, on looking down into the black gorge before him, "For God's sake, don't think of taking me down that coal-pit at this time of night!" The road down the Gateshead High Street is almost as steep as the roof of a house, and up the Newcastle Side, as the street there is called, it is little better. During many centuries the traffic north and south passed along this dangerous and difficult route, across the old bridge which spans the river in the bottom of the valley. For some thirty years the Newcastle Corporation had discussed various methods of improving the communication between the towns; and the discussion might have gone on for thirty years more, but for the advent of railways, when the skill and enterprise to which they gave birth speedily solved the difficulty and bridged the ravine. The local authorities adroitly took advantage of the opportunity, and insisted on the provision of a road for ordinary vehicles and foot passengers in addition to the railroad. In this circumstance originated one of the most remarkable peculiarities of the High-Level Bridge, which serves two purposes, being a railway above, with a carriage roadway underneath.

The breadth of the river at the point of crossing is 515 feet, but the length of the bridge and viaduct between the Gateshead station and the terminus on the Newcastle side is about 4000 feet. It springs from Pipewell Gate Bank, on the south, directly across to Castle Garth, where, nearly fronting the bridge, stands the fine old Norman keep of the *New* Castle, now nearly eight hundred years old; and a little beyond it is the spire of St. Nicholas Church, with its light and graceful Gothic crown, the whole forming a grand architectural group of unusual historic interest. The bridge passes completely over the roofs of the houses which fill both sides of the valley, and the extraordinary height of the upper parapet, which is about 130 feet above the bed of the river, offers a prospect to the passing traveler the like of which is perhaps nowhere else to be seen. Far below lie the queer chares and closes, the wynds and lanes of old Newcastle; the water is crowded with pudgy, black coal keels; and, when there is a lull in the great clouds of smoke which usually obscure the sky, the funnels of steamers and the masts of the shipping may be seen far down the river. The old bridge lies so far beneath that the passengers crossing it seem like so many bees passing to and fro.

The first difficulty encountered in building the bridge was in securing a solid foundation for the piers. The dimensions of the piles to be driven were so huge that the engineer found it necessary to employ some extraordinary means for the purpose. He called Nasmyth's Titanic steam-hammer to his aid—the first occasion, we believe, on which this prodigious power was employed in bridge pile-driving. A temporary staging was erected for the steam-engine and hammer apparatus, which rested on two keels, and, notwithstanding the newness and stiffness of the machinery, the first pile was driven on the 6th of October, 1846, to a depth of 32 feet in four minutes. Two hammers of 30 cwt. each were kept in regular use, making from 60 to 70 strokes per minute, and the results were astounding to those who had been accustomed to the old style of pile-driving by means of the ordinary pile-frame, consisting of slide, ram, and monkey. By the old system the pile was driven by a comparatively small mass of iron descending with great velocity from a considerable height—the velocity being in excess and the mass deficient, and calculated, like the momentum of a cannon-ball, rather for destructive than impulsive action. In the case of the steam pile-driver, on the contrary, the whole weight of a heavy mass is delivered rapidly upon a driving-block of several tons weight placed directly over the head of the pile, the weight never ceasing, and the blows being repeated at the rate of a blow a second, until the pile is driven home. It is a curious fact, that the rapid strokes of the steam-hammer evolved so much heat, that on many occasions the pile-head burst into flame during the process of driving. The elastic force of steam is the power that lifts the ram, the escape permitting its entire force to fall upon the head of the driving-block; while the steam above the piston on the upper part of the cylinder, acting as a buffer or recoil-spring, materially enhances the effect of the downward blow. As soon as one pile was driven, the traveler, hovering overhead, presented another, and down it went into the solid bed of the river with almost as much ease as a lady sticks pins into a cushion. By the aid of this formidable machine, what before was among the most costly and tedious of engineering operations was rendered simple, easy, and economical.

When the piles had been driven and the coffer-dams formed and puddled, the water within the inclosed spaces was pumped out by the aid of powerful engines, so as to lay bare the bed of the river. Considerable difficulty was experienced in getting in the foundations of the middle pier, in consequence of the water forcing itself through the quicksand beneath as fast as it was removed. This fruitless labor went on for months, and many expedients were tried. Chalk was thrown in in large quantities outside the piling, but without effect. Cement concrete was at last put within the coffer-dam until it set, and the bottom was then found to be secure. A bed of concrete was laid up to the level of the heads of the piles, the foundation course of stone blocks being commenced about two feet below low water, and the building proceeded without farther difficulty. It may serve to give an idea of the magnitude of the work when we state that 400,000 cubic feet of ashlar, rubble, and concrete were worked up in the piers, and 450,000 cubic feet in the land-arches and approaches.

The most novel feature of the structure is the use of cast and wrought iron in forming the double bridge, which admirably combines the two principles of the arch and suspension, the railway being carried over the back of the ribbed arches in the usual manner, while the carriage-road and footpaths, forming a long gallery or aisle, are suspended from these arches by wrought-iron vertical rods, with horizontal tie-bars to resist the thrust. The suspension-bolts are inclosed within spandril pillars of cast iron, which give great stiffness to the superstructure. This system of longitudinal and vertical bracing has been much admired, for it not only accomplishes the primary object of securing rigidity in the roadway, but at the same time, by its graceful arrangement, heightens the beauty of the structure. The arches consist of four main ribs, disposed in pairs, with a clear distance between the two inner arches of 20 feet 4 inches, forming the carriage-road, while between each of the inner and outer ribs there is a space of 6 feet 2 inches, constituting the footpaths. Each arch is cast in five separate lengths or segments, strongly bolted together. The ribs spring from horizontal plates of cast iron, bedded and secured on the stone piers. All the abutting joints were carefully executed by machinery, the fitting being of the most perfect kind. In order to provide for the expansion and contraction of the iron arching, and to preserve the equilibrium of the piers without disturbance or racking of the other parts of the bridge, it was arranged that the ribs of every two adjoining arches resting on the same pier should be secured to the springing-plates by keys and joggles; while on the next piers, on either side, the ribs remained free, and were at liberty to expand or contract according to tem-

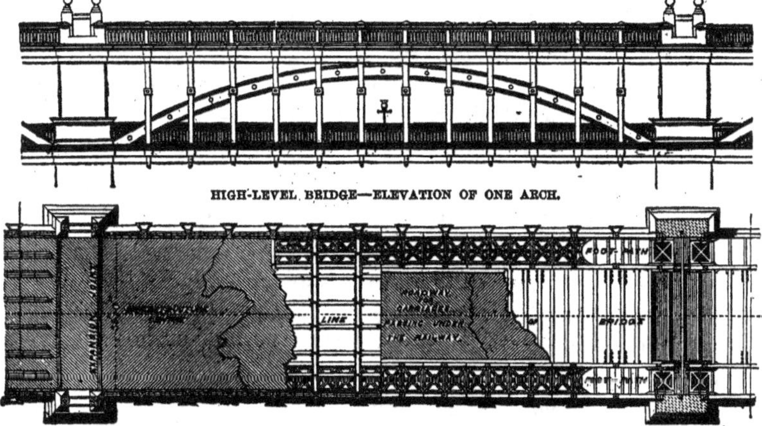

HIGH-LEVEL BRIDGE—ELEVATION OF ONE ARCH.

PLAN OF ONE ARCH.

perature—a space being left for the purpose. Hence each arch is complete and independent in itself, the piers having simply to sustain their vertical pressure. The arches are six in number, of 125 feet span each, the two approaches to the bridge being formed of cast-iron pillars and bearers in keeping with the arches.

The result is a bridge that for massive solidity may be pronounced unrivaled. It is one of the most magnificent and striking of the bridges to which railways have given birth, and has been worthily styled "the King of railway structures." It is a monument of the highest engineering skill of our time, with the impress of power grandly stamped upon it. It will also be observed from the drawing placed as the frontispiece to this Life, that the High-Level Bridge forms a very fine object in a picture of great interest, full of striking architectural variety and beauty. The bridge was opened on the 15th of August, 1849. A few days after, the royal train passed over it, halting for a few minutes to enable her majesty to survey the wonderful scene below. In the course of the following year the queen opened the extensive stone viaduct across the Tweed above described, by which the last link was completed of the continuous line of railway between London and Edinburg. Over the entrance to the Berwick station, occupying the site of the once redoubtable Border fortress, so often the deadly battle-ground of the ancient Scots and English, was erected an arch under which the royal train passed, bearing in large letters of gold the appropriate words, "*The last act of the Union.*"

The warders at Berwick no longer look out from the castle walls to descry the glitter of Southron spears. The bell-tower, from which the alarm was sounded of old, though still standing, is deserted; the only bell heard within the precincts of the old castle being the railway porter's bell announcing the arrival and departure of trains. You see the Scotch Express pass along the bridge and speed southward on the wings of steam. But no alarm spreads along the Border now. Northumbrian beeves are safe. Chevy Chase and Otterburn are quiet sheep-pastures. The only men-at-arms on the battlements of Alnwick Castle are of stone. Bamborough Castle has become an asylum for shipwrecked mariners, and the Norman Keep at Newcastle has been converted into a Museum of Antiquities. The railway has indeed consummated the Union.

CHAPTER XVIII.

CHESTER AND HOLYHEAD RAILWAY—MENAI AND CONWAY BRIDGES.

WE have now to describe briefly another great undertaking, begun by George Stephenson, and taken up and completed by his son, in the course of which the latter carried out some of his greatest works—we mean the Chester and Holyhead Railway, completing the railway connection with Dublin, as the Newcastle and Berwick line completed the connection with Edinburg. It will thus be seen how closely Telford was followed by the Stephensons in perfecting the highways of their respective epochs; the former by means of turnpike roads, and the latter by means of railways.

George Stephenson surveyed a line from Chester to Holyhead in 1838, and at the same time reported on the line through North Wales to Port Dynallen, as proposed by the Irish Railway Commissioners. His advice was strongly in favor of adopting the line to Holyhead, as less costly and presenting better gradients. A public meeting was held at Chester in January, 1839, in support of the latter measure, at which he was present to give explanations. Mr. Uniacke, the mayor, in opening the proceedings, observed that it clearly appeared that the rival line through Shrewsbury was quite impracticable. Mr. Stephenson, he added, was present in the room, ready to answer any questions which might be put to him on the subject; and "it would be better that he should be asked questions than required to make a speech; for, though a very good engineer, he was a bad speaker."

One of the questions then put to Mr. Stephenson related to the mode by which he proposed to haul the passenger-carriages over the Menai Suspension Bridge by horse-power; and he was asked whether he knew the pressure the bridge was capable of sustaining. His answer was that "he had not yet made any calculations, but he proposed getting data which would enable him to arrive at an accurate calculation of the actual strain upon the bridge during the late gale. He had, however, no hesitation in saying that it was more than twenty times as much as the strain of a train of carriages and a locomotive engine. The only reason why he proposed to convey the carriages over by horses was in order that he might, by distributing the weight, not increase the wavy motion. All the train would be on at once, but distributed. This he thought better than passing them linked together, by a locomotive engine." It will thus be observed that the practicability of throwing a rigid railroad bridge across the Straits had not yet been completed.

The Dublin Chamber of Commerce passed resolutions in favor of Stephenson's line after hearing his explanations of its essential features. The project, after undergoing much discussion, was at length embodied in an act passed in 1844, and the work was brought to a successful completion by his son, with several important modifications, including the grand original feature of the tubular bridges across the Menai Straits and the estuary of the Conway. Excepting these great works, the construction of this line presented no unusual features, though the remarkable terrace cut for the accommodation of the railway under the steep slope of Penmaen Mawr is worthy of a passing notice.

About midway between Conway and Bangor, Penmaen Mawr forms a bold and almost precipitous headland, at the base of which, in rough weather, the ocean dashes with great fury. There was not space enough between the mountain and the strand for the passage of the railway; hence in some places the rock had to be blasted to form a terrace, and in others sea walls had to be built up to the proper level, on which to form an embankment of sufficient width to enable the road to be laid. A tunnel of 10½ chains in length was cut through the headland itself; and on its east and west sides the line was formed by a terrace cut out of the cliff, and by embankments protected by sea walls, the terrace being three times interrupted by embankments in its course of about a mile and a quarter. The road lies so close under the steep mountain face that it was even found necessary at certain places to protect it against possible accidents from falling stones, by means of a covered way. The terrace on the east side of the headland was, however, in some measure, protected against the roll of the sea by the mass of stone run out from the tunnel, which formed a deep shingle-bank in front of the wall.

PENMAEN MAWR. [By Percival Skelton, after his original Drawing.]

The part of the work which lies to the westward of the headland penetrated by the tunnel was exposed to the full force of the sea, and the formation of the road at that point was attended with great difficulty. While the sea wall was still in progress, its strength was severely tried by a strong northwesterly gale which blew in October, 1846, accompanied with a spring tide of 17 feet. On the following morning it was found that a large portion of the rubble was irreparably injured, and 200 yards of the wall were then replaced by an open viaduct, with the piers placed edgeways to the sea, the openings between them being spanned by ten cast-iron girders 42 feet long. This accident farther induced the engineer to alter the contour of the sea wall, so that it should present a diminished resistance to the force of the waves.

But the sea repeated its assaults, and made farther havoc with the work, entailing heavy expenses and a complete reorganization of the contract. Increased solidity was then given to the masonry, and the face of the wall underwent farther change. At some points outworks were constructed, and piles were driven into the beach about 15 feet from the base of the wall for the purpose of protecting its foundations and breaking the force of the waves. The work was at length finished after about three years' anxious labor; but Mr. Stephenson confessed that if a long tunnel had been made in the first instance through the solid rock of Penmaen Mawr, a saving of from £25,000 to £30,000 would have been effected. He also said he had arrived at the conclusion that in railway works engineers should endeavor as far as possible to avoid the necessity of contending with the sea;* but if he were ever again compelled to go within its reach, he would adopt, instead of retaining walls, an open viaduct, placing all the piers edgeways to the force of the sea, and allowing the waves to break upon a natural slope of beach. He was ready enough to admit the errors he had committed in the original design of this work; but he said he had always gained more information from studying the causes of failures and endeavoring to surmount them, than he had done from easily-won successes. While many of the latter had been forgotten, the former were indelibly fixed in his memory.

But by far the greatest difficulty which Robert Stephenson had to encounter in executing this railway was in carrying it across the Straits of Menai and the estuary of the Conway, where, like his predecessor Telford, when forming his high road through North Wales, he was under the necessity of resorting to new and altogether untried methods of bridge construction. At Menai, the waters of the Irish Sea are perpetually vibrating along the precipitous shores of the Strait, rising and falling from 20 to 25

* The simple fact that in a heavy storm the force of impact of the waves is from one and a half to two tons per square foot, must necessarily dictate the greatest possible caution in approaching so formidable an element. Mr. R. Stevenson (Edinburg) registered a force of three tons per square foot at Skerryvore during a gale in the Atlantic, when the waves were supposed to run twenty feet high.

feet at each successive tide, the width and depth of the channel being such as to render it available for navigation by the largest ships. The problem was to throw a bridge across this wide chasm —a bridge of unusual span and dimensions—of such strength as to be capable of bearing the heaviest loads at high speeds, and of such a uniform height throughout as not in any way to interfere with the navigation of the Strait. From an early period Mr. Stephenson had fixed upon the spot where the Britannia Rock occurs, nearly in the middle of the channel, as the most eligible point for crossing, the water width from shore to shore at high water being there about 1100 feet.

The engineer's first idea was to construct the bridge of two cast-iron arches of 350 feet span each. There was no novelty in this idea; for, as early as the year 1801, Mr. Rennie prepared a design of a cast-iron bridge across the Strait at the Swilly Rocks, the great centre arch of which was to be 450 feet span; and at a later period, in 1810, Telford submitted a design of a similar bridge at Inys-y-Moch, with a single cast-iron arch of 500 feet. But the same objections which led to the rejection of Rennie's and Telford's designs proved fatal to Robert Stephenson's, and his iron-arched railway bridge was rejected by the Admiralty. The navigation of the Strait was under no circumstances to be interfered with; and even the erection of scaffolding from below, to support the bridge during construction, was not to be permitted. The idea of a suspension bridge was dismissed as inapplicable, a degree of rigidity and strength greater than could be secured by any

bridge erected on the principle of suspension being considered an indispensable condition of the proposed structure.

Mr. Stephenson next considered the expediency of erecting a bridge by means of suspended centering, after the ingenious method proposed by Telford in 1810,* by which the arching was to be carried out by placing equal and corresponding voussoirs on opposite sides of the pier at the same time, tying them together by horizontal tie-bolts. The arching, thus extended outward from each pier and held in equilibrium, would have been connected at the crown with the extremity of the arch advanced in like manner from the adjoining pier. It was, however, found that this method of construction was not applicable at the crossing of the Conway, and it was eventually abandoned. Various other plans were suggested; but the whole question remained unsettled even down to the time when the company went before Parliament in 1844 for power to construct the proposed bridges. No existing kind of structure seemed to be capable of bearing the severe extension to which rigid bridges of the necessary spans would be subjected, and some new expedient of engineering therefore became necessary.

Mr. Stephenson was then led to reconsider a design which he had made in 1841 for a road bridge over the River Lea at Ware, with a span of 50 feet, the conditions only admitting of a platform 18 or 20 inches thick. For this purpose a wrought-iron platform was devised, consisting of a series of simple cells, formed of boiler-plates riveted together with angle-iron. The bridge was not, however, carried out after this design, but was made of separate wrought-iron girders composed of riveted plates.† Recurring to his first idea of this bridge, the engineer thought that a stiff platform might be constructed, with sides of strongly-trussed frame-work of wrought iron, braced together at top and bottom with plates of like material riveted together with angle-iron, after a method adopted by Mr. Rendel in stiffening the suspension

* See "Lives of the Engineers," vol. ii., p. 445. It appears that Mr. Fairbairn suggested this idea in his letter to Mr. Stephenson, dated the 3d of June, 1845, accompanied by a drawing. See his "Account of the Construction of the Britannia and Conway Tubular Bridges," etc. London, 1849.

† Robert Stephenson's narrative of the early history of the design, in Edwin Clark's "Britannia and Conway Tubular Bridges," vol. i., p. 25, London, 1850.

bridge at Montrose with wooden trellis-work a few years before; and that such platform might be suspended by strong chains on either side to give it increased security. "It was now," says Mr. Stephenson, "that I came to regard the tubular platform as a beam, and that the chains should be looked upon as auxiliaries." It appeared to him, nevertheless, that without a system of diagonal struts inside, which of course would have prevented the passage of trains *through* it, this kind of structure was ill suited for maintaining its form, and would be very liable to become lozenge-shaped. Besides, the rectangular figure was deemed objectionable, from the large surface which it presented to the wind.

It then occurred to him that circular or elliptical tubes might better answer the intended purpose; and in March, 1845, he gave instructions to two of his assistants to prepare drawings of such a structure, the tubes being made with a double thickness of plate at top and bottom. The results of the calculations made as to the strength of such a tube were considered so satisfactory, that Mr. Stephenson says he determined to fall back upon a bridge of this description on the rejection of his design of the two cast-iron arches by the Parliamentary Committee. Indeed, it became evident that a tubular wrought-iron beam was the only structure which combined the necessary strength and stability for a railway, with the conditions deemed essential for the protection of the navigation:

"I stood," says Mr. Stephenson, "on the verge of a responsibility from which, I confess, I had nearly shrunk. The construction of a tubular beam of such gigantic dimensions, on a platform elevated and supported by chains at such a height, did at first present itself as a difficulty of a very formidable nature. Reflection, however, satisfied me that the principles upon which the idea was founded were nothing more than an extension of those daily in use in the profession of the engineer. The method, moreover, of calculating the strength of the structure which I had adopted was of the simplest and most elementary character; and whatever might be the form of the tube, the principle on which the calculations were founded was equally applicable, and could not fail to lead to equally accurate results."*

* Robert Stephenson's narrative in Clark's "Britannia and Conway Tubular Bridges," vol. i., p. 27.

Mr. Stephenson accordingly announced to the directors of the railway that he was prepared to carry out a bridge of this general description, and they adopted his views, though not without considerable misgivings.

While the engineer's mind was still occupied with the subject, an accident occurred to the *Prince of Wales* iron steam-ship, at Blackwall, which singularly corroborated his views as to the strength of wrought-iron beams of large dimensions. When this vessel was being launched, the cleet on the bow gave way in consequence of the bolts breaking, and let the vessel down so that the bilge came in contact with the wharf, and she remained suspended between the water and the wharf for a length of about 110 feet, but without any injury to the plates of the ship, satisfactorily proving the great strength of this form of construction. Thus Mr. Stephenson became gradually confirmed in his opinion that the most feasible method of bridging the strait at Menai and the river at Conway was by means of a hollow tube of wrought iron. As the time was approaching for giving evidence before Parliament on the subject, it was necessary for him to settle some definite plan for submission to the committee.

"My late revered father," says he, "having always taken a deep interest in the various proposals which had been considered for carrying a railway across the Menai Straits, requested me to explain fully to him the views which led me to suggest the use of a tube, and also the nature of the calculations I had made in reference to it. It was during this personal conference that Mr. William Fairbairn accidentally called upon me, to whom I also explained the principles of the structure I had proposed. He at once acquiesced in their truth, and expressed confidence in the feasibility of my project, giving me at the same time some facts relative to the remarkable strength of iron steam-ships, and invited me to his works at Millwall to examine the construction of an iron steam-ship which was then in progress."*

The date of this consultation was early in April, 1845, and Mr. Fairbairn states that, on that occasion,

"Mr. Stephenson asked whether such a design was practicable, and whether I could accomplish it; and it was ultimately arranged

* "Robert Stephenson's narrative in Clark's "Britannia and Conway Tubular Bridges," vol. i., p. 27.

that the subject should be investigated experimentally, to determine not only the value of Mr. Stephenson's original conception (of a circular or egg-shaped wrought-iron tube, supported by chains), but that of any other tubular form of bridge which might present itself in the prosecution of my researches. The matter was placed unreservedly in my hands; the entire conduct of the investigation was intrusted to me; and, as an experimenter, I was to be left free to exercise my own discretion in the investigation of whatever forms or conditions of the structure might appear to me best calculated to secure a safe passage across the Straits."*

Mr. Fairbairn then proceeded to construct a number of experimental models, for the purpose of testing the strength of tubes of different forms. The short period which elapsed, however, before the bill was in committee, did not admit of much progress being made with those experiments; but from the evidence in chief given by Mr. Stephenson on the subject on the 5th of May following, it appears that the idea which prevailed in his mind was that of a bridge with openings of 450 feet (afterward increased to 460 feet), with a roadway formed of a hollow wrought-iron beam about 25 feet in diameter, presenting a rigid platform suspended by chains. At the same time, he expressed the confident opinion that a tube of wrought iron would possess sufficient strength and rigidity to support a railway train running inside of it without the help of the chains.

While the bill was still in progress, Mr. Fairbairn proceeded with his experiments. He first tested tubes of a cylindrical form, in consequence of the favorable opinion entertained by Mr. Stephenson of tubes in that shape, extending them subsequently to those of an elliptical form.† He found tubes thus shaped more or less defective, and proceeded to test those of a rectangular kind. After the bill had received the royal assent, on the 30th of June, 1845, the directors of the company, with great liberality, voted a sum for the purpose of enabling the experiments to be

* "Account of the Construction of the Britannia and Conway Tubular Bridges." By W. Fairbairn, C.E., London, 1849.

† Mr. Stephenson continued to hold that the elliptical tube was the right idea, and that sufficient justice had not been done to it. A year or two before his death, Mr. Stephenson remarked to the author that, had the same arrangement for stiffening been adopted to which the oblong rectangular tubes owe a great part of their strength, a very different result would have been obtained.

prosecuted, and upward of £6000 were thus expended to make the assurance of their engineer doubly sure.

Mr. Fairbairn's tests were of the most elaborate and eventually conclusive character, bringing to light many new and important facts of great practical value. The due proportions and thicknesses of the top, bottom, and sides of the tubes were arrived at after a vast number of separate trials, one of the results of the experiments being the adoption of Mr. Fairbairn's invention of rectangular hollow cells in the top of the beam for the purpose of giving it the requisite degree of strength. About the end of August it was thought desirable to obtain the assistance of a mathematician, who should prepare a formula by which the strength of a full-sized tube might be calculated from the results of the experiments made with tubes of smaller dimensions. Professor Hodgkinson was accordingly called in, and he proceeded to verify and confirm the experiments which Mr. Fairbairn had made, and afterward reduced them to the required formulæ, though Mr. Fairbairn states that they did not appear in time to be of any practical service in proportioning the parts of the largest tubes.*

Mr. Stephenson's time was so much engrossed with his extensive engineering business that he was in a great measure precluded from devoting himself to the consideration of the practical details, which he felt were safe in the hands of Mr. Fairbairn —"a gentleman," as he stated to the Committee of the Commons, "whose experience was greater than that of any other man in England." The results of the experiments were communicated to him from time to time, and were regarded by him as exceedingly satisfactory. It would appear, however, that while Mr. Fairbairn urged the sufficient rigidity and strength of the tubes without the aid of chains, Mr. Stephenson had not quite made up his mind upon the point. Mr. Hodgkinson, also, was strongly inclined to retain them.† Mr. Fairbairn held that it

* "Mr. Fairbairn's Account," p. 22.

† The following passage occurs in Robert Stephenson's report to the directors of the Chester and Holyhead Railway, dated the 9th of February, 1846: "You will observe in Mr. Fairbairn's remarks that he contemplates the feasibility of stripping the tube entirely of all the chains that may be required in the erection of the bridge; whereas, on the other hand, Mr. Hodgkinson thinks the chains will be an essential, or, at all events, a useful auxiliary, to give the tube the requisite strength and rigid-

was quite practicable to make the tubes "sufficiently strong to sustain not only their own weight, but, in addition to that load, 2000 tons equally distributed over the surface of the platform—a load ten times greater than they will ever be called upon to support."

It was thoroughly characteristic of Mr. Stephenson, and of the caution with which he proceeded in every step of this great undertaking—probing every inch of the ground before he set his foot down upon it—that he should, early in 1846, have appointed his able assistant, Mr. Edwin Clark, to scrutinize carefully the results of every experiment, whether made by Mr. Fairbairn or Mr. Hodgkinson, and subject them to a separate and independent analysis before finally deciding upon the form or dimensions of the structure, or upon any mode of procedure connected with it. That great progress had been made by the two chief experimenters before the end of 1846 appears from the papers on the subject read by Messrs. Fairbairn and Hodgkinson before the British Association at Southampton in September of that year. In the course of the following month Mr. Stephenson had become satisfied that the use of auxiliary chains was unnecessary, and that the tubular bridge might be made of such strength as to be entirely self-supporting.*

ity. This, however, will be determined by the proposed additional experiments, and does not interfere with the construction of the masonry, which is designed so as to admit of the tube, with or without chains. The application of chains as an auxiliary has occupied much of my attention, and I am satisfied that the ordinary mode of applying them to suspension bridges is wholly inadmissible in the present instance; if, therefore, it be hereafter found necessary or desirable to employ them in conjunction with the tube, another mode of employing them must be devised, as it is absolutely essential to attach them in such a manner as to preclude the possibility of the smallest oscillation."

* In a letter of Mr. Fairbairn to Mr. Stephenson, dated July 18th, 1846, he says: "To get rid of the chains will be a desideratum; and I have made the tube of such strength, and intend putting it together upon such a principle, as will insure its carrying a dead weight, equally distributed over its hollow surface, of 4000 tons. With a bridge of such powers, what have we to fear? and why, in the name of truth and in the face of conclusive facts, should we hesitate to adopt measures calculated not only to establish the principle as a triumph of art, but, what is of infinitely more importance to the shareholders, the saving of a large sum of money, nearly equal to half the cost of the bridge? I have been ably assisted by Mr. Clark in all these contrivances; but in a matter of such importance we must have your sanction and support."—"Mr. Fairbairn's Account," p. 93.

While these important discussions were in progress, measures were taken to proceed with the masonry of the bridges simultaneously at Conway and the Menai Strait. The foundation-stone of the Britannia Bridge was laid by Mr. Frank Forster, the resident engineer, on the 10th of April, 1846; and on the 12th of May following that of the Conway Bridge was laid by Mr. A. M. Ross, resident engineer at that part of the works. Suitable platforms and workshops were also erected for proceeding with the punching, fitting, and riveting of the tubes; and when these operations were in full progress, the neighborhood of the Conway and Britannia Bridges presented scenes of extraordinary bustle and industry. On the 11th of July, 1847, Mr. Clark informed Mr. Stephenson that "the masonry gets on rapidly. The abutments on the Anglesea side resemble the foundations of a great city rather than of a single structure, and nothing appears to stand still here." About 1500 men were employed on the Britannia Bridge alone, and they mostly lived upon the ground in wooden cottages erected for the occasion. The iron plates were brought in ship-loads from Liverpool, Anglesea marble from Penmon, and red sandstone from Runcorn, in Cheshire, as wind and tide, and shipping and convenience, might determine. There was an unremitting clank of hammers, grinding of machinery, and blasting of rock going on from morning to night. In fitting the Britannia tubes together not less than 2,000,000 of bolts were riveted, weighing some 900 tons.

The Britannia Bridge consists of two independent continuous tubular beams, each 1511 feet in length, and each weighing 4680 tons, independent of the cast-iron frames inserted at their bearings on the masonry of the towers. These immense beams are supported at five places, namely, on the abutments and on three towers, the central of which is known as the Great Britannia Tower, 230 feet high, built on a rock in the middle of the Strait. The side towers are 18 feet less in height than the central one, and the abutments 35 feet lower than the side towers. The design of the masonry is such as to accord with the form of the tubes, being somewhat of an Egyptian character, massive and gigantic rather than beautiful, but bearing the unmistakable impress of power.

The bridge has four spans—two of 460 feet over the water,

CONSTRUCTION OF THE MAIN BRITANNIA TUBE ON THE STAGING.

and two of 230 feet over the land. The weight of the longer spans, at the points where the tubes repose on the masonry, is not less than 1587 tons. On the centre tower the tubes lie solid; but on the land towers and abutments they lie on roller-beds, so as to allow of expansion and contraction. The road within each tube is 15 feet wide, and the height varies from 23 feet at the ends to 30 feet at the centre. To give an idea of the vast size of the tubes by comparison with other structures, it may be mentioned that each length constituting the main spans is twice as long as London Monument is high; and if it could be set on end in St. Paul's Church-yard, it would reach nearly 100 feet above the cross.

The Conway Bridge is, in most respects, similar to the Britannia, consisting of two tubes of 400 feet span, placed side by side, each weighing 1180 tons. The principle adopted in the construction of the tubes, and the mode of floating and raising them, was nearly the same as at the Britannia Bridge, though the general arrangement of the plates is in many respects different.

It was determined to construct the shorter outer tubes of the Britannia Bridge on scaffoldings in the positions in which they were permanently to remain, and to erect the larger tubes upon wooden platforms at high-water-mark on the Caernarvon shore, from whence they were to be floated in pontoons—in like manner as Rennie had floated into their places the centerings of his Waterloo and other bridges—and then raised into their proper places by means of hydraulic power, after a method originally suggested by Mr. Edwin Clark. The tubes of the Conway Bridge also were to be constructed on shore, and floated to their places on pontoons, as in the case of the main centre tubes of the Britannia Bridge.

CONWAY BRIDGE. [By Percival Skelton.]

The floating of these tubes on pontoons, from the places where they had been constructed to the recesses in the masonry of the towers, up which they were to be hoisted to the places they were permanently to occupy, was an anxious and exciting operation. The first proceeding of this nature was at Conway, where Mr. Stephenson directed it in person, assisted by Captain Claxton, Mr. Brunel, and other engineering friends. On the 6th of March, 1848, the pontoons bearing the first great tube of the up-line were floated round quietly and majestically into their place between the towers in about twenty minutes. Unfortunately, one of the sets of pontoons had become slightly slued by the stream, by which the Conway end of the tube was prevented from being brought home, and five anxious days to all concerned intervened before it could be set in its place. In the mean time, the presses and raising machinery had been fitted in the towers above, and the lifting process was begun on the 8th of April, when the immense mass was raised 8 feet, at the rate of about 2 inches a minute. On the 16th the tube had been raised and finally lowered into its permanent bed; the rails were laid within it; and on the 18th Mr. Stephenson passed through with the first locomotive. The second tube was proceeded with on the removal of the first from the platform, and was completed and floated in seven months. The rapidity with which this second tube was constructed was in no small degree owing to the Jacquard punching-machine, contrived for the purpose of punching the holes for the rivets by Mr. Roberts, of Manchester. The tube was finally fixed in its permanent bed on the 2d of January, 1849.

The floating and fixing of the great Britannia tubes was a still more formidable enterprise, though the experience gained at Conway rendered it easy compared with what it otherwise would have been. Mr. Stephenson superintended the operation of floating the first in person, giving the arranged signals from the top of the tube on which he was mounted, the active part of the business being performed by a numerous corps of sailors, under the immediate direction of Captain Claxton. Thousands of spectators lined the shores of the Strait on the evening of the 19th of June, 1849. On the land attachments being cut, the pontoons began to float off; but one of the capstans having given way from the too great strain put upon it, the tube was brought home again for the night.

By next morning the defective capstan was restored, and all was in readiness for another trial. At half past seven in the evening the tube was afloat, and the pontoons swung out into the current like a monster pendulum, held steady by the shore guide-lines, but increasing in speed to almost a fearful extent as they neared their destined place between the piers.

"The success of this operation," says Mr. Clark, "depended mainly on properly striking the 'butt' beneath the Anglesey tower, on which, as upon a centre, the tube was to be veered round into its position across the opening. This position was determined by a 12-inch line, which was to be paid out to a fixed mark from the Llanfair capstan. The coils of the rope unfortunately overrode each other upon this capstan, so that it could not be paid out. In resisting the motion of the tube, the capstan was bodily dragged out of the platform by the action of the palls, and the tube was in imminent danger of being carried away by the stream, or the pontoons crushed upon the rocks. The men at the capstan were all knocked down, and some of them thrown into the water, though they made every exertion to arrest the motion of the capstan-bars. In this dilemma, Mr. Charles Rolfe, who had charge of the capstan, with great presence of mind called the visitors on shore to his assistance; and handing out the spare coil of the 12-inch line into the field at the back of the capstan, it was carried with great rapidity up the field, and a crowd of people, men, women, and children, holding on to this huge cable, arrested the progress of the tube, which was at length brought safely against the butt and veered round. The Britannia end was then drawn into the recess of the masonry by a chain passing through the tower to a crab on the far side. The violence of the tide abated, though the wind increased, and the Anglesey end was drawn into its place beneath the corbeling in the masonry; and as the tide went down, the pontoons deposited their valuable cargo on the welcome shelf at each end. The successful issue was greeted by cannon from the shore and the hearty cheers of many thousands of spectators, whose sympathy and anxiety were but too clearly indicated by the unbroken silence with which the whole operation had been accompanied."*

By midnight all the pontoons had been got clear of the tube, which now hung suspended over the waters of the Strait by its

* "The Britannia and Conway Tubular Bridges." By Edwin Clark. Vol. ii., p. 683-4.

two ends, which rested upon the edges cut in the rock for the purpose at the base of the Britannia and Anglesey towers respectively, up which the tube had now to be lifted by hydraulic power to its permanent place near the summit. The accuracy with which the gigantic beam had been constructed may be inferred from the fact that, after passing into its place, a clear space remained between the iron plating and the rock outside of it of only about three quarters of an inch!

Mr. Stephenson's anxiety was, of course, very great up to the time of effecting this perilous operation. When he had got the first tube floated at Conway and saw all safe, he said to Captain Moorsom, "Now I shall go to bed." But the Britannia Bridge was a still more difficult enterprise, and cost him many a sleepless night. Afterward describing his feelings to his friend Mr. Gooch, he said, "It was a most anxious and harassing time with me. Often at night I would lie tossing about, seeking sleep in vain. The tubes filled my head. I went to bed with them and got up with them. In the gray of the morning, when I looked across the Square,* it seemed an immense distance across to the houses on the opposite side. It was nearly the same length as the span of my tubular bridge!" When the first tube had been floated, a friend observed to him, "This great work has made you ten years older." "I have not slept sound," he replied, "for three weeks." Sir F. Head, however, relates that, when he revisited the spot on the following morning, he observed, sitting on a platform overlooking the suspended tube, a gentleman, reclining entirely by himself, smoking a cigar, and gazing, as if indolently, at the aerial gallery beneath him. It was the engineer himself, contemplating his newborn child. He had strolled down from the neighboring village, after his first sound and refreshing sleep for weeks, to behold in sunshine and solitude that which, during a weary period of gestation, had been either mysteriously moving in his brain, or, like a vision—sometimes of good omen and sometimes of evil—had, by night as well as by day, been flitting across his mind.

The next process was the lifting of the tube into its place, which was performed very deliberately and cautiously. It was raised by powerful hydraulic presses, only a few feet at a time,

* No. 34 Gloucester Square, Hyde Park, where he lived.

and carefully under-built, before being raised to a farther height. When it had been got up by successive stages of this kind to about 24 feet, an extraordinary accident occurred, during Mr. Stephenson's absence in London, which he afterward described to the author in as nearly as possible the following words: "In a work of such novelty and magnitude, you may readily imagine how anxious I was that every possible contingency should be provided for. Where one chain or rope was required, I provided two. I was not satisfied with 'enough:' I must have absolute security, so far as that was possible. I knew the consequences of failure would be most disastrous to the company, and that the wisest economy was to provide for all contingencies, at whatever cost. When the first tube at the Britannia had been successfully floated between the piers, ready for being raised, my young engineers were very much elated; and when the hoisting apparatus had been fixed, they wrote to me, saying, 'We are now all ready for raising her: we could do it in a day, or in two at the most.' But my reply was, No; you must only raise the tube inch by inch, and you must build up under it as you rise. Every inch must be made good. Nothing must be left to chance or good luck. And fortunate it was that I insisted upon this cautious course being pursued; for, one day, while the hydraulic presses were at work, the bottom of one of them burst clean away! The cross-head and the chains, weighing more than 50 tons, descended with a fearful crash upon the press, and the tube itself fell down upon the packing beneath. Though the fall of the tube was not more than nine inches, it crunched solid castings, weighing tons, as if they had been nuts. The tube itself was slightly strained and deflected, though it still remained sufficiently serviceable. But it was a tremendous test to which it was put, for a weight of upward of 5000 tons falling even a few inches must be admitted to be a very serious matter. That it stood so well was extraordinary. Clark immediately wrote me an account of the circumstance, in which he said, 'Thank God you have been so obstinate; for if this accident had occurred without a bed for the end of the tube to fall on, the whole would now have been lying across the bottom of the Straits.' Five thousand pounds extra expense was caused by this accident, slight though it might seem. But careful provision was made against future failure; a new and improved cylinder was provided; and the work was very soon advancing satisfactorily toward completion."*

When the queen first visited the Britannia Bridge, on her return from the North in 1852, Robert Stephenson accompanied her majesty and Prince Albert over the works, explaining the principles on which the bridge had been built, and the difficulties which had attended its erection. He conducted the royal party to near the margin of the sea, and, after describing to them the incident of the fall of the tube, and the reason of its preservation, he pointed with pardonable pride to a pile of stones which the workmen had there raised to commemorate the event. While nearly all the other marks of the work during its progress had been obliterated, that cairn had been left standing in commemoration of the caution and foresight of their chief.

The floating and raising of the remaining tubes need not be described in detail. The second was floated on the 3d of December, and set in its permanent place on the 7th of January, 1850. The others† were floated and raised in due course; on

* The hydraulic presses were of an extraordinary character. The cylinders of those first constructed were of wrought iron (cast iron being found altogether useless), not less than 8 inches thick. They were tested by being subjected to an internal pressure of 3 or 3½ tons to the circular inch. The pressure was such that it squeezed the fibres of the iron together; so that, after a few tests of this character, the piston, which at first fitted it quite closely, was found considerably too small. "A new piston," says Mr. Clark, "was then made to suit the enlarged cylinder; and a farther enlargement occurring again and again with subsequent use, the new pistons became as formidable an obstacle as the cylinders. The wrought-iron cylinder was on the point of being abandoned, when Mr. Amos (the iron manufacturer), having carefully gauged the cylinder inside and out, found to his surprise that, although the internal diameter had increased considerably, the external diameter had retained precisely its original dimensions. He consequently persevered in the construction of new pistons, and ultimately found that the cylinder enlarged no longer, and to this day it continues in constant use. Layer after layer having attained additional permanent set, sufficient material was at length brought into play, with sufficient tenacity to withstand the pressure; and thus an obstacle, apparently insurmountable, and which threatened at one time to render much valuable machinery useless, was entirely overcome. The workman may be excused for calling the stretched cylinder stronger than the new one, though it is only stronger as regards the amount of its yielding to a given force."—Clark, vol. i., p. 306. The hydraulic presses used in raising the tubes of the Britannia Bridge, it may be remembered, were afterward used in starting the *Great Eastern* from her berth on the shore at Milwall, where she had been built.

† While the preparations were in progress for floating the third tube, Mr. Stephenson received a pressing invitation to a public railway celebration at Darlington, in honor of his old friend, Edward Pease. His reply, dated the 15th of May, 1850, was

MENAI BRIDGE. [By Percival Skelton, after his original Drawing.]

the 5th of March Mr. Stephenson put the last rivet in the tube, and passed through the completed bridge, accompanied by about

as follows: "I am prevented having the pleasure of a visit to Darlington on the 22d, owing to that or the following day having been fixed upon for floating the next tube at the Menai Straits; and as this movement depends on the tide, it is, of course, impossible for me to alter the arrangements. I sincerely regret this circumstance, for every early association connected with my profession would have tended to render my visit a gratifying one. It would, moreover, have given me an opportunity of saying publicly how much the wonderful progress of railways was dependent upon the successful issue of the first great experiment, and how much that issue was influenced by your great discernment, and your confidence in my late revered father. In my remembrance you stand among the foremost of his patrons and early advisers; and I know that throughout his life he regarded you as one of his very best friends. One of the things in which he took especial delight was in frequently and very graphically describing his first visit to Darlington, on foot, to confer with you on the subject of the Stockton and Darlington Railway."

a thousand persons, drawn by three locomotives. The bridge was found almost entirely rigid, scarcely showing the slightest deflection. When, in the course of the day, a train of 200 tons of coal was allowed to rest with all its weight, for two hours, in the centre of the eastern land tube, the deflection was only four tenths of an inch, or less than that produced upon the structure by half an hour's sunshine;* while the whole bridge might with safety, and without injury to itself, be deflected to the extent of 13 inches. The bridge was opened for public traffic on the 18th of March. The cost of the whole work was £234,450.

The Britannia Bridge is one of the most remarkable monuments of the enterprise and skill of the present century. Robert Stephenson was the master spirit of the undertaking. To him belongs the merit of first seizing the ideal conception of the structure best adapted to meet the necessities of the case, and of selecting the best men to work out his idea, himself watching, controlling, and testing every result by independent check and counter-check. And, finally, he organized and directed, through his assistants, the vast band of skilled workmen and laborers who were for so many years occupied in carrying his magnificent original conception to a successful practical issue.

But it was not accomplished without the greatest anxiety and mental pressure. Mr. Clark has well observed that few persons who merely witness the results of the engineer's labors can form any conception of the real difficulties overcome, and the intense anxiety involved in their elaboration. "If the stranger," he says, "who contemplates the finished reality, requires so much thought

* The effect of sunshine in deflecting the bridge is very curious. When the first main tube was tested, ballast-wagons loaded with iron were drawn into the centre and left standing there. The first 20 tons increased the deflection an eighth of an inch, and with 50 tons the deflection was 9 inches. After standing all night, the deflection in the morning was found to be only 8⅝ inches. How was this to be accounted for? Mr. Clark says: "This was attributed at the time to an error made in the reading; but this, and many other anomalies in the deflection, were afterward fully accounted for by local changes of temperature. *A gleam of sunshine* on the top of the tube raised it on one occasion nearly an inch in half an hour with 200 tons at the centre, the top plates being expanded by increase of temperature, while the lower plates remained constant from radiation to the water immediately beneath them. In a similar manner, the tube was drawn sidewise to the extent of an inch from *the sun shining on one side*, and returned immediately as clouds passed over the sun, being, in fact, a most delicate thermometer in constant motion, both vertically and laterally."

to appreciate its principles and comprehend its detail, what weary hours must he have undergone who first conceived its bold proportions—who, combating, almost alone, every prejudice that assailed him, and with untiring labor discussing every objection, listening to every opinion, and embodying every inquiry, at length matured, step by step, this noble monument?" On the occasion of raising the last tube into its place, Mr. Stephenson declared, in reply to the felicitations of a large company who had witnessed the proceedings with intense interest, that not all the triumph which attended this great work, and the solution of the difficult problem of carrying a rigid roadway across an arm of the sea at such a height as to allow the largest vessels to pass with all their sails set beneath it, could repay him for the anxieties he had gone through, the friendships he had compromised, and the unworthy motives which had been attributed to him; and that, were another work of the same magnitude offered to him with like consequences, he would not for worlds undertake it!

The Britannia Bridge was indeed the result of a vast combination of skill and industry. But for the perfection of our tools, and the ability of our mechanics to use them to the greatest advantage—but for the matured powers of the steam-engine—but for the improvements in the iron manufacture, which enabled blooms to be puddled of sizes before deemed impracticable, and plates and bars of immense size to be rolled and forged—but for these, the Britannia Bridge would have been designed in vain. Thus it was not the product of the genius of the railway engineer alone, but of the collective mechanical genius of the English nation.

CONWAY BRIDGE—FLOATING THE FIRST TUBE.

VIEW IN TAPTON GARDENS. [By Percival Skelton.]

CHAPTER XIX.

CLOSING YEARS OF GEORGE STEPHENSON'S LIFE—ILLNESS AND DEATH—CHARACTER.

In describing the completion of the series of great works detailed in the preceding chapter, we have somewhat anticipated the closing years of George Stephenson's life. He could not fail to take an anxious interest in the success of his son's designs, and he paid many visits to Conway and to Menai during the progress of the bridges. He was present on the occasion of the floating and raising of the first Conway tube, and there witnessed a proof of the soundness of Robert's judgment as to the efficiency and strength of the structure, of which he had at first expressed some doubt; but before the like test could be applied at the Britannia Bridge, George Stephenson's mortal anxieties were at an end, for he had then ceased from all his labors.

Toward the close of his life, George Stephenson almost entirely withdrew from the active pursuit of his profession. He devoted himself chiefly to his extensive collieries and lime-works, taking a local interest only in such projected railways as were calculated to open up new markets for their products.

At home he lived the life of a country gentleman, enjoying his garden and grounds, and indulging his love of nature, which, through all his busy life, had never left him. It was not until the year 1845 that he took an active interest in horticultural pursuits. Then he began to build new melon-houses, pineries, and vineries, of great extent; and he now seemed as eager to excel all other growers of exotic plants in his neighborhood, as he had been some thirty years before to surpass the villagers of Killingworth in the production of cabbages and cauliflowers. He had a pine-house built 68 feet in length and a vinery 140 feet. Workmen were constantly employed in enlarging them, until at length he had no fewer than ten glass forcing-houses. He did not take so much pleasure in flowers as in fruits. At one of the county agricultural meetings he said that he intended yet to grow pineapples at Tapton as big as pumpkins. The only man to whom he would "knock under" was his friend Paxton, the gardener to the Duke of Devonshire; but he was so old in the service, and so skillful, that he could scarcely hope to beat him. Yet his "Queen" pines did take the first prize at a competition with the duke, though this was not until shortly after his death, when the plants had become fully grown. Stephenson's grapes also took the first prize at Rotherham, at a competition open to all England. He was extremely successful in producing melons, having invented a method of suspending them in baskets of wire gauze, which, by relieving the stalk from tension, allowed nutrition to proceed more freely, and better enabled the fruit to grow and ripen.

He also took much pride in his growth of cucumbers. He raised them very fine and large, but he could not make them grow straight. Place them as he would, notwithstanding all his propping and humoring of them by modifying the application of heat and the admission of light, they would still insist on growing crooked in their own way. At last he had a number of glass cylinders made at Newcastle, and into these the growing cucumbers were inserted, when at last he succeeded in growing them perfectly straight. Carrying one of the new products into his house one day, and exhibiting it to a party of visitors, he told them of the expedient he had adopted, and added, "I think I have bothered them noo!"

Farming operations were also carried on by him with success. He experimented on manure, and fed cattle after methods of his own. He was very particular as to breed and build in stock-breeding. "You see, sir," he said to one gentleman, "I like to see the *coo's* back at a gradient something like this" (drawing an imaginary line with his hand), "and then the ribs or girders will carry more flesh than if they were so—or so." When he attended the county agricultural meetings, which he frequently did, he was accustomed to take part in the discussions, and he brought the same vigorous practical mind to bear upon questions of tillage, drainage, and farm economy which he had before been accustomed to exercise on mechanical and engineering matters.

All his early affection for birds and animals revived. He had favorite dogs, and cows, and horses; and again he began to keep rabbits, and to pride himself on the beauty of his breed. There was not a bird's nest in the grounds that he did not know of; and from day to day he went round watching the progress which the birds made with their building, carefully guarding them from harm. His minute knowledge of the habits of British birds was the result of a long, loving, and close observation of nature.

At Tapton he remembered the failure of his early experiment in hatching birds' eggs by heat, and he now performed it successfully, being able to secure a proper apparatus for maintaining a uniform temperature. He was also curious about the breeding and fattening of fowls; and when his friend Edward Pease, of Darlington, visited him at Tapton, he explained a method which he had invented of fattening chickens in half the usual time. The chickens were confined in boxes, which were so made as to exclude the light. Dividing the day into two or three periods, the birds were shut up at the end of each after a heavy feed, and went to sleep. The plan proved very successful, and Mr. Stephenson jocularly said that if he were to devote himself to chickens he could soon make a little fortune.

Mrs. Stephenson tried to keep bees, but found they would not thrive at Tapton. Many hives perished, and there was no case of success. The cause of failure was long a mystery to the engineer; but one day his acute powers of observation enabled him to unravel it. At the foot of the hill on which Tapton House stands, he saw some bees trying to rise up from among the grass, laden with honey and wax. They were already exhausted, as if with long flying; and then it occurred to him that the height at which the house stood above the bees' feeding-ground rendered it difficult for them to reach their hives when heavy laden, and hence they sank exhausted. He afterward incidentally mentioned the circumstance to Mr. Jesse, the naturalist, who concurred in his view as to the cause of failure, and was much struck by the keen observation which had led to its solution.

George Stephenson had none of the habits of the student. He read very little; for reading is a habit which is generally acquired in youth, and his youth and manhood had been, for the most part, spent in hard work. Books wearied him and sent him to sleep. Novels excited his feelings too much, and he avoided them, though he would occasionally read through a philosophical work on a subject in which he felt particularly interested. He wrote very few letters with his own hand. Nearly all his letters were dictated, and he avoided even dictation when he could. His greatest pleasure was in conversation, from which he gathered most of his imparted information.

It was his practice, when about to set out on a journey by railway, to walk along the train before it started, and look into the carriages to see if he could find "a conversible face." On one of such occasions, at the Euston Station, he discovered in a carriage a very handsome, manly, and intelligent face, which he afterward found was that of the late Lord Denman. He was on his way down to his seat at Stony Middelton, in Derbyshire. Stephenson entered the carriage, and the two were shortly engaged in interesting conversation. It turned upon chronometry and horology, and the engineer amazed his lordship by the extent of his knowledge on the subject, in which he displayed as much minute information, even down to the latest improvements in watch-making, as if he had been bred a watchmaker and lived by the trade. Lord Denman was curious to know how a man whose time must have been mainly engrossed by engineering had gathered so much knowledge on a subject quite out of his own line, and he asked the question. "I learned clockmaking and watchmaking," was the answer, "while a working-man at Killingworth, when I made a little money in my spare hours by cleaning the pitmen's clocks and watches; and since then I have kept up my information on the subject." This led to farther questions, and then he proceeded to tell Lord Denman the interesting story of his life, which held him entranced during the remainder of the journey.

Many of his friends readily accepted invitations to Tapton House to enjoy his hospitality, which never failed. With them he would "fight his battles o'er again," reverting often to his battle for the locomotive; and he was never tired of telling, nor were his auditors of listening to, the lively anecdotes with which he was accustomed to illustrate the struggles of his early career. While walking in the woods or through the grounds, he would arrest his friends' attention by allusion to some simple object—such as a leaf, a blade of grass, a bit of bark, a nest of birds, or an ant carrying its eggs across the path—and descant in glowing terms on the creative power of the Divine Mechanician, whose contrivances were so exhaustless and so wonderful. This was a theme upon which he was often accustomed to dwell in reverential admiration when in the society of his more intimate friends.

One night, when walking under the stars, and gazing up into the field of suns, each the probable centre of a system, forming the Milky Way, a friend observed, "What an insignificant creature is man in sight of so immense a creation as this!" "Yes!" was his reply: "but how wonderful a creature also is man, to be able to think and reason, and even in some measure to comprehend works so infinite!"

A microscope which he had brought down to Tapton was a source of immense enjoyment, and he was never tired of contemplating the minute wonders which it revealed. One evening, when some friends were visiting him, he induced each of them to puncture his skin so as to draw blood, in order that he might examine the globules through the microscope. One of the gentlemen present was a teetotaler, and Stephenson pronounced his blood to be the most lively of the whole. He had a theory of his own about the movement of the globules in the blood, which has since become familiar. It was, that they were respectively charged with electricity, positive at one end and negative at the other, and that they thus attracted and repelled each other, causing a circulation. No sooner did he observe any thing new than he immediately set about devising a reason for it. His training in mechanics, his practical familiarity with matter in all its forms, and the strong bent of his mind, led him first of all to seek for a mechanical explanation; and yet he was ready to admit that there was a something in the principle of *life*—so mysterious and inexplicable—which baffled mechanics, and seemed to dominate over and control them. He did not care much, either, for abstruse mechanics, but only for the experimental and practical, as is usually the case with those whose knowledge has been self-acquired.

Even at his advanced age the spirit of frolic had not left him. When proceeding from Chesterfield Station to Tapton House with his friends, he would almost invariably challenge them to a race up the steep path, partly formed of stone steps, along the hill-side. And he would struggle, as of old, to keep the front place, though by this time his "wind" greatly failed him. He would occasionally invite an old friend to take a wrestle with him on the lawn, to keep up his skill, and perhaps to try some new "knack" of throwing. In the evening he would sometimes indulge his visitors by reciting the old pastoral of "Damon and Phyllis," or singing his favorite song of "John Anderson my Joe."

But his greatest enjoyment on such occasion was "a crowdie." "Let's have a crowdie night," he would say; and forthwith a kettle of boiling water was ordered in, with a basin of oatmeal. Taking a large bowl, containing a sufficiency of hot water, and placing it between his knees, he poured in oatmeal with one hand, and stirred the mixture vigorously with the other. When enough meal had been added, and the stirring was completed, the crowdie was made. It was then supped with new milk, and Mr. Stephenson generally pronounced it "capital!" It was the diet to which he had been accustomed when a working-man, and all the dainties with which he had become familiar in recent years had not spoiled his simple tastes. To enjoy crowdie at his years, besides, indicated that he still possessed that quality on which no doubt much of his practical success in life had depended—a strong and healthy digestion.

He would also frequently invite to his house the humbler companions of his early life, and take pleasure in talking over old times with them. He never assumed any of the bearings of the great man on such occasions, but treated his visitors with the same friendliness and respect as if they had been his equals, sending them away pleased with themselves and delighted with him. At other times, needy men who had known him in their youth would knock at his door, and they were never refused access. But if he had heard of any misconduct on their part, he would rate them soundly. One who knew him intimately in private life has seen him exhorting such backsliders, and denouncing their misconduct and imprudence, with the tears streaming down his cheeks. And he would generally conclude by opening his purse, and giving them the help which they needed "to make a fresh start in the world."

His life at Tapton during his later years was occasionally diversified by a visit to London. His engineering business having become limited, he generally went there for the purpose of visiting friends, or "to see what there was fresh going on." He found a new race of engineers springing up on all sides—men who knew him not; and his London journeys gradually ceased to yield him pleasure. A friend used to take him to the opera, but by the end of the first act he was generally observed in a profound slumber. Yet on one occasion he enjoyed a visit to the Haymarket, with a party of friends on his birthday, to see T. P. Cooke in "Black-eyed Susan"—if that can be called enjoyment which kept him in a state of tears during half the performance. At other times he visited Newcastle, which always gave him great pleasure. He would, on such occasions, go out to Killingworth and seek up old friends, and if the people whom he knew were too retiring and shrunk into their cottages, he went and sought them there. Striking the floor with his stick, and holding his noble person upright, he would say, in his own kind way, "Well, and how's all here to-day?" To the last he had always a warm heart for Newcastle and its neighborhood.

Sir Robert Peel, on more than one occasion, invited George Stephenson to his mansion at Drayton, where he was accustomed to assemble round him men of the highest distinction in art, science, and legislation, during the intervals of his Parliamentary life. The first invitations were respectfully declined; but Sir Robert again pressing him to come down to Tamworth, where he would meet Buckland, Follett, and others well known to both, he at last consented.

Stephenson's strong powers of observation, together with his native humor and shrewdness, imparted to his conversation at all times much vigor and originality. Though mainly an engineer, he was also a profound thinker on many scientific questions, and there was scarcely a subject of speculation or a department of recondite science on which he had not employed his faculties in such a way as to have formed large and original views. Mr. Sopwith, F.R.S., has informed us that the conversation at Drayton, on one occasion, turned on the theory of the formation of coal, in the course of which Stephenson had an animated discussion with Dr. Buckland. But the result was, that Dr. Buckland, a much greater master of tongue-fence, completely silenced him. Next morning, before breakfast, when he was walking in the grounds deeply pondering, Sir William Follett came up and asked what he was thinking about. "Why, Sir William, I am thinking over that argument I had with Buckland last night. I know I am right, and that, if I had only the command of words which he has, I'd have beaten him." "Let me know all about it," said Sir William, "and I'll see what I can do for you." The two sat down in an arbor, where the astute lawyer made himself thoroughly acquainted with the points of the case, entering into it with the zeal of an advocate about to plead the interests of his client. After he had mastered the subject, Sir William said, "Now I am ready for him." Sir Robert Peel was made acquainted with the plot, and adroitly introduced the subject of the controversy after dinner. The result was, that in the argument which followed, the man of science was overcome by the man of law. "And what do *you* say, Mr. Stephenson?" asked Sir Robert, laughing. "Why," said he, "I say this, that of all the powers above and under the earth, there seems to me to be no power so great as the gift of the gab."

One Sunday, when the party had just returned from church, they were standing together on the terrace near the Hall, and observed in the distance a railway flashing along, tossing behind its long white plume of steam. "Now, Buckland," said Stephenson, "I have a poser for you. Can you tell me what is the power that is driving that train?" "Well," said the other, "I suppose it is one of your big engines." "But what drives the engine?" "Oh, very likely a canny Newcastle driver." "What do you say to the light of the sun?" "How can that be?" asked the doctor. "It is nothing else," said the engineer: "it is light bottled up in the earth for tens of thousands of years—light, absorbed by plants and vegetables, being necessary for the condensation of carbon during the process of their growth, if it be not carbon in another form—and now, after being buried in the earth for long ages in fields of coal, that latent light is again brought forth and liberated, made to work as in that locomotive, for great human purposes."*

During the same visit Mr. Stephenson one evening repeated his experiment with blood drawn from the finger, submitting it to the microscope in order to show the curious circulation of the globules. He set the example by pricking his own thumb; and the other guests, by turns, in like manner gave up a small portion of their blood for the purpose of ascertaining the comparative liveliness of their circulation. When Sir Robert Peel's turn came, Stephenson said he was curious to know "how the blood

* This was a favorite notion of George Stephenson's, and he held that what produced light and heat had originally been light and heat. Mr. Fearon, solicitor, has informed the author that he accompanied Stephenson on one of his visits to Belgium, when it seemed to him that the engineer did not take much interest in the towns, churches, or public buildings of Belgium, probably because he knew little of history, and they recalled no associations with the past. One day the party went to see the beautiful Hôtel de Ville at Brussels, but Stephenson did not seem moved by it. On passing out of the square, however, by the little street which leads toward the Montague de la Cour, his interest was thoroughly roused by the sight of an immense fat pig hung up in a butcher's shop. He immediately took out his foot-rule, measured the pig, and expressed a desire to have some conversation with the butcher as to how it had been fed. The butcher accordingly waited upon them at the hotel, and told all he knew about the feeding of the pig; and then, says Mr. Fearon, "George went off into his favorite theory of the sun's light, which he said had fattened the pig; for the light had gone into the pease, and the pease had gone into the fat, and the fat pig was like a field of coal in this respect, that they were, for the most part, neither more nor less than bottled sunshine."

globules of a great politician would conduct themselves." Sir Robert held forth his finger for the purpose of being pricked; but once and again he sensitively shrunk back, and at length the experiment, so far as he was concerned, was abandoned. Sir Robert Peel's sensitiveness to pain was extreme, and yet he was destined, a few years after, to die a death of the most distressing agony.

In 1847, the year before his death, George Stephenson was again invited to join a distinguished party at Drayton Manor, and to assist in the ceremony of formally opening the Trent Valley Railway, which had been originally designed and laid out by himself many years before. The first sod of the railway had been cut by the prime minister in November, 1845, and the formal opening took place on the 26th of June, 1847, the line having thus been constructed in less than two years.

What a change had come over the spirit of the landed gentry since the time when George Stephenson had first projected a railway through that district! Then they were up in arms against him, characterizing him as the devastator and spoiler of their estates, whereas now he was hailed as one of the greatest benefactors of the age. Sir Robert Peel, the chief political personage in England, welcomed him as a guest and friend, and spoke of him as the chief among practical philosophers. A dozen members of Parliament, seven baronets, with all the landed magnates of the district, assembled to celebrate the opening of the railway. The clergy were there to bless the enterprise, and to bid all hail to railway progress, as "enabling them to carry on with greater facility those operations in connection with religion which were calculated to be so beneficial to the country." The army, speaking through the mouth of General A'Court, acknowledged the vast importance of railways, as tending to improve the military defenses of the country. And representatives from eight corporations were there to acknowledge the great benefits which railways had conferred upon the merchants, tradesmen, and working classes of their respective towns and cities.

In the spring of 1848 George Stephenson was invited to Whittington House, near Chesterfield, the residence of his friend and former pupil, Mr. Swanwick, to meet the distinguished American, Emerson. On being introduced to each other they did not immediately engage in conversation; but presently Stephenson jumped up, took Emerson by the collar, and, giving him one of his friendly shakes, asked how it was that in England we could always tell an American. This led to an interesting conversation, in the course of which Emerson said how much he had every where been struck by the haleness and comeliness of the English men and women, from which they diverged into a discussion of the influences which air, climate, moisture, soil, and other conditions exercised on the physical and moral development of a people. The conversation was next directed to the subject of electricity, on which Stephenson launched out enthusiastically, explaining his views by several simple and some striking illustrations. From thence it gradually turned to the events of his own life, which he related in so graphic a manner as completely to rivet the attention of the American. Afterward Emerson said "that it was worth crossing the Atlantic were it only to have seen Stephenson —he had such force of character and vigor of intellect."

The rest of George Stephenson's days were spent quietly at Tapton, among his dogs, his rabbits, and his birds. When not engaged about the works connected with his collieries, he was occupied in horticulture and farming. He continued proud of his flowers, his fruits, and his crops, while the old spirit of competition was still strong within him. Although he had for some time been in delicate health, and his hand shook from nervous debility, he appeared to possess a sound constitution. Emerson had observed of him that he had the lives of many men in him. But perhaps the American spoke figuratively, in reference to his vast stores of experience. It appeared that he had never completely recovered from the attack of pleurisy which seized him during his return from Spain. As late, however, as the 26th of July, 1848, he felt himself sufficiently well to be able to attend a meeting of the Institute of Mechanical Engineers at Birmingham, and to read to the members his paper "On the Fallacies of the Rotatory Engine."

It was his last public appearance. Shortly after his return to Tapton he had an attack of intermittent fever, from which he seemed to be recovering, when a sudden effusion of blood from the lungs carried him off, on the 12th of August, 1848, in the sixty-seventh year of his age. When all was over, Robert wrote to Edmund Pease, "With deep pain I inform you, as one of his oldest friends, of the death of my dear father this morning at 12 o'clock, after about ten days' illness from severe fever." Mr. Starbuck, who was also present, wrote: "The favorable symptoms of yesterday morning were toward evening followed by a serious change for the worse. This continued during the night, and early this morning it became evident that he was sinking. At a few minutes before 12 to-day he breathed his last. All that the most devoted and unremitting care of Mrs. Stephenson* and the skill of medicine could accomplish has been done, but in vain."

George Stephenson's remains were followed to the grave by a large body of his work-people, by whom he was greatly admired and beloved. They remembered him as a kind master, who was ever ready actively to promote all measures for their moral, physical, and mental improvement. The inhabitants of Chesterfield evinced their respect for the deceased by suspending business, closing their shops, and joining in the funeral procession, which was headed by the corporation of the town. Many of the surrounding gentry also attended. The body was interred in Trinity Church, Chesterfield, where a simple tablet marks the great engineer's last resting-place.

TRINITY CHURCH, CHESTERFIELD.

* The second Mrs. Stephenson having died in 1845, George married a third time in 1848, about six months before his death. The third Mrs. Stephenson was an intelligent and respectable lady, who had for some years officiated as his housekeeper.

The statue of George Stephenson, which the Liverpool and Manchester and Grand Junction Companies had commissioned, was on its way to England when his death occurred; and it served for a monument, though his best monument will always be his works. The statue referred to was placed in St. George's Hall, Liverpool. A full-length statue of him, by Bailey, was also erected, a few years later, in the noble vestibule of the London and Northwestern Station, in Euston Square. A subscription for the purpose was set on foot by the Society of Mechanical Engineers, of which he had been the founder and president. A few advertisements were inserted in the newspapers, inviting subscriptions; and it is a notable fact that the voluntary offerings included an average of two shillings each from 3150 working-men, who embraced this opportunity of doing honor to their distinguished fellow-workman.

But the finest and most appropriate statue to the memory of George Stephenson is that which was erected in 1862, after the design of John Lough, at Newcastle-upon-Tyne. It is in the immediate neighborhood of the Literary and Philosophical Institute, to which both George and his son Robert were so much indebted in their early years; close to the great Stephenson locomotive foundery established by the shrewdness of the father; and in the vicinity of the High-Level Bridge, one of the grandest products of the genius of the son. The head of Stephenson, as expressed in this noble work, is massive, characteristic, and faithful; and the attitude of the figure is simple, yet manly and energetic. It stands on a pedestal, at the respective corners of which are sculptured the recumbent figures of a pitman, a mechanic, an engine-driver, and a plate-layer. The statue appropriately stands in a very thoroughfare of working-men, thousands of whom see it daily as they pass to and from their work; and we can imagine them, as they look up to Stephenson's manly figure, applying to it the words addressed by Robert Nicoll to Robert Burns, with perhaps still greater appropriateness:

"Before the proudest of the earth
We stand, with an uplifted brow;
Like us, thou wast a toiling man—
And we are noble, now!"

The portrait prefixed to this volume gives a good indication of

George Stephenson's shrewd, kind, honest, manly face. His fair, clear countenance was ruddy, and seemingly glowed with health. The forehead was large and high, projecting over the eyes, and there was that massive breadth across the lower part which is usually observed in men of eminent constructive skill. The mouth was firmly marked, and shrewdness and humor lurked there as well as in the keen gray eye. His frame was compact, well knit, and rather spare. His hair became gray at an early age, and toward the close of his life it was of a pure silky whiteness. He dressed neatly in black, wearing a white neckcloth; and his face, his person, and his deportment at once arrested attention, and marked the Gentleman.

TABLET IN TRINITY CHURCH, CHESTERFIELD.

VICTORIA BRIDGE, MONTREAL.

CHAPTER XX.

ROBERT STEPHENSON'S VICTORIA BRIDGE, LOWER CANADA—ILLNESS AND DEATH.

George Stephenson bequeathed to his son his valuable collieries, his share in the engine manufactory at Newcastle, and his large accumulation of savings, which, together with the fortune he had himself amassed by railway work, gave Robert the position of an engineer millionaire—the first of his order. He continued, however, to live in a quiet style; and although he bought occasional pictures and statues, and indulged in the luxury of a yacht, he did not live up to his income, which went on accumulating until his death.

There was no longer the necessity for applying himself to the laborious business of a Parliamentary engineer, in which he had now been occupied for some fifteen years. Shortly after his father's death, Edward Pease recommended him to give up the more harassing work of his profession; and his reply (15th of June, 1850) was as follows:

"The suggestion which your kind note contains is quite in accordance with my own feelings and intentions respecting retirement; but I find it a very difficult matter to bring to a close so complicated a connection in business as that which has been established by twenty-five years of active and arduous professional duty. Comparative retirement is, however, my intention, and I trust that your prayer for the Divine blessing to grant me happiness and quiet comfort will be fulfilled. I can not but feel deeply grateful to the Great Disposer of events for the success which has hitherto attended my exertions in life, and I trust that the future will also be marked by a continuance of His mercies."

Although Robert Stephenson, in conformity with this expressed intention, for the most part declined to undertake new business, he did not altogether lay aside his harness, and he lived to repeat his tubular bridges both in Egypt and Canada. The success of the tubular system, as adopted at Menai and Conway, was such as to recommend it for adoption wherever great span was required, and the peculiar circumstances connected with the navigation of the Nile and the St. Lawrence may be said to have compelled its adoption in carrying railways across both those rivers.

Two tubular bridges were built after our engineer's designs across the Nile, near Damietta, in Lower Egypt. That near Benha contains eight spans or openings of 80 feet each, and two centre spans, formed by one of the largest swing-bridges ever constructed, the total length of the swing-beam being 157 feet, a clear waterway of 60 feet being provided on either side of the centre pier. The only novelty in these bridges consisted in the road being carried upon the tubes instead of within them, their erection being carried out in the usual manner by means of workmen, materials, and plant sent out from England. The Tubular Bridge constructed in Canada, after Mr. Stephenson's designs, was of a much more important character, and deserves a fuller description.

The important uses of railways had been recognized at an early period by the inhabitants of North America, and in the course of about thirty years more than 25,000 miles of railway, mostly single, were constructed in the United States alone. The Canadians were more deliberate in their proceedings, and it was not until the year 1840 that their first railway, 14 miles in length, was constructed between Laprairie and St. John's, for the purpose of connecting Lake Champlain with the River St. Lawrence. From this date, however, new lines were rapidly projected; more particularly the Great Western of Canada, and the Atlantic and St. Lawrence (now forming part of the Grand Trunk), until in the course of a few years Canada had a length of nearly 2000 miles of railway open or in course of construction, intersecting the provinces almost in a continuous line from Rivière du Loup, near the mouth of the St. Lawrence, to Port Sarnia, on the shores of Lake Huron.

But there still remained one most important and essential link to connect the lines on the south of the St. Lawrence with those on the north, and at the same time place the city of Montreal in direct railway connection with the western parts of Canada. The completion of this link was also necessary in order to maintain the commercial communication of Canada with the rest of the world during five months in every year; for, though the St. Lawrence in summer affords a splendid outlet to the ocean—toward which the commerce of the colony naturally tends—the frost in winter is so severe, that during that season Canada is completely frozen in, and the navigation hermetically closed by the ice.

The Grand Trunk Railway was designed to furnish a line of land communication along the great valley of the St. Lawrence at all seasons, following the course of the river, and connecting the principal towns of the colony. But stopping short on the north shore, nearly opposite Montreal, with which it was connected by a dangerous and often impracticable ferry, it was felt that, until the St. Lawrence was bridged by a railway, the Canadian system of railways was manifestly incomplete. But how to bridge this wide and rapid river! Never before, perhaps, was a problem of such difficulty proposed for solution by an engineer. Opposite Montreal, the St. Lawrence is about two miles wide, running at the rate of about ten miles an hour; and at the close of each winter it carries down the ice of 2000 square miles of lakes and rivers, with their numerous tributaries.

As early as the year 1846, the construction of a bridge at Montreal was strongly advocated by the local press as the only means of connecting that city with the projected Atlantic and St. Lawrence Railway. But the difficulties of executing such a work seemed almost insurmountable to those best acquainted with the locality. The greatest difficulty was apprehended from the tremendous shoving and pressure of the ice at the break-up of winter. At such times, opposite Montreal, the whole river is packed with huge blocks of ice, and it is often seen piled up to a height of from 40 to 50 feet along the banks, placing the surrounding country under water, and occasionally doing severe damage to the massive stone buildings erected along the noble river front of the city.

But no other expedient presented itself but a bridge, and a survey was made accordingly at the instance of the Hon. John Young, one of the directors of the railway. A period of colonial depression having shortly after occurred, the project slept for a time, and it was not until six years later, in 1852, when the Grand Trunk Railway was under construction, that the subject was again brought under discussion. In that year, Mr. Alexander M. Ross, who had superintended the construction of Robert Stephenson's tubular bridge at Conway, visited Canada, and inspected the site of the proposed structure, when he at once formed the opinion that a tubular bridge carrying a railway was the most suitable means of crossing the St. Lawrence, and connecting Montreal with the lines on the north of the river.

The directors felt that such a work would necessarily be of a most formidable and difficult character, and before coming to any conclusion they determined to call to their assistance Mr. Robert Stephenson, as the engineer most competent to advise them in the matter. Mr. Stephenson considered the subject of so much interest and importance that, in the summer of 1853, he proceeded to Canada to inquire as to all the facts, and examine carefully the site of the proposed work. He then formed the opinion that a tubular bridge across the river was not only practicable, but by far the most suitable for the purpose intended, and early in the following year he sent an elaborate report on the whole subject to the directors of the railway. The result was the adoption of his recommendation and the erection of the Victoria Bridge, of which Robert Stephenson was the designer and engineer, and Mr. A. M. Ross the joint and resident engineer in directly superintending the execution of the undertaking. The details of the plans were principally worked out in Mr. Stephenson's office in London, under the superintendence of his cousin, Mr. George Robert Stephenson, while the iron-work was for the most part constructed at the Canada Works, Liverpool, from whence it was shipped, ready for being fixed in position on the spot.

The Victoria Bridge is, without exception, the greatest work of its kind in the world. For gigantic proportions, and vast length and strength, there is nothing to compare with it in ancient or modern times. The entire bridge, with its approaches, is only about sixty yards short of *two miles* in length, being five times longer than the Britannia Bridge across the Menai Straits, seven and a half times longer than Waterloo Bridge, and more than ten times longer than Chelsea Bridge. The two-mile tube across the St. Lawrence rests on twenty-four piers, which, with the abutments, leave twenty-five spaces or spans for the several parts of the tube. Twenty-four of these spans are 242 feet wide; the centre span—itself a huge bridge—being 330 feet. The road is carried within the tube 60 feet above the level of the river, so as not to interfere with its navigation.

As one of the principal difficulties apprehended in the erection of the bridge was that arising from the tremendous "shoving"

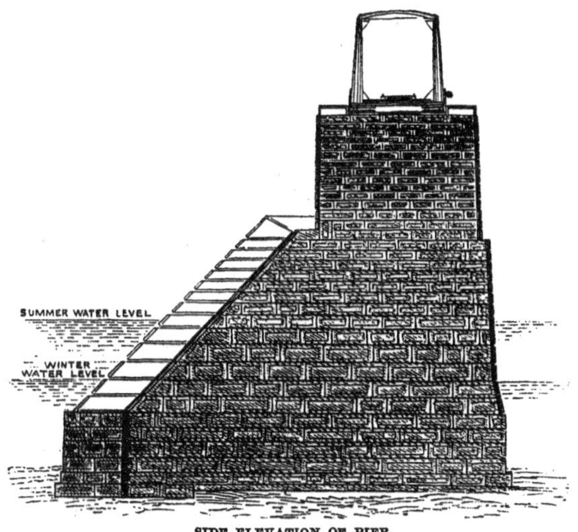

SIDE ELEVATION OF PIER.

and ramming of the ice at the break-up of winter, the plans were carefully designed so as to avert all danger from this cause. Hence the peculiarity in the form of the piers, which, though greatly increasing their strength for the purpose intended, must be admitted to detract considerably from the symmetry of the structure as a whole. The western face of each pier—that is, the up-river side—has a large wedge-shaped cutwater of stone-work, presenting an inclined plane toward the current, for the purpose of arresting and breaking up the ice-blocks, and thereby preventing them from piling up and damaging the tube carrying the railway. The piers are of immense strength. Those close to the abutments contain about 6000 tons of masonry each, while those which support the great centre tube contain about 12,000 tons. The former are 15 feet wide, and the latter 18. Scarcely a block of stone used in the piers is less than seven tons in weight, while many of those opposed to the force of the breaking-up ice weigh fully ten tons.

As might naturally be expected, the getting in of the foundations of these enormous piers in so wide and rapid a river was attended with many difficulties. To give an idea of the water-power of the St. Lawrence, it may be mentioned that when the river comes down in its greatest might, large stone boulders weighing upward of a ton are rolled along by the sheer force of the current. The depth of the river, however, was not so great as might be supposed, varying from only five to fifteen feet during summer, when the foundation-work was carried on.

The method first employed to get in the foundations was by means of dams or caissons, which were constructed on shore, floated into position, and scuttled over the places at which the foundations were to be laid, thus at once forming a nucleus from which the dams could be constructed. The first of such dams was floated, got into position, scuttled, and sunk, and the piling fairly begun, on the 19th of June, 1854. By the 15th of the following month the sheet-piling and puddling was finished, when the pumping of the water out of the inclosed space by steam-power was proceeded with, and in a few hours the bed of the river was laid almost dry, the toe of every pile being distinctly visible. By the 22d the first stone of the pier was laid, and on the 14th of August the masonry was above water-level.

The getting in of the foundations of the other piers was proceeded with in like manner, though frequently interrupted by storms, inundations, and collisions of timber-rafts, which occasionally carried away the moorings of the dams. Considerable difficulty was in some places experienced from the huge boulder-stones lying in the bed of the river, to remove which sometimes cost the divers several months of hard labor. In getting in the foundations of the later piers, the method first employed of sinking the floating caissons in position was abandoned, and the dams were constructed of "crib-work,"* which was found more con-

* The dams of "crib-work" were formed by laying flattened pine logs along the

venient, and less liable to interruption by accident from collision or otherwise.

By the spring of 1857 a sufficient number of piers had been finished to enable the erection of the tubes to be proceeded with. The operations connected with this portion of the work were also of a novel character. Instead of floating the tubes between the piers and raising them into position by hydraulic power, as at Conway and Menai, which the rapid current of the St. Lawrence would not permit, the tubes were erected *in situ* on a staging prepared for the purpose, as shown in the following engraving.

Floating scows, each 60 feet by 20, were moored in position,

WORKS IN PROGRESS, 1857—VIEW FROM ABOVE THE SOUTH ABUTMENT.

whole outer edge of the work, and at intervals of from 5 to 10 feet parallel therewith throughout the whole of the breadth, connected with transverse timbers firmly treenailed and notched into them. When one course was formed, another was laid upon and firmly treenailed to it. After two or three courses were laid, transverse timbers were placed over them close together, so as to form a flooring, on which stone was placed to suit the crib as the work progressed. When the under side of the crib touched the bottom, it was carefully filled with loose stones and clay puddle to the water level. The process of puddling and pumping out the water, and building up the pier within the dam thus formed, then proceeded in the usual manner. In some cases a powerful steam dredge was employed to clear out the puddle-chambers.

and kept in their place by piles sliding in grooves. These piles, when firmly fixed in the bed of the river, were bolted to the sides of the scows, and the tops were leveled to receive the sills upon which the framing carrying the truss and platform was erected. Timbers were laid on the lower chords of the truss, forming a platform 24 feet wide, closely planked with deals. The upper chords carried rails, along which moved the "travelers" used in erecting the tubes. The plates forming the bottom of each tube having been accurately laid and riveted, and adjusted to level and centre by oak wedges, the erection of the sides was next proceeded with, extending outward from the centre on either side, this work being closely followed by the plating of the top. Each tube between the respective pairs of piers was in the first place erected separate and independent of its adjoining tubes; but after completion, the tubes were joined in pairs and firmly bolted to the masonry over which they were united, their outer ends being placed upon rollers so arranged on the adjoining piers that they might expand or contract according to variations of temperature.

The work continued to make satisfactory progress down to the spring of 1858, by which time fourteen out of the twenty-four piers were finished, together with the formidable abutments and approaches to the bridge. Considerable apprehensions were entertained as to the security of the piers and the unfinished parts of the work at the usual breaking-up of the ice. We take the following account from a letter written by Mr. Ross to Mr. Stephenson descriptive of the scene.

"On the 29th of March, the ice above Montreal began to show signs of weakness, but it was not until the 31st that a general movement became observable, which continued for an hour, when it suddenly stopped, and the water rose rapidly. On the following day, at noon, a grand movement commenced; the waters rose about four feet in two minutes, up to a level with many of the Montreal streets. The fields of ice at the same time were suddenly elevated to an incredible height; and so overwhelming were they in appearance, that crowds of the townspeople, who had assembled on the quay to watch the progress of the flood, ran for their lives. This movement lasted about twenty minutes, during which the jammed ice destroyed several portions of the quay wall, grinding the hardest blocks to atoms. The embanked approaches to the Victoria Bridge had tremendous forces to resist. In the full channel of the stream, the ice in its passage between the piers was broken up by the force of the blow immediately on its coming in contact with the cutwaters. Sometimes thick sheets of ice were seen to rise up and rear on end against the piers, but by the force of the current they were speedily made to roll over into the stream, and in a moment after were out of sight. For the two next days the river was still high, until on the 4th of April the waters seemed suddenly to give way, and by the following day the river was flowing clear and smooth as a mill-pond, nothing of winter remaining except the masses of bordage ice which were strewn along the shores of the stream. On examination of the piers of the bridge, it was found that they had admirably resisted the tremendous pressure; and though the timber "crib-work" erected to facilitate the placing of floating pontoons to form the dams was found considerably disturbed and in some places seriously damaged, the piers, with the exception of one or two heavy stone blocks, which were still unfinished, escaped uninjured. One block of many tons' weight was carried to a considerable distance, and must have been torn out of its place by sheer force, as several of the broken fragments were found left in the pier."

Toward the end of January, 1859, the plating of the bottom of the great central tube was begun. The execution of this part of the undertaking was of a very formidable and difficult character. The gangs of men employed upon it were required to work night and day, though the season was mid-winter, as it was of great importance to the navigation that the staging should be removed by the time that the ice broke up and the river became open. The night gangs were lighted at their work by wood-fires filling huge braziers, the bright glow of which illumined the vast snow-covered ice-field in the midst of which they worked at so lofty an elevation; and the sight as well as the sounds of the hammering and riveting, the puffing of the steam-engines, and the various operations thus carried on, presented a scene the like of which has rarely been witnessed. The work was not conducted without considerable risk to the men, arising from the intense cold. The temperature was often 20° below zero, and notwithstanding that they all worked in thick gloves, and that care was taken to protect every exposed part, many of them were severely frostbitten. Sometimes, when thick mist rose from the river, they would become covered with icicles, and be driven from their work.

Notwithstanding these difficulties, the laying of the great central tube made steady progress. By the 17th of February the first pair of side-plates was erected; on the 28th, the bottom was riveted and completed; 180 feet of the sides was also in place,

ERECTION OF MAIN CENTRAL TUBE.

and 100 feet of the top was plated; and on the 21st of March the whole of the plating was finished. A few days later the wedges were knocked away, and the tube hung suspended between the adjoining piers. On the 18th of May following the staging was all cleared away, with the moored scows and the crib-work, and the centre span of the bridge was again clear for the navigation of the river.

The first stone of the bridge was laid on the 22d of July, 1854. The works continued in progress for a period of five and a half years, until the 17th of December, 1859, when the first train passed over the bridge; and on the 25th of August, 1860, it was formally opened for traffic by the Prince of Wales. It was the greatest of Robert Stephenson's bridges, and worthy of being the crowning and closing work of his life. But he was not destined to see its completion. Two months before the bridge was finished he had passed from the scene of all his labors.

We have little to add as to the closing events in Robert Stephenson's life. Retired in a great measure from the business of an engineer, he occupied himself for the most part in society, in yachting, and in attending the House of Commons and the Clubs. It was in the year 1847 that he entered the House of Commons as member for Whitby; but he does not seem to have been very regular in his attendance, and only appeared on divisions when there was a "whip" of the party to which he belonged. He was a member of the Sewage and Sanitary Commissions, and of the Commission which sat on Westminster Bridge. He very seldom addressed the House, and then only on matters relating to engineering. The last occasions on which he spoke were on the Suez Canal* and the cleansing of the Serpentine.

* Mr. Stephenson entertained a very strong opinion as to the inexpediency of making this canal, and the impracticability of keeping it open except at an enormous expense. Of course it was possible to make the canal provided there was money enough raised for the purpose. But, even if made, he held that it would not long be used, for there would not be traffic enough to pay working expenses. In 1846, Mr. Stephenson carefully examined the country along the line of the proposed canal, from Tineh on the Mediterranean, to Suez on the Red Sea, in company with the agents of M. Talabot, a French engineer, and M. de Negrelli, an Austrian engineer. They ascertained that there was no difference of level between the two seas, and that consequently a canal capable of being scoured by the waters of either was impracticable. On the occasion of Captain Pim's reading a paper on the subject of the revived project of the canal before the Geographical Society on the 11th of April, 1859, Mr. Stephenson took part in the discussion which followed. He held that any harbor constructed at Port Said, however far it might be extended into the sea, would only act as a mud-trap, and that it would be impracticable to keep such a port open. Mr. George Rennie had compared the proposed breakwater at Pelusium with the break-

Besides constructing the railway between Alexandria and Cairo, he was consulted, like his father, by the King of Belgium as to the railways of that country; and he was made Knight of the Order of Leopold because of the improvements which he had made in locomotive engines, so much to the advantage of the Belgian system of inland transit. He was consulted by the King of Sweden as to the railway between Christiana and Lake Miösen, and in consideration of his services was decorated with the Grand Cross of the Order of St. Olaf. He also visited Switzerland, Piedmont, and Denmark, to advise as to the system of railway communication best suited for those countries. At the Paris Exhibition of 1855 the Emperor of France decorated him with the Legion of Honor in consideration of his public services; and at home the University of Oxford made him a Doctor of Civil Laws. In 1855 he was elected President of the Institute of Civil Engineers, which office he held with honor and filled with distinguished ability for two years, giving place to his friend Mr. Locke at the end of 1857.

Mr. Stephenson was frequently called upon to act as arbitrator

water at Portland, on which Mr. Stephenson observed, "Why, at Portland, the stones are carried out from the shore and thrown into the sea, but at Pelusium there is no solid shore, and all the stones must be brought 100 miles. Can there be any comparison between a breakwater at Portland and one in the Mediterranean on a lee-shore, where there is no stone and no foundation whatever? It is only the silt of the Nile. The Nile brings down millions of tons of mud yearly, and hence the Delta formed at its mouth. The moment you construct a harbor at Port Said and project piers into the sea, you immediately arrest the course of the mud, and will never be able to keep the port open. It would be the most extraordinary thing in the world to project two jetties into an open sea on a lee-shore, which has for almost three months in the year a northeast wind blowing upon it. There is no seaman, except in fair weather, who would venture to approach such a place. To render it at all accessible and safe, there must be a harbor of refuge made, and we know from experience in our own country what a large question that would open up. But even suppose such a harbor to be made. The current carries the mud of the Nile in an easterly direction; and if you provide a harbor of refuge, which means a quiescent harbor, it will act merely as a gigantic mud-trap. I believe it to be nearly if not absolutely true, that there is no large harbor in the world maintained on the delta of a large river. Any such harbor would be silted up in a few years. And whoever has traveled over the district between Port Said and Suez, and seen the moving sands, must see that it would be necessary to dredge, not only that harbor, but the canal itself." Mr. Stephenson's conclusion accordingly was that the scheme was impracticable, that it would not justify the expenditure necessary to complete it, and that, if ever executed, it would prove a commercial failure.

between contractors and railway companies, or between one company and another, great value being attached to his opinion on account of his weighty judgment, his great experience, and his upright character; and we believe his decisions were invariably stamped by the qualities of impartiality and justice. He was always ready to lend a helping hand to a friend, and no petty jealousy stood between him and his rivals in the engineering world. The author remembers being with Mr. Stephenson one evening at his house in Gloucester Square when a note was put into his hand from his friend Brunel, then engaged in his fruitless efforts to launch the *Great Eastern*. It was to ask Stephenson to come down to Blackwall early next morning, and give him the benefit of his judgment. Shortly after six next morning Stephenson was in Scott Russell's building-yard, and he remained there until dusk. About midday, while superintending the launching operations, the balk of timber on which he stood canted up, and he fell up to his middle in the Thames mud. He was dressed as usual, without great-coat (though the day was bitter cold), and with only thin boots upon his feet. He was urged to leave the yard and change his dress, or at least dry himself; but, with his usual disregard of health, he replied, "Oh, never mind me; I'm quite used to this sort of thing;" and he went paddling about in the mud, smoking his cigar, until almost dark, when the day's work was brought to an end. The result of this exposure was an attack of inflammation of the lungs, which kept him to his bed for a fortnight.

He was habitually careless of his health, and perhaps he indulged in narcotics to a prejudicial extent. Hence he often became "hipped," and sometimes ill. When Mr. Sopwith accompanied him to Egypt in the *Titania*, in 1856, he succeeded in persuading Mr. Stephenson to limit his indulgence in cigars and stimulants, and the consequence was that by the end of the voyage he felt himself, as he said, "quite a new man." Arrived at Marseilles, he telegraphed from thence a message to Great George Street, prescribing certain stringent and salutary rules for observance in the office there on his return. But he was of a facile, social disposition, and the old associations proved too strong for him. When he sailed for Norway in the autumn of 1859, though then ailing in health, he looked a man who had still plenty of life in him. By the time he returned his fatal illness had seized him. He was attacked by congestion of the liver, which first developed itself in jaundice, and then ran into dropsy, of which he died on the 12th of October, in the fifty-sixth year of his age. He was buried by the side of Telford in Westminster Abbey, amid the departed great men of his country, and was attended to his resting-place by many of the intimate friends of his boyhood and his manhood. Among those who assembled round his grave were some of the greatest men of thought and action in England, who embraced the sad occasion to pay the last mark of their respect to this illustrious son of one of England's greatest working-men.

It would be out of keeping with the subject thus drawn to a conclusion to pronounce any panegyric on the character and achievements of George and Robert Stephenson. These, for the most part, speak for themselves; and both were emphatically true men, exhibiting in their lives many valuable and sterling qualities.

No beginning could have been less promising than that of the elder Stephenson. Born in a poor condition, yet rich in spirit, he was from the first compelled to rely upon himself, every step of advance which he made being conquered by patient labor. Whether working as a brakesman or an engineer, his mind was always full of the work in hand. He gave himself thoroughly up to it. Like the painter, he might say that he had become great "by neglecting nothing." Whatever he was engaged upon, he was as careful of the details as if each were itself the whole. He did all thoroughly and honestly. There was no "scamping" with him. When a workman, he put his brains and labor into his work; and when a master, he put his conscience and character into it. He would have no slop-work executed merely for the sake of profit. The materials must be as genuine as the workmanship was skillful. The structures which he designed and executed were distinguished for their thoroughness and solidity; his locomotives were famous for their durability and excellent working qualities. The engines which he sent to the United States in 1832 are still in good condition; and even the engines built by him for the Killingworth Colliery, upward of thirty years since, are working there to this day. All his work was honest, representing the actual character of the man.

He was ready to turn his hand to any thing—shoes and clocks, railways and locomotives. He contrived his safety-lamp with the object of saving pitmen's lives, and periled his own life in testing it. With him to resolve was to do. Many men knew far more than he, but none was more ready forthwith to apply what he did know to practical purposes. It was while working at Willington as a brakesman that he first learned how best to handle a spade in throwing ballast out of the ships' holds. This casual employment seems to have left upon his mind the most lasting impression of what "hard work" was; and he often used to revert to it, and say to the young men about him, "Ah, ye lads! there's none o' ye know what *wark* is." Mr. Gooch says he was proud of the dexterity in handling a spade which he had thus acquired, and that he has frequently seen him take the shovel from a laborer in some railway cutting, and show him how to use it more deftly in filling wagons of earth, gravel, or sand. Sir Joshua Walmsley has also informed us that, when examining the works of the Orleans and Tours Railway, Stephenson, seeing a large number of excavators filling and wheeling sand in a cutting, at a great waste of time and labor, went up to the men and said he would show them how to fill their barrows in half the time. He showed them the proper position in which to stand so as to exercise the greatest amount of power with the least expenditure of strength; and he filled the barrow with comparative ease again and again in their presence, to the great delight of the workmen. When passing through his own workshops he would point out to his men how to save labor and get through their work skillfully and with ease. His energy imparted itself to others, quickening and influencing them as strong characters always do, flowing down into theirs, and bringing out their best powers.

His deportment to the workmen employed under him was familiar, yet firm and consistent. As he respected their manhood, so they respected his masterhood. Although he comported himself toward his men as if they occupied very much the same level with himself, he yet possessed that peculiar capacity for governing which enabled him always to preserve among them the strictest discipline, and to secure their cheerful and hearty services. Mr. Ingham, M.P. for South Shields, on going over the workshops at Newcastle, was particularly struck with this quality of the master in his bearing toward his men. "There was nothing," said he, "of undue familiarity in their intercourse, but they spoke to each other as man to man; and nothing seemed to please the master more than to point out illustrations of the ingenuity of his artisans. He took up a rivet, and expatiated on the skill with which it had been fashioned by the workman's hand—its perfectness and truth. He was always proud of his workmen and his pupils; and, while indifferent and careless as to what might be said of himself, he fired up in a moment if disparagement were thrown upon any one whom he had taught or trained."

In manner, George Stephenson was simple, modest, and unassuming, but always manly. He was frank and social in spirit. When a humble workman, he had carefully preserved his sense of self-respect. His companions looked up to him, and his example was worth much more to many of them than books or schools. His devoted love of knowledge made his poverty respectable, and adorned his humble calling. When he rose to a more elevated station, and associated with men of the highest position and influence in Britain, he took his place among them with perfect self-possession. They wondered at the quiet ease and simple dignity of his deportment; and men in the best ranks of life have said of him that "he was one of Nature's gentlemen."

Probably no military chiefs were ever more beloved by their soldiers than were both father and son by the army of men who, under their guidance, worked at labors of profit, made labors of love by their earnest will and purpose. True leaders of men and lords of industry, they were always ready to recognize and encourage talent in those who worked for and with them. Thus it was pleasant, at the openings of the Stephenson lines, to hear the chief engineers attributing the successful completion of the works to their assistants; while the assistants, on the other hand, ascribed the principal glory to their chiefs.

George Stephenson, though a thrifty and frugal man, was essentially unsordid. His rugged path in early life made him careful of his resources. He never saved to hoard, but saved for a purpose, such as the maintenance of his parents or the education of his son. In his later years he became a prosperous and even a wealthy man; but riches never closed his heart, nor stole away the elasticity of his soul. He enjoyed life cheerfully, because hopefully. When he entered upon a commercial enterprise, whether for others or for himself, he looked carefully at the ways and means. Unless they would "pay," he held back. "He would have nothing to do," he declared, "with stock-jobbing speculations." His refusal to sell his name to the schemes of the railway mania—his survey of the Spanish lines without remuneration—his offer to postpone his claim for payment from a poor company until their affairs became more prosperous, are instances of the unsordid spirit in which he acted.

Another marked feature in Mr. Stephenson's character was his patience. Notwithstanding the strength of his convictions as to the great uses to which the locomotive might be applied, he waited long and patiently for the opportunity of bringing it into notice; and for years after he had completed an efficient engine, he went on quietly devoting himself to the ordinary work of the colliery. He made no noise nor stir about his locomotive, but allowed another to take credit for the experiments on velocity and friction which he had made with it upon the Killingworth railroad. By patient industry and laborious contrivance he was enabled, with the powerful help of his son, almost to do for the locomotive what James Watt had done for the condensing engine. He found it clumsy and inefficient, and he made it powerful, efficient, and useful. Both have been described as the improvers of their respective engines; but, as to all that is admirable in their structure or vast in their utility, they are rather entitled to be described as their inventors. They have both tended to increase indefinitely the mass of human comforts and enjoyments, and to render them cheap and accessible to all. But Stephenson's invention, by the influence which it is daily exercising upon the civilization of the world, is even more remarkable than that of Watt, and is calculated to have still more important consequences. In this respect it is to be regarded as the grandest application of steam-power that has yet been discovered.

George Stephenson's close and accurate observation provided him with a fullness of information on many subjects which often appeared surprising to those who had devoted to them a special study. On one occasion the accuracy of his knowledge of birds came out in a curious way at a convivial meeting of railway men in London. The engineers and railway directors present knew each other as railway men and nothing more. The talk had been all of railways and railway politics. Stephenson was a great talker on those subjects, and was generally allowed, from the interest of his conversation and the extent of his experience, to take the lead. At length one of the party broke in with, "Come, now, Stephenson, we have had nothing but railways! can not we have a change, and try if we can talk a little about something else?" "Well," said Stephenson, "I'll give you a wide range of subjects; what shall it be about?" "Say *birds' nests!*" rejoined the other, who prided himself on his special knowledge of the subject. "Then birds' nests be it." A long and animated conversation ensued: the bird-nesting of his boyhood—the blackbird's nest which his father had held him up in his arms to look at when a child at Wylam—the hedges in which he had found the thrush's and the linnet's nests—the mossy bank where the robin built—the cleft in the branch of the young tree where the chaffinch had reared its dwelling—all rose up clear in his mind's eye, and led him back to the scenes of his boyhood at Callerton and Dewley Burn. The color and number of the birds' eggs—the period of their incubation—the materials employed by them for the walls and lining of their nests, were described by him so vividly, and illustrated by such graphic anecdotes, that one of the party remarked that, if George Stephenson had not been the greatest engineer of his day, he might have been one of the greatest naturalists.

His powers of conversation were very great. He was so thoughtful, original, and suggestive. There was scarcely a department of science on which he had not formed some novel and sometimes daring theory. Thus Mr. Gooch, his pupil, who lived with him when at Liverpool, informs us that when sitting over the fire, he would frequently broach his favorite theory of the sun's light and heat being the original source of the light and heat given forth by the burning coal. "It fed the plants of which that coal is made," he would say, "and has been bottled up in the earth ever since, to be given out again now for the use of man." His son Robert once said of him, "My father flashed his bull's eye full upon a subject, and brought it out in its most vivid light in an instant: his strong common sense and his varied experience, operating on a thoughtful mind, were his most powerful illuminators."

The Bishop of Oxford related the following anecdote of him at a recent public meeting in London: "He heard the other day of an answer given by the great self-taught man, Stephenson, when he was speaking with something of distrust of what were called competitive examinations. Stephenson said, 'I distrust them for this reason—they will lead, it seems to me, to an unlimited power of cram;' and he added, 'Let me give you one piece of advice—never to judge of your goose by its stuffing!'"

George Stephenson had once a conversation with a watchmaker, whom he astonished by the extent and minuteness of his knowledge as to the parts of a watch. The watchmaker knew him to be an eminent engineer, and asked how he had acquired so extensive a knowledge of a branch of business so much out of his sphere. "It is very easily to be explained," said Stephenson; "I worked long at watch-cleaning myself, and when I was at a loss, I was never ashamed to ask for information."

His hand was open to his former fellow-workmen whom old age had left in poverty. To poor Robert Gray, of Newburn, who acted as his brideman on his marriage to Fanny Henderson, he left a pension for life. He would slip a five-pound note into the hand of a poor man or a widow in such a way as not to offend their delicacy, but to make them feel as if the obligation were all on his side. When Farmer Paterson, who married a sister of George's first wife, Fanny Henderson, died and left a large young family fatherless, poverty stared them in the face. "But ye ken," said our informant, "*George struck in fayther for them.*" And perhaps the providential character of the act could not have been more graphically expressed than in these simple words.

On his visit to Newcastle, he would frequently meet the friends of his early days, occupying very nearly the same station in life, while he had meanwhile risen to almost world-wide fame; but he was not less hearty in his greeting of them than if their relative position had remained the same. Thus, one day, after shaking hands with Mr. Brandling on alighting from his carriage, he proceeded to shake hands with his coachman, Anthony Wigham, a still older friend, though he only sat on the box.

Robert Stephenson inherited his father's kindly spirit and benevolent disposition. We have already stated that he was often called in as an umpire to mediate between conflicting parties, more particularly between contractors and engineers. On one occasion Brunel complained to him that he could not get on with his contractors, who were never satisfied, and were always quarreling with him. "You hold them too tightly to the letter of your agreement," said Stephenson; "treat them fairly and liberally." "But they try to take advantage of me at all points," rejoined Brunel. "Perhaps you suspect them too much?" said Stephenson. "I suspect all men to be rogues," said the other, "till I find them to be honest." "For my part," said Stephenson, "I take all men to be honest till I find them to be rogues." "Ah! then, I fear we shall never agree," concluded Brunel.

Robert almost worshiped his father's memory, and was ever ready to attribute to him the chief merit of his own achievements as an engineer. "It was his thorough training," we once heard him say, "his example, and his character, which made me the man I am." On a more public occasion he said, "It is my great pride to remember that, whatever may have been done, and however extensive may have been my own connection with railway development, all I know and all I have done is primarily due to the parent whose memory I cherish and revere."* To Mr. Lough, the sculptor, he said he had never had but two loves—one for his father, the other for his wife.

Like his father, he was eminently practical, and yet always open to the influence and guidance of correct theory. His main consideration in laying out his lines of railway was what would best answer the intended purpose, or, to use his own words, to secure the maximum of result with the minimum of means. He was pre-eminently a safe man, because cautious, tentative, and experimental; following closely the lines of conduct trodden by his father, and often quoting his maxims.

In society Robert Stephenson was simple, unobtrusive, and modest, but charming and even fascinating in an eminent degree. Sir John Lawrence has said of him that he was, of all others, the man he most delighted to meet in England—he was so manly yet gentle, and withal so great. While admired and beloved by men of such calibre, he was equally a favorite with women and children. He put himself upon the level of all, and charmed them

* Address as President of the Institution of Civil Engineers, January, 1856.

no less by his inexpressible kindliness of manner than by his simple yet impressive conversation.

His great wealth enabled him to perform many generous acts in a right noble and yet modest manner, not letting his right hand know what his left hand did. Of the numerous kindly acts of his which have been made public, we may mention the graceful manner in which he repaid the obligations which both himself and his father owed to the Newcastle Literary and Philosophical Institute when working together as fellow experimenters many years before in their humble cottage at Killingworth. The Institute was struggling under a debt of £6200, which impaired its usefulness as an educational agency. Mr. Stephenson offered to pay one half the sum provided the local supporters of the Institute would raise the remainder, and conditional also on the annual subscription being reduced from two guineas to one, in order that the usefulness of the institution might be extended. His generous offer was accepted and the debt extinguished.

Both father and son were offered knighthood, and both declined it. During the summer of 1847, George Stephenson was invited to offer himself as a candidate for the representation of South Shields in Parliament. But his politics were at best of a very undefined sort. Indeed, his life had been so much occupied with subjects of a practical character that he had scarcely troubled himself to form any decided opinion on the party political topics of the day, and to stand the cross-fire of the electors on the hustings might possibly have proved an even more distressing ordeal than the cross-questioning of the barristers in the Committees of the House of Commons. "Politics," he used to say, "are all matters of theory—there is no stability in them; they shift about like the sands of the sea; and I should feel quite out of my element among them." He had, accordingly, the good sense respectfully to decline the honor of contesting the representation of South Shields.

We have, however, been informed by Sir Joseph Paxton that, although George Stephenson held no strong opinions on political questions generally, there was one question on which he entertained a decided conviction, and that was the question of Free Trade. The words used by him on one occasion to Sir Joseph were very strong. "England," said he, "is, and must be, a shopkeeper; and our docks and harbors are only so many wholesale shops, the doors of which should always be kept wide open." It is curious that his son should have taken precisely the opposite view of this question, and acted throughout with the most rigid party among the Protectionists, supporting the Navigation Laws and opposing Free Trade, even to the extent of going into the lobby with Colonel Sibthorp, Mr. Spooner, and the fifty-three "cannon-balls," on the 26th of November, 1852. Robert Stephenson to the last spoke in strong terms as to the "betrayal of the Protectionist party" by their chosen leader, and he went so far as to say that he "could never forgive Peel."

But Robert Stephenson will be judged in after times by his achievements as an engineer rather than by his acts as a politician; and, happily, these last were far outweighed in value by the immense practical services which he rendered to trade, commerce, and civilization, through the facilities which the railways constructed by him afforded for free intercommunication between men in all parts of the world. Speaking in the midst of his friends at Newcastle in 1850, he observed:

"It seems to me but as yesterday that I was engaged as an assistant in laying out the Stockton and Darlington Railway. Since then, the Liverpool and Manchester, and a hundred other great works have sprung into existence. As I look back upon these stupendous undertakings, accomplished in so short a time, it seems as though we had realized in our generation the fabled powers of the magician's wand. Hills have been cut down and valleys filled up; and when these simple expedients have not sufficed, high and magnificent viaducts have been raised, and, if mountains stood in the way, tunnels of unexampled magnitude have pierced them through, bearing their triumphant attestation to the indomitable energy of the nation, and the unrivaled skill of our artisans."

As respects the immense advantages of railways to mankind there can not be two opinions. They exhibit, probably, the grandest organization of capital and labor that the world has yet seen. Although they have unhappily occasioned great loss to many, the loss has been that of individuals, while, as a national system, the gain has already been enormous. As tending to multiply and spread abroad the conveniences of life, opening up new fields of industry, bringing nations nearer to each other, and thus promoting the great ends of civilization, the founding of the railway system by George Stephenson and his son must be regarded as one of the most important events, if not the very greatest, in the first half of this nineteenth century.

THE STEPHENSON MEMORIAL SCHOOLS, WILLINGTON QUAY.

INDEX.

Accident, G. Stephenson's stage-coach, 389.
Accidents in coal-mines, 175, 196.
Adam, Mr., counsel for Liverpool and Manchester Railway Bill, 265.
Adhesion of wheel and rail, 82, 152, 156, 165.
Albert, Prince, an early traveler by rail, 390.
Alderson, Mr., counsel against Liverpool and Manchester Railway Bill, 268, 271, 274, 275.
Allcard, Wm., 283.
Alton Grange, G. Stephenson's house at, 344.
Ambergate, land-slip at, 372; lime-works at, 394, 395.
Anderson, Dr., his early advocacy of railroads, 73.
Arnold, Dr., on railways, 390.
Atmospheric railways, 402, 403, 426–428.

Bald, Robert, mining engineer, 198, 212.
Barrow, Sir John, on railway speed, 262.
Beaumont, Mr., his wooden wagon-ways, 48.
Belgium, railways in, 382; G. Stephenson's visits to, 382, 383, 415.
Benton Colliery and village, 138, 140, 151.
Berkeley, Mr., on railways, 341.
Berwick, Royal Border Bridge at, 430.
Bird-nesting, G. Stephenson's love of, 106, 109, 380, 491.
Black Callerton Colliery, 109, 116, 117.
Blackett, Mr. Wylam, 102, 153, 154, 157–161.
Blast, the steam, its invention, 170.
Blenkinsop, Mr., Leeds, his locomotive, 155–157, 162.
Blisworth Cutting, 355.
Boiler, the multitubular, its invention, 316–318.
Booth, Henry, 256, 312, 318, 319.
Boulton, Matthew, his tubular boiler, 316–318.
Boulton and Watt, and the locomotive, 63–68.
Bradshaw, Mr., his opposition to Liverpool and Manchester line, 255, 258.
Braithwaite and Ericsson's "Novelty," 322–324.
Brake, G. Stephenson's self-acting, 334, 398.
Brakeing of colliery engines, 116–118, 131.
Brandling, Messrs., 184, 191, 192, 431.
Brandreth's "Cycloped," 322.
Bridge building, rapid progress of, 431, 432.
Bridges—Royal Border, 430; High-Level, Newcastle, 431; Britannia (Menai), 439–442; Conway, 451; Victoria, Lower Canada, 476.
Britannia Bridge, North Wales, 449, 452–459.
Brougham, William, counsel for Liverpool and Manchester Bill, 262, 265.
Bruce, Mr., R. Stephenson's schoolmaster, 141.
Brunel, I. K., 423–427, 486.
Brunton's "Mechanical Traveler," 157.
Brussels, railway celebrations at, 383, 416.
Buckland, Dr., 467.
Bull Bridge, near Ambergate, 373.
Bull, Edward, his Cornish engine, 76; William, partner of Trevithick, 76, 88.
Burrell, G. Stephenson's partner, 207.
Burstall's "Perseverance," 322, 326.

Callerton Colliery and village, 109, 116, 117.
Canada, railways in, *Pref.*, v., 476.
Canal Companies' opposition to railways, 260, 341.
Cardiff and Merthyr Railroad, 73.
Carrying stock of railways, *Pref.*, ix., 334.
Cattle brought to London by rail, *Pref.*, xx.
Chapman's locomotive, 157, 163.
"Charlotte Dundas," the first practical steam-boat, 70.
Chat Moss, surveying on, 252, 264; railway constructed on, 283–288.
Chester and Birkenhead Railway, 402; and Holyhead Railway, 438.
Chesterfield, town of, 395, 471.
Clanny, Dr., his safety-lamp, 179, 196.
Clark, Edwin, R. Stephenson's assistant, 448.
Claycross Colliery, 394, 420.
Coach, first railway, 240.
Coal, working of, 100, 101; supply of, to London, *Pref.*, xxv.; haulage of, 153, 161; supply of, by railways, 386, 392.
Coal Railways, G. Stephenson on, 393.
Cochrane, Lord, and Peruvian revolution, 89.
Coe, William, 116, 117, 121, 125.
Coffin, Sir Isaac, on railways, 280.
Collieries, G. Stephenson's, at Snibston, 344; at Claycross, 392.
Colombia, R. Stephenson's residence in, 301–308.
Companies, joint-stock railway, 339, 404.
Contractors and railways, 353, 360, 361, 493.
Conversation, G. Stephenson's love of, 463, 491.
Conway, tubular bridge at, 450, 451.
Cooper, Sir A., R. Stephenson's interview with, 350.
Cornish engineers, early, 75, 76.
Correspondence, G. Stephenson's, 297, 379, 380.
Crib-work, Victoria Bridge, 479, 480.
Cropper, Isaac, Liverpool, 293, 313, 325.
"Crowdie night," a, 465.
Croydon and Merstham Railroad, 74, 216.
Cubitt, W., evidence of, on Liverpool and Manchester Railway, 272.
Cugnot, N., his road locomotive, 60.
Curr, John, his cast-iron tram-way, 50.
Cuttings—Olive Mount, 291; Tring, 354; Blisworth, 355; Ambergate, 372; Oakenshaw, 372.

Darlington, railway projected at, 218.
Darwin, Erasmus, his fiery chariot, 53–59.
Davy, Sir H., on Trevithick's steam-carriage, 79; his paper on fire-damp, 179; his safety-lamp, 189; testimonial to, 191; his lamp compared with Stephenson's, 195.
Denman, Lord, 463.
Derby, Earl of, and Liverpool and Manchester Railway, 252, 258, 280.
Dewley Burn Colliery, 107–111.
Direct lines, rage for, 408.
Dixon, John, assists in survey of Stockton and

Darlington Railway, 219, 236; resident engineer Liverpool and Manchester Railway, 283.
Dodds, Ralph, Killingworth, 132, 139.
Dutton Viaduct, 366.

East Coast route to Scotland, 426.
Edgeworth, R. L., early speculations on railways, 56, 57.
Eggs, brought to London by rail, *Pref.*, xxii.
Egypt, R. Stephenson's tubular bridges in, 507; Suez Canal, 484, 485.
Electric telegraphing on railways, *Pref.*, xiii.
Emerson, G. Stephenson's meeting with, 469, 470.
Ericsson's "Novelty," 322-324.
Evans, Oliver, his steam-carriage, 71, 72; his boiler, 77.
Explosions from fire-damp, 175.

Fairbairn, William, C.E., early friendship with G. Stephenson, 124, 125; experiments on iron tubes for R. Stephenson, 446.
Fire-damp, explosions of, 175.
Fish brought to London by rail, *Pref.*, xxi.
Fitch, John, American engineer, 71.
Food brought to London by rail, *Pref.*, xix.
Forth-Street Works, Newcastle, 232, 396.
Foster, Jonathan, Wylam, 158.
Foundations—of bridge on the Derwent, 372; of High-Level Bridge, Newcastle, 434; of Victoria Bridge, Montreal, 479.
Free Trade, G. Stephenson's notions of, 494, 495.
Friction, G. Stephenson's early experiments in, 202; and gradients, 400.
Frolic, G. Stephenson's love of, 135, 375, 465.

Gauge of railways, 234, 424.
"Geordy" safety-lamp, 175-195.
Gilbert, Davies, and Trevithick, 79, 82, 83.
Giles, Francis, C.E., his evidence against Liverpool and Manchester Railway Bill, 273, 275, 289.
Gooch, Thomas, C.E., 277, 295, 328, 330.
Government and railways, 337, 338.
Gradients and friction, 202, 400.
Grand Allies, Killingworth, 135.
Grand Junction Railway, 341, 365.
Grand Trunk Railway, Canada, 476.
Gray, Thomas, and the locomotive, 156, 311.
Great Western Railway, 340, 342, 424.
Greenwich Railway opened as a "show," *Pref.*, xv.
Gurney, Goldsworthy, 171, 317.

Hackworth, T., and the steam-blast, 174; his locomotive "Sanspareil," 322, 324, 325, 326.
Half-lap joint, G. Stephenson's, 200.
Harrison, Mr., counsel against Liverpool and Manchester Bill, 265, 272, 276.
Harvey, Mr., engineer, Hayle, 76.
Hedley, William, Wylam, 159, 160, 171.
Henderson, Fanny, G. Stephenson's first wife, 118, 123, 125, 127.
Heppel, Kit, Killingworth, 132, 135.
Hetton Railway constructed by G. Stephenson, 208.
High-Level Bridge, Newcastle, 433.
Hindmarsh, Miss, G. Stephenson's second wife, 214.
Hodgkinson, Professor, his calculations as to strength of iron tubes, 447.
Holyhead, railway to, 438.
Hornblower, Jonathan, 75, 76.
Horticulture, G. Stephenson's experiments in, 460, 461.
Horse traction on railways, 46, 57, 74, 150, 166, 234, 240.
Howick, Lord, his support of atmospheric railways, 427; G. Stephenson's interview with, 428, 429.
Hudson, George, the "Railway King," 407, 411.
Huskisson, Mr., an early advocate of railways, 278, 280; fatal accident to, 331.
Hydraulic press used to lift the tubes at the Britannia Bridge, 456.

Ice-flood at Montreal, 481, 482.
Inclined planes, self-acting, 149, 150, 162.
India, railways in, *Pref.*, iv.
Iron bridge building, progress in, 432, 443.
Italian railways, *Pref.*, iv.

James, William, surveys Liverpool and Manchester Railway, 248; visit to Killingworth, 250; arrangement with Stephenson and Losh, 251; compelled to relinquish the survey, 253, 254.
James, W. H., his tubular boiler, 317.
Jameson, Professor, Edinburg, 213.
Jessop, William, his cast-iron edge-rail, 51.
Joy, Mr., counsel for Liverpool and Manchester Bill, 265, 268.

Keelmen of the Tyne, 101, 102.
Kent, opposition to railways in, 342.
Killingworth, 126, 129; High Pit, 131; locomotive, 168; underground machinery 198; visited by Edward Pease, 230; W. James, 250; promoters of Liverpool and Manchester Railway, 257.
Kilmarnock and Troon tram-road, 206.
Kilsby Tunnel, 342, 357-361, 363.

Lambton, Mr. (Earl of Durham), 225.
Lamp, invention of the safety, 175.
Land-slip at Ambergate, 372.
Landlords and railways, 223, 252, 341, 352, 469.
Lardner, Dr., on undulating lines, 400.
Leicester and Swannington Railway, 343.
Leopold, King, G. Stephenson's interviews with, 382, 383, 416.
Lime-works at Ambergate, 394, 395.
Littleborough Tunnel, 368.
Liverpool and Manchester Railway projected, 247; survey by W. James, 249; George Stephenson appointed engineeer, 254; virulent opposition, 259, 260; the bill in committee, 265; rejected, 277; renewed application, 278; the bill passed, 280; the railway constructed, 281; discussion as to the power to be employed to work the line, 311; prize offered for the best locomotive, 314; the competition at Rainhill, 322; triumph of the "Rocket," 326; public opening of the railway, 330; its success, 332.
Locke, Joseph, C.E., resident engineer on Liverpool and Manchester Railway, 283.
Locomotive engine gradually perfected, 47; Sir I. Newton's idea, 53; Darwin's, 53-59; Cugnot's, 60-63; James Watt's, 60, 64; William Murdock's model locomotive, 66; William Symington's model, 68-70; Oliver Evans's 71; Richard Trevithick's steam-carriage and first locomotive, 77-82; Blenkinsop's Leeds locomotive, 155; Blackett's Wylam locomotive, 157-161; Stephenson's Killingworth locomotive, 164-170; farther improvements by Stephenson, 201, 202; locomotives constructed for Stockton and Darlington Railway, 235; the "Rocket," 319; farther improvements in locomotives, 335; number of locomotives in the United Kingdom, *Pref.*, ix., x.; self-feeding apparatus of, *ib.*, xiv.
Locomotive workshops at Newcastle, the Stephensons', 232, 396.

London and Birmingham Railway, 349–364.
London, railways in, opening of the Greenwich line, *Pref.*, xv.; magnitude of suburban traffic, *ib.*, xvi.; new lines opened, *ib.*, xvi.; population increased by, *ib.*, xviii.; provisioning of London, *ib.*, xix.; coal supply of, *ib.*, xxv.
Losh, Mr. Stephenson's partner, 201, 233.
Lough's statue of G. Stephenson, 472.

Mackworth, Sir H., his sailing wagon, 52.
Mail service by railway, *Pref.*, xxvi.
Manchester, railways projected in connection with, 340; and Leeds Railway, 366.
Mania, the railway, 405, 406.
Maps—of Newcastle district, 98; Stockton and Darlington Railway, 224; Liverpool and Manchester Railway, 250–251; Leicester and Swannington Railway, 343; London and Birmingham Railway, 354; Midland Railway, 370; Straits of Menai, 442.
Mechanics' Institutes, G. Stephenson at meetings of, 397.
Menai, bridge over Straits of, 439.
Merchandise, traffic of London, *Pref.*, xxvi.
Merstham tram-road, 74, 217.
Merthyr tram-road, 73; Trevithick's locomotive tried on, 80.
Middlesborough-on-Tees, growth of, 245.
Midland Railway, 370.
Milk brought to London by rail, *Pref.*, xxiv.
Miller, Mr., Dalswinton, and steam navigation, 70.
Montreal, Victoria Bridge at, 476.
Moore, Francis, his patent for steam-carriages, 63.
Morecambe Bay, G. Stephenson's proposed line across, 376.
Moss, Chat (see *Chat Moss*).
Multitubular boiler, invention of the, 318.
Murdock, William, his model locomotive, 66; Watt discourages his application to the subject, 67, 77.
Murray, Matthew, and the Leeds locomotive, 155.

Nasmyth's steam-hammer first applied to pile-driving, 434.
Navvies, Railway, 362.
Newcastle-on-Tyne, early history, 97; Literary and Philosophical Institute, 142, 185, 189, 209, 494; Mechanics' Institute, 397; High-Level Bridge, 431.
Newcastle and Berwick Railway, 426.
Newcomen's atmospheric engine, 100.
Neville's tubular boiler, 317, 318.
Newton, Sir I., his idea of steam locomotion, 53.
Nicholson's steam-jet, 82, 171.
Nile, R. Stephenson's tubular bridges over the, 475.
North Midland Railway, 370, 373, 374.
North, Roger, description of early tram-roads, 49.
Northampton, opposition of, to railways, 342.
Northumberland Atmospheric Railway, 427.
"Novelty" locomotive, 323.

Oaks Pit Colliery explosion, 195.
Offices, Stephenson's London, 381, 407.
Old Quay Navigation, Liverpool, 256.
Olive Mount Cutting, 291.
Openings of railways—Hetton, 209; Stockton and Darlington, 236; Liverpool and Manchester, 330; London and Birmingham, 384; in Midland Counties, 384; East Coast route to Scotland, 426, 437; Britannia Bridge, 458; Trent Valley, 469.
Opposition to railways—in country districts, 337, 341; at Northampton, 342; in Kent, 342; at Eton, 342; to London and Birmingham, 350.
Organization—of early railways, 330, 333; of modern railways, *Pref.*, xi.
Outram's railway, first use of stone blocks, 51.

Parliament and railways, 338, 406, 410.
Parr Moss, railway across, 288.
Passenger-carriage, the first, 240.
Passenger-traffic, beginnings of, *Pref.*, vii., xv., 240, 241, 333, 338; of London, *Pref.*, xvii.
Pease, Edward, promotes Stockton and Darlington Railway, his character, 222; anticipations concerning railways, 225; intercourse with George Stephenson, 227, 229, 230, 231, 232; assists George Stephenson with capital, 232; faith in the locomotive, 235, 246; letter to Robert Stephenson, 306, 307.
Peel, Sir R., on undulating lines, 409, 410; G. Stephenson's visit to, 467.
Penmaen Mawr, railway under, 439.
Pen-y-darran, Trevithick's locomotive made and tried at, 80–82.
Permanent way, *Pref.*, viii., xi., 159, 200.
Peruvian mining, Trevithick's adventures in connection with, 87.
Petherick, J., his description of Trevithick's steam-carriage, 78, 79.
Phillips, Sir Richard, on railroads, 217.
Pile-driving by steam, 434.
Pitmen, habits and character of Newcastle, 100, 101.
Plate-ways, 50, 82.
Politics, G. and R. Stephenson's, 494.
Population of London, how influenced by railways, *Pref.*, xviii.
Postal service and railways, *Pref.*, xxvii.
Potatoes brought to London by rail, *Pref.*, xxiii.
Poultry brought to London by rail, *Pref.*, xxii.
Primrose Hill Tunnel, 356.
Professional charges, G. Stephenson's, 382.
Provisioning of London, *Pref.*, xix.
Pyrenean pastoral, 418.

Quarterly Review on railway speed, 263.
Queen, the, her first use of the railway, 390; opens the High-Level and Royal Border Bridges, 437; visits the Britannia Bridge, 456.

Rails—stone blocks first used, 48; planks, 48; plates of iron, 50; cast-iron rails, 50; flanched rails, 51; tram-plates at Merthyr, 81; Wylam wagon-way, 153; rack rail, 156, 157, 159, 160; heavier cast-iron rails used, 160; roughly laid, 200; Stephenson's half-lap joint, 200; Stephenson recommends wrought-iron rails, 233; temporary rails in constructing roads, 284; Vignolles's and Ericsson's central friction, 311; strained by high speed, 399.
Railway locomotive (see *Locomotive*).
Railway king, the, 407, 411.
Railway speed (see *Speed*).
Railway speculation and mania, 374, 401–405.
Railways, length of, constructed, *Pref.*, iii.; in India, *ib.*, iv.; in United States, *ib.*, vi.; carrying stock of, *ib.*, ix.; effects of, *ib.*, xv.; in London, *ib.*, xv.; number of workmen employed on, *ib.*, xxviii.
Railways constructed and opened—Cardiff and Merthyr, 73; Sirhowy, 73; Wandsworth, Croydon, and Merstham, 73, 74; Wylam, 160; Kilmarnock and Troon, 206; Hetton, 207; Stockton and Darlington, 224; Liverpool and Manchester, 247; Canterbury and Whitstable, 339; Grand Junction, 340, 365; Leicester and Swannington, 343; London

and Birmingham, 349; Manchester and Leeds, 366; Midland, 370; in Belgium, 382; Chester and Birkenhead, 402; Newcastle and Darlington, 412; Newcastle and Berwick, 414, 426; Royal North of Spain, 417; Chester and Holyhead, 438; Trent Valley Railway, 469; Grand Trunk, Lower Canada, 476.
Rainhill, locomotive contest at, 322.
Ramsbottom's locomotive self-feeding apparatus, *Pref.*, xiv.
Rastrick, Mr., C.E., 153, 312, 315.
Ravensworth, Lord, 135, 192.
Rennie, John, C.E., 220, 221; Messrs. Rennie and Liverpool and Manchester line, 279, 281.
Residential area of London, enlarged by railways, *Pref.*, xvii.
Richardson, Thomas, Lombard Street, 230, 232, 266, 267, 307.
Road locomotion—Stevin's sailing-coach, 52; Mackworth's and Edgeworth's sailing-wagons, 52, 53, 57; Cugnot's road locomotive, 61; Murdock's model, 66; Symington's steam-carriage, 68; Oliver Evans's locomotive, 71, 72; Trevithick's steam-carriage, 77; G. Stephenson's views of locomotion on common roads, 202–205; House of Commons report in favor of, 338.
Robins at Alton Grange, anecdote of, 381.
"Rocket" locomotive, the, 319–328.
Roscoe, Mr., his farm on Chat Moss, 282, 283.
Ross, A. M., joint engineer of Victoria Bridge, Montreal, 477.
Royal Border Bridge, Berwick, 429.

Safety-lamp—Dr. Clanny's, 179; George Stephenson's first lamp, 180; second and third lamps, 186; Sir H. Davy's paper on fire-damp, 179; his lamp, 187; dates when lamps produced, 188; controversy Davy *v.* Stephenson, 187; comparative merits of lamps, 195.
Safety of railway traveling, *Pref.*, x.
Sailing-coaches and wagons, 52, 53, 57.
Saint Fond on colliery wagon roads, 49.
Saint Lawrence River, Victoria Bridge across, 476–484.
Sandars, Mr., Liverpool and Manchester Railway, 248, 253, 254, 255, 262, 263, 297, 313.
Sankey Viaduct, 292, 293.
"Sanspareil" locomotive, Hackworth's, 324, 325.
Scarborough, railway to, 374.
Screw-propeller patented by Trevithick, 86.
Seguin, M., his tubular boiler, 317, 318.
Self-feeding apparatus of boilers, *Pref.*, xiv.
Sheep carried to London by rail, *Pref.*, xxi.
Sibthorp, Col., on railways, 341, 390, 391.
Signaling of railway trains, *Pref.*, xi.
Simplon, Midland Railway compared with road over the, 371.
Sirhowy Railroad, 73.
Snibston, George Stephenson's sinking for coal at, 344.
Sopwith, Mr., F.R.S., 416, 467.
South Devon atmospheric railway, 428.
Spain, George Stephenson's visit to, 418.
Spankie, Mr. Sergeant, counsel for Liverpool and Manchester Railway Bill, 271.
Speculation in railways, 374, 401; G. Stephenson on, 406, 407; R. Stephenson and, 425.
Speed, railway, *Pref.*, viii.; on Liverpool and Manchester line, 332; George Stephenson on, 398, 399.
Spur-gear, George Stephenson's, 164, 165.
Stage-coach traveling, *Pref.*, vii., 337, 387, 389.
Statues of George Stephenson, 472.
Steam-blast, invention of the, 168, 170; rival claims, 170, 171; of the "Rocket," 320.
Steam-boat, the first working, 70.
Stephenson family, the—Robert and Mabel, George's father and mother, 103–105; brothers and sisters, 111, 112; old Robert, 123; maintained by his son George, 129.
Stephenson, George, birth and birthplace, 103, 104; his parents, 105; boyhood, 107–110; fireman and engine-man, 109–113; learns to read, 114; learns to brake, 116, 117; makes and mends shoes and "falls in love," 118; thrashes a bully, 119, 120; self-improvement, 121; removes to Willington, 122; marries Fanny Henderson, 123; studies mechanics, perpetual motion, 124; cleans clocks, 125; birth of only son and removal to Killingworth, 126; death of his wife, 127; goes to Scotland, his pump boot, 128; returns to Killingworth, *ibid.*; brakesman at West Moor pit, 129; joins in a brakeing contract, 130, 131; cures a pumping-engine, 132–134; appointed engine-wright, 135; education of his son, 139–141; his cottage at West Moor, 146; the sun-dial, 148, 149; studies the locomotive, 151, 161–163; his first traveling-engine, 163–170; invents his safety-lamp, 179–186; improves underground machinery at Killingworth, 198; patent for improved rails and chairs, 200, 201; experiments on friction, 202; constructs Hetton Railroad, 208; marries Elizabeth Hindmarsh, 214; appointed engineer of the Stockton and Darlington Railway, 228, 229; commences locomotive factory at Newcastle, 232; supplies locomotives to Stockton and Darlington Railway, 235; appointed engineer to Liverpool and Manchester Railway, 254; obstructions to the survey, 259, 260; his evidence in committee, 266; bill rejected, 277; reappointed engineer, 281; construction of Liverpool and Manchester Railway, 282–295; battle of the locomotive, 310–315; triumph of the "Rocket" at Rainhill, 319–328; organization of the railway traffic, 333; improvements of the locomotive, 335; the self-acting brake, 334, 398; leases the Snibston estate, 344; engineer of Manchester and Leeds Railway, 366; engineer of North Midland, 371; of York and North Midland, 373; quickness of observation, 375; proposed line across Morecambe Bay, 376; immense labors, 377; extensive correspondence, 379, 380; London office, 381; visits to Belgium, 382, 383; leases Claycross estate and colliery, 394; on railway speculation, 406, 407; third visit to Belgium, 415; visit to Spain, 417; interview with Lord Howick, 428, 429; life in retirement at Tapton, 460; visit to Sir Robert Peel, 467; theory about sun's light, 468; illness and death, 470; statues of, 472; characteristics, 487–492.
Stephenson, Robert, his birth, 126; boyhood and education, 140–143; boyish tricks, 143, 144; scientific amusements, 145; teaches algebra, 148; joint production with his father of a sun-dial, 148, 149; assists his father in safety-lamp experiments, 181, 184; Newcastle Institute, 209; apprenticed as coal-viewer, 209; coal-pit explosion, narrow escape, joint studies with his father, 210; sent to Edinburg University, 211; his notes of lectures, 212; life in Edinburg, 213; geological excursion in the Highlands, return to Killingworth, 213, 214; assists Mr. James in survey of Liverpool and Manchester Railway, 252; makes drawings for engines, 301; engages with Colombian Mining Association, and residence in South America, 301–306; resigns his situation, 306; meeting with Trevithick at Cartagena, 308; shipwreck, 308; tour in the United States, and return home, 309; co-operates with his father in the locomotive competition, 315; builds the "Rocket," 319; engineer of Leicester and Swannington Rail-

way, 343; engineer of London and Birmingham Railway, 349; marriage to Miss Sanderson, 353; report on atmospheric system, 404; succeeds his father generally as engineer, 421; his extensive practice, 422, 423; his caution, 425, 448, 456; engineer of High-Level Bridge, Newcastle, 431; engineer of Chester and Holyhead Railway, 438; designs the first iron tubular bridge, 444; opens the Britannia Bridge, 457; designs tubular bridges over the Nile, 475; designs the Victoria Tubular Bridge, Lower Canada, 477; member of House of Commons, 484; honors, 485; present at launch of "Great Eastern," 486; illness and death, 487; characteristics, 492–494.
Stevin's sailing-coach, 52.
Stockton and Darlington Railway projected and surveyed, 222; Edward Pease, promoter, 222; act obtained, 224; George Stephenson resurveys and constructs line, 228, 229; line opened, 236; coal-traffic, 239; first passenger-traffic, 240, 241; growth of Middlesborough, 245.
Straits of Menai, bridge over, 441.
Strathmore, Earl of, 135, 192.
Suez Canal, Robert Stephenson's opinion of, 484, 485.
Summers and Ogle's tubular boiler, 317.
Sun-dial at Killingworth, 148, 149, 396.
Sun's light and coal formation, G. Stephenson's ideas on, 468, 491.
Sunshine, effect of, on tubes of Britannia Bridge, 458.
Superheated steam, Trevithick's use of, 91.
Swanwick, Frederick, G. Stephenson's secretary, 297, 299, 315.
Sylvester, Mr., on maximum speed, 264.
Symington, William, his working model of a road locomotive, 68; co-operation with Miller of Dalswinton in applying power to boats, 70; his misfortunes and death, 70.

Tapton House, George Stephenson's residence at, 392, 395, 460.
Telegraph signaling on railways, *Pref.*, xiii.
Thames Tunnel begun by Trevithick, 85, 86.
Thirlwall, William, engineer, 108.
Thomas, Mr., of Denton, on railways, 73.
Traffic, passenger, beginnings of, *Pref.*, vi., xv., 240, 241, 333, 385, 388; cattle, *Pref.*, xx.; coal, *ib.*, xxv., 153, 161, 386, 392; food, *Pref.*, xix.; merchandise, *ib.*, xxvi.; poultry, etc., *ib.*, xxii.; postal, *ib.*, xxvi.
Train service of London, *Pref.*, xvii.
Tram-ways, early, 48, 49, 73, 106, 152.
Trevithick, Richard, birth and education, 74; engineering ability in youth, 75; partner with Andrew Vivian at Camborne, 76; his improved engine and boiler, 77; his steam-carriage for roads, 77–79; carriage exhibited in London, 79, 80; constructs the first railway locomotive, 80; dredges the Thames by steam-power, 83; his high-pressure engines and new patents, 83, 84; partly constructs a Thames tunnel, 85, 86; returns to Camborne, new patents, 86; his tubular boiler, engines for Peru, 86, 87; goes to Lima, received with honors, 88; civil war and ruin, 89; meets Robert Stephenson at Cartagena, 90; shipwreck and return to England, 91; new inventions, his last days and death in poverty, 92, 93; his character, his important inventions, *ibid.*; his locomotive, 152, 153, 170, 317.
Tring Cutting, 354.
Trinity Church, Chesterfield, G. Stephenson's burial-place, 471.
"Tubbing" in coal-pits, 344.
Tubes, floating of, at Conway, 451, 452; at Menai Strait, 452; lifting of the, 455; erection of, at Victoria Bridge, Montreal, 480.
Tubular boilers by various inventors, 317.
Tubular bridges—over Menai Straits, 443; at Conway, 451, 452; at Damietta and Benha, Lower Egypt, 475; at Montreal, 480.
Tunnels—at Liverpool, 290; at Primrose Hill, 356; at Kilsby, 357; at Littleborough, 368.
Turner, Rev. William, Newcastle, 185.

Undulating Railways, theory of, 400.
United States, railways in, *Pref.*, v.
Uvillé, M., and Trevithick, 87–89.

Vegetables carried to London by rail, *Pref.*, xxiii.
Viaducts—Sankey, 292; Dutton, 366; Berwick, 430; Newcastle, 431.
Victoria Bridge, Montreal, 477.
Vignolles, Charles, C.E., 279, 291, 311.
Vivian, Andrew, Trevithick's partner, 76.

Walker, James, C.E., report on fixed and locomotive engines, 312.
Wallsend, 97.
Walmsley, Sir Joshua, 418, 419.
Waters, Mr., Gateshead, 158.
Watt, James, his model locomotive, 60; his scheme of 1784, 64, 65; discourages application of steam to locomotion, 67.
"Way-leave" tram-ways, 49.
Wellington, Duke of, and railways, 330–332, 390.
West Moor Colliery, 177, 214.
Wharncliffe, Lord, and George Stephenson, 135, 367.
Wheat carried to London by rail, *Pref.*, xx.
Whinfield, Mr., Gateshead, 154.
Wigham, John, G. Stephenson's teacher, 138.
Williams, Mr. Scorrier, his gratitude to Trevithick, 77.
Willington Quay, G. Stephenson at, 122.
Wind, power of, employed in locomotion, 52, 57.
Wood, Nicholas, testimony concerning Stephenson's invention of the steam-blast, 171–173; makes drawing for Stephenson's safety-lamp, 180; assists in experiments, 180, 185, 189, 196, 198; in colliery explosions, 210; on the locomotive, 262, 314, 315.
Woolf, Cornish engineer, 84, 317.
Workmen, railway, *Pref.*, xxviii., 336, 362.
Wylam Colliery and village, 102–104; wagon-way, 153.

York and North Midland Railway, 373, 374; public opening of, 384.
Young, Arthur, on early tram-ways, 49.

THE END.

BOOKS OF TRAVEL AND ADVENTURE

PUBLISHED BY

HARPER & BROTHERS, NEW YORK.

HARPER & BROTHERS will send any of the following Works by mail, postage free, to any part of the United States, on receipt of the Price.

HARPER'S CATALOGUE OF TRAVEL-BOOKS *is one of the literary curiosities of the day, exhibiting at a glance the contributions of modern travel to geographical and other knowledge. Commencing with South Africa, and marking on a map the tracks of these travelers, the reader will be astonished to see how thoroughly they cover the length and breadth of Africa. Livingstone, Ellis, Burton, Du Chaillu, Reade, Andersson, Speke, Davis, Wilson, and others, have within a few years explored Africa pretty thoroughly; Egypt and the Holy Land have been repeatedly described in late times; Layard had given us the revelations of the Euphrates and the Tigris valleys; Atkinson had written his admirable accounts of Siberia, illustrated by his own most brilliant pencil; Huc and others described China; and now a hitherto almost unknown portion of the very heart of Asia is opened to us by the delightful book of Vámbéry.*—N. Y. JOURNAL OF COMMERCE.

Livingstone's Zambesi. Narrative of an Expedition to the Zambesi and its Tributaries; and of the Discovery of Lakes Shirwa and Nyassa, 1858–1864. By DAVID and CHARLES LIVINGSTONE. With Map and Illustrations. 8vo, Cloth, $5 00.

Dr. Livingstone's South Africa. Missionary Travels and Researches in South Africa; including a Sketch of Sixteen Years' Residence in the Interior of Africa, and a Journey from the Cape of Good Hope to Loando on the West Coast; thence across the Continent, down the River Zambesi, to the Eastern Ocean. By DAVID LIVINGSTONE, LL.D., D.C.L. With Portrait, Maps by Arrowsmith, and numerous Illustrations. 8vo, Cloth, $4 50.

Social Life of the Chinese: With some Account of their Religious Governmental, and Business Customs and Opinions. With special but not exclusive reference to Fuhchau. By Rev. JUSTUS DOOLITTLE, Fourteen Years Member of the American Board. With over 150 Illustrations. In Two Volumes, 12mo, Cloth, Beveled Edges, $5 00.

The Story of the Great March: Diary of General Sherman's Campaign through Georgia and the Carolinas. By Brevet Major GEORGE WARD NICHOLS, Aid-de-Camp to General Sherman. With a Map and numerous Illustrations, and an Appendix, containing Official Reports by Major-General Sherman, Quarter-master and Commissary Reports, &c. Twenty-second Edition. 12mo, Cloth, Beveled Edges, $2 00.

Captain Hall's Arctic Researches and Life among the Esquimaux. Arctic Researches and Life among the Esquimaux: being the Narrative of an Expedition in Search of Sir John Franklin, in the Years 1860, 1861, and 1862. By CHARLES FRANCIS HALL. With Maps and 100 Illustrations. 8vo, Cloth, $5 00.

Vámbéry's Central Asia. Travels in Central Asia. Being the Account of a Journey from Teheran across the Turkoman Desert, on the Eastern Shore of the Caspian, to Khiva, Bokhara, and Samarcand, performed in the Year 1863. By ARMINIUS VÁMBÉRY. With Map and Woodcuts. 8vo, Cloth, $4 50.

Reade's Savage Africa. Western Africa: Being the Narrative of a Tour in Equatorial, Southwestern, and Northwestern Africa; with Notes on the Habits of the Gorilla; on the Existence of Unicorns and Tailed Men; on the Slave Trade; on the Origin, Character, and Capabilities of the Negro, and of the future Civilization of Western Africa. By W. WINWOOD READE. With Illustrations and a Map. 8vo, Cloth, $4 00.

Speke's Africa. Journal of the Discovery of the Source of the Nile. By Captain JOHN HANNING SPEKE. With Maps and Portraits, and numerous Illustrations, chiefly from Drawings by Captain GRANT. 8vo, Cloth, uniform with LIVINGSTONE, BARTH, BURTON, &c. Price $4 00.

Du Chaillu's Africa. Explorations and Adventures in Equatorial Africa: with Accounts of the Manners and Customs of the People, and of the Chase of the Gorilla, the Crocodile, Leopard, Elephant, Hippopotamus, and other Animals. By PAUL B. DU CHAILLU, Corresponding Member of the American Ethnological Society; of the Geographical and Statistical Society of New York; and of the Boston Society of Natural History. With numerous Illustrations. 8vo, Cloth, $5 00.

Squier's Central America. The States of Central America: Their Geography, Topography, Climate, Population, Resources, Productions, Commerce, Political Organization, Aborigines, &c., &c. Comprising Chapters on Honduras, San Salvador, Nicaragua, Costa Rica, Guatemala, Belize, the Bay Islands, the Mosquito Shore, and the Honduras Inter-Oceanic Railway. By E. G. SQUIER, formerly Chargé d'Affaires of the United States to the Republics of Central America. With numerous Original Maps and Illustrations. A New and Enlarged Edition. 8vo, Cloth, $4 00.

Squier's Nicaragua. Nicaragua: Its People, Scenery, Monuments, Resources, Condition, and proposed Canal. With 100 Maps and Illustrations. By E. G. SQUIER, formerly Chargé d'Affaires of the United States to the Republics of Central America. A Revised Edition. 8vo, Cloth, $4 00.

Squier's Waikna. Waikna; or, Adventures on the Mosquito Shore. By SAMUEL A. BARD. With a Map of the Mosquito Shore, and upward of 60 original Illustrations. 12mo, Cloth, $1 50.

Burton's City of the Saints. The City of the Saints; and Across the Rocky Mountains to California. By Captain RICHARD F. BURTON, Fellow and Gold Medalist of the Royal Geographical Societies of France and England; H. M. Consul in West Africa; Author of "The Lake Regions of Central Africa." With Maps and numerous Illustrations. 8vo, Cloth, $3 50.

Burton's Lake Regions of Central Africa. The Lake Regions of Central Africa. A Picture of Exploration. By RICHARD F. BURTON, Captain H.M.I. Army; Fellow and Gold Medalist of the Royal Geographical Society. With Maps and Engravings on Wood. 8vo, Cloth, $3 50.

Atkinson's Amoor Regions. Travels in the Regions of the Upper and Lower Amoor, and the Russian Acquisitions on the Confines of India and China. With Adventures among the Mountain Kirghis; and the Manjours, Manyargs, Toungouz, Touzemtz, Goldi, and Gelyaks; the Hunting and Pastoral Tribes. By THOMAS WITLAM ATKINSON, F.G.S., F.R.G.S., Author of "Oriental and Western Siberia." With a Map and numerous Illustrations. 8vo, Cloth, $3 50.

Andersson's Okavango River. The Okavango River. A Narrative of Travel, Exploration, and Adventure. By CHARLES JOHN ANDERSSON, Author of "Lake Ngami." With a Steel Portrait of the Author, numerous Woodcuts, and a Map, showing the Regions explored by Andersson, Cumming, Livingstone, and Du Chaillu. 8vo, Cloth, $3 50.

Stephens's Travels in Central America. Travels in Central America, Chiapas, and Yucatan. By J. L. STEPHENS. With a Map and 88 Engravings. 2 vols., 8vo, Cloth, $6 00.

Stephens's Travels in Yucatan. Incidents of Travel in Yucatan. By J. L. STEPHENS. 120 Engravings, from Drawings by F. CATHERWOOD. 2 vols., 8vo, Cloth, $6 00.

Stephens's Travels in Egypt. Travels in Egypt, Arabia Petræa, and the Holy Land. By J. L. STEPHENS. Engravings. 2 vols., 12mo, Cloth, $3 00.

Stephens's Travels in Greece. Travels in Greece, Turkey, Russia, and Poland. By J. L. STEPHENS. Engravings. 2 vols., 12mo, Cloth, $3 00.

Arizona and Sonora. The Geography, History, and Resources of the Silver Region of North America. By SYLVESTER MOWRY, late Lieutenant United States Army, late United States Boundary Commissioner, &c. With Illustrations. 12mo, Cloth, $1 50.

"**From Dan to Beersheba**;" or, The Land of Promise as it now Appears. Including a Description of the Boundaries, Topography, Agriculture, Antiquities, Cities, and Present Inhabitants of that Wonderful Land. With Illustrations of the Remarkable Accuracy of the Sacred Writers in their Allusions to their Native Country. By Rev. J. P. NEWMAN, D.D. Maps and Engravings. 12mo, Cloth, $1 75.

Hunting in South Africa. African Hunting from Natal to the Zambesi, including Lake Ngami, the Kalahari Desert, &c., from 1852 to 1860. By WILLIAM CHARLES BALDWIN, Esq., F.R.G.S. With Illustrations by James Wolf and J. B. Zwecker. 12mo, Cloth, $1 50.

Wyoming; Its History, Stirring Incidents, and Romantic Adventures. By GEORGE PECK, D.D. With Illustrations. 12mo, Cloth, $1 75.

Journal of a Residence on a Georgia Plantation in 1838–1839. By FRANCES ANNE KEMBLE. 12mo, Cloth, $1 50.

Three Years in Japan. The Capital of the Tycoon: A Narrative of a Three Years' Residence in Japan. By Sir RUTHERFORD ALCOCK, K.C.B., Her Majesty's Envoy Extraordinary and Minister Plenipotentiary in Japan. With Maps and numerous Illustrations. 2 vols., 12mo, Cloth, $3 50.

The Sioux War. History of the Sioux War and Massacres of 1862 and 1863. By ISAAC V. D. HEARD. With Portraits and Illustrations. 12mo, Cloth, $1 75.

Crusoe's Island: A Ramble in the Footsteps of Alexander Selkirk. With Sketches of Adventure in California and Washoe. By J. Ross Browne. With Illustrations. 12mo, Cloth, $1 75.

Davis's Carthage. Carthage and Her Remains: Being an Account of the Excavations and Researches on the Site of the Phœnician Metropolis in Africa and other Adjacent Places. Conducted under the Auspices of Her Majesty's Government. By Dr. Davis, F.R.G.S. Profusely Illustrated with Maps, Woodcuts, Chromo-Lithographs, &c., &c. 8vo, Cloth, $4 00.

Lamont's Seasons with the Sea-Horses. Seasons with the Sea-Horses; or, Sporting Adventures in the Northern Seas. By James Lamont, Esq., F.G.S. With Map and Illustrations. 8vo, Cloth, $3 00.

Life and Adventure in the South Pacific. By Jones. With Illustrations. 8vo, Cloth, $1 50.

Pfeiffer's Last Travels and Autobiography. The Last Travels of Ida Pfeiffer: inclusive of a Visit to Madagascar. With an Autobiographical Memoir of the Author. Translated by H. W. Dulcken. Steel Portrait. 12mo, Cloth, $1 50.

Lord Elgin's Mission to China, &c. Narrative of Lord Elgin's Mission to China and Japan in 1857, '58, '59. By Laurence Oliphant, Secretary to Lord Elgin. Illustrations. 8vo, Cloth, $3 50.

Life in Spain. Past and Present. By Walter Thornbury, Author of "Every Man his own Trumpeter," "Art and Nature," "Songs of the Cavaliers and Roundheads," &c. With Illustrations. 12mo, Cloth, $1 50.

The Prairie Traveller. A Hand-Book for Overland Emigrants. With Maps, Illustrations, and Itineraries of the Principal Routes between the Mississippi and the Pacific. By Randolph B. Marcy, U. S. Army. Published by Authority of the War Department. 16mo, Cloth, $1 00.

Ellis's Madagascar. Three Visits to Madagascar during the Years 1853—1854—1856. Including a Journey to the Capital, with Notices of the Natural History of the Country and of the Present Civilization of the People. By the Rev. William Ellis, F.H.S., Author of "Polynesian Researches." Illustrated by a Map and Woodcuts from Photographs, &c. 8vo, Cloth, $3 50.

Fankwei; or, The San Jacinto in the Seas of India, China, and Japan. By William Maxwell Wood, M.D., U.S.N., late Surgeon of the Fleet to the United States East India Squadron, Author of "Wandering Sketches in South America, Polynesia," &c., &c. 12mo, Cloth, $1 50.

Page's La Plata. La Plata: The Argentine Confederation and Paraguay. Being a Narrative of the Exploration of the Tributaries of the River La Plata and Adjacent Countries, during the Years 1853, '54, '55, and '56, under the orders of the United States Government. By Thomas J. Page, U.S.N., Commander of the Expedition. With Maps and numerous Engravings. 8vo, Cloth, $5 00.

The Land and the Book; or, Biblical Illustrations drawn from the Manners and Customs, the Scenes and the Scenery of the Holy Land. By W. M. Thomson, D.D., Twenty-five Years a Missionary of the A.B.C.F.M. in Syria and Palestine. With two elaborate Maps of Palestine, an Accurate Plan of Jerusalem, and *several Hundred Engravings*, representing the Scenery, Topography, and Productions of the Holy Land, and the Costumes, Manners, and Habits of the People. Two elegant Large 12mo Volumes, Cloth, $5 00.

www.ingramcontent.com/pod-product-compliance
Lightning Source LLC
LaVergne TN
LVHW021319110826
845150LV00003B/617

* 9 7 8 1 4 2 5 5 5 7 5 7 7 *